A Pentecostal Hermeneutic
Spirit, Scripture and Community

A PENTECOSTAL HERMENEUTIC

SPIRIT, SCRIPTURE AND COMMUNITY

KENNETH J. ARCHER

CPT Press
Cleveland, Tennessee USA

Published by CPT Press
900 Walker ST NE
Cleveland, TN 37311
email: cptpress@pentecostaltheology.org
website: www.pentecostaltheology.org

First published by Continuum in the Journal of Pentecostal Theology
Supplement Series (28) 2005.

ISBN-10: 0981965113
ISBN-13: 9780981965116

Contents

Chapter 7

PREFACE

This monograph is a slightly revised version of my doctoral thesis entitled, 'Forging A New Path: A Contemporary Pentecostal Hermeneutical Strategy for the 21st Century' undertaken at the University of St Andrews, Scotland and successfully defended in 2001. I am honored to have the dissertation published in the Journal of Pentecostal Theology Supplemental series because many of those whose work have been published in the series have contributed to me personally and shaped my theological understanding. I offer this monograph to the larger Christian community as a testimony of the rich theological tradition called Pentecostalism. I also hope this study will be a blessing to my fellow Pentecostals worldwide as we continue to share our story.

The purpose of this monograph is to present a critically informed contemporary Pentecostal hermeneutical strategy that is rooted in Pentecostal identity, in its stories, beliefs and practices. The contemporary hermeneutical strategy is anchored in the Pentecostal community's identity while simultaneously being a critical hermeneutical strategy for the interpretation of Scripture in the production of a praxis-oriented theology. The contemporary strategy recognizes the combined contributions of the Spirit, Scripture and community in a dialogical interdependent interpretive process. The primary interpretive method is narrative, which is explored in relation to community identity and in relation to biblical interpretation.

Pentecostalism was a paramodern movement. The interpretive method of early Pentecostals testifies to this reality. As Pentecostals entered academic communities, their interpretive method became both mainstream and modernistic through the adaptation of the historical critical method(s). The proposed hermeneutic moves beyond the impasse created by modernity and pushes Pentecostals into the contemporary context by critically re-appropriating early Pentecostal ethos and interpretive practices for a contemporary Pentecostal community.

PREFACE TO THE PAPERBACK EDITION

The appearance of this edition comes with great celebration on my part and much tedious editorial work on the part of others. Allow me to express my deep gratitude to John Christopher Thomas and Lee Roy Martin for their editorial assistance. About twenty years ago Chris Thomas had a vision for making available quality Pentecostal academic work at affordable prices. With CPT Press he, joined by Lee Roy Martin, has recovered that vision. I am thrilled to have my monograph published in a durable paperback binding and readable typeset that is reasonably price. Also, I appreciate graduate assistants, Shawn Hitt, Wes Hunter and Chris Rouse, along with seminary graduate Robb Blackaby, who worked diligently on the monograph.

I am especially pleased that this paperback edition will be affordable to majority world readers, as well as students. To my delight, Gary Flokstra, director of 4 the World Resource Distributors (4WRD), contacted me in late February 2009, asking if my monograph was available in paperback at a reasonable rate. He has communicated his intention to place copies of this work in Pentecostal colleges in the majority world. His interest, along with other affirmations, testifies to the importance of making the work available in a reasonably priced edition. This CPT Press paperback edition will help to realize my desire for an affordable publication of my monograph.

Interestingly, unbeknownst to Gary, his father Jerry Flokstra was my biblical hermeneutics teacher when I was student at Central Bible College. 'Brother' Flokstra, as we called him, raised serious concerns about Pentecostals' adoption of Dispensationalism and wondered if Pentecostals might need to reflect upon the broader issues of hermeneutics. He whetted my appetite for future study of 'Pentecostal' hermeneutics. It is my hope that this monograph will continue to contribute to the ongoing dialogue concerning Pentecostal/charismatic hermeneutics and theological method.

Finally, I would like to thank all my colleagues at the Church of God Theological Seminary for their encouragement. They continue to play an important role in my theological reflection and work. I want to express my continued sincere gratitude to my wife, Melissa, and our sons, Trent and Tyler, for all their support.

Kenneth J. Archer
March 2009

ACKNOWLEDGEMENTS

I want to thank the Lord Jesus Christ for his liberating salvation. Hope and healing have been graciously extended to me in numerous ways by means of the Holy Spirit and the Pentecostal community. I am truly grateful for all the Lord has done.

There are many people who have helped me during this academic journey. I am particularly grateful for the support of two of my professors from Ashland Theological Seminary, Dr JoAnn Ford Watson and Dr O. Kenneth Walther. They believed in me and encouraged me to pursue a PhD.

Professor Richard Bauckham, my doctoral supervisor, provided the helpful guidance that enabled me to complete the thesis. I enjoyed and still miss the times spent in his office at St Mary's College discussing the early stages of my research and other theological concerns that were on my heart. Dr D. William Faupel of Asbury Theological Seminary deserves special recognition because he spent many hours with me going over various drafts of the thesis. His comments on both the content and structure of the drafts enabled me to develop further my writing style and argumentation.

Dr John Christopher Thomas of the Church of God Theological Seminary has been a special friend who has personally provided me with prayerful counsel and encouragement. Dr Eugene Gibbs of Ashland Theological Seminary conversed often with me about Pentecostalism and Hermeneutics. His encouraging friendship often provided much needed opportunities for laughter. He also proofread the final draft of the thesis. Likewise, Rev Robert Rosa, Dean of Student Life at Ashland Seminary, has walked through every facet of this process with me and is indeed my closest Pentecostal brother in the Lord.

Rev Andrew Hamilton, close friend and fellow postgraduate student at St Mary's College, served along side me as Associate Pastor of Mohicanville Community Church. He provided intellectually stimulating conversation and Christian companionship as we labored together in the local church. A word of thanks must also be extended to the congregation of Mohicanville Community Church who have allowed me to complete this thesis while serving as their pastor.

To my parents, Ken and Charlotte Archer, I owe a debt of gratitude for all their love, support and encouragement. My in-laws, Rev Norman and Nancy Beetler, who introduced me to Pentecost and have been my spiritual anchor, have sacrificed financially to enable Melissa and I to fulfill the call of God upon our lives. Dad Beetler has been and still is my primary theological dialogue partner even though we often (lovingly) disagree.

Finally and most importantly I want to thank my wife, Melissa Archer. Melissa has sacrificed greatly in so many ways so that I could accomplish the task of researching and writing this thesis. She is a wonderful mother to our sons, a gifted teacher and my best friend. As a fourth generation Pentecostal, she has played a vital role in my life as a passionate narrator of the Pentecostal story. I could not have completed this project without her cheering me on to the finish line.

I want to dedicate this 'book' to my two sons, Trenton Charles Archer and Tyler Russell Archer. You both have been a blessing to me in so many ways! I am proud of you and love you. You have been blessed with a rich heritage of the Pentecostal faith, and it is my prayer that you both will continue serving the Lord and sharing the Pentecostal story.

Abbreviations

ABD	David Noel Freedman (ed.), *The Anchor Bible Dictionary* (New York: Doubleday, 1992)
DPCM	*Dictionary of Pentecostal and Charismatic Movements*
JPT	*Journal of Pentecostal Theology*
JPTSup	*Journal of Pentecostal Theology Supplement Series*
JSSR	*Journal for the Scientific Study of Religion*
JSNT	*Journal for the Study of the New Testament*
JSNTSup	*Journal for the Study of the New Testament Supplement Series*
NovT	*Novum Testamentum*
Pneuma	*Pneuma: The Journal of the Society for Pentecostal Studies*
TDNT	Gerhard Kittel and Gerhard Friedrich (eds.), *Theological Dictionary of the New Testament* (trans. Geoffrey W. Bromiley; 10 vols., Grand Rapids, MI: Eerdmans, 1964–)

INTRODUCTORY REMARKS FOR THE READERS

Critical to our survival and our ability to speak to and be heard by the larger church is our willingness to engage in hermeneutical self-understanding.[1]

Cecil M. Robeck

Purpose of the Monograph

The purpose of this monograph is to articulate a constructive contemporary Pentecostal hermeneutical strategy. This hermeneutical strategy emerges out of the very ethos of the early Pentecostal community and will enable the Pentecostal community to engage critically Scripture and society as it continues to embody its missional objective into the 21st century. In order to achieve this goal, I embarked upon a quest for Pentecostal self-understanding and its influence upon biblical interpretation. The Pentecostal tradition, although still relatively young when compared to other historic Christian traditions, is now in a position to examine critically its own identity, hermeneutical posture and its relationship to other Christian communities. Pentecostals are being called upon by various Christian traditions to offer distinct contributions concerning contemporary theology and hermeneutical practice. It is my prayerful concern that this monograph will contribute to the ongoing discussion concerning 'Pentecostal' hermeneutics and theology.

Cecil Robeck's quote with which this introduction begins sums up the rationale for this important study. North American Pentecostals have just begun to respond to the general call that we need to reflect critically upon our identity as a movement. This work recognizes the vital importance of Robeck's concern. Furthermore, if Pentecostals want to be taken seriously by other academic Christian

---

[1] Cecil M. Robeck, Jr., 'Taking Stock of Pentecostalism: The Personal Reflections of a Retiring Editor', *Pneuma* 15.1 (Spring 1993), p. 60.

communities and offer insights from their own tradition to the larger Christian community, we must respond with the appropriate academic language while maintaining our own identity and language. Pentecostal identity (who we are as a community) needs to be addressed so that we are in a better position to explain to other communities who we are and why we act as we do. Pentecostal identity, however, will be addressed as it relates to Pentecostal hermeneutical concerns since the primary focus of this monograph is hermeneutics.

In this work I will present and defend the argument that inherently within the emergence of early Pentecostalism was a biblical theological hermeneutical strategy that was different than both academic modernistic Fundamentalism and liberalism. The early Pentecostal hermeneutic must be retrieved and retained in order for the movement to mature as a Christian theological tradition. This early hermeneutical strategy will, however, be critically re-appropriated and presented as a contemporary hermeneutical strategy.

Generally, Pentecostalism is categorized as one of many 'Evangelical' sub groups. Along with this classification, Pentecostal identity is primarily construed as an extension of the Protestant evangelical tradition. The logical argument that follows is that Pentecostal method(s) of biblical interpretation should be the same as academic Evangelicals. This construal, however, undermines the vitality and authenticity of the early Pentecostal movement as a protest to mainline Protestantism. I will demonstrate that there existed an authentic and distinct early Pentecostal hermeneutical strategy that was rooted in its self-identity and manifested through its interpretation of the Bible. The early biblical interpretive method was shaped by the Pentecostal community's identity, thus creating a distinct hermeneutical strategy.

If Pentecostals want to be taken seriously as a restoration movement with something vital to offer the greater Christian community, then the movement must embark upon a journey of hermeneutical self-understanding. It is not enough just to adopt and use academic methods of biblical interpretation stamped with the approval of the Evangelical community in order to prove the legitimacy of their interpretations, for there are Christian traditions other than Evangelicalism that Pentecostals can dialogically engage for mutual benefit. Pentecostals need to come to grips with what it means to be 'Pentecostal'. In turn, this will affect their understanding and interpretation of reality in general and of Scripture in particular.

As will be demonstrated, early Pentecostalism came from the margins of society. Most Pentecostals were not trained academically in university religion departments or academic seminaries. In time, however, Pentecostals ventured into these arenas of learning which were often hostile to their own identity. This author will not argue that Pentecostals need to return naively to their early biblical interpretive method(s). However, I do believe that the Pentecostal community needs to retrieve the praxis-driven spiritual ethos of the early Pentecostal movement and re-present it from a contemporary post-critical and Pentecostal perspective. Hence, the strategy that will emerge will be an approach to scriptural interpretation that is anchored in Pentecostal identity and informed by contemporary concerns.

Pentecostals, both in the academy and in the local congregation cannot (nor should they desire to) return to a pre-critical interpretation of Scripture. Yet neither will the hermeneutic of modernity (historical criticism) uncritically wed to Pentecostal identity enable them to speak to the current or future Christian community's engagement with Scripture in a manner by which they can be taken seriously (by both the academy and more importantly by the Pentecostal laity). Pentecostals desire to use their intellectual ability and spiritual gifts in a critical manner. Simply stated, the *thesis* of this study is that there exists within early Pentecostalism an authentic Pentecostal approach to interpretation that is rooted in and guided by Pentecostal identity which can be retrieved and critically re-appropriated within the current postmodern context.

I will demonstrate that the Pentecostal tradition can stand on its own feet as an authentic Christian restoration movement and that it can critically offer insightful helps, particularly in the area of hermeneutics, to our sisters and brothers in other Christian traditions. We are all aware that exegetical methodologies alone cannot completely validate an interpretation of Scripture. Hermeneutics is not just concerned with the horizon of the biblical text and the methods used to interpret this document, but it also must consider the contribution of the present horizon of the reader in community. Pentecostals have been primarily concerned with the use of proper exegetical methodologies in their quest to discover the determinate meaning entombed in the biblical text. Consequently, little attention has been paid to the identity of the 'Pentecostal' readers and hearers and their creative contribution in the production of meaning. This study attempts to explain the identity of the early Pentecostal community and its contribution to the production of meaning while addressing current hermeneutical concerns that have arisen within the Pentecostal community. Furthermore this writer will offer a contemporary Pentecostal hermeneutical strategy for the 21ˢᵗ century.

Focus and Limitation of the Study

The focus of this study will be limited by a number of factors. The primary historical investigation will examine the first generation of Pentecostals. Pentecostalism emerged on the time line at the turn of the twentieth century in North America. Thus from a historical and geographical perspective the descriptive analysis of early Pentecostal identity and interpretive practice will be limited to the early twentieth-century North American context.

However, the philosophical and theological issues related to hermeneutics have arisen within global contemporary Pentecostal academic communities. Yet in order to make this analysis manageable I have limited the investigation of hermeneutical concerns to contemporary North American English-speaking Pentecostal communities (primarily those with historical connections to the Azusa Street Revival that took place in Los Angeles, California between 1906–1909).

The focus of the study is Pentecostal communal identity and how that affects their interpretation of Scripture. The argument will be advanced that the early Pentecostals were a mature counter-cultural paramodern movement protesting modernity and in turn had forged a distinct hermeneutical response to the crises created by modernity. In the earliest stages of the movement there can be found an authentic Pentecostal hermeneutical approach which can be retrieved and re-appropriated for contemporary Pentecostal community. The current hermeneutical approach of most academic Pentecostals has been to embrace modern assumptions and practices about hermeneutics from an Evangelical perspective. I believe that this practice will only continue to transform Pentecostals into mainstream neo-fundamentalists, undermining Pentecostal identity and practice.

Review of Flow of Argument

In chapter one I place the beginnings of Pentecostalism in its social and religious context. In addition, I also identify the primary social and theological influences that gave rise to the movement. Pentecostalism is shown to be a counter-cultural paramodern movement located on the margins of North American society. The major concern of this chapter will be to demonstrate that Pentecostalism as a paramodern movement was a spiritual and social protest to modernistic liberalism and modernistic Protestant cessationist orthodoxy. The 'Full Gospel' message and the lifestyle it generated was the catalyst that caused others to convert to Pentecostalism.

Chapter two discusses the hermeneutical context of early Pentecostalism. Here I argue that the Pentecostals forged an alternative path in response to Fundamentalists and liberals. The Pentecostals' continuation of holiness praxis in confrontation with liberalism and Fundamentalism created a fertile context out of which a Pentecostal hermeneutic emerged. Much attention will be given to the hermeneutical practices of the various Protestant groups with recognition that the controversy between Fundamentalism and liberalism was a result of an intellectual paradigm shift. In response to the paradigm shift the Pentecostals cut a third path.

The thesis of the third chapter is that the early Pentecostals used the same biblical interpretive method as Wesleyan and Keswickian holiness folk—the 'Bible Reading Method'. Pentecostals used this method to develop their doctrinal understanding of the baptism in the Holy Spirit which differed from both the Wesleyan and Keswickian understanding. To substantiate this argument a thorough analysis of early Pentecostal interpretation is presented. The Pentecostals did not create a new method of interpreting the Bible, but they did use this pre-critical interpretive method from a Pentecostal perspective, which in turn made it a unique (Pentecostal) way of reading and interpreting the Bible.

In Chapter four, I argue that the uniqueness of the Pentecostal hermeneutic was the distinct narrative tradition from which the Bible Reading Method was used. The Central Narrative Convictions will be identified and related to the Pentecostal story, which is the primary hermeneutical context through which Scripture was interpreted. In this chapter, the early Pentecostal ethos can be clearly heard, thus enabling the present reader to have a better grasp of Pentecostal communal self-identity.

The Pentecostal hermeneutic is rooted in the narrative tradition of the community. The Pentecostal narrative tradition has a cohesive theological structure and is centered upon the dramatic story of God's dynamic involvement in their community. The early hermeneutical strategy emphasized the importance of a controlling story that included the necessity and immediacy of experience in the interpretation of Scripture. This chapter, therefore, should lead readers to the conclusion that there does exist an authentic Pentecostal hermeneutic working within early Pentecostalism.

Chapter five will focus on current Pentecostal discussions concerning hermeneutical issues. Among these many conversations, two prominent positions have emerged within the Pentecostal community. The majority of Pentecostals embrace the position that Pentecostals need to use evangelically and academically acceptable methods (a modified historical-critical approach of modernity) which attempts to avoid 'sectarian' epistemological categorization and strive for universally acceptable rationalistic foundations. The minority position recognizes Pentecostalism as an authentic Christian movement whose identity cannot be submerged into Evangelicalism without losing important aspects of Pentecostal identity. I will side with the minority position.

Finally, chapter six unfolds a contemporary Pentecostal hermeneutical strategy which takes very seriously early Pentecostal identity and hermeneutical practices. The strategy cannot be reduced to a rigid method or attempt to return to the pre-critical early Bible Reading Method. It will embrace the 'Pentecostal Story' as the primary hermeneutical context and critically re-appropriate insightful interpretive practices of the early Pentecostals into a contemporary hermeneutical strategy. The hermeneutical strategy will be a narrative approach to interpretation that embraces a tridactic negotiation for meaning between the biblical text, Pentecostal community and the Holy Spirit. Meaning is arrived at through the dialectical process based upon an interdependent dialogical relationship between Scripture, Spirit and community. Furthermore, the strategy will invite dialogue with other communities (both Christian and non-Christian). Hence, this hermeneutical strategy and interpretation of Scripture will be open to the critique of other traditions. The articulation of a Pentecostal hermeneutic is not an attempt to isolate Pentecostals from critique, nor is it an attempt to arrive at some neutral method that in and of itself demonstrates the validity of Pentecostal doctrine (such as tongues as the initial physical evidence of Spirit baptism). The strategy will be critical and draw on contemporary academic hermeneutical concerns. The Pentecostal hermeneutic will be offered as a strategy for interpreting Scripture and reality in a critical manner. The hermeneutic strategy is product of the Pentecostal community, thus making it a Pentecostal hermeneutical strategy.[2]

My Personal Hermeneutical Journey: Traveling through the First Naïveté and into the Second Naïveté

I began my Christian faith journey in June of 1982 at an Assembly of God church located in Wellington, Ohio. My cousin, who prior to his conversion had been one of my drinking buddies, invited me to attend the Wellington Assembly of God church with him and his wife. I was nineteen and had serious problems with alcohol. My life had hit bottom so I decided to go with them to church. After all, what did I have to lose? Two weeks later in response to the closing 'altar call' I accepted Jesus as my Lord and Savior.

Even though I was raised and confirmed as a Roman Catholic and attended Catechism and Mass weekly with my family until I was fourteen, I had never taken Christianity as a lifestyle very seriously (I believed in God yet lived as though God did not exist). From age thirteen to nineteen, I engaged in a lifestyle of promiscuity and drugs, which I knew (through my pietistic mother) were forbidden to Christians, and it was precisely the pursuit of these temporarily pleasurable escapes of reality that almost destroyed my life.

Because of my mother's prayers (my mom had become a charismatic Catholic who meet regularly with a small group of Christians for prayer and bible study, and as a teenager I had often found

---

[2] This was made possible by participating in the Society for Pentecostal Studies and presenting portions of this study to the Society.

her prayer list of family members who needed to be 'saved' and to my surprise my name was on it) and Christian witness, the grace of the living God was extended to me. I began to explore the Christian faith as a lifestyle. The loving-kindness of the Pentecostal congregation in Wellington convinced me to convert to the Pentecostal Christian faith, which meant that I needed to change my lifestyle. I knew that Jesus had forgiven me and accepted me. I knew the living God loved me not because the Bible said so but more importantly because this particular Pentecostal community showed me so. It was this community that nurtured and discipled me into the Pentecostal Christian way of life where holiness was the norm not the exception. I was rebaptized by immersion in water, filled with the Holy Spirit with the biblical sign of tongues and responded to numerous altar calls further experiencing God's sanctifying grace. While attending this church, I was called into pastoral ministry. I also was privileged to date and later marry the pastor's daughter. This congregation was a typical popularistic (and some what fundamentalistic) Pentecostal community that passionately loved Jesus and compassionately reached out to the sick, sinful and struggling in society. It was this community that encouraged me to go to Bible college and prepare for full-time pastoral ministry.

I attended Central Bible College, an Assembly of God college in Springfield, Missouri. I will always be grateful for the college and many of the faculty members because they were willing to accept me as a student on academic probation and teach me basic learning skills. The college provided an opportunity for me to acquire the basic learning skills of reading and writing as well as provide an atmosphere for further Pentecostal spiritual formation. It was here that I first became indoctrinated into classical Pentecostalism from a more fundamentalist perspective. I also began to be introduced to modern critical biblical scholarship and philosophical reasoning. I graduated with a major in Bible and a minor in biblical Greek and had accumulated a 3.3 grade point average. During my final year at Central Bible College, I was encouraged by some teachers to go on and do graduate work.

After graduation I became the senior pastor in the Pentecostal church in Wellington where I had been converted. As the pastor I began to run into strong fundamentalist arguments that rejected women in leadership positions. This ran contrary to early Pentecostal practice and belief. I began a quest into the various interpretive arguments that whet my appetite for further theological studies.

I enrolled at Ashland Theological Seminary in Ashland, Ohio, after being in pastoral ministry for 3 years in Wellington. In order to enroll full-time at Ashland Seminary I had to resign from Wellington and find another congregation that would allow me to attend Seminary. We (Melissa and I) began pastoring a small Assemblies of God missions church in Twinsburg, Ohio.

At Ashland Theological Seminary I encountered an evangelical pietistic faculty who were much more open to academic and critical scholarship than what I had encountered at Central Bible College. At Ashland Seminary my critical thinking skills were awakened, and I began to assess my Pentecostal faith critically in the safety of a conservative evangelical Seminary. I became much more aware of the influences of modernity upon Christian belief and practice. The evangelical perspective of the historical critical method was affirmed with an ongoing critique of the liberal presupposition beliefs that gave rise to the method. During my last year I had taken upper level courses which introduced me to various theoretical concepts influenced by modernity that pushed me to rethink my Pentecostal and even Christian faith. I had not yet figured out how to be a critical thinking practitioner and remain a faithful Pentecostal Christian. I had entered the wilderness of criticism only wishing that I could somehow return to my paramodern pre-critical Pentecostal beliefs, which of course was impossible.

I graduated from Ashland Theological Seminary with a Master of Divinity with an interdisciplinary major in theology, Church history and philosophy. My critical thinking skills where strengthened, which enabled me to graduate with high honors (3.9). I was encouraged by faculty to pursue a PhD.

One of the faculty members at Ashland Seminary suggested Professor Richard Bauckham as a possible supervisor for my PhD research. I had become aware of Bauckham through reading his work on Jürgen Moltmann for a course in contemporary theology. I also knew he was a committed Christian and scholar. These were two extremely important attributes that I was looking for in a supervisor. I wrote Professor Bauckham and explained to him my desire to engage in hermeneutics and Pentecostalism. He was interested and extended an invitation to me to become one of his research students.

My year of postgraduate research at St Mary's College, University of St Andrews only exasperated my struggle. However, with the help of the Holy Spirit, my Christian research supervisor Professor Bauckham and 'post'-critical academic Pentecostals (whom I meet through the Society of Pentecostal Studies), I eventually crossed the desert of skeptical (modern and or postmodern) criticism. I had journeyed through the wilderness of the first naïveté (both pre-critical and then modernistic scientific Biblicism) and entered into the 'second naïveté'.[3]

The second naïveté is a post-critical stance in which I recognize that commitment to community is not an option but a reality, and my participation in a Christian community shapes my view of reality. I am not suggesting that one cannot understand other views of reality, but I am saying that one's participation in a community nevertheless makes life meaningful. From my Pentecostal post-critical stance, Scripture is affirmed as a self-authenticating meta-narrative which offers readers an opportunity to enter into a verbally construed world and view reality from its perspective. Scripture creates a world so that one can encounter the mediated transforming presence of the living God, but it does so through open-ended conversation with its readers. Therefore, hermeneutical inquiry is always with us[4] and 'the very heart of hermeneutics is the conversation'.[5]

---

[3] Paul Ricoeur, *The Symbolism of Evil* (New York, NY: Harper and Row, 1967), p. 351.

[4] Ricoeur, *The Symbolism of Evil*, p. 351, writes, 'But if we can no longer live the great symbolisms of the sacred in accordance with the original belief in them, we can, we modern men, aim at a second naïveté in and through criticism. In short, it is by *interpreting* that we can *hear* again' (his emphasis).

[5] W. Randolph Tate, *Biblical Interpretation: An Integrated Approach*, (Peabody, MA: Hendrickson, rev. edn, 1997), p. xvi. See also James K.A. Smith, *The Fall of Interpretation: Philosophical Foundations for a Creationist Hermeneutic* (Downers Grove, IL: InterVarsity, 2000) who argues that hermeneutics is part of God's good creation of humanity not a result of the fall of humanity.

1

DEFINING PENTECOSTALISM: A DIVERSE AND PARADOXICAL ENDEAVOR

The Pentecostal movement is diverse, volatile and mercurial … it is highly paradoxical.[1]

Harvey Cox

The gestation of Pentecostalism took place during the social chaos and revivalistic vigor of the late nineteenth century in North America. Yet, it was during the volatile first decade of the twentieth century in the United States that the Pentecostal movement was birthed. Presently, Pentecostalism exists as a highly complex, theologically multi-cultural organism that has literally covered the earth.[2] The bewildering diversity and paradoxical complexity of contemporary Pentecostalism stems from its diverse origins.[3]

Pentecostalism originated in multiple in geographic locations with both Kansas and Los Angeles claiming to be its birthplace.[4] Pentecostalism as a movement is also diverse theologically. Initially,

---

[1] Harvey Cox, *Fire from Heaven: The Rise of Pentecostal Spirituality and the Reshaping of Religion in the Twenty-first Century*, (Reading, MA: Addison-Wesley Publishing Company, 1995), p. 184.

[2] For statistical information see David B. Barrett, 'Statistics, Global' in Stanley M. Burgess and Gary B. McGee (eds.), *DPCM* (Grand Rapids, MI: Zondervan, 1988), pp. 810–30. Also C. Peter Wagner, 'Church Growth' in *DPCM*, pp. 180–95.

[3] See Vinson Synan (ed.), *Aspects of Pentecostal-Charismatic Origins* (Plainfield, NJ: Logos International, 1975). This volume of essays examines the non-Wesleyan, the Wesleyan Holiness, and black origins (to list just three) of Pentecostalism.

[4] Peter W. Williams, *America's Religions: Traditions and Cultures* (New York: Macmillan, 1990), p. 262. Williams makes an important observation about the similarity between the Radical Reformation, the Great Awakening and Pentecostalism concerning their multiple origins.

Pentecostals came from the Wesleyan Holiness tradition, but then some Keswickian people or 'Finished Work' adherents embraced Pentecostalism (which caused the first major theological uproar among early Pentecostals).[5] Pentecostals were not a homogeneous ethnic group either. From the very beginning, the movement was multi-racial. Hence, there exists a hardy debate about who was the 'first' real founder of the Pentecostal movement and what 'theological' doctrines are distinctly Pentecostal.

Some historians have argued that Charles Fox Parham was the founder of Pentecostalism and have claimed Topeka, Kansas as the birthplace of the movement.[6] However, other historians claim an African-American origin with William Seymour as the founder and the Azusa Street Mission in Los Angeles, California as the birthplace.[7] At the heart of this controversy is the definition of 'Pente-

---

[5] Vinson Synan, 'Classical Pentecostalism' in *DPCM*, pp. 220–21.

[6] Charles W. Conn, *Like a Mighty Army Moves the Church of God* (Cleveland, TN: Church of God Publishing House, 1955), p. 25; Sarah F. Parham, *The Life of Charles F. Parham: Founder of the Apostolic Faith Movement* (Joplin, MO: Hunter, 1930 reprint 1969), pp. 51–56; James R. Goff, Jr., *Fields White Unto Harvest: Charles F. Parham and the Missionary Origins of Pentecostalism* (Fayetteville, AR: The University of Arkansas Press, 1988). Goff asserts that 'Parham is the key to any interpretation of Pentecostal origins' and that Parham not Seymour should be viewed as the founder of the Pentecostal movement (p. 16 and p. 11). See his introduction for a review of current historiographies on Pentecostalism and his rationale for Parham as founder. Goff is the definitive biographer of Parham.

[7] Leonard Lovett, 'Black Origins of the Pentecostal Movement' in V. Synan (ed.), *Aspects of Pentecostal-Charismatic Origins* (Plainfield, NJ: Logos International, 1975), pp. 123-41; James S. Tinny, 'Exclusivist Tendencies in Pentecostal Self-Definition: A Critique from Black Theology', *The Journal of Religious Thought* 36.1 (Spring-Summer, 1979), pp. 32–53; *idem*, 'Competing Strains of Hidden and Manifest Theologies in Black Pentecostalism' (a paper presented to the Society for Pentecostal Studies held November 14, 1980 at Oral Roberts University, Tulsa, OK.); Leonard Lovett, 'Black Holiness-Pentecostalism: Implications for Ethics and Social Transformation' (PhD Dissertation, Emory University, 1979). Lovett states, 'the United Holy Church continued from its inception in 1885 with only a name change' and that 'the Azusa Street Revival was no more than confirmation of a phenomenon which had already begun among Black holiness-Pentecostals' (pp. 50–52). Therefore, Azusa Street is the birthplace of the contemporary movement (p. 53); Eric Lincoln and Lawrence H. Mamiya, *The Black Church in the African American Experience* (Durham, NC: Duke University Press, 1990). They argue that 'the black Pentecostals have a unique historical origin ... they trace their origins not to white denominations, but to a movement initiated and led by a black minister ... these black Pentecostals began not as a separatist movement, but as part of a distinctly interracial movement from which whites subsequently withdrew' (p. 76). Also of extreme importance is Walter J. Hollen-

costal' and which geographical location had the most significant impact on the spread of Pentecostalism. Also one must acknowledge that early Pentecostalism contains Trinitarian and Oneness ('Jesus only') groups,[8] Wesleyan Holiness and Finished Work groups.[9] Therefore, 'there was no one direct line of development for all of Pentecostalism nor was there any one historical pattern for all groups'.[10] Yet it is this diversity along with Pentecostalism's ability to adapt without losing its essential beliefs and practices that has aided in its growth.

In order to grasp an essential understanding of early Pentecostalism, this writer will recognize it as a diffuse group of restorationist revivalistic movements,[11] held together by a common doctrinal commitment to the 'Full Gospel' message[12] and a passionate em-

---

weger's influence upon the understanding of Pentecostalism and its origins. In his work, *The Pentecostals* (Peabody, MA: Hendrickson, 1972), Hollenweger's first sentence states, 'The origins of the Pentecostal movement go back to a revival amongst the Negroes of North America at the beginning of the present century' (p. xiv). Under his supervision three important works were written which deal with Pentecostal origins: Douglas J. Nelson, 'For Such A time as This: The Story of Bishop William J. Seymour and the Azusa Street Revival: A Search for Pentecostal Roots' (Unpublished PhD Thesis, University of Birmingham, England, 1981). This is the definitive biography on Seymour. Secondly, Ian MacRoberts, *The Black Roots and White Racism of Early Pentecostalism in the U.S.A.* (New York: St. Martin's Press, 1988); thirdly, D. William Faupel, *The Everlasting Gospel: The Significance of Eschatology in the Development of Pentecostal Thought* (JPTSup, 10; Sheffield: Sheffield Academic Press, 1996). Also Hollenweger's influence can be felt upon the *Journal of Pentecostal Theology* (Sheffield: Sheffield Academic Press). See the first issue, 1992, where he has the first article.

[8] David A. Reed, *In Jesus' Name: The History and Beliefs of Oneness Pentecostals* (JPTSup, 31; Blandford Forum, UK: Deo Publishing, 2008). p. 174. Reed's monograph is an extensive revision with substantial new information of his 'Origins and Development of the Theology of Oneness Pentecostalism in the United States' (Ph.D. Dissertation, Boston University, 1978); J.L. Hall, 'A Oneness Pentecostal Looks at Initial Evidence' in Gary B. McGee (ed.), *Initial Evidence: Historical and Biblical Perspectives on the Pentecostal Doctrine of Spirit Baptism* (Peabody, MA: Hendrickson, 1991), pp. 168–88.

[9] R.A. Riss, 'Finished Work Controversy' in *DPCM*, pp. 306–309.

[10] H.N. Kenyon, 'An Analysis of Racial Separation within the Early Pentecostal Movement' (MA thesis, Baylor University, TX, 1979), p. 9.

[11] Edith Blumhofer, *Restoring the Faith: The Assemblies of God, Pentecostalism, and American Culture* (Chicago, IL: University of Illinois Press, 1993) argues that 'restorationism is often the basic component of a Pentecostal movement' (p. 4).

[12] This is a reference to the five or four-fold understanding of the work of Jesus as Savior, Sanctifier, Spirit Baptizer, Healer, and soon coming King. See Donald Dayton, *Theological Roots of Pentecostalism* (Peabody, MA: Hendrickson, 1987),

phasis upon the ecstatic religious experiences associated with Spirit baptism.[13] Also of extreme importance was the contribution of Wesleyan Holiness slaves. African slave spirituality and worship has helped to shape Pentecostalism's dynamic experiential characteristics.[14] Harvey Cox observes correctly:

> No responsible historian of religion now disputes that Pentecostalism was conceived when essentially African and African American religious practices began to mingle with the poor white southern Christianity that sprang from a Wesleyan lineage. But ... a fierce debate still simmers about when and where the birth actually took place.[15]

---

which presents both a historical and theological analysis of Pentecostalism through this theological prism. The 'Full Gospel' is the common matrix for Pentecostal doctrine and identity.

[13] Augustus Cerillo, Jr., 'The Origins of American Pentecostalism', *Pneuma* 15.1 (Spring, 1993), pp. 77-88. This present author is following his suggestion with slight modification in order to examine Pentecostalism 'as a diffuse group of movements, however, connected by doctrinal commitment or single religious experience' (p. 87).

[14] Leonard Lovett, 'Black Holiness-Pentecostalism' in *DPCM*, points out that 'it is primarily in worship form, religious expression, and lifestyle, rather than a codified belief system that Black-holiness-Pentecostalism shares in the rich tradition and legacy of black slave religion' (pp. 76–77). Steven J. Land in his *Pentecostal Spirituality: A Passion for the Kingdom* (JPTSup, 1; Sheffield: Sheffield Academic Press, 1993) identifies the origin of Pentecostalism's spirituality as a product of the 'black spirituality of the former slaves in the United States encountering the specific Catholic spirituality of the movement's grandfather, John Wesley' (p. 35).

[15] Cox, *Fire From Heaven*, p. 149. The fierce debate concerning the birth of Pentecostalism refers to who should be acknowledged as the founder of the movement (Charles Fox Parham [white] or William Seymour [black]) and which Christian tradition had the primary influence upon Pentecostalism. Scholars have presented a variety of theories as to which earlier religious movements and individual(s) gave birth to Pentecostalism. Cerillo, 'The Origins of American Pentecostalism', p. 77, states that these theories are always 'constructed around some combination of sociological, ideological, racial, and providential causes'. Presently, there are four competing views concerning the origin of the movement in North America. Goff, in his *Fields White unto Harvest*, argues stringently for Parham as the originator. Along with Goff, this group argues that Parham developed Pentecostalism's unique doctrine of Spirit baptism initially evidenced by speaking in an unlearned tongue and that Parham was the first person to preach the 'Full Gospel' message. Also see Robert M. Anderson, *Vision of the Disinherited: The Making of American Pentecostalism* (Peabody, MA: Hendrickson, 1979), pp. 252–57. The second view, which has been predominantly influenced by W.J. Hollenweger and James Tinney, argues for 'black roots'. They argue that Pentecostalism was birthed during the Azusa Street revival under the leadership of William

Social and Theological Influences

Pentecostalism began as and continues to be a complex, heterogeneous and eclectic movement in both theological and social composition.[16] During the period that ran roughly from the American Civil War to the Great Depression, American society was caught in the vortex of change as mass immigration, urbanization and industrialization re-sculptured the North American landscape.[17] As a result, societal problems became much more complicated and acute. Yet 'most public-spirited Protestants still felt that the key to a better life together lay in personal moral reform'.[18] Thus the most prevalent evangelical Protestant attempts to reform urban life was based on principles of private action and personal responsibility.[19]

Seymour, an African-American. For this group, not to acknowledge Seymour and Azusa Street as the origin is an attempt to rewrite history with a racial bias that undermines the importance of Black Christian influence on and contribution to Pentecostalism. See also, L. Lovett, 'Black Origins of the Pentecostal Movement' and Jean-Jacques Suurmound, *Word and Spirit at Play: Towards a Charismatic Theology* (London: SCM Press Ltd., 1994), pp. 5–7. A third view opts for a 'leaderless leadership' in which no one 'main personality can be said to be the originator of the movement'. This view is presented by L. Grant McClung, Jr. (ed.), *Azusa Street and Beyond: Pentecostal Missions and Church Growth in the Twentieth Century*, (South Plainfield, NJ: Bridge Publishing, 1986), p. 4. The Pentecostal movement spontaneously erupted in several places simultaneously. Thus it is a 'child of the Holy Ghost'. Finally, there exist those like V. Synan, *The Holiness-Pentecostal Movement in the United States* (Grand Rapids, MI: Eerdmans, 1971), p 168, who argues for an interracial origin:

> Despite some controversy over the matter, it can safely be said that Parham and Seymour share roughly equal positions as founders of modern Pentecostalism. Parham laid the doctrinal foundations of the movement, while Seymour served as the catalytic agent for its popularization. In this sense, the early Pentecostal movement could be classed as neither 'Negro' nor 'White', but as interracial.

I agree with those who argue for the Azusa Street Mission under the leadership of William Seymour as the birthplace for the Pentecostal movement.

[16] Anderson, *Vision of the Disinherited: The Making of American Pentecostalism*, p. 165.

[17] William M. Menzies, *Anointed to Serve: The Story of the Assemblies of God* (Springfield, MO: Gospel Publishing House, 1971), pp. 18–20. Also see George M. Marsden, *Understanding Fundamentalism and Evangelicalism* (Grand Rapids, MI: Eerdmans, 1991), chapter one.

[18] Mark A. Noll, *A History of Christianity in the United States and Canada* (Grand Rapids, MI: Eerdmans, 1992), p. 295.

[19] Noll, *A History of Christianity*, p. 304.

Restorationist Revivalism's Influence upon Pentecostalism

Revival was the means to transform the individual, implant the principles of private action and personal responsibility, and thereby, change society. In North America, 'the popular belief was that the individual was the basic religious unit'.[20] This meant that denominational affiliation was ultimately a matter of personal preference, which resulted in weakened denominational structures. The people's strongest religious loyalties were not to denominations or even local congregations but to attractive, anointed revivalistic preachers. For evangelicals, revival was the selected means for transforming and healing America's deadly societal illnesses. Many, like D.L. Moody, believed that the only hope for the United States was revival.[21] Hence, revivalism was an outgrowth of American 'rugged individualism' that targeted the individual to bring about societal change.

Revivalism was not necessarily a rejection of the intellect, but it was the means for emphasis upon emotion throughout early American Evangelicalism.[22] Revivalistic preachers emphasized the necessity of a personal conscious conversion experience. These preachers were concerned with orthodox belief, but they were even more concerned about a heartfelt conversion experience. By emphasizing a personal salvation experience, they appealed to the emotions, which placed individual experience at center stage.[23] Both Blacks and Whites were attracted to revivalistic Christianity because it was lively, emotional, fervid and powerfully encouraging to peo-

---

[20] Marsden, *Understanding Fundamentalism and Evangelicalism*, p. 17.

[21] George M. Marsden, *Fundamentalism and American Culture: The Shaping of Twentieth-Century Evangelicalism, 1870–1925* (New York: Oxford University Press, 1980), p. 38.

[22] Marsden, *Fundamentalism and American Culture*. He highlights the fact that all newer evangelical movements after the Civil War have a base in some form of Charles Finney's 'social religious meeting'. 'Finney's revivals marked the beginning of the attempt to build a new Christian community united by intense feeling. The focal point for this emphasis was the "social religious meeting", small groups gathered for prayer, Bible study, witnessing and song' (p. 45). However, John Wesley's Methodist class societies were doing the same thing.

[23] C.C. Goen, *Revivalism and Separatism in New England, 1740–1800: Strict Congregationalists and Separate Baptists in the Great Awakening* (Middletown, CT: Wesleyan University Press, 1987), pp. 8–35, reference to p. 15. Goen describes the innovations of Revivalism during the Great Awakening. Most of these revivalistic characteristics were also a part of the revivalistic preachers of the American frontier.

ple caught in the intolerable economic and social conditions of the day.[24] By the last decade of the nineteenth century, Methodism was the largest body of Protestant Christians.[25] However, 'the Pentecostal movement was not particularly Methodist in origin even though some of the leaders and many members of various Pentecostal sects had been Methodist. The same could be said of those who had been Baptist, Presbyterian and Episcopalian.'[26]

Pentecostalism emerged from the social chaos and revivalistic fervor that characterized the beginning of twentieth-century America. During the height of 'come-outism'[27] Pentecostalism appeared

---

[24] Frederick A. Norwood, *The Story of American Methodism: A History of the United Methodists and Their Relations* (Nashville, TN: Abingdon, 1974), pp. 165–66.

[25] Norwood, *The Story of American Methodism,* p. 301. Donald W. Dayton, 'Yet Another Layer of The Onion or Opening the Ecumenical Door to let the Riffraff in', *The Ecumenical Review* 40.1 (January 1988). Dayton argues that, 'Methodism (and the holiness movement and even Pentecostalism) have always been "movements" for the renewal of Christianity rather than churches, though they have often had to lapse back into ecclesiastical structures' (pp. 109–10).

[26] Norwood, *The Story of American Methodism*, p. 300.

[27] Come-outism was the pejorative title applied to the radical Wesleyan Holiness preachers who were calling people out of established Methodist churches to become a part of the independent holiness churches. At the heart of the come-outers' concern was the holiness doctrine of entire sanctification. The 'come-outism' movement began in the 1880's, hit its high point in the last decade of the nineteenth century, and continued into the first decade of the twentieth century (Norwood, *The Story of Methodism*, p. 300). The 'textbook' of come-outism was John P. Brooks, *The Divine Church* first published in 1887. Brooks was a loyal Methodist who had edited *The Banner of Holiness.* 'In 1885 he left the Methodist church denouncing the "easy, indulgent, accommodating, mammonized" kind of Wesleyanism which tolerated church parties, festivals, and dramatic presentations and "erected gorgeous and costly temples to gratify its pride"' (Synan, *The Holiness-Pentecostal Movement in the United States,* pp. 42–54, cited p. 46). Many people agreed with Brooks and thus 'come-outism' was not an option but a necessity. Blumhofer writes, 'This persuasion (the come-outism articulated by Brooks) molded the subculture in which Pentecostal views flourished' (*Restoring the Faith,* pp. 14, 29. cited p. 14, parenthetical statement added). However, it was not only the more radical holiness preachers who believed the mainline Christian traditions were backslidden. The prominent higher life (Keswickian) preacher A.J. Gordon, challenged the Evangelical Alliance for the United States held in Washington, D.C. in 1887 with these words: 'It's not an orthodox creed which repels the masses, but an orthodox greed'. Gordon challenged the conference to recognize that the masses' complaint was against the Protestant Christians who were hoarding money (Grant Wacker, 'The Holy Spirit and the Spirit of the Age in American Protestantism, 1880–1910', *The Journal of American History* 72.1 [June 1985], p. 46). Therefore many of the more radical evangelicals agreed with the holiness preachers that the mainline denominations were backslidden beyond

on American soil. The Pentecostal movement first sprouted in the geographical regions that were most familiar with revivalistic Christianity and were most often subject to troubling change and conflict; namely, the South, Midwest and Far-west.[28] With the exception of New England, Pentecostalism became a national movement almost immediately.

Holiness Influences upon Pentecostalism

The roots of the Pentecostal movement were firmly entrenched within the Holiness movements, both the Wesleyan Holiness movement (which was Pentecostalism's immediate predecessor)[29] and the

---

recovery and to associate with them was sinful (Blumhofer, *Restoring the Faith*, p. 29).

[28] Williams, *America's Religions*, pp. 261–62. Cf. Synan, *The Holiness-Pentecostal Movement in the United States*. 'It is a matter of record that the most radical elements in the holiness movement were in the rural South and Midwest and that most holiness denominations began in those regions from 1895–1900' (p. 52).

[29] Marsden, *Understanding Fundamentalism and Evangelicalism*, p. 42, states,

'The holiness movement was actually a variety of movements growing out of the teachings of John Wesley … holiness groups usually were concerned not only with personal purity but also with responsibilities toward the poor … holiness organizations … were leaders in Protestant care for the poor and evangelism to the outcasts'.

Cf. Donald W. Dayton, 'The Limits of Evangelicalism: The Pentecostal Tradition' in D.W. Dayton and R.K. Johnston (eds.), *The Variety of American Evangelicalism* (Downers Grove, IL: InterVarsity, 1991), pp. 36–56: 'Pentecostalism is to be understood as a radical wing of the Wesleyan/holiness movement of the late nineteenth century' (p. 49). See also Synan, *The Holiness-Pentecostal Movement in the United States*, who argues persuasively for the same thesis as D. Dayton. See also Anderson, *Vision of the Disinherited*, chapter two 'The Holiness Background', pp. 28–46. Anderson, like Synan and Dayton, emphasizes that Pentecostalism's immediate origins are located in the more radical phases of the Holiness movements. He states, 'The outstanding characteristics of the Holiness movement—literal-minded Biblicism, emotional fervor, puritanical mores, enmity toward ecclesiasticism, and above all belief in a 'Second Blessing' in Christian experience—were inherited and perpetuated by the Pentecostals'. 'Except for speaking in tongues, in the early days there was little to distinguish the Pentecostal believer from his holiness brethren' (p. 28). The only Pentecostal denominations in existence prior to 1910 were those groups which were swept into the movement as an already existing holiness body and up until 1910, most Pentecostals accepted without question the three works of grace. Two well-known Pentecostal denominations which were first Holiness denominations (embracing entire sanctification as a second work of grace) are The Church of God in Christ (COGIC) under the leadership of Charles Mason and the Church of God, Cleveland, Tennessee. Both denominations adhere to three works of grace and understand the third work as 'the baptism of the Holy Spirit' which is usually accompanied by tongues. Prior to

and the Keswickian higher life movement.[30] These Holiness movements 'were committed to the idea that conversion ought to be followed by another landmark religious experience, and they both
called this experience the baptism of the Holy Spirit'.[31] Both

---

embracing Pentecostalism, they would have understood the second work of grace
(sanctification) as the baptism in the Holy Spirit. See the articles in *DPCM* for a
brief history of these denominations. The Wesleyan Holiness movement was an
attempt to recapture John Wesley's doctrine of sanctification. They emphasized
that moral perfection was an achievable reality, which was recognized as a distinct
second act of grace and they identified the second act of grace as the baptism of
the Holy Spirit. The purpose of the Holy Spirit baptism experience was to eradicate inbred sin, thus enabling one to live a life of moral perfection. The baptism
in the Holy Spirit was framed in puritistic concepts. See Anderson, *Vision of the
Disinherited*, Appendix One, pp. 289–90, for a clear, concise, chronological defini-
tional scheme for the different views concerning the three 'Acts of Grace'. See
also Paul M. Bassett, 'The Theological Identity of North American Holiness
Movement: Its Understanding of the Nature and Role of The Bible' in Dayton
and Johnston (eds.), *The Variety of American Evangelicalism*, pp. 72–108.

[30] For recent discussions of the Higher Life movement see Ernest R. Sandeen, *The Roots of Fundamentalism: British and American Millenarianism, 1880–1930*
(Chicago, IL: The University of Chicago Press, 1970), pp. 132–87. Marsden, *Fundamentalism and American Culture*, pp. 72–101. D.W. Bebbington, *Evangelicalism in
Modern Britain: A History from the 1730s to the 1980s* (London: Unwin Hyman Ltd.),
pp. 151–80. For the Higher Life movement's impact on Pentecostalism see W.M.
Menzies, 'The Non-Wesleyan Origins of the Pentecostal Movement' in Synan
(ed.), *Aspects of Pentecostal-Charismatic Origins*, pp. 81–98. E.D. Waldvogel (Blumhofer), 'The Overcoming Life: A Study in the Reformed Evangelical Origins of
Pentecostalism' (PhD dissertation, Harvard University, 1977). E.D. Blumhofer,
'Purity and Perfection: A Study in The Pentecostal Perfectionist Heritage', in
Richard Hughes (ed.), *The American Quest for the Primitive Church* (Urbana, IL: University of Illinois, 1988), pp. 257–82. Higher Life movements advocated a second
work of grace yet unlike the Wesleyan Holiness groups they understood this second work in terms of power and also called it 'The baptism of The Holy Spirit'.
The experience or 'enduement of power' enabled one to be an effective 'soul
winner'. Thus they emphasized Christian service and framed the baptism experience with 'power' concepts, and so sanctification was still understood to be a
progressive process. For a discussion pertaining to the contemporary positions of
these holiness groups, dispensational and Reformed see Dieter *et al.*, *Five Views
On Sanctification* (Grand Rapids, MI: Zondervan, 1987). See also Henry H. Knight
III, 'From Aldersgate to Azusa: Wesley and the Renewal of Pentecostal Spirituality', *JPT* 8 (April, 1996), pp. 82–98. Knight's important article discusses J.
Wesley's development of a uniquely Protestant understanding of holiness and
then the appropriation of Wesley's teaching on holiness by three prominent holiness strands: the Methodist theology of Phoebe Palmer, the Arminianized Calvinism of Charles Finney and the Reformed holiness teaching of the Keswick movement.

[31] Grant Wacker, 'The Holy Spirit and the Spirit of the Age in American Protestantism, 1880–1910', *The Journal of American History* 72.1 (June 1985), p. 48.

movements regarded this baptism experience as biblical and essential in maintaining a victorious life over sin in the present age. Furthermore, 'for those involved, it was neither primarily Wesleyan nor Reformed, but essentially *Christian*'.[32] Pentecostals, like the various Holiness groups, proclaimed that holiness of heart and life was a crisis experience that followed the conversion experience and was apprehended and maintained by faith. Yet unlike most other Holiness groups, Pentecostals adamantly preached a third distinct blessing of the Holy Spirit, which they also called 'The baptism of the Holy Spirit'. This Spirit-baptism was an enduement of power for proclamation and demonstration of the Gospel and was initially evidenced by speaking in unlearned tongues.[33]

The Pentecostals shared a similar theological and sociological context with the Holiness movements. They preached restorative revivalistic messages and affirmed the necessity of a Spirit baptism experience that was subsequent to salvation and a clean heart. Their worship services (especially the Pentecostals and some of the Wesleyan Holiness folk) were interracial and included physical healings and the manifestation of tongues.[34] Marsden points out that even though there were clear distinctions between these movements, all three were essentially conservative on most points of theology and were actively involved in revivalism. Even though these groups had significant differences concerning 'the baptism of the

---

[32] Blumhofer, 'Purity and Preparation', p. 266.

[33] Knight, 'From Aldersgate to Azusa', p. 93. Knight points out that the three blessing 'soteriology' was the teaching of the earliest Pentecostal leaders, Charles Parham, W.J. Seymour, C.H. Mason, G.B. Cashwell, and Florence Crawford.

[34] Concerning 'restorative revivalism' see Blumhofer, *Restoring the Faith*, p. 12, where she defines restorationism as 'the impulse to restore the primitive or original order of things as revealed in Scripture, free from the accretions of church history and tradition'. Marsden in *Understanding Fundamentalism and Evangelicalism*, p. 43, writes, 'Pentecostals insisted that true heart religion be evidenced by unmistakable signs of the Spirit's radical transforming power, especially the pentecostal signs of faith healing and speaking in tongues'. Mark A. Noll, 'Christianity and Culture in America' in Howard C. Kee, *Christianity: A Social and Cultural History* (New York: Macmillan, 1991), p. 731, observes, 'Meetings at Azusa Street, which went on for three years, were marked by spontaneous prayer and preaching, a nearly unprecedented cooperation between Blacks and Whites, and the active participation of women'.

Holy Spirit' (resulting in many controversies and divisions among them), they were united in their common opposition to modernity.[35]

Pentecostalism, like the Wesleyan Holiness movement(s) from which it first emerged, was a populist movement *protesting* the evils of modernity and the cold cerebral Christianity of the mainline Protestant traditions.[36] The Holiness and Pentecostal people represented a conservative counterweight among the lower income people groups to the liberal thinking of the upper and middle socio-economic classes.[37] By 'coming out' of the older mainline churches, these people were *protesting* the innovative 'modernistic' developments and protecting old time revivalistic Christianity, which they perceived as being in danger of extinction in America.[38] The Pentecostal and Holiness movements were not direct descendants of old-school Presbyterianism but were instead products of Wesleyan thought. 'The structures of Wesleyan thought were not characteristically those of the tradition of "Protestant orthodoxy"' and so 'these movements are not classical Protestantism but protests against it'.[39]

---

[35] Marsden, *Understanding Fundamentalism and Evangelicalism*, pp. 39–44, cited p. 44.

[36] Cox, *Fire From Heaven*, p. 75, 'the real enemy was the "coldness" of conventional religion'.

[37] Synan, *The Holiness-Pentecostal Movement*, p 58.

[38] Anderson, *Vision of the Disinherited*, p. 223. Cf. Synan, *The Holiness-Pentecostal Movement*, pp. 52–53, who argues that the Holiness groups which began after 1894 were a 'religious revolt which paralleled the political and economic revolt of populism' and so 'both the holiness and the populist movements were protests against the Eastern establishments'.

[39] Dayton, 'Yet Another Layer of the Onion', pp. 98–99. He writes, 'two of the ten volumes in the original Oxford edition of Princetonian B.B. Warfield's collected works are devoted to the intense refutation of all sorts of contemporary "perfectionisms" from Ritschl through Methodism and Oberlin to the major "holiness" teachers of the late nineteenth century'. Dayton believes that

> one of the major causes of misunderstandings of Wesley's doctrine of Christian perfection is that the Western categories of 'perfection' are used to interpret what is derived more fundamentally from Eastern categories. Wesley's thought is as Catholic as it is Protestant not only in the sense that it ultimately derives from the '*via media*' of Anglicanism, but also in the fact that he self-consciously used Catholic sources, *and the fundamental shape of his thought moves more in a Catholic than magisterial Protestant direction* (p. 98, italics added).

Melvin E. Dieter, in a paper presented to the Society for Pentecostal Studies on November 11, 1988, entitled, 'The Wesleyan/Holiness And Pentecostal Movements: Commonalities, Confrontation and Dialogue' argues that 'the ulti-

Pentecostalism was a development of Wesleyan thought. Pentecostalism could not have come from the Reformed tradition. It was
Wesleyan thought impacting the Reformed tradition that produced
the Keswick movement. Although the Holiness and Pentecostal
movements sided with the Fundamentalists (Old school Princeton
orthodoxy) against Modernism, the Wesleyan Holiness and Pentecostal movements came into existence in protest against Presbyterian orthodoxy. This is especially true of Pentecostalism even
though it shares with Fundamentalism an opposition to modernity.

Modernity's Influence upon Pentecostalism

The impact of rationalistic modernity upon Protestant Christianity
pushed many Evangelicals into various forms of theological liberalism.[40] The particular innovations of modernity that challenged traditional Christianity were as follows: 1) evolutionary theory in both its
biological and social applications which diminished the supernatural
and personal aspects of God; 2) higher criticism which undermined
the authority of Scripture; and 3) comparative religion studies which
relativized Christianity and deprived it of its unique and absolute
character.[41] Modernistic North America made economic upward
mobility an achievable possibility for many people and thus the
older frontier denominations (like Methodism) became more mainstream and increasingly more concerned with middle class values
(formality in worship, ornate buildings, Victorian values).[42]

Pentecostalism was protesting the secularized social order produced by modernity and the spiritually sterile mainline denominations that attempted to accommodate the worldview of modernity.[43]

---

mate charge that Warfield and his friends leveled against the movement (New-
school revivalistic Calvinism of C. Finney and others) was that it was really
'Methodist' (p. 7).

[40] Timothy P. Weber, *Living in the Shadow of The Second Coming: American Premillennialism, 1875–1982* (Chicago: The University of Chicago Press, 1987), p. 86.

[41] See Anderson, *Vision of the Disinherited,* p. 31 and Marsden, *Fundamentalism
and American Culture*, pp. 25–26.

[42] Anderson, *Vision of the Disinherited,* p. 31.

[43] Blumhofer, *Restoring the Faith*, pp. 98–99. Pentecostals took seriously the
biblical injunctions to simple dress and detachment toward material things. Their
strong ethic of separation and intense community bond through shared religious
community experiences (which were ridiculed by those who did not embrace
Pentecostalism), nurtured a strong distaste for traditional churches. Pentecostals
often described traditional denominations as 'dead' or 'cold' or 'lukewarm'.

'Pentecostalism' then 'may be viewed as one small part of a wide-spread, long-term protest against the whole thrust of modern urban-industrial capitalistic society'.[44] Fundamentalism appealed to the 'respectable' Protestant and Anglo-European working class whose ambitions and desires were essentially middle-class Victorian.[45] Pentecostalism attracted 'the [socially] disinherited both black and white, in areas of the country least affected by the forces of modernization'[46] and 'spread most rapidly among the self disciplined lower to middle socio-economic classes. *But an ardent desire for the unmediated experience of the Holy Spirit was still a more universal characteristic of those who became Pentecostals?* (emphasis added).[47] The Pentecostals longed for and would not settle for anything less than an experiential manifestation of the Spirit's 'direct divine, incontrovertible intervention which did not rely on the intellect or feeling but on a sign of the presence of the Holy Ghost which both the individual experiencing it and all who were looking on would know that "the work had been done"'.[48]

---

[44] Anderson, *Vision of the Disinherited*, p. 223.

[45] Marsden, *Fundamentalism and The American Culture*, p. 202. Pentecostalism and the radical holiness groups usually existed on the fringes of society.

[46] Williams, *America's Religions*, p. 263. Marsden, *Understanding Fundamentalism and Evangelicalism*, pp. 42–43, 'Pentecostalism … was even more radical (than the Holiness groups) in its teachings and more prone to attract the socially disinherited'.

[47] Mark A. Noll, *A History of Christianity in the United States and Canada* (Grand Rapids, MI: Eerdmans, 1992), p. 387. On the same page, Noll, to help underscore the passionate desire of Pentecostals to experience the Spirit, records the testimony of Alice Reynolds, a teenager who was baptized in the Spirit on Easter Sunday, 1907 in Indianapolis:

The wrath of God's presence in the service deeply moved me, until there was a complete melting of the reserve that had held me back from a full surrender to God … Spontaneously I rose to my feet, lifting my hands with a glad note of praise, 'Thank God for the baptism in the Holy Spirit; praise, O praise the Lord!' … As this praise came from my lips, for the first time in my life I sank to the floor … In a few moments my jaws began to tremble, and the praise that was literally flooding my soul came forth in languages I had never known.

One can find countless number of testimonies similar to this one in any early Pentecostal publication. See also E.L. Blumhofer, *Pentecost in My Soul: Explorations in the Meaning of Pentecostal Experience in the Assemblies of God* (Springfield, MO: Gospel Publishing House, 1989) for a collection of Spirit baptism testimonies.

[48] Dieter, 'The Wesleyan/Holiness and Pentecostal Movements', p. 18.

The Pentecostal movement was formed from the margins of mainstream society and was birthed as an 'oppressed people' who yearned for a desire to see the glory of God. Cold cerebral orthodoxy could not liberate them from an oppressive society.[49] Pentecostalism has always belonged to the more marginalized members of society.[50] Because early Pentecostals came predominantly from the lower socio-economic strata of society, they tended to be classified as pre-modern, anti-intellectual and anti-social. Yet in practice, Pentecostals were a paramodern, counter-culture movement.

In an era of the 'war to end all wars', Pentecostals were Pacifists. In an era when women were excluded from public voice, Pentecostals were ordaining women as ministers. In an era of the KKK (Ku Klux Klan), Pentecostal blacks and whites were worshipping together.[51]

Thus, many early Pentecostals were characterized by a radical paramodern counter-culture identity.

The personal testimonies of the earliest Pentecostals were ones of tremendous sacrifice and great endurance, all for the sake of the 'Full Gospel message'. Pentecostals worshiped in renovated saloons, railway cars, abandoned warehouses, tents, schoolhouses, private homes and open fields.[52] These early pioneers,[53] which in-

---

[49] Cheryl Bridges Johns, 'The Adolescence of Pentecostalism: In Search of a Legitimate Sectarian Identity', *Pneuma* 17.1 (Spring, 1995), pp. 13–14.

[50] Blumhofer, *Pentecost in My Soul*, p. 15, 'With few exceptions, they (Pentecostals) were neither highly educated nor economically prosperous. Few if any held positions of social or cultural influence'.

[51] C.B. Johns, 'The Adolescence of Pentecostalism', pp. 4–5. Johns' writes, 'because of its ecstatic religious practices and its "abnormal" social behavior, Pentecostalism was opposed by the society at large and by the established churches ... Yes, Pentecostals were different from the dominant culture, but they were *like one another* in speech, dress, values'. Concerning the pacifistic stance of early Pentecostals, see D.J. Wilson, 'Pacifism' in *DPCM*, pp. 658–60. Early Pentecostals were generally but not universally pacifistic, and most Pentecostal denominations held to pacifism as the 'official position' of the denomination. Two influential pacifistic Pentecostal leaders were Donald Gee, who became chairman of the British Assemblies of God, and Charles H. Mason, Bishop of the Church of God in Christ (Memphis, Tennessee). Mason, as a result of being a (black) pacifist, was put in prison and accused of being a German sympathizer during the war (pp. 658–59).

[52] Anderson, *Vision of the Disinherited*, p. 77 and Grant Wacker, 'Character and Modernization of North American Pentecostalism', a paper presented to the Society for Pentecostal Studies, 1991, p. 3.

cluded women, often lived in extreme poverty and would venture out into the world passionately preaching the Gospel to whoever would listen. Pentecostals literally desired to evangelize the world in their generation. A.J. Tomlinson[54] articulated this passion during his address to the 1912 General Assembly of the Church of God, Cleveland, Tennessee, with these words:

> This is the time when everyone that can preach or conduct a prayer meeting ought to be out in the field. We speak in the fear of God, from a sincere heart, when we say that the world ought to be evangelized in our generation, and we should not dare to thrust this responsibility on a future generation ... The fields are before us and white unto harvest. It is time to push out into new territory. Foreign countries should be occupied, and the gospel given to them as rapidly as possible.[55]

Many responded to the 'call' and set out 'by faith' to evangelize the lost. They often 'set out with little or no money, seldom knowing where they would spend the night, or how they would get their next meal, sleeping in barns, tents and parks' and often 'bands of workers would pool their funds, buy a tent or rent a hall and live communally in the meeting place, subsisting at times on flour and water, or rice, or sardines and sausages'.[56] Howard Goss, an early

---

[53] See Anderson, *Vision of the Disinherited*, chapter six titled 'Apostles and Prophets' for an interpretive summary of the information he gleaned from his compilation of biographical material of 45 leaders who joined the Pentecostal movement during its earliest years. Anderson utilized this material to support a 'social deprivation theory' as the primary means of understanding the beginning and continued growth of Pentecostalism. No one disagrees about the socio-economic and culturally diverse origins of the earliest people who became Pentecostals. A critique of the social deprivation model will come later in this chapter. For the biographical stories of seven Pentecostal pioneers who shaped the British Pentecostal movement and whose ministries encircled the world see Colin C. Whittaker, *Seven Pentecostal Pioneers*, (Springfield, MO: Gospel Publishing House, 1985).

[54] Tomlinson was elected as the first general overseer of the Church of God (Cleveland, Tenn.) in 1907. See H.D. Hunter, 'Tomlinson, Ambrose Jessup' in *DPCM*, pp. 846–48.

[55] Lewis J. Willis (compiler), *Assembly Addresses of the General Overseers: Sermons that Guided the Church*, (Cleveland, Tennessee: Pathway Press, 1986), p. 20.

[56] Anderson, *Vision of the Disinherited*, p. 77. Anderson (p. 78) offers the following story in order to illustrate the typical privations endured by many of the Pentecostal pioneers:

pioneer, 'acknowledged that the very "foundation for the vast Pentecostal Movement" had been laid by loners and free lancers, by missionaries without board support and by pastors without degrees or salaries or "restful holidays"'.[57]

The Pentecostal evangelists moved from town to town by walking, hopping delivery wagons, jumping freight trains, or bumming rides. They traveled throughout the land often warning sinners from courthouse steps, city parks, dance halls, gambling houses and red light districts about the coming wrath of God. They challenged Christians to be prepared for the second coming of Jesus, which they believed would take place very soon.[58]

C. Downey articulated this eschatological fervor which motivated the early Pentecostal people and preachers to evangelize the world and 'pentecostalize' Christians:

> This Gospel of the Kingdom shall be preached in all the world for a witness unto all nations: and then shall the end come. We believe under God this is the great message for these days. Baptized Saints are confidently assured that we are on the threshold

---

The story of Walter J. Higgins who, together with his wife, accepted the pastorate of a Pentecostal assembly in Morehouse, Missouri. They were provided with living quarters in a crawl-up attic furnished with one iron bed, one table, and several wooden crates for chairs. They lived on sorghum molasses and potatoes three times a day, and Higgins went about his duties with the soles of his shoes literally worn through to his feet. Small wonder many Pentecostal preachers worked at manual labor to support themselves.

[57] Wacker, 'Character and Modernization', p. 17.

[58] Anderson, *Vision of The Disinherited*, p. 78. Anderson argues that the central theme of the early Pentecostal movement was 'Jesus is coming soon'. D.W. Faupel in his, *The Everlasting Gospel* builds on Anderson's contribution of Pentecostalism being a millenarian movement. Yet Faupel does not accept social deprivation as the best explanation for Pentecostalism's genesis. His thesis is that 'American Pentecostalism can be best understood as the emergence of a millenarian belief system that resulted from a paradigm-shift which took place within nineteenth century Perfectionism' (p. 18). Faupel uses a biological model to organize and present his material. His theological historiography is the most thorough presentation of early Pentecostalism. E. Blumhofer, building on her early work and drawing upon the insights of G. Wacker, argues that Pentecostalism is best understood by means of a restorationist motif.

of the greatest event in the history of the world, viz: The imminent appearing of Jesus Christ.[59]

Thus, Pentecostals moved along the fringes of the established denominations, appealing to the 'independents' and 'come-outers'
whose theological preferences had already marginalized them from
mainline traditions and had predisposed them to accept the logic of
the Pentecostal 'Full Gospel message'.[60] They infiltrated nonde-
nominational and independent churches, Holiness associations, and,
when possible, denominational churches in order 'to proclaim the
full and final restoration of New Testament Christianity'.[61]

The Pentecostal message offered wholeness and healing because
it presented a frame of reference for understanding human experience and defining ultimate concerns.[62] This, in turn, instilled both
hope and purpose in the hearts of the listeners because the preachers and teachers 'assured all who would listen that none had fallen
too low to look up and discover dignity and status as a child of
God'.[63] D.W. Myland, an early Pentecostal pioneer and interpreter
of the movement, wrote in 1910:

> God sent this latter rain to gather up all the poor and outcast,
> and make us love everybody … He poured it out upon the little
> sons and daughters, and servants and handmaidens … God is
> taking the despised things, the base things and being glorified in
> them.[64]

---

[59] C.W. Downey, 'The Gospel of the Kingdom', *The Word and Witness* 10
(March 20, 1914), p. 2, cited in Faupel, *The Everlasting Gospel*, p. 21.

[60] Faupel *The Everlasting Gospel*, p. 14, argues that, 'the baptism in the Holy
Spirit evidenced by speaking in an unknown tongue, the only unique feature of
Pentecostalism, proved to be the final piece of a larger interlocking puzzle which
had been painfully put together, piece by piece, within nineteenth century Perfectionism'.

[61] Blumhofer, *Restoring the Faith*, p. 84. Faupel, *The Everlasting Gospel*, pp. 14–
15, points out that by 1909 the Pentecostal message and movement had spread
throughout the USA and was established in at least 50 countries of the world.
Thus the message had found a receptive audience in nearly every nation in the
world. However, not everyone responded favorably to the presence of the Pentecostal evangelists in their communities and churches.

[62] Blumhofer, *Restoring the Faith*, p. 92.

[63] Blumhofer, *Restoring the Faith*, p. 84.

[64] Cited in Cox, *Fire from Heaven*, p. 67.

The Pentecostal revivalist message of end time restoration brought wholeness to those who lived on the fringes of modernistic society.

The humanization of those who were socially and economically marginalized came by means of Scripture filtered through the worldview of the Pentecostal community. The practice of affirming one another as brother and sister as well as the practice of reinforcing the behavior codes of conduct (similar to the Holiness standards) while allowing anyone in the community to participate in the service (through testimonies, songs and at times even preaching), also contributed to the process of becoming whole.[65]

Society influenced those who would become Pentecostals, and no one denies that the earliest Pentecostals were the oppressed, marginalized, poor working classes of society. Revivalist restoration preaching and practices brought meaning to their lives. However, their passion for the Kingdom of God was fueled by 'their reading' of the biblical meta-narrative and not necessarily because they were socially deprived. Their social cultural milieu contributed to 'how' they read Scripture as well as to 'what' themes they heard in Scripture. Thus, their social situation enabled the Pentecostal pioneers to 'hear' and 'long for' themes in Scripture which were being ignored or were viewed as unacceptable by both the Fundamentalists and the liberals of that era. An 'eschatological intensity' and 'existential identification' with the 'Full Gospel message' of the New Testament Apostolic Christianity shaped Pentecostals.[66]

In sum, 'Pentecostalism' emerged as an identifiable Christian restorationist revivalistic movement within the first decade of the twentieth century. The major theological themes of renewal held by Holiness movements (Wesleyan and Keswickian) were absorbed

---

[65] See Frank Bartleman with forward by Vinson Synan, *Azusa Street: The Roots of Modern-day Pentecost*, (South Plainfield, NJ: Bridge Publishing, 1980). This book is a reprint of Bartleman's 1925 history entitled, *How "Pentecost" Came to Los Angeles*. Bartleman offers an eyewitness interpretive account of Los Angeles revivals and also discusses the worship services of these revivals. See pp. 53–60 for his description of services at the Azusa street mission. Pentecostal services were not leaderless, but the leaders, like Seymour, did allow for a high degree of involvement by the laity in the services.

[66] M.W. Dempster, 'The Search For Pentecostal Identity', *Pneuma* 15.1 (Spring, 1993), p. 1.

and synthesized into the 'Full Gospel message', which by 1919 became entirely identified with the Pentecostals.[67]

The Pentecostals' social location was predominantly from the lower social and economic strata of American society. Yet, as American church historian Mark Noll has pointed out, the most universal characteristic of early Pentecostals was their passionate desire for an unmediated experience with the Holy Spirit.[68] They sought to establish a deep and personal relationship with Jesus Christ through Spirit baptism. Their religious passion was shaped and facilitated by their restorationist reading of the New Testament narrative. Frank J. Ewart, an early leader within Pentecostalism, expressed this perspective when he wrote:

> Although this movement was based squarely and completely on Scripture, its very heartbeat was an *experience* and not some theological premise that had been developed after years of study and re-evaluation. It had no affiliation with modern theology (emphasis added).[69]

Ewart's comment is consistent with early Pentecostal understanding; that is, they saw themselves as scripturally sound and at odds with both liberal theology and Protestant orthodoxy. The Pentecostal movement was a protest both against modernity and against mainline Christianity. Their emphasis on the baptism of the Holy Spirit and healing separated them from the Fundamentalists. Therefore, the Scripture read through the marginalized Wesleyan Holiness eyes from a restorationist and revivalistic perspective was the primary cause of the Pentecostal movement.

---

[67] Timothy L. Smith writes in his *Called unto Holiness: The Story of the Nazarenes; The Formative Years,* (Kansas City, MO: Nazarene Publishing House, 1962), p. 320, that 'the spread of Pentecostalism teaching on the "baptism in the Holy Spirit" [the third Blessing] with signs following afterwards, (speaking in tongues), caused the Nazarene General Assembly of 1919 to drop the word 'Pentecostal' from the denomination's name, in order to avoid identification with the new movement'.

[68] Noll, *A History of Christianity*, p. 387. See also footnote 49 above.

[69] Frank J. Ewart, *The Phenomenon of Pentecost* (Hazelwood, MO: Word Aflame Press, 1947, Revised 1975), p. 39.

The 3-D View of Pentecostalism

Sociologists, psychologists and many historians have predominantly explained the origin, attraction and expansion of the Pentecostal movements through the utilization of some form of Social Deprivation theory, which includes social disorganization and/or psychologically defective individuals.[70] The projection of Pentecostalism in 3-D[71] does not enhance ones view of this religious movement. When Pentecostalism is viewed in 3-D, all one sees is a gross reductionism that eclipses, ignores, or completely dismisses the religious claims of the Pentecostals.[72] Their religious experiences are generally viewed as some sort of a personality defect resulting from socio-economic deprivation. This is especially emphasized when the Pentecostals being analyzed were members of racial minority groups (Black and Hispanic) and White Appalachian folk who had not yet made it into middle class status.[73] For example, R. Anderson argues that:

> Most pentecostal converts came from peasant roots, and it may well be that those whose religious heritage was other than that of evangelical-pietistic Protestantism were predisposed to Pentecostalism by the mystical, supernatural, even animistic and magical notions common to those who live close to the soil ... There is no doubt, however, that material and social deprivation plus an

---

[70] Virginia H. Hine, 'The Deprivation and Disorganization Theories of Social Movements' in I.I. Zarestsky and M.P. Leone (eds.), *Religious Movements in Contemporary America* (Princeton, NJ: Princeton University Press, 1974), pp. 646–61 with reference to p. 646. Her article was based upon case studies of Pentecostalism in the USA, Mexico, Haiti, and Columbia. For a succinct review and critique of the historical development of social movement theories with a special emphasis on the impact on interpreting Pentecostalism, see Albert G. Miller, 'Pentecostalism as a Social Movement: Beyond The Theory Of Deprivation', *JPT* 9 (1996), pp. 98–119.

[71] I am using '3-D' as an abbreviation for deprivation, disorganization, and defective.

[72] Miller, 'Pentecostalism as a Social Movement', p. 114.

[73] Luther P. Gerlach, 'Pentecostalism: Revolution or Counter-Revolution?' in Zaretsky and Leone (eds.), *Religious Movements in Contemporary America*, pp. 669–99, with reference to pp. 669–70. Gerlach and Hine worked together for a number of years researching Pentecostalism. They have presented their definitive work for the spread of Pentecostalism (and the Black Power Movement) in their monograph called *People, Power, Change: Movements of Social Transformation* (Indianapolis, IN; Bobbs-Merril Educational Publishing, 1970).

animistic religious outlook combined to predispose most of the recruits to the early Pentecostal movement.[74]

Anderson explains the initial origin and ongoing expansion of Pentecostalism by means of the Social Deprivation theory. Anderson argues that Pentecostals were socially discontent because they were enormously frustrated with their very low social position in society.[75] Pentecostals came largely from rural-agrarian origins (even though they were diverse in racial and ethnic origin) and could not adjust to the shock of transplantation as a result of mass urbanization. This social condition of disorganization was exasperated due to 'their generally low social status' and 'poor or no education'.[76] He concludes his monograph by restating this controlling thesis: 'the root source of Pentecostalism was social discontent'.[77]

Anderson's statistical information and historical presentation of the first twenty-five years of Pentecostalism is helpful.[78] Unfortunately, by analyzing this information entirely through the Social Deprivation theory, he reduces the early Pentecostals' quest for a deeper spiritual walk with Jesus as a personal weakness rather than a serious faith claim. Thus, 'their religious beliefs or their native exegesis was taken as less than an accurate explanation of why they were attracted to this movement'.[79] Why individuals were attracted to Pentecostalism may have had more to do with how they read and interpreted Scripture and their religious quest, than being deprived. It would appear that Anderson recognizes the religious factor when he writes:

---

[74] Anderson, *Vision of the Disinherited*, pp. 135, 228.

[75] Anderson, *Vision of the Disinherited*, p. 154.

[76] Anderson, *Vision of the Disinherited*, pp. 226–27.

[77] Anderson, *Vision of the Disinherited*, p. 240.

[78] Anderson, *Vision of the Disinherited*, p. 229, recognizes that his 'hard statistical evidence' can only account for the origins. Thus when he discusses the continued growth of the movement (which draws adherents from the middle and upper middle class); he writes,

'The neo-Pentecostals do not suffer a material deprivation of the early Pentecostals, but they suffer a real or imagined deprivation of respect and prestige … Pentecostals, old and new, have typically testified that before their conversion to Pentecostalism they felt empty and hungry for God or for something they could not articulate. In short, they felt deprived'.

[79] Miller, 'Pentecostalism as a Social Movement', p. 114.

By far the most important difference between those working poor who became Pentecostals and the much greater number who did not was the religious orientation of the former … the vast majority of recruits to Pentecostalism came from the Holiness movement, from emotional, evangelical, and revivalistic Protestant backgrounds or from the more crudely superstitious forms of Catholicism.[80]

However, Anderson (along with many others) believes that the real cause of the movement is Social Deprivation, and that Pentecostalism serves as another example of the Church-sect Theory.[81] For he asserts that, 'the Pentecostal movement fits the classical pattern of sects that arise primarily among the socially deprived and [then] later developed "churchly" characteristics as the deprivation of its membership is ameliorated'.[82]

Pentecostal identity was forged by the fiery restorative revivalistic preaching of the Full Gospel message (which places great emphasis on millenarian theology and ecstatic experiences) and was molded in an expressively experiential celebrative worship (which witnessed the charismatic gifts—healings and tongues—as a present reality in their community). This belief and practice lends itself to Social Deprivation analysis.[83] Thus, Pentecostalism is explained as some kind of defense or compensation mechanism of persons suffering from societal stresses, economic problems and/or psychological deficiencies.[84] Those who became Pentecostal did so because they were deprived, disorganized and/or defective.

When Social Deprivation models are used to explain the *cause* and *continued* growth of Pentecostalism, the movement's sole function is reduced merely to existing as a *Haven of the Masses.*[85] This haven exists for those who cannot find the source of gratification

[80] Anderson, *Vision of the Disinherited*, p. 228.

[81] See Philip D. Kenneson, *Beyond Sectarianism: Re-Imagining Church and World* (Harrisburg, PA: Trinity Press International, 1999), for a brief overview and discussion of sociological use of church-sect type.

[82] Anderson, *Vision of the Disinherited*, p. 228.

[83] Hine, 'The Deprivation and Disorganization', p. 652.

[84] Gerlach, 'Pentecostalism: Revolution or Counter-Revolution?', p. 674.

[85] The title of Christian Lalive d'Epinay's monograph, *Haven of the Masses: A Study of the Pentecostal Movement in Chile* (London: Lutterworth, 1969).

from society at large.[86] 'Such a view', writes V. Hine, 'is based upon the as yet unproven assumption that political, economic, or social rewards are more satisfying than religious ones'.[87] Therefore, the 3-D view does not take seriously the religious concerns or the cultural exegesis of Scripture as a convincing explanation as to why these people were attracted to the Pentecostal movement. This 3-D view fails to recognize Pentecostals as normal functioning members of society (who are yet at odds with modernity's worldview) who choose to become Pentecostal due to their deep religious hunger and understanding of Scripture.[88] It also fails to account for the discrepancies in the research data.

Anthropologists V. Hine and L. Gerlach initially accepted Social Deprivation and Defect theories as the way to explain the cause and growth of Pentecostalism. However, they abandoned these as 'the' primary and 'necessary' cause because they found no evidence to support their first proposition that 'Pentecostalism was best explained as a haven for the disorganized or confused'.[89] Gerlach states that the 'only thing which does distinguish Pentecostals from the general American population is their specific religious practice and belief' and so 'this cannot then be used to prove them generally defective'.[90] Yet, it is precisely the seemingly unusual belief of Pentecostals (as articulated through the Full Gospel message) and their practices (tongues, trances, dancing, exorcisms, healings) that encourage sociologists, historians (like Anderson) and psychologists to view the Pentecostals as 'havens' for those who cannot cope in the established societal order.[91]

---

[86] Gerlach, 'Pentecostalism: Revolution or Counter-Revolution?', p. 670.

[87] Hine, 'The Deprivation and Disorganization', p. 652.

[88] Gerlach, 'Pentecostalism: Revolution or Counter-Revolution?', p. 671, asks:

how do we know that people are sufficiently deprived, disorganized, devitalized, or defective enough to join or start a movement or sect? Easy! You know that they have reached this condition after they do join or start this activity. Why do they join? Well, because they are deprived, disorganized, devitalized. The trick in getting such tautology accepted is to separate statements about effect and presumed cause by pages of description.

[89] Gerlach, 'Pentecostalism: Revolution or Counter-Revolution?', p. 675. See also Gerlach and Hine, 'Five Factors Crucial to the Growth and Spread of a Modern Religious Movement', *JSSR* 7.1 (Spring, 1968), pp. 23–40.

[90] Gerlach, 'Pentecostalism: Revolution or Counter-Revolution?', p. 679.

[91] Gerlach, 'Pentecostalism: Revolution or Counter-Revolution?', p. 670.

In her article, 'The Deprivation and Disorganization Theories of Social Movements', Hine demonstrates in a thoroughly systematic manner the inadequacy of the Social Deprivation and Disorganization models as they relate to Pentecostalism. She first defines the model used for analysis and then presents actual Pentecostal case studies, which reveal the model's inability to account for all of the conflicting data. A brief review of her research article follows. Concerning the Social Disorganization model, Hine writes:

> There is no question but that the intimacy and emotional support provided by the Pentecostal type of group interaction is a highly successful solution for individuals experiencing social dislocation or family disruption. Nevertheless, the fact that Pentecostalism spreads as effectively among groups where family organization is strong would suggest that while social disorganization may be considered a *facilitating* factor ... It cannot be viewed as [a] necessary [factor].[92]

Pentecostalism does spread among the dislocated, but it also flourishes among life-long urbanites and spreads in small rural communities (in both North and Latin America) where family ties have not been disrupted. In fact, in some case studies, the very functioning of tribal and village social structure facilitated the spread of Pentecostalism.[93] Thus, the Social Disorganization theory does not adequately explain the cause and spread of the Pentecostal movement.

Social Deprivation, embracing both status and economics, is the most common explanation for the rise and growth of all types of social movements.[94] Therefore, one is not surprised to find Social Deprivation as the primary theory used to explain Pentecostalism's origin and growth. Because this theory embraces the church-sect typology, Pentecostalism is generally classified as a sect.[95] However, Hine's and Gelach's research indicates that even though the first Pentecostal wave attracted people from lower socio-economic groups, the recent and still continuing wave of Pentecostalism is

[92] Hine, 'The Deprivation and Disorganization', pp. 650–51.
[93] Hine, 'The Deprivation and Disorganization', pp. 648–49.
[94] Hine, 'The Deprivation and Disorganization', p. 651.
[95] Gerlach and Hine, 'Five Factors Crucial to the Growth', p. 23.

attracting members from the middle and upper middle class who are not suffering from socio-economic deprivation.

In addition, Hine shows that the characteristics typically associated with the 'sect type' and 'economically disinherited' (such as the emphasis on the religious experience, lay leadership, confessional basis for membership, high degree of membership participation, reliance on spontaneous leading of the Holy Spirit in organizational concerns, home meetings, etc.) are found more often within contemporary Pentecostal churches of middle and upper class converts than the older established Pentecostal churches. 'The more routinized "church-like" Pentecostal groups are often those churches whose membership is characteristically drawn from the lower socio-economic levels'.[96] Thus Social Deprivation and church-sect typology cannot entirely account for or provide an accurate analysis of Pentecostalism. Pentecostalism appears to be an anomaly.

Hine's research challenges Anderson's assertion that:

> The poorer, more dislocated and despised, the more marginal and highly mobile people are in the social order, the more extreme will be their ecstatic response ... Today ecstasy is most pronounced in independent storefront Pentecostal missions among blacks and recent Hispanic immigrants.[97]

Hine's research indicates that religious ecstasy is also found to be active in Anglo middle class Pentecostal communities, especially when they are not directly affiliated with the more historic Pentecostal denominations of the first wave.[98]

Hine and Gerlach's research is not attempting to say that the Pentecostal movement is presently only drawing adherents from the middle and upper middle class. Pentecostalism still draws adherents from the lower socio-economic groups. However, it is not exclusively drawing from that category. There are many Pentecostal

---

[96] Hine, 'The Deprivation and Disorganization', p. 656.

[97] Anderson, *Vision of the Disinherited*, p. 231.

[98] See Margaret M. Poloma's, 'By their Fruits ...: A Sociological Assessment Of the Toronto Blessing', a paper presented to the Annual Meeting of the Society for Pentecostal Studies, University of Toronto, Ontario, Canada, March 7–9, 1996. Poloma's statistical analysis demonstrates that middle and upper middle class people, with a post-high school education, desired, sought and experienced ecstatic Christian religious experiences which they then reported had changed their lives.

communities in both America and other countries that are not economically and socially deprived. Hence, socio-economic deprivation
cannot be *the necessary cause* for the spread of Pentecostalism.

Hine recognizes the usefulness of these models, but deprivation
and disorganization should be considered as *facilitating* rather than
causal factors when analyzing the movement. Hine and Gerlach argue that a more satisfying explanation for an individual's conversion
to Pentecostalism can be found in the study of the movement's re-
cruitment patterns.[99] In other words, the 'explanation for the spread
of the movement is to be sought within the dynamics of the movement itself'.[100] Hine and Gerlach define a movement as:

> A group of people who are organized for, ideologically moti-
> vated by, and committed to a purpose which implements some
> form of personal or social change; who are actively engaged in
> the recruitment of others; and whose influence is spreading in
> opposition to the established order within which it originated.[101]

Because they shifted their emphasis from seeking a purely external
cause from outside the movement to analyzing the internal infrastructure of the movement (due to the inability of Social Deprivation to account for all the inconsistencies of the data), Gerlach and
Hine saw Pentecostalism as both the cause and effect of individual
and social change.[102] They suggest a better approach to understanding Pentecostalism (and other movements) would be to consider it
as a 'cause of change' instead of a 'reaction to change'.[103] From this
perspective Pentecostalism is not reactionary but revolutionary.

Pentecostalism does generate individual and social change, and
no doubt societal changes contributed to its persuasive polemics.
Therefore, 'instead of assuming that "strange religious behavior" by
North Americans is a consequence of deprivation or personality
defects, examine such behavior as a commitment to religious
movement and to change'.[104] Unusual behavior, then, is not necessarily a defense or compensation mechanism; rather, it should be

---

[99] Hine, 'The Deprivation and Disorganization', p. 660.
[100] Gerlach and Hine, 'Five Factors Crucial to the Growth', p. 23.
[101] Gerlach and Hine, *People, Power, Change*, p. xvi.
[102] Gerlach, 'Pentecostalism', p. 680.
[103] Gerlach, 'Pentecostalism', p. 672.
[104] Gerlach, 'Pentecostalism', p. 672.

seen as transforming activity. From this perspective, Gerlach describes 'Pentecostalism not as a sect activity and an opiate for the deprived but as a far-flung movement of change'.[105] Pentecostalism as a movement encourages personal transformation that is revolutionary in nature.

Pentecostalism is a revolutionary movement calling for personal and social transformation. Pentecostals were and continue to be motivated by the 'Full Gospel message', which is in direct opposition to modernity's conception of reality (the established order of society). People (predominantly Holiness Christians) were attracted to Pentecostalism because of its seemingly scriptural message and supernatural signs. Pentecostalism was not just a reinterpretation of the 'old time religion'. Pentecostal celebrative worship services, with tongues, trances, exorcisms, dancing and healings, were transforming activities of commitment to a new movement, rather than simply attempting to preserve the old ways. The Full Gospel message was birthed as marginalized Christian peoples from the Anglo and African slave Holiness communities read Scripture with revivalistic restorative lenses. Thus, Pentecostalism originated due to the logical coherence of the Five/Four Fold Pentecostal message validated by the supernatural signs amongst the community and in direct opposition to the predominate worldview of modernity. It was the collision of Scripture, signs (Spirit) and societal worldviews that caused and continues to cause the spread of the movement motivated by the passionate desire for an unmediated experiential encounter with Jesus. The following testimony serves to reiterate the important role that religious experience had within the Pentecostal community.

PENTECOSTAL EXPERIENCE

Sister Lucy M. Leatherman writes from 231 Second Avenue, N.Y. ... her testimony will be an interest to all. 'While seeking the baptism with the Holy Ghost in Los Angeles, after Sister Ferrell laid hands on me, I praised and praised God and saw my Savior in the heavens. And as I praised, I came closer and closer, and I was so small. By and by I swept into the wound in His side, and He was not only in me but I in Him, and there I found that rest that passeth all understanding, and He said to me that,

105 Gerlach, 'Pentecostalism', p. 674.

you are in the bosom of the Father. He said I was clothed upon and in the secret place of the Most High. But I said, Father, I want the gift of the Holy Ghost, and the heavens opened and I was overshadowed, and such power came upon me and went through me. He said, Praise Me, and when I did, angels came and ministered unto me. I was passive in His hands, and by the eye of faith I saw angel hands working on my vocal cords, and I realized they were loosing me. I began to praise Him in an unknown tongue ... Anywhere with Jesus I will gladly go. On land or sea, what matter where, Where Jesus is 'tis heaven there.'[106]

No doubt social deprivation was an important facilitating and for some an enabling factor, but it was not the cause of one's conversion to Pentecostalism. People embraced the new Pentecostal faith because of its 'scripturally' appealing message and its self-authenticating and community validating religious experience(s).

The Early Pentecostal Worldview: A Paramodern Perspective

A worldview may be defined as an overarching conceptual perspective from which one interprets reality, thus making human experience meaningful or understandable. A worldview consists of a cluster of basic assumptions (whether consciously recognized or not) through which one arranges thoughts, responds to experiences and interprets reality in a meaningful manner.[107] Worldviews will vary from culture to culture and from time period to time period, yet a worldview will inevitably exist within every person who is rooted in a particular historical time period. Thus one's cultural environment will be the primary contributor to one's worldview. However one's worldview can be reconfigured.

At the turn of the century, the Pentecostal worldview functioned within the broader 'Christian worldview' and on the fringes of the modernistic worldview.[108] The heart of the traditional Christian

---

[106] William Seymour (ed.), *The Apostolic Faith* 1.3 (1906), p. 4.

[107] L. Russ Bush, *A Handbook for Christian Philosophy* (Grand Rapids, MI: Zondervan, 1991), p. 322.

[108] Modernity, modern age, modernism are all used as synonyms and will be defined from a historical perspective. The modern age began with the Renais-

worldview would be the incarnate, crucified and risen Son of God—Jesus of Nazareth.[109] Pentecostals advocated the traditional Christian concept of God, and they saw humanity as fallen and in need of a Savior. The Pentecostal community also emphasized pietistic themes like the priesthood of all believers, the authoritative role of Scripture in defining doctrinal praxis and the necessity of the continued miraculous involvement of God in creation (signs and wonders).[110]

In other words, the first Pentecostal communities were made up of prior Holiness Christians who embraced Pentecostal doctrines and practices that were not entirely different from what they had believed prior to being identified among the Pentecostal community. In fact, the Pentecostal Full Gospel message and belief system differs little in the expression of its themes from the Holiness message and to some degree, the broader evangelical Protestant Christianity found in North America. Yet there is one major exception, as historian Goff notes: 'the emphasis on such divine intervention was unusually high'. He argues that the baptism in the Holy Spirit evidenced in speaking in other tongues (the new and unique doctrine of Pentecostalism) along with the emphasis on divine healing serve to illustrate the supernatural emphasis within Pentecostalism.[111] Thus from the outside, the Pentecostal and Holiness communities all look the same. However, as Goff points out, there was a significant degree of opposition against the Pentecostal communities from these closest sisters.[112] Physical persecution by others was a common occurrence against the early Pentecostals.[113]

---

sance/ Enlightenment and has come under serious questioning during the crisis of the 21st Century. See Bryan S. Turner (ed.), *Theories of Modernity and Postmodernity* (London: Sage Publications Ltd., 1990). Thomas C. Oden, *Agenda for Theology: After Modernity ... What?* (Grand Rapids, MI, 1990). Stanley J. Grenz, *A Primer on Postmodernism* (Grand Rapids, MI: Eerdmans, 1996).

[109] Ronald H. Nash, *World-Views in Conflict: Choosing Christianity in a World of Ideas* (Grand Rapids, MI: Zondervan, 1992), pp. 32–33.

[110] By doctrinal praxis, this writer is emphasizing the fact that the Pentecostal community's concern for practical doctrine affected how they lived and behaved in society and functioned in the Pentecostal community. Thus their doctrine is praxis driven and scripturally concerned.

[111] Goff, *Fields White unto Harvest*, p. 12.

[112] Goff, *Fields White unto Harvest*, p. 13.

[113] For few examples of violence against Assembly of God ministers see, 'The night God Stopped the Angry mob', *Assemblies of God Heritage* (Spring, 1983), p.

The following report from *The New York Times,* printed Monday, June 8, 1908, serves both to illustrate the outsiders' views of Pentecostalism and to underscore the important themes of the Pentecostal community's worldview.

"'HOLY GHOSTERS" WIN WHITES AND NEGROS:' New sect with Quarters in Forty-first street speaks a strange tongue: SAY WORLD WILL END SOON: 'Chief Saint' Sturtevant, One Time Longshoreman, Aided in his meetings By White and Colored Deaconesses.

For more than a year whites and negroes have been conducting what is described on the board outside as 'The Full Gospel of Holiness Mission' at 325 West Forty-first Street and holding daily meetings. Because of their strong faith in the power of the Holy Ghost to save sinners in the neighborhood and the frequent use of the name in their teaching the mission has become known as the 'Holy Ghosters.'

The services begin each night with an open-air address at Thirty-seventh Street and Eighth Avenue at 7:30 o'clock. Prayers are read by a tall surpliced negro called 'Chief Saint Sturtevant' and a white woman called Sister Williams. These are followed by hymns, sung to the accompaniment of a harmonium, in which black and white deaconesses take part, all wearing short white jackets and black bonnets with flowering veils. In the course of the service a prayer is delivered by a white boy, said to be 6 years old, but who looks older, in which he exhorts all the sinners standing by to repent while there is yet time, as the end of all things is at hand. After a collection has been taken up the Holy Ghosters march to their meeting place in Forty-first Street, which consists of two rooms on the ground floor opening on the street.

Last night when the mission service began at 8:30 o'clock, the room was thronged with men and women of all ages, white and

6–7; 'Beating In Texas Follows Ministry to Blacks', *Assemblies of God Heritage* (Spring, 1986), p. 5; and 'Violent Persecution In The Hills: W.C. Long's "Diehards" Survive Fires, Bullets, and Bombs in the 1920s', *Assemblies of God Heritage* (Winter 1983), p. 3.

black, all sitting together. Some had come out of curiosity, while others were members of the mission. Chief Saint G.C. Deekon (*sic*), a white man, formerly a 'longshoreman, who has renounced that calling, opened the meeting by giving out a hymn, 'There is Peace In My Soul.' This was sung by the congregation, accompanied by Sister Williams on an organ.

The most peculiar part of the service was the 'language of unknown tongues', which Sister Williams Saint Deekon (*sic*), and others of the Holy Ghosters appeared to be able to speak and understand. To the stranger within the gates it seemed a mixture of Italian, Syrian, Arabic, modern Greek, and the gibberish of the Coney Island barkers.

The belief of the missioners is that the world is at an end of its career under the present sinful conditions, that the Messiah is coming soon, and those who wish to understand his preaching must learn the new religion and language.

The Full Gospel Holiness Mission attracts numbers of people of all kinds, who come out of curiosity and listen to the service, which strongly resembles an old-fashion camp meeting.[114]

This journalistic report captures important themes that are a part of the 'Pentecostal culture'.[115] These themes are theological: revivalistic preaching; Spirit baptism (tongues); immediacy of the second coming of Jesus (millenarian) and are praxis related: interracial and

---

[114] *New York Times* (Monday, June 8, 1908), p. 5, columns 3–4. See also the less favorable reports in the *Los Angeles Times* (April 18, 1906), and (September 19, 1906), concerning the Azusa Street Mission. See the *Los Angeles Times* (July 23, 1906), concerning the Pentecostal New Testament Church in Los Angeles. Cox states that 'Newspapers lampooned what they called the "fanaticism and unseemly contortions" allegedly going on at the Pentecostal revivals and were especially disturbed by the interracial character of the meetings' in *Fire From Heaven*. The quote is found among the photos sandwiched between pp. 78 and 79 at the end of part one.

[115] Culture is to be understood as similar to worldview yet in a more particular sense. 'Culture is "a system of patterned values, meanings, and beliefs that give cognitive structure to the world, provide a basis for coordinating and controlling human interactions, and constitute a link as the system is transmitted to one generation to the next"'. Neil J. Smelser, 'Culture: Coherent or Incoherent' in R. Munch and N. J. Smelser (eds.), *Theory of Culture* (University of California Press, 1992), cited in Vernon K. Robbins, *The Tapestry of Early Christian Discourse: Rhetoric, Society and Ideology* (London and New York: Routledge, 1996), p. 4.

unsegregated worship, community involvement in service which included women and children! However, the reporter emphasized the interracial and unsegregated, gender inclusive involvement within the service with the 'most peculiar part' as being the manifestation of unknown tongues. The reporter also connected this Full Gospel Holiness mission of the northeastern state, New York, with the more southern-styled Holiness camp meetings. Hence, this revealed the close connection with Holiness Christianity. Tongues, however, became the most recognizable identifying feature of early Pentecostalism.

The central theme of the early Pentecostal worldview was the persistent emphasis upon the supernatural (charismatic) manifestations of the Spirit within the worshiping community. Grant Wacker argues that the framework in which speaking in tongues should be analyzed is the 'thoroughly experiential supernatural conceptual horizon'. Wacker states that 'what made pentecostalism unique … was its preoccupation with events that seemed starkly supernatural'.[116] This preoccupation with the manifestation of 'signs and wonders' was produced through the dialectic tension of supernaturalism and ecstasy,[117] which was generated within a *Pentecostal cultural reading of Scripture*. These ecstatic experiences (Spirit baptism with tongues, divine healing and unsegregated celebrative worship services) offered tangible evidence that the person and community had a direct encounter with the living God.[118] The countless reports[119] of healings, trances (falling out in the spirit), tongues and other tangible miracles functioned like a life changing sacrament for those believers who witnessed and experienced these unforgettable moments of

---

[116] Grant Wacker, 'The Functions of Faith in Primitive Pentecostalism', *Harvard Theological Review* 77 (1984), p. 360.

[117] Wacker, 'The Functions of Faith', p. 360.

[118] A common repeated phrase concerning the Azusa revival was 'the color line was washed away in the Blood'. Marsden in *Understanding Fundamentalism And Evangelicalism* states that, 'It [Pentecostalism] was for a time, in fact, the only portion of Protestantism to be integrated racially' (p. 43).

[119] See Cox, *Fire From Heaven*, pp. 67–78. He writes, 'One can hardly open a book of pentecostal reminiscence from the vertiginous years that followed the Azusa Street revival without signs and wonders tumbling out of the pages' (p. 69).

transforming grace.[120] However, Spirit baptism did not just cause people to change their religious affiliation, 'it changed everything. They literally saw the whole world in a new light. Spirit baptism was not just an initiation rite, it was a mystical encounter.'[121] Thus, this scripturally narrated supernaturalistic worldview 'offered common people a *transforming* perception of reality that invested life with meaning ...' (emphasis added).[122]

The supernaturalistic environment of Pentecostal culture was in direct opposition to the dominant modernistic, naturalistic world-view and the greatest point of contention among its closest sisters—the Holiness folk and their cousins—the Fundamentalists.[123] The Pentecostal community was on a direct collision course with modernity and cessationist Christianity.

Modernity could be characterized as 'Descartes' autonomous, rational substance encountering Newton's mechanistic world'.[124] Modernity's humanistic (the mastery of all naturalistic and super-naturalistic forces), positivistic (science and instrumental reasoning as the sole arbiter of truth) and naturalistic mechanistic universe (the material universe is the sum total of reality),[125] could only per-

---

[120] Grant Wacker, 'Marching to Zion: Religion in a Modern Utopian Community', *Church History* 54.4 (Dec. 1985), pp. 469–511, reference to p. 510. Wacker states that those who were sick but were not healed

> bore the stigma of a second class citizenship ... [because the person had] inadequate faith at best and a sinful heart at worst. Even so they interpreted their ability to persevere, to endure pain without resorting to worldly medicines or physicians, as confirmation of the genuineness of their salvation and the perfection of their sanctification (p. 511).

[121] Cox, *Fire From Heaven*, p. 70.

[122] Blumhofer, *Restoring the Faith*, p. 9.

[123] For the Holiness folk, it challenged their doctrinal understanding of the baptism of the Holy Spirit and for the Fundamentalists, it challenged their doctrinal argument of the cessation of miracles, justification by faith alone and prohibiting women from preaching (exhorting) or teaching men and being a pastor of a congregation. The most notorious polemic against miracles (divine healing in particular) was B.B. Warfield's *Counterfeit Miracles* (New York: Charles Scribner's Sons, 1918).

[124] Stanley J. Grenz, *A Primer on Postmodernism*, p. 3.

[125] See Brian Fay's helpful conceptual analysis of how the modern age refashioned (the premodern) western religious understanding of humanity as fallen and in need of divine revelation and/or a savior (what he calls 'The Self-estrangement Theory') with the humanistic variant of the estrangement theory. The humanistic variant (made possible by the Enlightenment) sees humans as fallen but only in a secular sense and redeemable through their own capacity to transform their own

ceive Pentecostals as overtly superstitious at best or psychologically deranged at worst. Yet, for the early Pentecostals, their cultural worldview presented a scripturally narrated gospel that 'resisted the lure of secular society and issued more than a superficial challenge to [the dominant] culture'.[126]

Ironically, this supernaturalistic worldview has been identified as the very reason for the overwhelming growth of the Pentecostal movement.[127] Margaret Poloma's sociological study of the Assemblies of God argues that Pentecostalism may be seen as an 'anthropological *protest* against modernity' (emphasis added) by 'providing a medium for encountering the supernatural'.[128] She characterizes the Pentecostal community by the 'belief in and experience of the paranormal as an alternate *Weltanschauung* for our instrumental rational modern society'. This is an anomaly to the dominant scientific worldview of our day, and yet it is precisely this supernaturalistic element that propels the growth of Pentecostalism within the modernistic age. Poloma states that the future of the Pentecostal movement 'rests not only in providing a medium for the encounter of the supernatural but in its continued ability to fuse the natural and supernatural, the emotional and rational, the charismatic and institutional in a decidedly postmodern way'.[129]

Pentecostalism should not be viewed as 'pre-modern' because it was born in the modernistic age. It shared characteristics of the so-called pre-modern era, but it relied upon the adaptation of modernistic language and belief to discover and articulate its practices and beliefs (thus it insisted on tangible, visible signs of the Holy Spirit's presence) even though it was in opposition to modernity. Pentecostalism should not be viewed as 'anti-modern' because it did not attempt to develop a 'critical' argument against modernity, which accepted the epistemological premise of modernity, that truth and

---

lives, with education, science and technology becoming the primary tools. *Critical Social Science: Liberation and Its Limits* (New York: Cornell University Press, 1987), chapter one, pp. 1–26.

[126] Blumhofer, *Restoring the Faith*, p. 9.

[127] Wacker, 'The Functions of Faith', pp. 374–75.

[128] Magaret Poloma, *The Assemblies of God at the Crossroads* (Knoxville, TN: University of Tennessee Press, 1989), p. 19.

[129] Poloma, *The Assemblies of God at the Crossroads*, pp. xvii-xx, first quote xvii, and second xix.

faith was based entirely upon 'objective historical evidence' in the manner of the Fundamentalists.[130] Pentecostals saw themselves as Fundamentalists, yet the 'Fundamentalists' seldom welcomed Pentecostals to their councils or saw them as allies.[131] 'Paramodern' would be a better way to classify early Pentecostalism.[132] This concept captures the fact that Pentecostalism emerged within modernity (a historically definitive time period), yet existed on the fringes of modernity (both in a sociological and economical sense and by its emphasis on physical evidence for the Spirit's presence—a modernistic slant on scientific experimentation language). Pentecostalism could never accept modernity's worldview completely, but it did utilize aspects of modernity (like technology, language, inductive reasoning) to advance the Pentecostal cause. Pentecostalism was (and is) a protest to the central features of modernity. The Pentecostal movement began as a paramodern movement protesting modernity and cessationist Christianity.

Summary

The purpose of this chapter has been to define Pentecostalism. This was done by examining three different perspectives of Pentecostalism: the social and religious context, social deprivation and by identifying the Pentecostal worldview. In the first section the primary influences that contributed to the shaping of Pentecostalism have been identified. These social and theological influences consisted of issues raised in dialogue with restorationist revivalism, both Wesleyan and Keswickian Holiness and modernity.

---

[130] Oden, *After Modernity*, p. 67, see also pp. 66–69.

[131] Marsden, *Fundamentalism and American Culture*, p. 94. Concerning the relationship between Fundamentalism and Pentecostalism, Marsden states that even though some Pentecostals saw themselves as Fundamentalists, Fundamentalists rejected the Pentecostals. Thus Fundamentalism has influenced Pentecostalism but Pentecostals had little if any influence upon the Fundamentalists. Synan writes in the introductory forward of *Azusa Street: The Roots of Modern-day Pentecost* that 'by 1928 [the Fundamentalists] had disfellowshiped all pentecostals from their ranks' (p. xxi).

[132] I prefer paramodern to submodern because the concept of submodern implies a parental hierarchical relational dependency of Pentecostalism with modernity. I am dependent upon Jackie David Johns for the term paramodern.

The second section was committed to addressing the claim that Pentecostalism emerged from the auspices of social deprivation. As has been demonstrated thus far, Pentecostalism is a diverse and often divergent movement. It is a movement that emerged on the margins of society. As stated in the main argument, some have sought to suggest that the primary catalyst of this movement was social depravation, social disorganization and/or psychologically defective individuals. While it was admitted that these might have had some influence in the emergence of Pentecostalism, this chapter demonstrated that if one holds these as primary catalysts the result is a gross reductionism that ignores the religious claims of Pentecostalism. The goal of this section was to show that Pentecostalism is more than a movement emerging from deprivation. It is a dynamic movement of which the 'Full Gospel' served as the primary catalyst convincing others to convert to Pentecostalism. Therefore, the Deprivation theory is a coincidental catalyst at most and only because Pentecostalism exists on the margins of society where social deprivation primarily exists.

Finally, by describing the Pentecostal worldview, it was concluded that Pentecostalism could never completely accept a modernistic worldview, or even a Christian cessationist worldview. However, it was acknowledged that Pentecostalism did in fact utilize certain aspects of modernity to advance its cause. Nevertheless, it has been concluded that early Pentecostalism was a paramodern movement which protested modernity. With this definition of the identity of Pentecostalism and its worldview, the task can now be undertaken to narrow this study by identifying the hermeneutical context of early Pentecostalism.

2

SHIFTING PARADIGMS: THE HERMENEUTICAL CONTEXT OF THE EARLY PENTECOSTALS

In ninety-nine out of a hundred cases, the meaning that the plain man gets out of the Bible is the correct one.[1]

R.A. Torrey

In the previous chapter, Pentecostalism was defined as a paramodern revivalistic, restorationist movement, held together by its common doctrinal commitment to the Full Gospel message. Pentecostalism had deep roots in the various Holiness camp meetings and the premillennial prophetic Bible conferences, which were of central importance to popularistic, revivalistic Christianity at the dawning of the twentieth century. The people, who came to be called Pentecostal, would later be acknowledged as the 'radical' wing of the various budding evangelical groups.[2]

The purpose of this chapter is to examine the hermeneutical context of the first generation of Pentecostals. The Pentecostals' continuation of Wesleyan Holiness praxis concerns in confrontation with Fundamentalist and liberal beliefs created a fertile context in which an authentic Pentecostal hermeneutic emerged. In order to understand the early Pentecostal hermeneutical method, Pentecostalism needs to be examined in its historical context, which gave rise to the Fundamentalist/Modernist debate.

---

[1] Cited in William G. Mcloughlin, Jr., *Modern Revivalism* (New York: Ronald Press, 1959), p. 372.

[2] See Blumhofer, *Restoring the Faith*, pp. 14–19.

Common Sense Realism: The Dominant Hermeneutical Context of the Early 19th Century

Traditional American biblical scholarship of the eighteenth and early nineteenth century witnessed dramatic changes during the 1880s-1920s. Robert W. Funk, in his presidential address to the Society of Biblical Literature, identified this time as the 'watershed' event that 'has affected the shape and course of [biblical] scholarship down to the present day'. By 'watershed', he was referring to that 'hypothetical point after which the lines in biblical scholarship were drawn very differently than in the preceding period'. Funk went on to say that 'the lines were significantly redrawn ... and our whole subsequent history has been shaped and to a large extent, tyrannized by the fresh demarcation'.[3] Funk was addressing the tremendous impact German higher criticism and the 'new science', which exposed Darwinism and 'the progressive, evolutionary spiral of human history', had upon traditional biblical scholarship. He correctly recognized that the greatest point of impact was upon 'the evangelical understanding and development of scripture'.[4] In America, the impact was dramatically felt and presented at the popular level throughout the country during the Fundamentalist and Modernist debates of the 1920s.[5]

Mark Noll demonstrates that prior to this 'watershed' period, traditional evangelical scholars held prominent positions in the academic community.[6] However, after 1900, evangelical scholars experienced a 'rapid decline' from their previous positions of 'relative strength'. According to Noll, the most important reason for this was due to 'the rise of the modern university in the United States'.[7]

---

[3] R.W. Funk, 'The Watershed of the American Biblical Tradition: The Chicago School, First Phase, 1892–1920', *Journal of Biblical Literature* 96 (1976), pp. 4–22, cited p. 7.

[4] Funk, 'The Watershed of the American Biblical Tradition', pp. 6 and 8.

[5] The most famous is the Scopes 'monkey trial' of 1925, which most historians regard as the deathblow to the Fundamentalist influence upon intellectual communities. See Marsden, *Fundamentalism and American Culture*, pp. 184–95.

[6] Mark Noll, *Between Faith and Criticism: Evangelicals, Scholarship, and the Bible in America* (Grand Rapids, MI: Baker Book House, 2nd edn, 1991), see chapter 3, cited p. 32.

[7] Noll, *Between Faith and Criticism*, pp. 32–33.

During the rapid expansion of modern American universities, biblical scholarship moved away from the traditional conservative intellectual British-American model and quickly embraced the ideals of the impressive German model for scholarship. The German model stressed a 'neutral scrupulous objectivity' along with a 'commitment to science in organic [naturalistic] evolutionary terms instead of mechanical, static ones'. This was fueled by a Hegelian 'iconoclastic progressive spirit', which assumed that better ideas were found in the present and that the earlier historical periods were 'primitive', hence insufficient and defective. The new scientific model of scholarship encouraged the 'rapid professionalization' of biblical scholars that required them to become 'specialized' and accountable to their 'academic peers' instead of the Christian communities to which they once belonged.[8] The process of 'professionalization' required biblical scholars to snatch the Bible from the hands of the Christian communities. For conservative intellectuals, this was extremely painful because the Bible had always been the 'Church's book', and the primary purpose of biblical scholarship was to contribute to the ongoing spirituality of the Christian community. Thus, 'to divorce study from the ecclesiastical community was to take something away from its [Scripture] essential character'.[9] This atmosphere created a 'central storm' around 'the source and the authority of Scripture'.[10]

Funk employed the watershed imagery in order to help visualize the significant changes that took place in biblical scholarship. Others have adapted Thomas Kuhn's[11] popular concept of a 'paradigm

---

[8] Noll, *Between Faith and Criticism*, pp. 33–34. Noll argues that Hegel more then Darwin caused the greatest concern for Evangelicals. This is due to the evangelical commitment to the authority and infallibility of Scripture, which of course was a primitive product.

[9] Noll, *Between Faith and Criticism*, p. 34. Noll states that up to 1875, 'virtually every American who could be called an expert in the study of Scripture sustained some kind of a denominational connection and devoted the results of biblical scholarship primarily to the ongoing spirituality of the church' (p. 33).

[10] Grant Wacker, 'The Demise of Biblical Civilization' in N. Hatch and M. Noll (eds.), *The Bible in America: Essays in Cultural History* (New York: Oxford University Press, 1982), pp. 121–38, cited p. 123.

[11] See Thomas Kuhn, *The Structure of Scientific Revolutions* (Chicago: University of Chicago Press, 1970, second edition). Marsden in his *Fundamentalism and American Culture* applies Kuhn's paradigm theory to Fundamentalism in order to explain the cohesiveness and the militant stance of this movement, see pp. 214–15. Fau-

shift' in order to explain the significance of the intellectual struggle which led to permanent changes concerning the biblical landscape. Timothy Weber writes, 'without pressing Kuhn's theory to extremes, it does, however, seem that something like a "paradigm shift" occurred in the world of [conservative intellectual] evangelical biblical scholarship during the last half of the nineteenth century'.[12] The 'paradigm shift' took place as the older scientific perceptual model of a static mechanical (deistic) universe gave way to the newer scientific model of an organic evolutionary and naturalistic universe. Henceforth, the static deistic empirical paradigm, which in America was built upon Common Sense Baconianism, was replaced by the naturalistic, developmental and more speculative scientific paradigm.[13] As worldviews changed, new ways of understanding the Bible emerged, and for many intellectual evangelical scholars, popularistic ministers and laity these 'scientific arguments' were simply unacceptable conclusions based upon naturalistic hypotheses.

Prior to the paradigm shift, Americans in general and Protestants in particular adhered to the concepts of Common Sense Realism and had a firm confidence in the inductive scientific method associated with Frances Bacon.[14] Common Sense reasoning 'permeated almost every faculty of the academy, institution of society and activity in [American] culture'.[15] The Baconian method of induction required one to look carefully at the evidence, determine what were the 'facts' and then classify these facts. One was not to superimpose hypotheses or theories upon the evidence, but only after thoroughly investigating the evidence through classification and generalization, would one discover the general law. The goal of this method was to

---

pel in his *The Everlasting Gospel*, argues that American Pentecostalism was a millenarian belief system which emerged as a result of a paradigm shift within the nineteenth-century holiness movement.

[12] Timothy Weber, 'The Two-Edged Sword: The Fundamentalist Use of the Bible' in Hatch and Noll (eds.), *The Bible in America*, pp. 101–20, cited p. 104. Weber uses William Newton Clark (1840–1912) as an example of a conservative who embraced liberalism as a result of the paradigm shift.

[13] Weber, 'The Two-Edged Sword', p. 103. Also see George Marsden, 'Everyone One's Own Interpreter?: The Bible, Science, and Authority in Mid-Nineteenth-Century America' in Hatch and Noll (eds.), *The Bible in America*, pp. 79–100.

[14] Marsden, 'Everyone One's own Interpreter?', p. 82.

[15] John C. Vander Stelt, *Philosophy and Scripture: A Study in Old Princeton and Westminster Theology* (Martlon, NJ: Mack, 1978), p. 12.

give humanity 'mastery over the forces of nature by means of scientific discoveries and inventions'.[16]

The Baconian method was considered to be an objective and empirical science that was deeply entrenched within conservative thinking because it was both scientific and supportive of evangelical faith.[17] Peirson, a premillennial dispensationalist and anti-modernist, demonstrated the importance of the Baconian objective empirical method at a major prophetic conference in 1895. He said,

> I like Biblical theology that does not start with superficial Aristotelian methods of reason, that does not begin with an hypothesis, and then wrap the facts and philosophy to fit the crook of our dogma, but a Baconian system, which first gathers the teachings of the word of God and then seeks to deduce some general law upon which the facts can be arranged.[18]

For conservative Protestants, the Bible, like nature, was a book of 'hard facts'; thus, the Baconian method served to discover objectively the plain (literal) meaning of Scripture.

Common Sense Realism,[19] as associated with Thomas Reid, argued that the human mind could really perceive what is actually there because the object contains the property that produces the sensation in the mind. In other words, the human mind perceives the real world directly.[20] Hence, one can know with certainty that something exists and what it is that exists. Reid argued that this was so because God had implanted within the mind of all people certain 'self-evident first principles' like the existence of God, the reality and existence of an external world and the uniformity of nature. These self-evident first principles are the starting point or founda-

---

[16] Bertrand Russell, *A History of Western Philosophy* (New York: NY: Simon and Schuster, 1972), p. 542. See also Robert Audi (ed.), *The Cambridge Dictionary of Philosophy* (New York, NY: Cambridge University Press, 1995), pp. 60–61.

[17] Marsden, 'Everyone One's own Interpreter?', pp. 82–84.

[18] 'The Coming of the Lord: The Doctrinal Center of the Bible' in *Addresses on the Second Coming of the Lord: Delivered at the Prophetic Conference, Allegheny, PA, December 3–6, 1895* (Pittsburgh, 1895), p. 82 also cited in G. Marsden, *Fundamentalism And American Culture*, p. 55.

[19] See 'Reid, Thomas' and 'Scottish common sense philosophy' in *The Cambridge Dictionary of Philosophy*, pp. 684–88 and 719.

[20] David Bebbington, *Evangelicalism in Modern Britain: A History from the 1730s to the 1980s* (Grand Rapids, MI: Baker Book House, 1989), p. 59.

tion on which knowledge is subsequently built. This Common Sense ability

> is not used here to indicate a power of general knowledge based on ordinary development and opportunities, but to mean a faculty of reason, a source of principles ... a capacity for certain original and intuitive judgments which may be used as a foundation for deductive reasoning.[21]

These self-evident principles need no further proof because one would be 'mad' to deny their existence.

Common Sense, then, implies that truth is static and not culturally derived. Truth is open to investigation irrespective of time or place, yet truth does not change—it remains constant. The 'Common Sense Baconian system assumed the stability of truth which could be known objectively by careful observers in any age or culture'.[22] Virtually all of the various Protestant seminaries, even though they held to different theological beliefs, used Common Sense reasoning because 'there prevailed a faith in immutable truth seen clearly by inductive scientific reasoning in scripture and nature alike'.[23] For Protestants, Common Sense philosophy wed to Baconian scientific method produced a confidence that one could discover the facts of Scripture as clearly as one could discover the facts of science. This 'enlightened' Common Sense approach reinforced the Protestant doctrine of the 'Perspicuity of Scripture'[24] and the traditional Western ideas of the perspicuity and immutability of

---

[21] John C. Vander Stelt, *Philosophy and Scripture*, p. 23 cited in Jon Ruthven, *On the Cessation of the Charismata: The Protestant Polemic on Postbiblical Miracles* (JPTSup, 3; Sheffield: Sheffield Academic Press, 1993), p. 46.

[22] Marsden, 'Everyone One's own Interpreter?', p. 92.

[23] Marsden, 'Everyone One's own Interpreter?', pp. 82, 92. 'From the liberal Unitarians at Harvard to the conservative Presbyterians at Princeton, among the moderate Calvinists of Yale, to their more radical perfectionist offspring at Oberlin, among Methodists and Baptists, and including the "gentlemen theologians" of the South' all relied upon common sense and the inductive method (p. 82).

[24] Roy A. Harrisville and Walter Sundberg, *The Bible in Modern Culture: Theology and Historical-Critical Method from Spinoza to Käsemann* (Grand Rapids, MI: Eerdmans, 1995), pp. 48, 185, 192–94. They correctly point out that this one doctrine (the Perspicuity of Scripture) 'is the driving force of American evangelicalism from the beginning' (p. 193). Marsden states in *Fundamentalism*, that 'there was a strong tradition in America that the Bible in the hands of the common person was of greater value than any amount of education' (p. 212).

truth.[25] Furthermore, Common Sense Baconianism was viewed as a practical and anti-elitist philosophy that enabled the common person to know the truth, and as a method, it brought together science and Scripture, faith and morality.[26]

In the wake of the paradigm shift that brought the demise of the old Common Sense consensus, American Protestants generally moved in one of three directions.[27] Modernists or liberals argued that the Bible's authority did not rest upon scientific or historical claims. For them, 'objective revelation' was not what authenticated Christianity; rather, its authenticity was found in 'personal experience'. Hence, the liberals based their theological understanding upon an experiential foundation. This 'experiential foundationalism' required 'an expressivist theory of religious language'. Experiential-expressivism understands 'religion and science to be incommensurable and thus finds no possible conflicts between them'.[28]

Moving in the opposite direction, but also relying on modernist philosophical theory as its foundation, was the conservative intellectuals—the academically informed Fundamentalist group. These men continued to reaffirm the 'factuality' and 'authority' of Scripture by appealing to the older yet modern 'scientific' model of Baconian Common Sense. They attacked the 'speculative hypotheses' of the new science, which they argued, was not really a true science. They saw the Bible as being scientific (in the sense of reporting facts accurately), whereas Darwinian evolution[29] was totally unscien-

---

[25] See Marsden 'Everyone One's own Interpreter?'

[26] Harrisville and Sundberg, *The Bible In Modern Culture*, p. 184.

[27] Marsden, 'Everyone One's Own Interpreter?', p. 95. The following information was adapted from Marsden.

[28] Nancey Murphy, *Beyond Liberalism and Fundamentalism: How Modern and Postmodern Philosophy Set the Theological Agenda* (Valley Forge, PA: Trinity Press International, 1996), p. 61. Her book demonstrates that the intellectual positions of the conservatives and the liberals were both built upon modern philosophical foundations and the philosophy of the modern period is primarily responsible for the bifurcation of Protestant Christian thought. She also demonstrates how these modern foundations have been called into question, thus contemporary Evangelicals who are the descendents of intellectual conservatism should move to postmodern approaches.

[29] It is important to point out that some conservative intellectuals like B.B. Warfield and James Orr affirmed a theistic but not a naturalistic evolutionary account of creation. This was something that later dispensational Fundamentalists would reject.

tific because it was based upon a mere hypothesis.[30] The Fundamentalists were desperately attempting to re-establish the 'old bal-
ance between scientific rationality and Scripture' and thus were an
academically enlightened anti-modernist movement. The conservative intellectuals built their theological understanding upon a scriptural foundation. Scriptural foundationalism takes a propositional
approach to religious language based upon a referential theory of
language. 'Propositionalism ... argues that the propositions of theology are commensurable with other kinds of knowledge, it also
creates problems of consistency with both science and history'.[31] In
order to resolve these apparent problems, the Fundamentalists appealed to the divine inspiration of Scripture—a supernatural act of
intervention by the living God.

The Wesleyan Holiness movement and the Pentecostals forged a
third route. From a paramodern perspective, they affirmed both the
objective nature of Scripture and the importance of personal experience as a means to reaffirm the supernatural inspiration of Scripture. Hence, the Holiness tradition and Pentecostals located the inspirational work of the Holy Spirit in both the past written document (Scripture) and in their present experience with Scripture. Inspiration was not limited to the Scripture in the sense that it was a
past document containing no errors, but it also included the present
ability of the Scripture to speak to the community. The community
experienced the Spirit through reading and living according to the
Scripture. Fundamentalists, however, located the inspirational work
of the Spirit in the past written document (Scripture) only. Marsden
declares, 'among these three positions much of American Protestantism still remains divided'.[32]

---

[30] Marsden, *Fundamentalism*, pp. 212–13.

[31] Murphy, *Beyond Liberalism and Fundamentalism*, p. 61.

[32] Marsden, 'Everyone One's Own Interpreter?', p. 95. M. Noll in his provocative book, *The Scandal of The Evangelical Mind* (Leicester, England: Inter-
Varsity Press, 1994) recognizes that 'Fundamentalism, dispensational premillennialism, the Higher Life movement and Pentecostalism were all evangelical strategies of survival in response to religious crises of the late nineteenth century' (p.
24).

The Conservative Approaches to Biblical Interpretation

In this section, the interpretive methods used by the conservative groups will be examined. These methods influenced the early Pentecostal interpretation and helped give rise to the Fundamentalist/Modernist debates of the 1920's. As will be demonstrated in the following chapter, the Pentecostals used the popularistic 'Bible Reading Method'. This method was an adaptation of the inductive approach, which was already in use by the various holiness groups.

Academic Anti-Modernist Fundamentalists
Between 1910 and 1915, twelve paperback volumes entitled *The Fundamentals: A Testimony of the Truth* were published. Over 3 million individual copies of *The Fundamentals* were freely distributed to pastors and church leaders in order to defend the 'fundamentals' or basic doctrines of conservative Protestant Christianity[33] against the growing influence of modernity.[34] Ironically, *The Fundamentals*, which contained over 100 articles, had no impact on the academic communities, including academic conservatives. This series was completely ignored by the academic periodicals of the day.[35] However, the presence of *The Fundamentals* was felt primarily amongst the Calvinistic revivalistic communities as well as the Wesleyan Holiness and Pentecostal communities. Thus *The Fundamentals* would find a receptive audience among the more popularistic revivalistic communities.

The authors of *The Fundamentals* came from various backgrounds and represented some of the 'leading conservative scholars at the start of the twentieth century'.[36] But, at least half of the authors

---

[33] In 1910, the Presbyterian General Assembly responded to modernism by passing a five-point resolution defining Protestant orthodoxy. To be a conservative or a fundamentalist, one had to affirm: (1) the inerrancy of Scripture, (2) the virgin birth of Christ, (3) a substitutionary doctrine of atonement, (4) the bodily resurrection of Christ, (5) the authenticity of biblical miracles. Most fundamentalist groups had lists of the basic doctrines, which they viewed as 'fundamental'. The fundamentalist groups were not all identical, yet they produced similar lists of fundamental beliefs, with the 'Inerrancy of Scripture' at the start of the list along with the second coming of Christ.

[34] Harrisville and Sundberg, *The Bible In Modern Culture*, p. 189.

[35] Noll, *Between Faith and Criticism*, p. 44.

[36] Noll, *A History of Christianity*, p. 381. Noll's list includes: Scottish theologian James Orr, Princeton Presbyterian B.B. Warfield, Anglican bishop H.C.G. Moule,

came from the more Reformed revivalistic traditions such as
Keswickian, dispensationalism and premillennialism. Yet, 'in order
to establish a self-consciously conservative coalition against modernism', dispensational premillennialism, which was the most con-
troversial issue among this coalition, was not promoted.[37] Hence,
there was a cooperative effort made by these authors to defend
what they understood to be the essential 'fundamentals' of the
Christian faith. In general, these articles were a competent restate-
ment of traditional conservative views,[38] presented in a highly po-
lemical tone, which attacked the 'naturalistic' presuppositions of
higher criticism and liberal theology. *The Fundamentals* was a critically
informed anti-criticism based on philosophical concerns of modernity that took academics and criticism very seriously. Yet, its preeminent concern remained that of reaching lost souls.[39]

Approximately one third of the articles in *The Fundamentals*[40] were
devoted to the defense of the inspiration and authority of Scripture.[41] James M. Gray wrote 'inspiration is not revelation' or 'illumination' or 'human genius'. Instead 'inspiration … is supernatural
throughout'. And 'the object of inspiration is not the inspiration of
men but the books—not the writers but the writings'.[42] L.W. Munhall explained the doctrine of verbal inspiration in this manner:

American dispensationalist C.I. Scofield, evangelist R.A. Torrey and Southern
Baptist E.Y. Mullins.

[37] Marsden, *Fundamentalism*, p. 119. B.B. Warfield being the most outspoken
against Keswickian higher life, dispensationalism and Divine healing. See *The
Works of Benjamin B. Warfield* (New York: Oxford University Press, 1931, reprint
1981, Baker Book House Co.) volume VIII.

[38] Noll, *A History of Christianity*, p. 381.

[39] Marsden, *Fundamentalism*, pp. 120–23.

[40] Another third of the articles dealt with traditional theological questions,
with the remaining articles being more difficult to classify. In 1917, *The Fundamentals: A Testimony To The Truth* was republished by The Bible Institute of Los Angeles, Los Angeles, Cal., which contains most of the original articles. The commit-
tee members in charge of this publication were primarily dispensationalists, with
the Keswickian dispensationalist R.A. Torrey serving as Executive Secretary. All
references of *The Fundamentals* will be to the 1917 publication.

[41] Noll, *Between Faith and Criticism*, p. 39.

[42] Torrey, *The Fundamentals*, 1917, II, p. 11. At the conclusion of Gray's article
is a long affectionate statement of admiration and affirmation of the intellectual
and spiritual character of the members of the General Assembly of the Presbyterian Church of America, of which he does not belong. Gray then quotes their
1893 resolution on the inspiration of Scripture as his closing remark.

the original writings, *ipsissima verba*, came through the penmen direct from God … The Bible…is the very Word of God, and consequently, wholly without error … [Because it is] God-breathed.[43]

For Munhall and the rest of the Fundamentalists, verbal inspiration means that the Scripture was the inerrant Word of God, a wholly supernatural event. 'This is fundamental to the Christian faith'.[44]

Noll states that Munhall's and Gray's articles were actually 'little more than abridged summaries of the Warfield-Hodge paper of 1881'.[45] There did not exist within North American Protestantism a fully developed systematic theology of the infallibility of Scripture until the creative efforts of the Princeton Calvinists, Hodge and Warfield.[46] Therefore, the Princeton theologians had a definitive influence upon the doctrine of the (verbal) inspiration of Scripture for conservative North American Protestant Christians.

The Princeton scholars drank deep from the well of Enlightenment thinking. Common Sense Realism and Baconian scientific method were totally embraced in order to defend Calvinistic theology and reconcile faith and reason, the supernatural and the natural.[47] Therefore 'Princeton was to be the crucible in which the great nineteenth-century evangelical theories of biblical inspiration and authority were forged'.[48]

The Princeton scholars were an academically Calvinistic conservative group within the fundamentalist coalition. They embraced Baconian Common Sense Realism and wed it to the traditional Reformed doctrine of the perspicuity of Scripture. This doctrine,

[43] Torrey, *The Fundamentals*, 1917, II, p. 45. Munhall quoted the 1893 resolution of the General Assembly of the Presbyterian Church in support of his argument that the original autographs were the inspired writings and not the translations. Like Munhall, the Fundamentalists' primary theological community was the conservative Presbyterians.

[44] Torrey, *The Fundamentals*, 1917, II, p. 44.

[45] Noll, *Between Faith and Criticism*, p. 40.

[46] James D. Hunter, *American Evangelicalism: Conservative Religion and the Quandary of Modernity* (New Brunswick: Rutgers University Press, 1983), p. 31.

[47] See Mark Noll, *The Princeton Theology, 1882–1921* (Grand Rapids: Baker Book House, 1983), pp. 30–35 and S. Ahlstrom, 'The Scottish Philosophy', *Church History* 24 (September 1995), pp. 257–72.

[48] Alister E. McGrath, *A Passion for the Truth: The Intellectual Coherence of Evangelicalism* (Downers Grove, IL: InterVarsity, 1996), p. 168.

which empowered the laity, simply meant that the 'common man' with common sense, aided by the Holy Spirit, was able to understand the plain meaning of Scripture related to all matters of salvation.[49]

B.B. Warfield was the chief architect of verbal inspiration and the inventor of the term inerrancy, which became the litmus test of Fundamentalism.[50] Warfield wrote:

> The Church, then, has held from the beginning that the Bible is the Word of God in such a sense that its words, though written by men and being indelibly impressed upon them the marks of their human origin, were written, nevertheless, under such an influence of the Holy Ghost as to be also the words of God, the adequate expression of His mind and will. It has always recognized that this conception of co-authorship implies that the Spirit's superintendence extends to the choice of the words by human authors [verbal inspiration], and preserves its product from everything inconsistent with a divine authorship—thus securing, among other things, that entire truthfulness which is everywhere presupposed in and asserted for scripture by the Biblical writers [inerrancy].[51]

Warfield saw inspiration as a supernatural influence of the Holy Spirit upon the biblical writers' mind so that they produced a divine product. Because the Bible is the inspired Word of God, it is factual in everything and cannot err.

Warfield argued that his doctrine rested upon the understanding of the biblical writers, which he retrieved through historical-grammatical exegesis. Warfield believed that verbal inspiration was virtually what the Church had always believed. He correctly recognized that the real issue was not what the biblical authors said about

---

[49] Harrisville and Sundberg, *The Bible in Modern Culture*, p. 185.

[50] Marsden, *Understanding Fundamentalism*, p. 156. For a sampling of B.B. Warfield's many writings on this subject see volume one 'Revelation and Inspiration' in *The Works of Benjamin B. Warfield*, reprint 1981. The following citations concerning Warfield are from this volume.

[51] 'The Real Problem of Inspiration' in *The Works of Benjamin B. Warfield*, p. 173. Warfield did not articulate a theory of dictation. See also Hodge and Warfield, *Inspiration* (Philadelphia: Presbyterian Board of Publication, 1881).

inspiration but the credibility of the Bible as a result of the scrutiny of biblical criticism.

> In order, therefore, to shake this doctrine, biblical criticism must show: either, that the New Testament writers did not claim inspiration; or that this claim was rejected by the contemporary church; or, that it is palpably negative by the fact that the books contained in it were forgeries; or, equally clearly negative by the fact that they contain along with the claims of errors of fact or contradictions of statement. The important question before us to-day (sic), then, is: Has biblical criticism proved any one of these positions?[52]

Warfield was convinced that his biblical doctrine of verbal inspiration was unshakable and could stand up under the scrutiny of biblical criticism. In fact, he argued that modern biblical criticism helped to establish the authenticity of the doctrine. Thus, he set out to demonstrate throughout the remainder of his article, 'Inspiration and Criticism' that 'modern biblical criticism has nothing valid to argue against the church doctrine of verbal inspiration'.[53] The Princetonians were not able to overthrow liberalism and their influence would be greater in the twentieth-century Evangelicalism than among the traditional academic institutions of the late nineteenth-century.[54]

Like the Princetonians, most of the authors of *The Fundamentals* were not opposed to critical academic analysis of Scripture.[55] They were opposed to the anti-supernatural presupposition held by the higher critics and the implications this had upon Scripture, as Canon Dyson Hague made clear in his article 'The History of the

---

[52] 'Inspiration and Criticism' in *The Works of Benjamin B. Warfield*, p. 400. These historical and philosophical arguments of verification are still accepted and used by some contemporary Evangelicals. For example, see the contemporary and popular evangelical textbook on hermeneutics by W. Klein, C. Blomberg and R. Hubbard, Jr., *Introduction To Biblical Interpretation* (Dallas: Word, 1993), which is a modified extension of Warfield's historical-grammatical exegetical method built upon the same philosophical foundation. Hence they address issues of pseudepigrapha, contradictions and authorial intent.

[53] *The Works of Benjamin B. Warfield*, p. 424.

[54] Marsden, *Understanding Fundamentalism*, p. 125.

[55] Some articles do reflect an anti-intellectual position; for example, see Philip Mauro, 'Modern Philosophy' in Torrey, *The Fundamentals*, 1917, IV, pp. 9–29.

Higher Criticism'. This article appeared first in the 1917 publication of *The Fundamentals*. Hague wrote:

> What the Conservative school oppose is not Biblical criticism, but Biblical criticism by rationalists ... [which is] neither expert nor scientific (p. 40). The Bible, in their view, was a mere human product. It was a stage in the literary evolution of a religious people (p. 20). It certainly was not given by inspiration of God, and is not the Word of the living God ... The Bible is either the Word of God, or it is not ... if their [Israel's] sacred literature was natural with mythical and pseudonymous admixtures; then the Bible is dethroned from its throne as the exclusive, authoritative, Divinely inspired Word of God (p. 32).[56]

James Orr, another important contributor to *The Fundamentals*, also addressed the important role presuppositions played in higher criticism. He believed that the presuppositions of the higher criticism, not the method itself, needed to be examined. He wrote:

> We are not bound to accept every wild critical theory that any critic may choose to put forward and assert ... We are entitled ... to look at the presuppositions on which criticism proceeds, and ask, How far is the criticism controlled by those presuppositions? ... [This] is my complaint against much of the current criticism of the Bible—not that it is criticism, but that it starts from the wrong basis, that it proceeds by arbitrary methods, and that it arrives at results which I think are demonstrably false results.[57]

The Fundamentalists' greatest point of contention with the liberals was that they were beginning their analysis of Scripture with 'unscientific hypotheses' and 'anti-supernatural' prejudices that reduce Scripture to the level of a naturalistic human book filled with myth and fables. Scripture, then, is perceived as an unhistorical and incorrect document.

The following statement by Orr correctly captures the effect presuppositions and methods have upon one's understanding of Scripture. However, it also reveals the important role historical veri-

---

[56] Torrey, *The Fundamentals*, 1917, I, pp. 9–42.
[57] Torrey, *The Fundamentals*, 1917, I, p. 97.

fication played in demonstrating the factuality and truthfulness of Scripture.

> A great deal here depends on your method of approach to these old narratives … Approach them in one way and you make them out to be a bundle of fables, legends, myths, without historical basis of any kind … Approach these narratives in another way and they are the oldest most precious tradition of our race … the word of God … not merely vehicles of great ideas, but presenting in their own archaic way … the memory of great historical truths.[58]

A preeminent concern of the conservatives, therefore, was to demonstrate the historical factuality of Scripture, because if it was not historically accurate it could not be true or teach truth. Hence, many of them called upon ancient history, modern philological discoveries and the testimony of archaeology in order to support the historical factuality of Scripture. For the Fundamentalists, criticism was not the problem; rather, it was the naturalistic evolutionary presuppositions along with the lack of factual hard evidence to substantiate the higher critics' conclusions. The Fundamentalists believed that if one would be open minded to miracles in the Bible (the supernatural) and inductively examine Scripture from a common sense, plain meaning perspective; one would recognize the Bible as a supernaturally inspired book—the very words of God.

The Fundamentalists had accepted and developed the apologetic defense of traditional Calvinistic Protestantism and the interpretation of Scripture upon the foundation of Baconian Common Sense Realism. Their 'historical grammatical exegetical method', which was an inductive plain meaning approach that desired to capture the

---

[58] Torrey, *The Fundamentals*, 1917, I. p. 232. Orr in this article was discussing the first 11 chapters of Genesis. Orr was a scholar who took modern biblical criticism very seriously and attempted to adjust his understanding of Scripture and biblical criticism without abandoning traditional Protestantism. He, like Warfield, did not embrace a literal six-day creationist view, but neither would he accept Darwinian evolutionary theory because this reduced the act of creation to a mere naturalistic and atheistic cause. See J. Orr, 'The Early Narratives Of Genesis' in Torrey, *The Fundamentals*, 1917, I, pp. 228–42, for his explanation of the agreement of Genesis with modern evolutionary science.

natural and intended sense of Scripture,[59] did not differ from other traditions except for the presuppositions that guided their study. All the conservative groups, who defended high views of Scripture (infallibility) and traditional views on the composition of the biblical writings, employed commonsensical inductive methods in ascertaining the plain or literal meaning of Scripture. They rejected the notion that parts of the Scripture could be mythical or folkloric. They affirmed the trustworthiness of Scripture in everything, for it could not contain errors of any kind.

The early revivalistic conservative groups that were the most heavily influenced by the Reformed tradition (Presbyterians, Baptists and dispensationalists), tended to take common sense to its painfully logical conclusion with the only acceptable interpretation being the one intended by the author. Hence, the Scriptures had no dual meanings (such as one literal and another spiritual or double meanings concerning OT prophecy), because Scripture could only have one meaning—the one intended by the original author.

The Popularistic Pre-critical Bible Reading Approach

Prior to the Modernist/Fundamentalist debates, the most common approach to reading the Bible among the Wesleyan Holiness and Keswickian movements was a pre-critical Bible reading approach that was an adaptation of the proof-text method. 'This approach consisted of stringing together a series of scriptural passages on a given topic'. This method was practiced in order to understand what God has said about that topic under investigation.[60] James H. Brookes, a noted Keswickian speaker and founder of the Niagara Prophecy Conferences, explained how to prepare a 'Bible Reading'.

> Have your reader select some word, as faith, repentance, love, hope, justification, sanctification and with the aid of a good concordance, mark down before the time of the meeting the references to the subject under discussion. These can be read as

---

[59] Hodge and Warfield, 'Inspiration', *Presbyterian Review* 2 (April 1881), pp. 225–60, reference to 237–38.

[60] Weber, 'The Two-Edged Sword', p. 110.

called for, thus presenting all the Holy Ghost has been pleased to reveal on the topic.[61]

This type of Bible reading was the practiced popularistic interpretive method used by laity and pastors to such an extent that it functioned in a service as a 'fundamentalist liturgy'.[62] From their perspective anyone could purchase a concordance and determine what God had said about the subject under investigation. In their minds, this eliminated the need for help from biblical scholars. All that the Christian needed, according to William Evans, a Bible teacher at Moody Bible Institute, was

> an English Bible; a devout and earnest spirit; a reverential and teachable mind; a willingness to do the will of God as it is revealed in the increasing knowledge of the Scriptures; the pursuance of a right, though simple method of reading and study— these are essentials for profit and pleasure in Bible study.[63]

Weber correctly recognizes that the Bible teachers in their zealous commitment argued that their beliefs were based on Scripture alone. Moreover, by stressing the inductive common sense reasoning, they 'oversold the perspicuity of the Bible and the role of the Spirit to such an extent that many [popularistic] fundamentalists were unable to explain, let alone tolerate, other points of view'.[64]

Proof-texting was also the primary theological method of the academic conservative Fundamentalists, but they practiced the proof text method in accordance with the historical critical position.[65] Of course, the academic Fundamentalists appealed to a dif-

---

[61] J. Brookes, *The Truth* 5 (1879), p. 314 as cited in Timothy P. Weber, *Living in the Shadow of the Second Coming* (Chicago: The University of Chicago Press, 1987), p. 37.

[62] Noll, *The Scandal of the Evangelical Mind*, p. 133.

[63] W. Evans, *Outline Study of The Bible* (Chicago: Bible Institute Colportage Association, 1913), pp. 15–16 as cited in Weber, 'The Two-Edged Sword', p. 111.

[64] Weber, 'The Two-Edged Sword', p. 116. However, Hunter in his *American Evangelicalism* demonstrates through statistical analysis that 'Bible reading is significantly higher among [contemporary] Evangelicals than among other groups in the Christian tradition' (p. 69). This is a result of the Evangelical conviction that the Bible is the vehicle for God's revelation and interpreting Scripture requires a prayerful commonsensical approach. See pp. 61–69.

[65] Proof-texting was a long established practice among Protestant Christianity. The academically trained Fundamentalists used proof-texting as a means to establish systematic and biblical doctrines. Yet the Fundamentalists used proof-texting

ferent set of presuppositions concerning the historical critical method. However, the practice of proof-texting was coming under significant scrutiny due to the influence of modern higher criticism. Proof-texting assumed that the Bible was equally inspired throughout and timeless in its teaching. Thus any verse of Scripture could be used as a proof to support a doctrinal position. One outspoken Modernist observed quite correctly that it is typical to find lists of Scripture citations following a discussion of a theological topic in the standard theological texts of the day. William Clarke wrote,

> even if a proof-text method were a good method in itself, it could not successfully be employed now, since the texts of the Bible have suffered such serious though unintended distortion. One thing is certain. Theology must seize upon the help of criticism and history and exegesis and all else that can show what the Bible really means. But no one of these has a word to say in favor of continuing the old, easy, superficial proof-text method.[66]

The conservatives, however, were not willing to abandon the proof-text method. Canon Dyson Hague recognized the consequences of higher criticism upon proof-texting as an interpretive methodology. He wrote,

> For up to the present time any text from any part of the Bible was accepted as a proof-text for the establishment of any truth of Christian teaching, and a statement from the Bible was considered an end to the controversy ... all Scripture was received by the great builders of our theological systems with that unassailable belief in the inspiration of its texts ... But now the higher critics think they have changed all that ... The Christian system, therefore, will have to be re-adjusted if not revolutionized, every text and chapter and book will have to be inspected and analyzed in light of its date, origin, and circumstances, and authorship, and so on, and only after it passed the examining board of the modern Franco-Dutch-German criticism will it be

---

from an anti-modern perspective, which was different from the more pre-modern approach of the Holiness groups.

[66] William Newton Clarke, *The Use of Scriptures in Theology* (Edinburgh: T. & T. Clark, 1907), pp. 35–36 as cited in Weber, 'The Two Edged-Sword', p. 107.

allowed to stand as a proof-text for the establishment of any Christian doctrine.[67]

Due to the philosophical and theological foundation of higher criticism, great doubt had been placed upon the trustworthiness, historical correctness, and reliability of Scripture. As a result, the higher critics were calling for the cessation of the 'science of systematic theology' based upon 'proof-texting and harmonies'. Yet Hague retorted to the higher critics that it would be out of the question to accept their verdict upon the proof-text method.[68] Why? According to R.A. Torrey, 'In ninety-nine out of a hundred cases, the meaning that the plain man gets out of the Bible is the correct one'.[69]

Noll argues that the conservatives who used the proof-text system actually believed that they were limiting the human element of error, because the practitioners were simply stringing together all that the Word of God said about the topic and then deducing a general principle. Thus, they thought they were not introducing human ideas but arriving, rather, at God's thoughts. This, according to Noll, 'was intellectual self-delusion' because

> ordinary human beings not inspired by the Holy Spirit had cut up the Bible into verses and that other ordinary human beings not inspired of the Holy Spirit were rearranging those verses to extract large-scale truths from the Scriptures meant that both the fundamentalist Bible Reading and the most important fundamentalist theological books partook fully in thoroughly natural and thoroughly human activity, even as they attempted to understand divine truth.[70]

Once again, we see the popularistic and academic conservatives' de-emphasis upon human involvement both in the production and interpretation of Scripture, which Noll and others have rightly criticized. A firm confidence in the harmony of Scripture also prevailed among them. The harmony of Scripture accepts a progressive un-

---

[67] Torrey, *The Fundamentals*, 1917, I, pp. 33–34.
[68] Torrey, *The Fundamentals*, 1917, I, p. 34.
[69] Cited in William G. Mcloughlin, Jr., *Modern Revivalism* (New York: Ronald Press, 1959), p. 372.
[70] Noll, *The Scandal of the Evangelical Mind*, p. 135.

folding of truth and rejects the notion that the Bible may contradict itself on any given subject.[71] One was expected to harmonize Scripture because 'everything [in Scripture] is in agreement with everything else, because the whole Bible was built in the thought of God ... its unity the unity of Divine plan and its harmony the harmony of a Supreme Intelligence'.[72]

The Synthetic Method

Conservative teachers did not encourage a haphazard, careless approach to Bible study, nor were they necessarily anti-intellectual. They believed there was a right way and wrong way to studying the Bible. Ordinary Christians, even when relying on common sense, could misread the Scriptures and come to wrong interpretations. In order to avoid faulty interpretation one must use a sound method.

The most popular method of Bible study used at the emerging 'Bible Institutes' was the inductive-synthetic method. James M. Gray's 'synthetic method' was a very popular method used by dispensational Fundamentalists. He developed his method in the 1880's while teaching at Moody Bible Institute, and in 1904 he published *How To Master the English Bible*.[73] Other Holiness revivalistic groups were using similar inductive-synthetic approaches, but Gray's will serve as an example of the synthetic method.

The synthetic approach stressed the importance of inductive method and reasoning. This approach to interpretation stressed that the Bible should be understood as a unified book before breaking it down into its individual parts. It also emphasized a close interrogation of the English syntax, grammatical structure, repetition of words and ideas of the text. Before studying a book or paragraph, one needed to have an overview or panoramic view of the Bible. Gray advised the Bible student to read the Bible through from Genesis to Revelation, reading each book in the Bible in its entirety in one setting. Then after the student had completed this task, he

---

[71] See Arthur T. Peirson, 'The Testimony of the Organic Unity of the Bible to Its Inspiration', Torrey, *The Fundamentals*, 1917, II, pp. 97–111. Peirson wrote, 'All the criticism of more than three thousand years has failed to point out one important or irreconcilable contradiction' within the Bible (p. 98). The law of non-contradiction continues to play a key role in contemporary reformed evangelical hermeneutics.

[72] Torrey, *The Fundamentals*, 1917, pp. 97–98.

[73] Weber, 'The Two-Edged Sword', p. 112.

could study each individual book in a very methodical manner. Weber succinctly explains Gray's method:

> Gray advised a five-step approach to individual book study: 1) read the book entirely at one sitting; 2) read it continuously (i.e., without regard to chapter or verse divisions); 3) read it repeatedly until one has a feel for the flow of the book; 4) read it independently of any outside aid or authority; 5) read it prayerfully. Once the whole was in hand, one could turn one's attention to a more detailed study of its component parts, the development of its themes, and even the meaning of individual words or phrases. After studying a number of books in this way, one would be able to consider common doctrines, overlapping ideas, and so on.[74]

The 'synthetic method' flourished among the Keswickian influenced Bible institutes, yet it was usually used in conjunction with dispensationalism. However, among Wesleyan Holiness communities, there emerged a 'synthetic approach' that did not embrace dispensationalism. One such approach was published in 1952. According to the author, Robert A. Traina, he learned this method while a student at The Biblical Seminary in New York, and the method 'reflects the primary approach of Wilber W. White, founder' of the Biblical Seminary. Traina identified White as 'the illustrious "father of inductive Bible study"'.[75] Traina's method was a thoroughly refined approach of the early inductive method. Traina's inductive method was published under the titled *Methodical Bible Study: A New Approach to Hermeneutics*.[76] His method was a thorough and exhaus-

---

[74] Weber, 'The Two-Edged Sword', pp. 112–13.

[75] R. Traina, 'Inductive Bible Study Reexamined in the Light of Contemporary Hermeneutics' in McCown and Massey (eds.), *Wesleyan Theological Perspectives*, Vol. 2: *Interpreting God's Word for Today* (Anderson, IN: Warner Press), p. 54.

[76] R. Traina, *Methodical Bible Study: A New Approach to Hermeneutics* (New York: Ganis and Harris, 1952). Traina served as Associate Professor of the English Bible at The Biblical Seminary in New York when his method was published and he later became Professor of English Bible at Asbury Theological Seminary, Kentucky. He had a PhD from Drew University. Asbury Seminary has a chair in honor of Traina, and his method is still being taught. A portion of this methodical method can be found in a very popular contemporary text on Evangelical hermeneutics, *Introduction to Biblical Interpretation* by W.W. Klein, C.L. Blomberg and R.L. Hubbard, Jr., (Dallas: Word, 1993). Unfortunately the authors never acknowledge Traina's work, but it seems clear that they are expanding on the

tive exegesis of the English translation of the Bible, written for students, pastors and laity of the revivalistic holiness traditions, but primarily those of a Wesleyan lineage.

The basic premise of his method was based upon his understanding that 'the Bible was an objective body of literature ...' and so one must use an approach that corresponds to it—an objective approach.[77] The objective approach used by Traina was induction because 'induction is objective and impartial', whereas 'deduction tends to be subjective and prejudicial'. Hence 'methodical Bible study is inductive Bible study'.[78] In his methodical approach, he covered four chapters: (1) Observation; (2) Interpretation; (3) Evaluation and Application and (4) Correlation. His approach could be understood as commonsensical literary analysis of Scripture in the tradition of historical-grammatical exegesis and the inductive method.[79]

Traina clearly distinguishes his method from various other approaches.[80] I will briefly touch upon his concerns with the literalist approach, historical approach, rationalistic interpretation and typological interpretation.[81]

Concerning the literalist (those in the popularistic Fundamentalists and dispensationalists camps, like James Gray and R.A. Torrey), Traina correctly recognized a fundamental flaw in their approach stemming from their philosophical foundation. He wrote:

> one of the main reasons for the error of the literalist is that he tends to equate the literal with the historical and the figurative with the unhistorical ... he inseparably relates the historical fact

methodical inductive method—see especially chapter six, 'General rules of Hermeneutics'. For example, compare their p. 164, which discusses the logical structural patterns that writers use in developing a logical line of thought, with Traina's discussion of literary structural relationships of Scripture on p. 28 in *Methodical Bible Study*.

[77] Traina, *Methodical Bible Study*, p. 7.

[78] Traina, *Methodical Bible Study*, p. 7.

[79] Traina, *Methodical Bible Study*, p. 180. Traina stated that 'the basic approach to the exposition of Scriptures should be the *grammatico-historical* ', which interprets the author's language 'by the laws of grammar and the facts of history' (pp. 181–82). It is important to note that the grammatical comes before the historical, which importantly illuminates the emphasis of his method!

[80] Traina, *Methodical Bible Study*, see pp. 167–81 for his detailed discussion of 'Some Erroneous Kinds of Interpretation'.

[81] Traina, *Methodical Bible Study*, pp. 169–76.

with its literary expression. He fails to realize that the literal and figurative approaches are not necessarily concerned respectively with fact and fiction. For they are simply two forms of literary expression ... the use of imagery to describe an event does not inevitably negate its historicity. Thus one may hold, for example, that Genesis 3 is figurative rather than literal and not necessarily imply thereby that it is substantially unhistorical rather than historical, or fictional rather than factual. The former decision involves literary interpretation; the latter concerns historical judgment. These two phases of exposition must be carefully distinguished.[82]

Traina's work is concerned with the historical context, but only as a means to understand the proper meaning of the words and the type of literary genre found in Scripture. Hence the historical setting or context is examined in order to understand the passage properly and in order to grasp the authors' intentions.[83] Traina was more concerned with the literary structure than traditional historical critical issues (source and tradition) or the 'real history' of the Hebrews.[84] He advocated that one must saturate oneself within the passage and see what is going on in the passage structurally, which is to say, he was concerned first with the literary world of the text. After one examined the literary features within their historical context, then one could move to historical questions that dealt with the world behind the text. The best exegete, according to Traina, is one who can develop a re-creative perception that allows the interpreter 'to stand in the shoes of Biblical authors in order to feel as they felt and to think as they thought'.[85] A thorough analysis of the literary structure and historical context in which the biblical passage emerged enabled one to see and *experience* the author's intended pur-

---

[82] Traina, *Methodical Bible Study*, pp. 175–76.

[83] It is on account of these two principles of exposition that Traina finds typological interpretation faulty, but he still finds it valuable and suggests 'to limit the exposition of Old Testament symbols [types] to those that are explained within the Scriptures themselves' (p. 176).

[84] Traina defines the historical approach as a study of the history of a certain people. For him, this fails to recognize the spiritual dimension of Scripture (see p. 172).

[85] Traina, *Methodical Bible Study*, p. 230. Traina presented a succinct summary of his method, pp. 229–31.

purpose.[86] Therefore, a pure rationalistic approach cannot grasp the experiential dimension of Scripture, nor affirm the mysterious and miraculous events discussed in Scripture.

Traina's methodical hermeneutic was an academically informed approach that had many similarities with the other early conservatives (commonsensical approach to language, trustworthiness of Scripture and induction as a scientific method). Yet his method attempted to avoid the principle of historical verification embraced in the nineteenth century and accepted as a foundational principle by both Fundamentalists and Modernists. His method is more in tune with the Wesleyan Holiness-Pentecostal beliefs than with the Princetonians, Fundamentalists and dispensationalists.[87] Unlike the Fundamentalists, Traina saw experience as an unavoidable and necessary asset. He argued that the 'Scriptures must be interpreted in light of experience' because 'Scriptures are the expression of experience'. His method attempted to be thoroughly inductive and primarily concerned with literary structure. He viewed Scripture more as a living work of art that can *affect* the reader, than as a dead historical artifact. His method, therefore, has much more in common with newer literary approaches (New Criticism) than the classical historical critical approaches.[88]

Dispensationalism

As noted earlier, James Gray's 'synthetic method' was also an inductive approach; but it, however, was intended to function within the theological interpretive grid known as dispensationalism. The Plymouth Brethren minister John Nelson Darby (1800–1882) imported dispensational premillennialism[89] to North America.[90] John Darby,

---

[86] Traina, *Methodical Bible Study*, p. 152.

[87] Traina, *Methodical Bible Study*, p. 139. Traina recognized that the interpretive process is influenced from the start by the experiences of the hermeneut. Thus, 'the peculiarities of one's own experience are invariably reflected in the interpretive process' (p. 138).

[88] For a discussion of Traina's methodical method and its relationship to contemporary hermeneutical methods that developed prior to 1972, see his two essays in *Interpreting God's Word For Today*, 1972, pp. 53–110. In his concluding remarks of the first essay, Traina stated, 'what is called for then, is a more comprehensive and holistic approach to an inductive interpretive methodology' (p. 79).

[89] For an overview of dispensationalism, see Marsden, *Fundamentalism and the American Culture*, pp. 48–62. Timothy P. Weber's *Living in the Shadow of the Second Coming* (Chicago: The University of Chicago Press, 1987, expanded edition) is the

prior to helping establish the Plymouth Brethren around 1830, was
an Anglican minister who had left the Church of Ireland because of
its waning spiritual condition. The Plymouth Brethren were a
loosely organized community of believers who met informally for
Bible study, prayer and communion.[91]

After the Civil War, futuristic premillennialism[92] began to grow
in popularity. John Darby came to America on various occasions
between 1866–1877 preaching and teaching his version of premillennialism called dispensationalism. Darby had met with a variety of
conservative ministers (who were primarily affiliated with the Calvinistic traditions) sharing his insights with them through his traditional Plymouth Brethren Bible study format. Many prominent and
popular leaders accepted his interpretive method (premillennial dispensationalism) and appreciated his emphasis upon laity's familiarity
of Scripture, but they declined in joining the Plymouth Brethren.
Instead, they disseminated dispensationalism to the conservative
revivalistic Christians throughout the various Bible Prophecy Con-

---

definitive study on premillennialism in American Evangelicalism. For a helpful
discussion on millennial views held in North American contemporary Evangelicalism, see Robert G. Clouse (ed.), *The Meaning of the Millennium: Four Views*
(Downers Grove, IL: InterVarsity, 1977).

[90] Weber, *Living in the Shadow of the Second Coming*, p. 17. Weber offers three
possibilities of how Darby came to develop dispensationalism. It may have come
from Edward Irving, or possibly a Miss MacDonald. Darby, however, claimed he
received this dispensational method all on his own. However, it is important to
recognize that the first two individuals mentioned are connected with early charismatic outpourings, which was a result of reading Scripture from a 'restorationist' perspective and emphasizing a futuristic premillennialism. Irving and/or
MacDonald most likely influenced Darby. See Larry Christenson, 'Pentecostalism's Forgotten Forerunner' in Vinson Synan's (ed.), Aspects *of Pentecostal-
Charismatic Origins*, pp. 15–37 and, David W. Dorries, 'Edward Irving and The
"Standing Sign" of Spirit Baptism' in Gary B. McGee's (ed.), *Initial Evidence: Historical and Biblical Perspectives On the Doctrine Of Spirit Baptism*, (Peabody, MA: Hendrickson, 1991), pp. 41–56.

[91] Noll, *A History of Christianity*, pp. 376–8. Weber, *Living in the Shadow*, pp. 16–
22.

[92] Premillennialists believed in a 'literal' thousand-year reign of Christ on
earth. This millennial reign will take place after Jesus' second coming and prior to
the complete recreation of heaven and earth. Not all premillennialists were or are
dispensationalists. Dispensationalists believed the same yet added a 'secret' rapture of the Church from the earth for seven years at which time God would pour
out his wrath, restore Israel, and then establish the millennium.

ferences held during the last quarter of the nineteenth century.[93] The most influential dispensational teaching came through the pen of C.I. Scofield, an American who adopted Darby's system. In 1909, Oxford University Press published the *Scofield Reference Bible.* Scofield's Study Bible has done more to spread the popularity of dispensationalism than any other piece of literature.[94]

The organizers of the Prophetic Bible Conferences were Calvinists, and many of them had embraced dispensationalism. Hence, dispensational premillennialism had strong Calvinistic ties and was primarily accepted first among clergy who held strong Calvinistic views.[95] However, not all the premillennialists involved in these conferences were dispensationalists, but most were, and after World War I, many of the newly formed Holiness groups (Wesleyan Holi-

---

[93] Marsden, *Fundamentalism and American Culture,* p. 46. There exists some ambiguity around whether Darby's dispensationalism gave rise to the Bible Prophecy Conference movement, or whether the conservative revivalistic Christian concern over end time prophecy promoted the Bible Prophecy movement which in turn, then became a vehicle for the spread of dispensationalism. See Noll, *A History of Christianity,* p. 377. But see Charles C. Ryrie, *Dispensationalism Today* (Chicago: Moody Press, 1965), who argues that 'The truth is that the calling of the prophetic conferences as a protest to modernity was the cause, and a gradual understanding of dispensationalism was the effect. The conferences led to dispensationalism not vice versa ... dispensationalism grew out of the *independent* study which resulted from the interest in prophecy' (p. 81). Ryrie reveals two important convictions held by dispensationalists. First, they believe the method is both biblical and literal method of interpretation. Secondly, they argue that dispensationalism was the result of independent scholars coming to similar understanding as a result of literally interpreting prophecy. Like Darby before him who argued that he came to his system as a result of private Bible study, Ryrie disavows any connection between the leaders of the prophetic conferences and Darby's influence. See his chapter 4, 'The Origins of Dispensationalism', especially pp. 81–82 and chapter 5, 'The Hermeneutics of Dispensationalism', especially pp. 86–90.

[94] Noll, *Between Faith And Criticism* writes, 'the Scofield Bible sold in breathtaking numbers and remains a mainstay of dispensational interpretation' (p. 58). Marsden in his *Fundamentalism* points out that the same group of Bible teachers and evangelists who promoted *The Fundamentals* were also promoting their own distinct view of dispensationalism—the most important being *The Scofield Reference Bible,* p. 119. No wonder Ernest Sandeen in his study on *The Roots of Fundamentalism* argues that 'as a result of the 1919 World's Conference on Christian Fundamentals, the millenarian movement had changed its name. The millenarians had become Fundamentalists' (p. 246, cited in Weber, *Living in the Shadow,* p. 162).

[95] Marsden, *Fundamentalism,* p. 46. Marsden writes, 'These early gatherings ... were clearly Calvinistic. Presbyterians and Calvinist Baptists predominated, while the number of Methodists was extremely small.'

ness, Keswick and Pentecostal) expressed their eschatology through dispensational theory.[96]

Prophetic Bible Conference leaders like Nathaniel West, James H. Brooks, William B. Erdman, Henry Parsons, A.J. Gordon, Rueben A. Torrey, James M. Gray, A.C. Dixon and C.I. Scofield were all activist evangelists who promoted a host of Bible conferences geared toward furnishing the laity with a better understanding of the prophetic portions of Scripture. Many of these men also held leadership positions within the newly emerging Bible Institutes (Moody Bible Institute, 1886; The Bible Institute of Los Angeles, 1907; and the Philadelphia College of the Bible, 1914, just to list a few). Thus, the Bible Institutes permanently institutionalized dispensational premillennialism and along with it, Fundamentalist concerns.[97] Yet, according to Marsden, 'dispensationalism was nevertheless the most distinctive intellectual product of emerging fundamentalism'.[98] Ironically, Noll sees dispensationalism as *the* scandal of the Evangelical mind.[99]

The dispensationalists embraced the Princetonian doctrine of the inspiration and authority of Scripture and their argument for interpreting Scripture according to its plain meaning-a historical grammatical approach with the emphasis on the historical.[100] Ironically, the Princetonians (Hodge, Warfield and Machen) were not concerned with premillennialism[101] and had rejected dispensationalism.[102] Yet due to their common reliance upon Baconian Common Sense Realism, they 'spoke the same language and defended the faith in similar fashion'.[103] This reliance upon the Princetonians'

[96] Noll, *A History of Christianity*, p. 378. See also the essay by Assembly of God historian William Menzies, 'Non Wesleyan Influences In The Pentecostal Revival From 1901 to 1910' in Vinson Synan (ed.), *Aspects of the Pentecostal-Charismatic Origins*, pp. 84–98. Menzies writes, 'It is at the point of eschatology that the fundamentalist influence [dispensational premillennialism] is perhaps most clearly discernible in the pentecostal movement' (p. 85).

[97] Marsden, *Understanding Fundamentalism and Evangelicalism*, pp. 40–41.

[98] Marsden, *Fundamentalism*, p. 44.

[99] Noll, *The Scandal of the Evangelical Mind*, p. 137.

[100] James D. Hunter, *American Evangelicalism*, p. 31.

[101] Alister McGrath, *Evangelicalism and the future of Christianity* (Downers Grove, IL: InterVarsity, 1995), pp. 29–30.

[102] See B.B. Warfield's review of R.A. Torrey's *What the Bible Teaches*, in *Presbyterian and Reformed Review* 10 (July 1899), pp. 562–64.

[103] Marsden, *Fundamentalism*, p. 118.

doctrine of Scriptural inspiration gave dispensationalism an intellectual accent. Hence dispensationalism was both 'scientific' because it used the Baconian method and 'supernatural' in the sense that Scripture had its origin from God and that God was in sovereign control of history.[104] Thus, the miracles recorded in the Bible were affirmed as historical fact. Yet, fundamentalist dispensationalists rejected any notion that the supernatural manifestations (miracles) or gifts of the Holy Spirit would continue after the death of the Apostles. Their 'supernaturalism' was concerned only with the miracles found in the Scripture, and the dispensationalists, in a similar manner as B.B. Warfield, argued for the *cessation* of the supernatural manifestations after the New Testament era.

The central feature of dispensationalism was and still is an emphasis upon the economy of God's dealing with humanity. Scofield emphasized this when he wrote:

> the dispensations are distinguished, exhibiting the majestic, progressive order of the divine dealings of God with humanity, 'the increasing purpose' which runs through and links together the ages from the beginning of the life of man to the end of eternity. Augustine said: 'Distinguish the ages, and the Scriptures harmonize.'[105]

A biblical dispensation or age as it is sometimes called 'is a period of time during which man is tested in respect of obedience to some *specific* revelation of the will of God'.[106] Unfortunately, humanity always fails the test and the dispensation ends in catastrophic judgment, which then opens the door for a new dispensation. Scofield represents all dispensationalists when he wrote: 'Each of the dispensations may be regarded as a new test of the natural man, and

---

[104] See Marsden, *Fundamentalism*, pp. 55–62 for a detailed discussion of the scientific method and pp. 63–71 for the supernatural aspect.

[105] *The Scofield Reference Bible* (New York: Oxford University Press, 1917, first published 1909), p. iii. For a dramatic visual presentation and explanation of dispensationalism see Clarence Larkin, *Dispensational Truth or God's Plan and Purpose In the Ages* (Philadelphia: Rev. Clarence Larkin Est., 1920). Larkin wrote in the forward that his book along with the charts were 'developed under the direction and guidance of the Holy Spirit' and was 'the outcome of over 30 years of careful and patient study of the Prophetic Scriptures, and aims to give not the opinions of men, but the teaching of the Word of God'.

[106] Scofield, *The Scofield Reference Bible*, p. 5.

each ends in judgment, marking his utter failure in every dispensation'.[107] Dispensationalists utilized this system to explain all historical change. Thus the Bible was used to interpret history and accentuate divine intervention. Antithetical to this view was Modernism that interpreted the Bible from naturalistic history.[108]

Historical periodization of Scripture was not new, but what separated dispensationalism from other futuristic Premillennialists was their rigid literal expectation that Old Testament prophecy will be fulfilled.[109]

> The prophetic writings are to be interpreted in the literal, natural and unforced meaning of the words' and 'all fulfilled prophecy has been fulfilled literally, not spiritually or allegorically ... this renders the study of prophecy simple. Zion and Jerusalem mean Zion and Jerusalem, not the church.[110]

Their argument for a literalistic approach to prophecy relied upon a strict distinction between the Church and Israel. This meant that God has two completely different plans operating in history, one for his 'earthly' chosen people, the Jewish race and one for his 'spiritual' people, the Church.[111] According to the dispensational view, the Church was not mentioned in the Old Testament, but came into existence as a result of the Jews rejecting Jesus, their Messiah, which opened the door for a new dispensation—the Church age or the age of grace.[112] Therefore, this present dispensation, 'The Church Age' is concerned only about *evangelizing* the lost. This age will end when Jesus returns with his raptured saints to set up his earthly kingdom in Jerusalem at which time he will restore all

---

[107] Scofield, *Rightly Dividing the Word of Truth* (New Jersey: Loizeaux Brothers, no date, first edition 1896), pp. 13–14. Scofield held that there were seven dispensations. Not all dispensationalists agreed on the exact number of dispensations, yet they were all in agreement that there were two distinct groups, the Hebrews and the Gentile church.

[108] Marsden, *Understanding Fundamentalism*, p. 41.

[109] Weber, *Living in the Shadow*, p. 17.

[110] C. I. Scofield (ed.), *The Scofield Bible Correspondence Course: Volume One, Old Testament* (Chicago: The Moody Bible Institute of Chicago, 1907), p. 128.

[111] Weber, *Living in the Shadow*, pp. 17–18. The key passage of dispensationalism was Daniel 9, the seventy weeks. See Marsden, *Fundamentalism*, pp. 52–54. Notice the chart on p. 53, which comes from Larkin's, *Dispensational Truth*.

[112] See Larkin, *Dispensational Truth*, pp. 19–21. Also Scofield, *The Scofield Bible Correspondence Course*, p. 128.

the Jews, his earthly people, to their land, thus literally fulfilling all Old Testament prophecy.[113]

Dispensationalism is an elaborate pessimistic theological system that appeals to a strict literalism of Old Testament prophetic fulfillment in order to justify its existence. The dispensationalists regarded their interpretive method as a literal or plain meaning approach, which was simply that of Common Sense.[114] This preference for the literal over the figurative (and typological) interpretation of prophecy became increasingly popular among all the premillennialists.[115] For the dispensationalist, Scripture was an encyclopedic puzzle in which no piece was too small in discerning God's plan for the ages. When Scripture was 'rightly divided' anyone could understand it; however, in order to rightly divide Scripture, one needed the help of a dispensational teacher and his charts. This is the great irony of dispensationalism: it argues for a common sense inductive approach to Bible study yet insists that one cannot interpret Scripture properly without the aid of dispensationalism.[116] When reading the Bible inductively, without the aid of the dispensational interpretive chart, one would have a difficult time arriving at the notion that God has two plans of redemption one for his earthly people Israel and one for his spiritual people the Church. Also one would have a difficult time understanding how the teachings of Jesus (such as the Sermon on the Mount) were not intended for the Christian community but instead for the millennial age that was to follow the Church age. Nor would one ever come to the conclusion that there was a great chasm of interrupted time between the 69th week and 70th week of Daniel's vision of the 'Seventy Weeks'.[117] Furthermore, the Church age became the great parenthesis to God's dealing with Israel, for the Church came into existence at the end of the 69th week, but it did not bring the inau-

---

[113] Dispensationalists predicted the re-establishment of the Jewish nation, thus dispensationalists have always been pro-Zionist. See Weber, *Living in the Shadow*, pp. 131–41.

[114] Marsden, *Fundamentalism*, p. 61.

[115] Bebbington, *Evangelicalism in Modern Britain*, p. 89.

[116] Timothy Weber, 'The Two Edged Sword: The Fundamentalist Use of the Bible' in N. Hatch and M. Noll (eds.), *The Bible In America: Essays in Cultural History* (New York: Oxford University Press, 1982), p. 114.

[117] See Daniel 9.20–27, the understanding of Daniel's vision is the capstone of the whole dispensational system.

guration of the 70th week. The 70th week will begin with the 'secret' rapture of the church from the earth. The following lengthy quotation is offered in order to illustrate this system with its emphasis on a so called 'literal' interpretation of Scripture, its separation of Israel and the Church and the key importance of the '70 weeks' of Daniel, which holds the system together.

> To understand the books of Daniel and Revelation and related scriptures such as Mt 24–25; Mk 13; Lk 21; 2 Th 2, and especially understand the time of the rapture and the second advent, one must clearly understand the 70 weeks of Daniel 9:24–27. Without doubt, all the above scriptures will be fulfilled during the last 7 years of this age known as 'Daniel's 70th week.' It must be understood, if we want clear truth, that Israel, and not the church, is the one dealt with in the 70th week, for Israel only was the one dealt with in the first 69 weeks. All the 69 weeks were literally fulfilled with Israel before the church age began. Not once was the NT church mentioned in their fulfillment of the 70th week of Dan 9:27; Mt 24:15-31; Lk 21:25-36 and Rev 4:1–19:21. The New Testament was not yet made and ratified by the Blood of Jesus Christ (Mt 26:28) until the end of the 69th week when the Messiah was cut off and crucified (Dan 9:26). The future 70th week will not and cannot begin until the NT church is raptured and God again begins to deal with 'thy people (Israel), and thy holy city (Jerusalem)' … All activity of the NT church will end before the 70th week begins.[118]

Dispensationalists were concerned with the exact sense of the printed word, thus they assumed an audience that could read and carefully follow their exposition of the biblical passage. Marsden argues that this emphasis upon the printed word 'is one of the principle things that distinguish fundamentalism from less intellectual forms of American revivalism' such as the Holiness and Pentecostal

---

[118] Finis Jennings Dake, *The Rapture and the Second Coming of Christ* (Atlanta, GA: Dake Bible Sales, 1977), p. 7. Even though Dake was not a participant in the early dispensational conferences, his works are consistent with traditional dispensational teaching. Dake's works (especially his annotated reference Bible) have been very influential among some Pentecostal communities.

groups.[119] 'Because of their emphasis on literal interpretations of prophecies, dispensationalists have been one of the groups most insistent on making the inerrancy of Scripture a test for true faith'.[120]

Not only did dispensationalism make a permanent distinction between how God deals with Israel and the Church, it also de-emphasized the Gospels and emphasized the Epistles because the Epistles were written for the Church. The Gospels were written to record Jesus' ministry for the Jews and as a result of their rejection of the Messiah, God turned to the Gentiles. Thus the Gospels (especially the Sermon on the Mount) were for the Jewish millennial kingdom that would come after the close of the Church age. The Epistles were written for the present Church age, hence the Gospels were viewed from a more Reformed perspective—as an objective declaration of the forgiveness of sin and not from an Anabaptist pietistic or Wesleyan perspective as a Christian way of life.

Dispensationalism wed to Common Sense Realism perpetuated the notion that propositional truth is found in the Epistles rather than the narrative portions of Scripture. They also, like the Reformed tradition, saw the Gospels functioning as an objective declaration of salvation and not like the Wesleyan Holiness and Pentecostal groups who saw the Gospels as a way of living the Christian life. For those in the dispensational camp, their 'canon within the canon' would be the New Testament Epistles, particularly Paul's letters. Unfortunately dispensationalism is still a popular method of interpretation amongst the laity of evangelical traditions today (and Dallas Theological Seminary), and the fascination with futuristic predictions continues to flourish in North America. During the 1970's the best selling book of any sort in the United States was the *Late Great Planet Earth* by Hal Lindsey. This book was an interpretation of world events from a traditional dispensational viewpoint.[121] More recently, Tim LaHaye's dispensational novel, *Left Behind: A*

---

[119] Marsden, *Fundamentalism*, p. 61. This further demonstrates that the dispensationalists were much more modern than the Holiness and Pentecostals.

[120] Marsden, *Understanding Fundamentalism*, p. 40.

[121] Noll, *The Scandal of the Evangelical Mind*, p. 140. Also, the Y2K craze encouraged a resurgence of dispensational thinking.

Novel of the Earth's Last Days, has spawned a plethora of subsequent books, tapes, movies and related materials.[122]

Clashing Worldviews: The Modernist/Fundamentalist Controversy[123]

The Modernist/Fundamentalist controversy concerning the nature and source of Scripture is best perceived as a 'clashing of world-views'. The Modernists attempted to adapt traditional Protestant Christianity to modern concepts of history, science and society. The Fundamentalists[124] attempted to re-present and defend nineteenth-century Reformed Protestantism. The Fundamentalists were in essence an academically critical, anti-modern response to liberalism[125] that later merged with more revivalistic popularistic Presbyterian and Baptist dispensational groups[126] who would emerge in the 1920's as militantly anti-modernist separatist fundamentalists.[127] The central issue in the Fundamentalist/Modernist debate was the source and authority of Scripture; however, seething beneath the surface was the more controlling factor—the understanding of history.[128]

The recasting of traditional Protestantism into a nineteenth-century modernistic mold created predominant characteristics that

---

[122] Tim F. LaHaye and Jerry B. Jenkins, *Left Behind : A Novel of the Earth's Last Days* (Wheaton, IL: Tyndale House Publishers, 1995). LaHaye's popularistic dispensational approach to eschatology is critiqued by Dale M. Coulter, 'Pentecostal Visions of the End: Eschatology, Ecclesiology and Fascination of the Left Behind Series', *JPT* 14.1 (October 2005), pp. 81–98.

[123] See Noll's, *A History of Christianity* chapter 14 for a discussion leading up to and following this controversy, specifically pp. 381–86.

[124] Noll, *A History of Christianity*, p. 383, notes that a Baptist named Curtis Lee Laws, editor, first coined the term Fundamentalist in 1920. Lee defined a Fundamentalist as one who was ready 'to do battle royal for the fundamentals'. He understood fundamentalism as 'a protest against that rationalistic interpretation of Christianity which seeks to discredit supernaturalism'. Fundamentalism is a complex phenomenon; see Marsden, *Fundamentalism* and Sandeen, *The Roots of Fundamentalism*.

[125] David Chidester, *Patterns of Power: Religion and Politics in America Culture* (Plainfield, NJ: Prentice-Hall, 1988), pp. 269–83.

[126] Noll, *Between Faith and Criticism*, p. 38.

[127] Marsden, *Fundamentalism*, p. 195. Marsden notes that this group is primarily made up of dispensationalists.

[128] Wacker, 'The Demise of Biblical Civilization', p. 123.

were easily identifiable. According to Claude Welch, the characteristics of the 'New Theology' were:

> the emphasis on divine immanence as a corrective to the Latin over emphasis on transcendence ... thus a different view of God's relationship to the natural and historical process and an evolutionary perspective; the understanding of revelation not as intrusion but as correlative to human discovery, as a process of God disclosing himself through genuine human means in a never-ending process of criticism and experiment; religious experience as a verifiable datum comparable to scientific data; the Bible as a document of religious experience and thus a different sort of authority.[129]

The 'New Theology' was the Modernists' attempt to salvage archaic Christianity from the death grip of the modern age. The Modernists argued that if Christianity was to survive, it must be reinterpreted in light of the rationalistic, naturalistic, instrumental modern age.[130] The Fundamentalists, however, saw 'New Theology' as the reincarnation of an 'old paganism'. J. Gresham Machen spoke for most Fundamentalists when he wrote:

> The liberal attempt at reconciling Christianity with modern science has really relinquished everything distinctive of Christianity, so that what remains is, in essentials, only the same indefinite type of religious aspiration which was in the world before Christianity came on the scene ... the apologist has really abandoned what he started out to defend. [131]

He spoke for all conservative Christians when he wrote, 'the chief modern rival of Christianity is "liberalism"'.[132]

---

[129] Claude Welch, *Protestant Thought in the Nineteenth Century* (New Haven, CT: Yale University Press, 1985), II, p. 232. Also see J.I. Packer, *Fundamentalism and the Word of God: Some Evangelical Principles* (Grand Rapids, MI: Eerdmans, 1992, first edition 1958), pp. 24–29. Packer writes, 'It was in protest against this radical refashioning of historic faith that "Fundamentalism" arose' (p. 27).

[130] Noll, *A History of Christianity*, pp. 373–76.

[131] J. Gresham Machen, *Christianity And Liberalism* (Grand Rapids, MI: Eerdmans, 1923), p. 7, cited in Packer, *Fundamentalism and the Word of God*, p. 27.

[132] Machen, *Christianity And Liberalism*, p. 53. Machen is recognized as the last of the old school Princeton Theologians, who later became Fundamentalism's finest intellect. For an important presentation of Machen and his understanding

By reading the highly publicized debates between the Fundamentalist pastor, John Roach Straton, DD (1875–1929) and the Unitarian modernist minister Charles F. Potter MA, STM (1885–1962), one can come to a better appreciation of how the Bible became the battlefront in this modernistic holy war.[133] The topics of the four debates were: 1) *The Battle over the Bible*; 2) *Evolution versus Creation*; 3) *The Virgin Birth—Fact or Fiction?* and 4) *Was Christ both God and Man?* The first debate was held at Calvary Baptist Church on December 20, 1923 and addressed the issue of whether or not the Bible was the infallible Word of God.[134]

Straton, the fundamentalist Baptist, argued that the Bible was indeed the infallible (free from all errors) Word of God.[135] He based his defense on the following proofs: 1) the inability of the Bible to be destroyed throughout history;[136] 2) the Bible's unique appeal to all races of people;[137] 3) archeological discoveries which overturn higher criticism's hypothetical conclusions;[138] 4) the Bible's remark-

---

of Christianity, see Harrisville and Sundberg, *The Bible In Modern Culture*, ch. 9, 'J. Gresham Machen: The Fundamentalist Defense', pp. 180–202. They write, 'If fundamentalism arose essentially as a protest movement, then J. Gresham Machen was its best theologian who walked the picket line' (p. 202).

[133] Editor Joel A. Carpenter writes in the preface,

> These debates, which took place in 1923–1924, were the most highly publicized events of the fundamentalist-modernist controversy before the Scopes Trial ... A series of fundamentalist rallies held at Straton's church so annoyed Potter ... that he challenged Straton to debate. Held before capacity audiences [three of them at Carnegie Hall], broadcast live on radio, and receiving major coverage of the press, these contests put the issues dividing modernists and fundamentalists squarely before the American public.

A facsimile of the publication of these debates are found in Joel A. Carpenter (ed.), *Fundamentalist Versus Modernist: The Debates Between John Roach Straton and Charles Francis Potter* (New York: Garland Publishing, 1988).

[134] John R. Straton and Charles F. Potter, *The Battle Over the Bible* (New York: George H. Doran Company, 1924). Inerrancy is still a real issue within the evangelical communities of North America; see Harold Lindsell, *The Battle for the Bible* (Grand Rapids, MI: Zondervan, fourteenth printing 1981, 1976). In the forward Harold J. Ockenga writes: 'It is apparent that those who surrender the doctrine of inerrancy inevitably move away from orthodoxy is indisputable ... [they] must ultimately yield the right to use the name "evangelical"'. Inerrancy has become the litmus test for Evangelical identity in North America.

[135] See Straton and Potter, *The Battle over the Bible*, pp. 13–51 for his lengthy argument.

[136] Straton and Potter, *The Battle over the Bible*, pp. 15–18.

[137] Straton and Potter, *The Battle over the Bible*, pp. 19–21.

[138] Straton and Potter, *The Battle over the Bible*, pp. 21–23.

able unity in all its diversity which necessitates one overseeing influence—namely God;[139] 5) the striking fact of the Bible's fulfilled prophecies which is the 'most conclusive proof for the divine origin and infallibility of the Bible';[140] 6) the Bible's own claims to be the Word of God;[141] and, 7) the Bible's self-authenticating authority.[142] According to Straton, these evidential proofs demonstrate that the Bible is 'divine in its origin and infallible in its content'.[143] Straton represented the conservative traditions. These were the concerns and traditional arguments of the early nineteenth-century and are still used by contemporary Evangelicals who embrace inerrancy.

Charles Potter rejected the infallibility (inerrancy) of the Bible. In his opening statement he asserted that he could affirm that 'the Bible is the best book' or even that 'we find God's Word in the Bible'. He rejected infallibility because it implied that 'every part of the Bible is the Word of God and therefore infallible' (inerrant). Thus Potter correctly stated, 'I do not have to prove that it is all wrong. If any part is wrong, or untrue, the Book is not infallible, as that word is commonly understood by English-speaking people.'[144]

Potter's argument involved three accusations (and he included scriptural citations). His accusations were the following: 1) the inaccuracies in the Bible, which are unscientific and unhistorical;[145] 2) the contradictions in the Bible;[146] and 3) the morally degrading ideas of God found in Scripture.[147] Potter's main argument against the infallibility of Scripture rested with the third issue:

> My main contention, however, on which I would be willing to base my entire argument, is not the scientific inaccuracies, nor even the fully recognized contradictions in the text of the Bible. If the Bible is the word of God, the scientific mistakes prove him ignorant and the contradictions prove him inconsistent … But my principle contention goes much deeper than that. It is

[139] Straton and Potter, *The Battle over the Bible*, pp. 23–26.
[140] Straton and Potter, *The Battle over the Bible*, pp. 26–32.
[141] Straton and Potter, *The Battle over the Bible*, pp. 32–36.
[142] Straton and Potter, *The Battle over the Bible*, pp. 36–51.
[143] Straton and Potter, *The Battle over the Bible*, p. 51.
[144] Straton and Potter, *The Battle over the Bible*, p. 52.
[145] Straton and Potter, *The Battle over the Bible*, pp. 59–60.
[146] Straton and Potter, *The Battle over the Bible*, pp. 60–61.
[147] Straton and Potter, *The Battle over the Bible*, pp. 61–62.

based on the morally degrading ideas of God which are contained in some parts of the Bible, where God is made by ignorant writers to sanction certain things which, if you and I did, we
would be put behind steel bars.[148]

Potter, like liberals in general, desired to liberate God from the
primitive texts that demoralized God. Potter used experience as the
foundation with rationalistic thinking as the basic infrastructure of
his argumentation. He believed these three arguments with scriptural citations and supported with scientific verification, created an
unshakable fortress that could not be overthrown by the naive arguments of the Fundamentalists. He believed that these arguments
demonstrated that 'the Bible is not literally inspired and not the infallible word of God'.[149]

Liberalism won the battle in the modern American universities,
but it failed to capture the *mind* and *heart* of revivalistic Protestant
Christianity.[150] Liberalism, in its attempt to throw off the dogmatic
theology of traditional Protestantism, clothed itself in the fashion-
able designs of Modernism and seemed to fail to recognize its own
style as faddish. Conversely, the Fundamentalists did more than
simply re-present 'orthodox doctrine'. They so immersed themselves in enlightened thought[151] that they too must be considered a
modern movement rather than a pre-modern movement. Granted,
Fundamentalism was in opposition to liberalism. However, Fundamentalism simply cannot be equated with 'a basic unaltered orthodoxy'.[152]

The Fundamentalists and the Modernists both shared a common
philosophical conviction, on which they built their 'evidential arguments'. The conviction was that only what was historically and objectively scientifically verifiable could be considered 'true' and thus
meaningful.[153] Both were overconfident in their claims. Thus,

---

[148] Straton and Potter, *The Battle over the Bible*, p. 61, also p. 58.

[149] Straton and Potter, *The Battle over the Bible*, p. 58, also p. 62.

[150] Noll, *A History of Christianity*, p. 374.

[151] Baconian Common Sense Realism.

[152] Alister McGrath, *Evangelicalism and the Future of Christianity*, p. 29.

[153] Timothy Cargal, 'Beyond Pentecostals and Hermeneutics in a Postmodern
Age', *Pneuma* 15.2 (1993), pp. 167–68. See also Daniel Patte, *What Is Structural
Exegesis?* (Philadelphia: Fortress Press, 1976), pp. 1–20.

modern fundamentalism is more akin to liberalism than either one of them would be willing to admit. Both tacitly assumed that faith was based on objective historical evidence and both were overconfident of their forms of evidence … liberal historicism and fundamentalist historicism remain to this day very much alike.[154]

Even though both groups assumed that historical verification would reveal the truth, they nevertheless were directly opposed to each other due to how each perceived history.

For the liberals, historical process was 'the bed of human perception' and knowledge was 'the product of a fluid social process'.[155] This meant that culture was a product of its own history and wholly conditioned by the historical setting in which it arose and exists. The historical process was driven from inside (immanence) and not a product of outside interference (transcendence). Therefore, the Modernists 'insisted that God's self-revelation is [was] mediated through the flow of history'. Furthermore, divine knowledge like ordinary knowledge 'must be found squarely within the historical process'.[156]

This new scientific paradigm altered the traditional understanding of the Bible. No longer was the Bible seen as a book of special revelation. Now it was seen as religious literature that contained a sprinkling of the Word of God. The authors of this religious literature were not infallible, because like all humans, they would have been fallible creatures. Consequently, the Bible was seen to have errors. Hence, the liberals would 'work and rework' the traditional

---

[154] Thomas C. Oden, *After Modernity … What? Agenda for Theology* (Grand Rapids, MI: Zondervan, 1990, forward by J.I. Packer), pp. 67–68. Oden wants to disassociate contemporary Evangelicalism from its early fundamentalist roots in order to challenge contemporary liberalism, and recapture an authentic orthodoxy. Oden is very disillusioned with modernity and does not believe that Fundamentalism is an adequate response to modernity because it 'conclusively belongs to the modern historicism' and has not become disillusioned with modernity, (pp. 66–69).

[155] See Wacker, 'The Demise of the Biblical Civilization', for an important contribution to the understanding of modernity's impact upon the understanding of historical process and how the conservatives dealt with this new idea (pp. 121–38, cited p. 125).

[156] Wacker, 'The Demise of the Biblical Civilization', pp. 125, 127.

doctrines of inspiration and authority of the Bible[157] in order to make it compatible with their new understanding of transcendence. Transcendence was now understood to be the inner causality of immanence. By reworking the traditional concept of transcendence, the liberals sought to salvage some semblance of Christianity.

Whereas the liberals' interpreted the Bible through the optic of human naturalistic historical process, the Fundamentalists would interpret the historical process through the optic of Scripture.[158] Traditional Protestantism understood Scripture to have originated through divine inspiration, an external supernatural event. Scripture was the result of God imposing himself upon the historical process through the mediation of human authors. This meant that Scripture was 'uncontaminated by the context in which it was received'.[159] From the Fundamentalists' perspective, the Modernists transformed Scripture into 'a promiscuous collection of disjointed documents, with … no significance beyond that of the time in which they were written'.[160]

One's concept of the historical process and of God's involvement with history became the seething issue beneath the raging storm surrounding the Bible. The Fundamentalists tried to overcome this storm by appealing to verbal or plenary inspiration. This was an attempt to appeal to an ahistorical supernatural phenomenon that escapes the modern notion of the historical process. However, historical verification from a Fundamentalists' perspective serves to validate the inerrancy of the Bible. Yet, as Oden correctly recognizes, Modernists also had ahistorical and antihistorical tendencies:

> There is a curious antihistorical quality about modernity. Since modernity has transcended the past, it thinks it can dismiss it, or control it with repressive hermeneutics. Biblical historical criticism, when accommodative to the assumptions of modernity, is repressive hermeneutics, unwilling to allow the text to speak through the modern sieve … It would be better if in social science, the values of modernity would be treated in the same way

---

[157] Wacker, 'The Demise of the Biblical Civilization', p. 124.
[158] Marsden, *Understanding Fundamentalism*, p. 41.
[159] Wacker, 'The Demise Of Biblical Civilization', p. 127.
[160] Wacker, 'The Demise of the Biblical Civilization', p. 132.

as any other social phenomenon, as if modernity had 'no privileged status as against its traditional or neo-traditional alternatives'.[161]

Summary

The Modernist/Fundamentalist controversy was a result of accepting similar philosophical views from the Enlightenment. The Fundamentalists built their argument with the aid of Common Sense Realism, and the Modernists built their arguments on naturalistic views and higher criticism. Fundamentalism drew its theological understanding from the Princeton theologians (Hodge and Warfield) who had relied upon Reid. The liberals, conversely, drew upon Schleiermacher and Kant. Hume is the pivotal skeptical philosopher who had 'called into question Locke's positive theories of both science and religious knowledge'. According to Murphy, 'Reid and Kant each responded to Hume's skepticism in their own way and in doing so each provided philosophical resources for the development of a theological tradition'[162]—Fundamentalism via Reid and liberalism via Kant. Both theological communities were 'modernistic', yet they came to antithetical conclusions about the authority and inspiration of Scripture. The impasse created by these modern and antimodern controversies could not be resolved. However, as Marsden suggests, there was another route being forged prior to and during the Fundamentalist/Modernist controversy. This route was a course that began being forged by the less 'intellectual' Methodist and Wesleyan Holiness groups. The path was continued then by the more 'popularistic' Pentecostals.[163] The Wesleyan Holiness and Pentecostals emphasized the practical and ethical understanding of Scripture. The Wesleyan Holiness and Pentecostals were more concerned with living faithfully and responsibly with God and less concerned about articulating a cognitive intellectual understanding of God. For historians like Marsden, the Wesleyan Holiness and Pentecostals are seen as less intellectual communities of faith. Yet, this may be to the Pentecostals' advantage. Since the Pentecostals

---

161 Oden, *After Modernity ... What?*, pp. 80–81.
162 Murphy, *Beyond Fundamentalism and Liberalism*, p. 5 and see pp. 11–85.
163 Marsden, *Fundamentalism*, p. 61.

were a paramodern movement, they had not immersed themselves in modernistic academic language and thought. Yes, they relied on Common Sense reasoning and argued for the supernatural inspiration of Scripture similar to the Fundamentalists. However, their concern was to live the Gospel faithfully before God, not to prove God's existence based upon philosophical argument. The Pentecostals, like the liberals, were very concerned about religious experience as authenticating Christianity. But unlike the liberals, who talked about 'religion of the heart' and experiencing God through the divine elements in the natural, Pentecostals would point to the supernatural signs of divine intervention taking place in their worship services (tongues and healing).[164] Hence, early Pentecostals were generating religious experience, whereas the liberals were simply talking about it.

The Pentecostals said yes to both the authority of Scripture and the authority of experience. This put Scripture and lived experience into a creative dialectical tension. Pentecostalism's lived experience was coloring their understanding of Scripture and Scripture was shaping their lived experiences.

Unfortunately, after the 1920's the Pentecostals would leave this more paramodern route and attempt to follow the modern path laid down by the Fundamentalists.[165] The Fundamentalists never accepted the Pentecostals. When Fundamentalism was reworked into Evangelicalism in the 1940's (National Association of Evangelicals) the Pentecostal communities were invited to join them as long as the Pentecostals were willing to change their doctrinal statements concerning inspiration. Inspiration had to be worded in the language of 'verbal inspiration' and embrace inerrancy. Hence the Pentecostals attempted to move away from the paramodern and embrace the modern. Pentecostals accepted the foundations of modernity and began immersing themselves in the language and concerns of modernistic thought. This modernistic foundation that they embraced had already been poured by the academic Fundamentalists at the turn of the twentieth century. The Pentecostals simply had to be educated into the modernistic thought and argument of the more 'intellectual' tradition.

---

[164] Marsden, *Understanding Fundamentalism and Evangelicalism*, p. 43.
[165] Marsden, *Fundamentalism*, p. 225.

The Pentecostals' continuation of Wesleyan Holiness praxis in confrontation with Fundamentalism and liberalism's beliefs created a fertile context in which an authentic Pentecostal hermeneutic emerged. In the next chapter, I will examine the exegetical method of the first generation of Pentecostals.

3

EARLY PENTECOSTAL BIBLICAL INTERPRETATION

Interpretation itself needs no defense; it is with us always, but like most intellectual activities, interpretation is interesting only when it is extreme.[1]

Jonathan Culler

The purpose of this chapter is to analyze the interpretive methods used by the first generation of Pentecostals. This analysis will demonstrate that the interpretive methods used by the first generation of Pentecostals were similar to those of the Holiness movements (Wesleyan and Keswickian) and like them, the Pentecostals used a premodern 'Bible Reading Method'. The analysis of the Pentecostal interpretive methods will begin by reviewing and challenging what some contemporary scholars have said about the interpretative strategy of the early Pentecostals. Then I will present a thorough examination of the interpretive methods of the first generation of Pentecostals.

Contemporary Explanations of the Interpretation of Scripture by Early Pentecostals

Contemporary scholars of Pentecostalism have explained the interpretative method of early Pentecostals as being 'literal', 'ahistorical' or 'pietistic' and generally involving some combination of these three. However, a 'literalistic hermeneutic' is the favored means of explaining the early Pentecostal interpretive method. These explanations will

---

[1] Umberto Eco *et al.*, *Interpretation and Overinterpretation* (ed., Stefan Collini; Cambridge University Press, 1992), p. 110.

be briefly examined in order to demonstrate that there exists some merit for these descriptive tautologies, yet they fail to explain the structure and significance of the Pentecostal hermeneutical strategy. They serve more as sweeping pejorative generalizations than accurate explanations of Pentecostal interpretation.

Russell Spittler

Russell P. Spittler, in his insightful essay entitled 'Are Pentecostals and Charismatics Fundamentalists?',[2] argues that these three communities of faith (Pentecostals, Charismatics and Fundamentalists) should be kept distinct even though they adhere to similar beliefs and practices. Concerning the Pentecostals and Fundamentalists, one of the interesting things that Spittler says they have in common is their approach to biblical interpretation. He writes,

> Pentecostals and Fundamentalists…are arch enemies when it comes to such matters as speaking in tongues and the legitimacy of expecting physical healing in today's world. But their approaches to the Bible, precritical and uncomplicated, are virtually identical. If the word *fundamentalism* gets defined only by biblical style, Pentecostals can be labeled fundamentalists without question.[3]

Spittler defines Fundamentalism's biblical style as '*an unbending literalism in biblical interpretation coupled with a theory of inspiration close to dictation*' (his emphasis).[4] Spittler suggests that '*an excessive use of Biblical literalism*' which came as a result of the Fundamentalists' influence upon early Pentecostalism 'has yielded some curious theological deviations' spe-

[2] Russell P. Spittler, 'Are Pentecostals and Charismatics Fundamentalists? A Review of American Uses of These Categories' in Karla Poewe (ed.) *Charismatic Christianity As A Global Culture* (Columbia, SC: The University of South Carolina, 1994), pp. 103–16.

[3] Spittler, 'Are Pentecostals and Charismatics Fundamentalists?', p. 106. He argues that we need to understand that what divides the two (Pentecostals and Fundamentalists) outweighs this similarity. He correctly points out some major differences between them. An important difference is that Fundamentalism 'mounts its arguments … in the form of creeds' whereas 'Pentecostals give testimonies'. Spittler states that 'there is a profound difference between the cognitive Fundamentalist and the experiential Pentecostal'. Spittler is correct, and this distinguishable feature impacts their interpretation of Scripture.

[4] Spittler, 'Are Pentecostals and Charismatics Fundamentalists?', p. 111.

cifically the theological position known as "Oneness Pentecostalism".[5]

This writer agrees with Spittler that Fundamentalism and Pentecostalism share a similar understanding of Scripture as the authoritative 'Word of God'. But to say that the method is an 'unbending literalism' is too simplistic a descriptive statement concerning the interpretive method.[6] Furthermore, Spittler's suggestion that this 'unbending literalism' was the reason for the emergence of Oneness Pentecostalism is incorrect. Fundamentalists vehemently rejected Oneness Pentecostals and Pentecostalism in general as heretical but not on the basis of their shared interpretive method. Their method was the pre-critical (which I would suggest is a better descriptive concept for the method than pietistic),[7] inductive and deductive Bible Reading Method.

---

[5] Spittler, 'Are Pentecostals and Charismatics Fundamentalists?', p. 111. Spittler believes that what led to Oneness Pentecostalism was 'the exegetical fact that at every place in the book of Acts where persons are baptized it is said they were baptized "in the name of Jesus." That was taken literally …' This writer agrees with Spittler on this point, but it must be remembered that it was the Book of Acts' baptismal formula over against the Book of Matthew's baptismal formula that was taken literally. In an earlier essay entitled 'Scripture and the Theological Enterprise: View from a Big Canoe' in Robert K. Johnston (ed.), *The Use of the Bible in Theology: Evangelical Options* (Atlanta, GA: John Knox Press, 1985) he declares that 'the use of Scripture in the Pentecostal heritage is a simple, natural, and revered, though often ahistorical, use of the words of Scripture both in the nourishment of personal piety and in setting a mandate for evangelicalism as chief agenda for the church' (p. 75). Spittler states that this pietistic approach needs to be used in conjunction with the historical exegetical method. Both are required for an accurate understanding of Scripture (see pp. 74–77).

[6] Spittler does not define 'literalism' in his essay. This also complicates an adequate understanding of their approach. See also Peter Williams, *America's Religions: Traditions and Cultures* (New York: Macmillan, 1990), who writes that Pentecostals 'read [scripture] with the same literalism that characterized the emerging Fundamentalist hermeneutic' (p. 261).

[7] I suggest that Spittler's usage of the word 'pietistic' is similar to Joel Green's definition of 'pre-critical'. Joel Green's description of a pre-critical mode of reading Scripture more accurately explains the hermeneutical posture of the first generation of Pentecostals. This writer is using pre-critical according to Green's definition found in his essay 'Hermeneutical Approaches to the New Testament Tradition' in J.D.G. Dunn and J.W. Rogerson (eds.), *Eerdmans Commentary on the Bible* (Grand Rapids, MI:. Eerdmans, 2003), p. 973. Green writes,

the Bible reading conducted by many people today can be characterized as 'precritical' insofar as it advances on the basis of the examined presumption that a NT text written, say, in the late first-century CE continues to possess an immediate and straightforward relevance in new times and situations. The text,

The Holiness and Pentecostal communities used this fluid method to come to an understanding of the 'literal' meaning of Scripture. This fluid method, however, was interwoven into their distinct Christian cultural worldviews, shaped by their central doctrinal convictions, and driven by distinguishable community concerns. Oneness Pentecostalism was a result of some Pentecostals' harmonizing the New Testament baptismal formulas in a new way.[8] Oneness Pentecostalism was not the result of an 'unbending literalism' but was the result of an unwillingness to embrace doctrinal statements like Trinity that were not directly supported by exact words or phrases in the New Testament, especially from the book of Acts. Hence, Oneness Pentecostals were unbending in their consistent rejection of the philosophical language of 'man-made creeds' which did not express a biblical understanding and/or language.[9] Of course the restorationist concern of what was and was not biblical was a community decision. The majority of Pentecostals remained Trinitarian because they did not view the Trinity as an unbiblical doctrine.

Spittler has implicitly made an insightful contribution to the understanding of the purpose of biblical interpretation for Pentecostals. He demonstrates that Pentecostal interpretation and theology always has 'an instrumental, missionary function', thus 'biblical understanding is held to be subordinate to and necessary for the preaching of

---

it is assumed, is transhistorical and transcultural. For persons operating in a pre-critical mode, the idea of 'interpretation' is itself problematic since, as it is often repeated, one needs only to read the NT in order to apprehend its message.

Green points out that a pre-critical approach ignores 'the sociolinguistic reality that all language is embedded in culture' and how or who 'decides when a text is to be taken in such a straightforwardly relevant way?' On the positive side, he states that a pre-critical reading 'underscores the importance of the faithful appropriation of scripture' and implies that Scripture is understandable, thus accessible to all persons, 'rather than those who possess accredited skills only'. Green is not defining pre-critical from a temporal chronological perspective (such as the pre-critical period followed by the critical and then post-critical), but instead he is using pre-critical to refer to one of four contemporary reading approaches. The other three are as follows: the scientific (historical-critical approaches), the contextual (what it meant in its cultural setting and then determine what it means today) and, the reactive (the readers influence and determine the meaning of the text). His concept of a Pre-critical reading would also apply to the various popularistic holiness groups' engagement with Scripture.

[8] Reed, *In Jesus' Name*, p. 174.

[9] See David Reed, 'Oneness Pentecostalism: Problems and Possibilities For Pentecostalism', *JPT* 11 (1997), pp. 81–83.

the Gospel'.[10] Spittler, as a Pentecostal, suggests that the primary purpose for biblical study is to produce 'an enhanced faith, hope, and love for both the individual and the community'.[11] Therefore, Pentecostal readings and theology primarily serve specific ecclesiastical functions, missionary outreach and community renewal, all of which are pietistic and more importantly Pentecostal concerns.

Grant Wacker

Grant Wacker explains early Pentecostal interpretation as a logical extension of their 'ahistorical outlook'.[12] This ahistorical outlook produced and reinforced the notion that the Bible had 'somehow escaped the vicissitudes of historical construction', thus the 'writers of the Bible had not been influenced in any truly significant way by the setting in which they lived'. This 'ahistorical outlook' encouraged Pentecostals to 'resist the relativistic assumptions of modern culture in general and of Biblical scholarship in particular'.[13]

Wacker exemplifies this ahistorical understanding of Scripture by citing Spittler. 'In the mind of the typical convert,…Scripture "dropped from heaven as a sacred meteor"'.[14] This 'conceptual ahistoricism led, then, to wooden principles of biblical interpretation'.[15] Wacker explains the wooden approach as 'the conviction that exege-

---

[10] Spittler, 'Scripture and the Theological Enterprise', p. 57.

[11] Spittler, 'Scripture and the Theological Enterprise', p. 77. He does not believe that 'exegesis', which he defines as 'merely the historical treatment of texts' (p. 75) is detrimental to Pentecostalism or for that matter Christianity. He is still a Pentecostal, ordained with the Assemblies of God. Spittler, who received a PhD from Harvard in 1973 in New Testament, gives an autobiographic testimony of his own encounter with the 'historical' texture of Scripture as a very beneficial experience for his Christian faith. Thus, Spittler acknowledges that 'the historical-critical method … is both legitimate and necessary but inadequate' (p. 76). It does not address piety (p. 77). The problem is that Spittler would use an exegetical approach that would be similar to Evangelicalism in general, the historical-grammatical approach, which is an attempt to explain the past meaning of the passage within and from its historical context and literary context. This is not the traditional historical-critical approach that he acknowledges (see p. 236, endnote 24).

[12] Grant Wacker, 'Functions of Faith in Primitive Pentecostalism', *Harvard Theological Review* 77 (1984), p. 365; see also footnote 11.

[13] Wacker, 'Playing for Keeps: The Primitivist Impulse in Early Pentecostalism' in *The American Quest for the Primitive Church*, p. 198.

[14] Wacker, 'Functions of Faith in Primitive Pentecostalism', p. 365. Spittler uses this analogy in his personal testimony of his understanding of Scripture before he encountered the historical nature of Scripture in graduate school, see his 'Scripture and the Theological Enterprise', p. 63.

[15] Wacker, 'Functions of Faith in Primitive Pentecostalism', p. 366.

sis is best when it is as rigidly literal as credibility can stand'.[16] He does not offer a descriptive explanation of this 'literalistic' approach, but he does list typical examples of Pentecostal practices in order to exemplify what this rigid literalism produced. He believes, for example, that an 'unflinching literal reading of Mark 16' became the basis for handling deadly snakes, drinking deadly poisons, and rejecting prescribed medication even if it meant the certain death of oneself or one's family member.[17] However, this writer believes this better illustrates that when Pentecostals interpreted the Bible, they did so in order to apply it directly to their immediate context.[18] Mark 16, 1 Corinthians 12 and 14, then, were understood as indicating what 'signs' should be evident among the Pentecostal community presently, not as past signs or gifts which happened within the New Testament church era. In other words, Pentecostals were not like classical Protestants or Fundamentalists when it came to interpreting the Bible. Classical Protestants and Fundamentalists read the Bible as a past inspired revelatory document, but the Pentecostals read the Bible as a presently inspired story.

Wacker further illustrates the early Pentecostal 'ahistorical literalistic' approach by citing an 'esteemed Pentecostal theologian'. The 'theologian' believed that angels (sons of God) engaged in sexual activity with women (the daughters of men), thus producing the giants as recorded in Genesis 6. This Pentecostal went on to say that this kind of activity 'still happens today'.[19] No doubt the implications of angels still cohabiting with women may alarm the contemporary Christian reader. But all of these cited interpretations from snake handling to divine healing by faith underscore that Pentecostals are noncessationists in their worldview. Pentecostals read Mark 16, picked up on the word 'signs' and argued that these signs should be a part of the 'Latter Rain' (Pentecostal) Christian community. Further, they argued that the presence of these 'signs' served as empirical evidence that God was present in their worship services. This reinforced

---

[16] Wacker, 'Functions of Faith in Primitive Pentecostalism', p. 365.

[17] Wacker, 'Functions of Faith in Primitive Pentecostalism', p. 366.

[18] G. Sheppard, 'Pentecostals and the Hermeneutics of Dispensationalism', *PNUEMA* 16.2 (1984), p. 22.

[19] Wacker, 'Functions of Faith in Primitive Pentecostalism', p. 366. Wacker is citing Hollenweger, *The Pentecostals*, p. 295.

their notion that they were not a new Christian sect but authentic Apostolic Christianity restored.

As for the angels cohabiting with women, this too serves to demonstrate that the Pentecostal worldview is more holistic and inclusive in its attempt to overcome the modernistic division of existence into separate 'spiritual and materialistic' realms. Furthermore, it challenges the traditional Protestant/Fundamentalist view that God does not presently perform miraculous signs. Pentecostalism recognizes the interaction between the spiritual realm (whether that is God and good angels or the Devil and evil angels) and the physical materialistic realm. For those who were cessationists, the Pentecostal scheme of reading was ridiculously abnormal. Yet, one must remember that Pentecostal snake handlers would not have come into existence without the Markan Jesus' testimony about signs following believers (Mk 16.14–20).[20] Nor would the incredible affirmation that (evil?) angels are still producing offspring if there was not a biblical story alluding to the possibility that they had once done so (the Genesis 6 story does not specifically say that this could not happen again).[21]

The Pentecostal reading of Scripture emanated from a popularistic paramodern understanding of Scripture and a paramodern understanding of God and the Devil's participatory interaction and felt influence upon the created world. Unlike Modernists and Fundamentalists, Pentecostals held that God and the 'supernatural realm' are very active within the physical realm.[22] Like Fundamentalists and Holiness folk, they read the passages in their Bibles as sacred Scripture. The various biblical genres were absorbed and dissolved into one category—'Holy Scripture'. The Bible was a gold mine. All that was needed to unearth the precious gold was the popularistic Bible Read-

---

[20] Mark 16.17-18, in the KJV reads, 'And these signs shall follow them that believe; In my name shall they cast out devils; they shall speak with new tongues; they shall take up serpents; and if they drink any deadly thing, it shall not hurt them; they shall lay hands on the sick and they shall recover'.

[21] Gordon J. Wenham, *Genesis 1–15* (WBC, 1; Waco, Texas: Word Books, 1987), offers three exegetical options for understanding this passage. He states that the oldest view and that of most modern commentators is that the 'sons of God' were nonhuman angelic beings of some kind (good or evil), pp. 139–43.

[22] The Modernists were not cessationists but held that only natural experiences that still happened today could account for the actual explanations of ancient religious experiential accounts. Stories like Genesis 6 were biblical myths, which never happened at all.

ing Method and sensitivity to the Holy Spirit's present revelatory guidance.

Wacker's characterization of the Pentecostal approach as ahistorical literalism does not adequately express the Pentecostal interpretive stance. They interpreted Scripture from a 'transhistorical and transcultural' perspective because they believed Scripture inherently possessed the ability to speak meaningfully in social settings different from the one in which it originated.[23]

The Pentecostal reading did confuse biblical narrative with modernistic historiography.[24] Like the Modernists, they were convinced that the biblical stories had to have actually happened in order to be 'true'. Unlike the liberals who argued that the stories were full of errors or were myths, they were convinced that the biblical stories happened just the way that they were told and could happen again. If the 'Sons of God' (fallen angels?) slept with women, then that is what actually happened. Thus they fused the ancient genre of biblical story with the modern assumptions of historiography.[25]

Wacker's penetrating essays contribute to contemporary hermeneutical concerns. They clearly demonstrate that the early Pentecostal worldview was thoroughly supernaturalistic and 'embodied a primordial urge toward disorder' which 'was out of step with the times'.[26]

---

[23] See n. 3 above.

[24] Modern historiography has to be written from a chronological, denotative manner that could be scientifically verifiable. It does not use the strategy of story in explaining past history.

[25] See W. Hollenweger, *The Pentecostals* (London: SCM Press, 1972), chapter 21, 'Back to the Bible!', especially pages 291–97 which exemplify this concern.

[26] Wacker, 'Functions of Faith in Primitive Pentecostalism', pp. 374–75. Also see his 'Playing for Keeps: The Primitivist Impulse in Early Pentecostalism'. In this essay he defines primitivism as 'any effort to deny history, or to deny the contingencies of historical existence, by returning to the time before time, to the golden age that preceded the corruptions of life in history' (p. 197). Then he goes on to argue how early Pentecostalism manifested three 'patterns of primitivism'. These three forms were what he calls philosophical primitivism, historical primitivism and ethical primitivism. Philosophical primitivism does not imply that Pentecostals were philosophical but that this belief 'existed at a preconceptual level' of their worldview (p. 198). Philosophical primitivism refers to the Pentecostal notion that they could know 'absolute truth' in a very personal manner which was 'unencumbered by the limitations of finite existence' (pp. 198–99). Historical primitivism was the Pentecostal notion that they replicated New Testament Christianity, which helps to explain why they found church history irrelevant, as exemplified in the 'Latter Rain' narrative (pp. 199–207). Ethical primitivism 'was a cluster of antimodern behavior patterns' which were patterned after the New Testament in order to

Their interpretations were to be both believable and livable yet they challenged the very foundations of modernity. Deconstructionism and Pentecostalism

> are consummatory, apocalyptic movements which dismantle the 'cathedral of modern intellect' and mock all forms of anthropological reductionism. Both mock the modernist conceit that humanity can construct a livable habitation utilizing the skill of rational analysis and problem solving.[27]

The Pentecostals were not full-fledged citizens of modernity. They were like the traveling circus sideshows, living on the margins of society and presenting to those who ventured into their tents an electrifying vision of Pentecost revisited.[28] The truthfulness of Scripture was discovered relationally, personally and experientially more so than 'scientifically'. They attempted to use the language and arguments of modernity, yet they always had a distinguishable accent that was neither premodern nor postmodern. They were a paramodern Christian community that attempted to deconstruct those elements of modernity and non-Pentecostal Christianity that they viewed as hostile. Pentecostal faith and interpretive practices cannot embrace the enlightened mind; 'like oil and water, they don't mix'.[29] A contemporary and critical Pentecostal reading that desires to embody the interpretation as well as explain it meaningfully should find a postmodern or post-critical approach more conducive to Pentecostal identity than the historical critical methods of enlightened modernity.[30]

---

bring about the power of New Testament Christianity. In short, 'the key to apostolic power was apostolic purity' (pp. 207–15, cited page 208).

[27] Cheryl Bridges Johns, 'Partners In Scandal: Wesleyan And Pentecostal Scholarship', *Wesleyan Theological Journal* 34.1 (1999), p. 17.

[28] I have in mind the movie entitled 'Leap of Faith', starring Steve Martin.

[29] Johns, 'Partners In Scandal: Wesleyan And Pentecostal Scholarship', p. 10.

[30] This writer would suggest that Pentecostalism, the Charismatic movement, the Neo Pentecostals, and Majority World Christianity all helped to contribute to the undermining of modernity's foundations. I do not have the space to demonstrate this idea. Conversely, one could argue that Pentecostalism, exported from Westernized America, brought about a modernizing influence to tribal peoples who converted to Pentecostalism.

David Reed and Donald Dayton

Finally, Donald Dayton and David Reed have suggested that the early Pentecostal interpretation exhibited a 'subjectivizing hermeneutic'.[31] In other words, it was a 'pietistic hermeneutic' which harmonized biblical interpretation and present religious experience.[32] Internal religious experience was the necessary 'subjective' counterpart to the external 'objective' text.[33] Pentecostalism, like Pietism, valued 'subjective' religious experience, which (even though they do not say this) implies from a modernistic perspective that they were more vulnerable to faulty interpretations. Hence, Pentecostals were more vulnerable to faulty interpretations because they embraced religious experience as a necessary component of their interpretive strategy.

This concern is especially felt when the 'subjectivizing hermeneutic' is compared to the 'objective and scientific' hermeneutic of the Enlightenment. Modernity has always defined objectivity over and against subjectivity and viewed subjectivity as potentially flawed. 'The assumption is that if the biblical text is approached from the stance of human experience, then the interpretation is more subjective; but if approached on the basis of logic and reason, the interpretation is more objective'.[34] The Modernist's desire to pretend to be a neutral interpreter by setting aside one's experience and/or presuppositions is a false illusion.[35] This writer agrees with both Reed and Dayton that there is a pietistic, experiential, heartfelt approach to interpretation among the Pentecostals. However, this writer strongly

---

[31] Dayton, *Theological Roots of Pentecostalism*, p. 23.

[32] Reed, *In Jesus' Name*, p. 32.

[33] Reed in 'Origins and Development of the Theology of Oneness Pentecostalism' (drawing upon Dayton) writes, 'Instead of objectively accepting the baptism of the Holy Spirit by faith, the believer has the experiential confirmation in the sign of speaking with other tongues' (p. 26). Reed believes that 'Pietism as a form of spirituality emphasizing the personal, subjective and experiential in religion, forms the broad base for understanding Oneness Pentecostalism' (p. 25). See also, *In Jesus' Name*, pp. 10, 32.

[34] F.L. Arrington, 'The Use of the Bible by Pentecostals', *Pneuma* 16.1 (1994), pp. 103–104.

[35] Anthony Thiselton, 'The New Hermeneutic' in I. Howard Marshall (ed.), *New Testament Interpretation* (Grand Rapids, MI: Eerdmans, 1977), p. 316. Also see Rudolf Bultmann's famous essay, 'Is Exegesis Without Presuppositions Possible?' in Schubert M. Ogden (ed. and trans.), *New Testament and Mythology and Other Basic Writings* (Philadelphia: Fortress Press, 1984), pp. 145–53.

disagrees that this is a subjective hermeneutic which may contaminate the objective truth.[36]

In sum, Pentecostals affirmed the necessity of religious experience for spiritual formation. As I shall demonstrate, the early Pentecostal reading method (exegesis) was similar to the Holiness communities (both Wesleyan and Keswickian). Pentecostals resisted higher criticism and attempted to eclipse modernity. Yet to say that the interpretative approach was a literalistic subjective hermeneutic serves more to devalue their reading ability than to explain accurately how they interpreted Scripture.

The Bible Reading Method: An Alternative Explanation

In this section, I shall present a descriptive analysis of the interpretive method used by the first generation of Pentecostals. The exegetical method will be inferred from sermons, Bible teachings, testimonials and Pentecostal historiographers.[37] This analysis will also demonstrate that the interpretive method used was similar to the Holiness movements (Wesleyan and Keswickian). The Pentecostals exegetical method was the 'Bible Reading Method'.

Early Pentecostals were not attempting to produce a systematic theology or exegetical commentaries. They were much more concerned with simply 'living the Christian life' and defending their understanding of the 'Apostolic Faith'. Thus, they attempted to retrieve

---

[36] I am not suggesting that Reed and Dayton imply such a notion, but from a Modernist's perspective it would.

[37] This analysis will be limited to a few representative individuals and selected works. The following individual's publications will serve as an influential and representative pool: Charles Fox Parham 1873–1929, William Joseph Seymour 1870–1922, Garfield Thomas Haywood 1880–1931, and Frank J. Ewart 1876–1947. A brief biographic account can be found on each of these individuals in the *DPCM*. I will also draw upon the three earliest Pentecostal historiographies that can be found in 'The Three Early Pentecostal Tracts' in Donald W. Dayton (ed.), *The Higher Christian Life* (New York: Garland Publishing, 1985). This volume contains the facsimiles of three of the earliest apologetic tracts of the Pentecostal movement: *The Latter Rain Covenant and Pentecostal Power* by D. Wesley Myland (1910); *The Spirit and The Bride* by G.F. Taylor (1907?); *The Apostolic Faith Restored* by B.F. Lawrence (1916). This, of course, is not an exhaustive list of all the first generation Pentecostals or publications, nor do all Pentecostals agree on all points of theological issues or interpretations yet they are significant and representative of contributing personalities among the first generation of Pentecostalism.

from the New Testament, a praxis-driven 'Jesus-centerism' Christianity.[38] Their biblical theology was pietistic and practical.[39] Pentecostalism, like 'pietism, has understood Christianity to be a living faith in Christ which is life-changing in nature'.[40]

The prime focus of Pentecostalism was on Jesus as the source of salvation, sanctification, healing and Spirit baptism. Jesus, through the Holy Spirit, enabled one to live a holy and productive Christian life. This Jesus-ology influenced Pentecostalism's interpretation of Scripture. Their pietistic concern is echoed in the words of W.J. Seymour: 'We are not fighting men or churches, but seeking to displace dead forms and creeds and wild fanaticism with living, practical Christianity'.[41] Thus, their battle cry was 'earnestly contend for the faith which was once delivered unto the saints' (Jude 3).[42]

In order to sift through their interpretive strategies, this writer will focus upon two uniquely important early doctrines that became central issues of Pentecostal identity: 1) the baptism in the Holy Spirit with the 'Bible evidence' of speaking in other tongues; and, 2) the Oneness or Jesus Only issue. Oneness Pentecostalism rejected the traditional Trinitarian view and asserted that Jesus is the totality of God in human form. Not all Pentecostals were of the 'Oneness'

[38] A term used by Reed in his 'Origins and Development of The Theology of Oneness Pentecostalism In the United States', pp. 2, 27–45. Jesus-centerism refers 'to that tendency within evangelical Protestantism to truncate, without really denying, the full scope of the theological understanding of God and the world into the person and work of Jesus Christ. Jesus becomes source of salvation and object of devotion and piety' (p. 2). For further development and expansion see, *In Jesus' Name*, pp. 33–36.

[39] Reed, 'Origins and Development of The Theology of Oneness Pentecostalism In the United States', pp. 2, 27–45.

[40] Henry H. Knight, *A Future for Truth: Evangelical Theology in a Postmodern World*, (Nashville: Abingdon Press, 1997), p. 24.

[41] *The Apostolic Faith*, 1.1 (Sept. 1906), p. 2 column 1.

[42] This biblical quotation appears on every first page of Seymour's publication, *The Apostolic Faith* and was a popular phrase among the Pentecostals. See also Sarah Parham's sermon titled 'Earnestly Contend for the Faith Once Delivered to the Saints' in Robert L. Parham (compiler), *Selected Sermons of the Late Charles F. Parham, Sarah E. Parham: Co-Founders of the Original Apostolic Faith Movement* (Baxter Springs, KS: Apostolic Faith Bible College, 1941), pp. 9–22. Sarah identified justification, sanctification, healing, the baptism of the Holy Spirit, the second coming (The Full Gospel), along with tithing, eternal life and unity as all being a part of the 'Faith' or message that was first held by New Testament Christians. She held that this was the doctrinal convictions of their *original* 'Apostolic Faith Movement' which 'was an evangelistic work, undenominational and Inter-denominational' (p. 22).

theological persuasion, but all Pentecostals would affirm the important experience of Spirit baptism and the centrality of Jesus in their personal salvific relationship with God. Hence the following analysis attempts to answer these questions: How are the early Pentecostals interpreting Scripture? And, what methods are they using in order to arrive at these innovative doctrines? By answering these questions this writer will demonstrate, through the analysis of the two doctrines, that the early Pentecostals developed their doctrinal understanding by utilizing the 'Bible Reading Method' from a Pentecostal point of view.

The Bible Reading Method was a commonsensical method that relied upon inductive and deductive interpretative reasoning skills. Once the biblical data was analyzed, it was then synthesized into a biblical doctrine. Harmonization was the acceptable and necessary way to synthesis all the biblical data on a particular subject.

In traditional scholastic Protestant Christianity, one developed a logically biblical doctrine with the preferred interpretive method, which was later dubbed the 'proof-texting system'.[43] The Bible Reading Method was a modified form of the proof-text system.[44] It in-

---

[43] See Jaroslav Pelikan, *From Luther To Kierkegaard* (St. Louis: Concordia, 1950), pp. 49–75, also see chapter two of this monograph.

[44] See B. Ramm's discussion on the proper use of 'proof texts' in his *Protestant Biblical Interpretation: A Textbook of Hermeneutics* (Grand Rapids, MI: Baker Book House, 1970, 3d rev. edn, 1993), pp. 172–78. Ramm argues that the Bible is a storehouse of facts and the 'theologian is a careful collector of the facts' (p. 173). Thus the theologian must collect and 'catalogue' the biblical topic into a 'systematic' and 'coherent' system. Thus proof-texting is necessary, but only acceptable if proper exegetical work has been done on the 'text'. He explains, 'the use of proof texts is perfectly legitimate ... [because] the conservative insists the citation of Scripture is nothing more than a special application of "foot-noting"'. However, it has been abused and so the proof-text must first be examined exegetically to make sure it really deals with the subject. His exegetical method would be a historical-grammatical approach from the Hodge-Warfield perspective, hence a modernistic and Fundamentalist approach. He refers to both Hodge and Calvin as examples of employing sound exegetical method, which enabled them to produce an orthodox biblical theology. Also see Klein, *Introduction to Biblical Interpretation* who states that 'there is nothing wrong with quoting verses to prove a point provided we understand them according to their contextual meaning (under the correct circumstances poof-texting can be valid)' (p. 160). For many contemporary conservative Evangelicals, the correct exegetical approach is to understand the passage from both the literary and historical context. Therefore, most academically trained Fundamentalist (Hodge-Warfield-Machen) and conservative Evangelicals desire to produce an exegetical theology, which then can be systematized. My point is that the early Pente-

volved looking up a specific word in an English Bible concordance, compiling an exhaustive list of its occurrences, and deducing a biblical truth based on the reading of the texts. This study will reveal that the interpretive method employed by Pentecostals was the Bible Reading Method, which they had inherited from their Wesleyan/Keswickian ancestors.

The focal point and primary concern of the Bible Reading Method was to synthesize the data into a doctrinal statement and thereby produce a biblical understanding concerning the topic or theme under investigation. Harmonization was the means to effective doctrinal synthesis and was used by the various Holiness groups. Even today, harmonization at some level is necessary for Christians who desire to have a canonically informed biblical and systematic theology. Harmonization, then, was an already established and accepted practice and was the final stage of the Bible Reading Method. The Bible Reading Method was the acceptable way of 'interpreting Scripture in light of Scripture'. The Pentecostal reading scheme was thoroughly popularistic, thus a 'pre-critical',[45] canonical and text centered synchronic approach from a revivalistic-restorationist biblicist perspective.[46] The early Pentecostals were using the same Bible Reading Method as their Holiness brothers and sisters, yet the method was being used from a Pentecostal perspective. By doing so they developed two unique doctrines: 1) Spirit baptism evidenced by speaking in tongues was the first innovative doctrine; and 2) water baptism in the name of Jesus only became the second innovation.

---

costals were concerned about both the 'historical-cultural' and 'grammatical' contexts of a passage, but they did not use the academically tutored historical-grammatical exegetical method. The Pentecostal proof-texting approach was synchronic—not diachronic—and was used primarily as a means to develop their doctrinal positions (like most other popularistic readings). Thus, they relied upon acceptable commentators like Adam Clarke for exegetical insight.

[45] See footnote 304 above.

[46] See Stephan J. Lennox, 'Biblical Interpretation in The American Holiness Movement, 1875–1920' (PhD dissertation, Drew University, 1992), for a thorough analysis of the Wesleyan Holiness approach to interpretation. Lennox argues that the holiness movement used the long standing 'Populist Hermeneutic' (explained in chapter two) while emphasizing certain Wesleyan ideas. For his explanation of the 'Bible Reading' method see pp. 214–15.

With Regard to Baptism in the Holy Spirit

When Frank Ewart wrote his historiography on Pentecostalism, he explained the hermeneutic of Charles Parham and his Bible students in order to help the reader understand how they arrived at their conclusion concerning the baptism in the Holy Spirit. Ewart wrote, 'Their adopted method was to select a subject, find all the references on it, and present to the class a scriptural summary of what the Bible had to say about the theme'.[47] Why is this statement on interpretive method so significant? First, the earliest Pentecostals did not explain their interpretive methodology in a programmatic manner. Ewart's statement is the closest thing that I have found that attempts to describe the Pentecostals' interpretive method. Second, it would appear that this method was assumed to be the primary way of developing a Bible doctrine. The typical and acceptable method of the Holiness movements was the same method used by Pentecostals. They used the inductive and deductive commonsense Bible Reading Method to develop their understanding of the baptism of the Holy Spirit as physically evidenced with speaking in other tongues. Thus, Ewart's statement serves more as an apologetic defense for the biblical credibility of the doctrine than as a description of their methodological interpretive approach.

Charles Fox Parham

The Bible Reading Method allowed Charles Fox Parham and his students to discover the 'biblical' solution to the heated debate of paramount importance for Wesleyan Holiness and Keswickian Christians. The Bible school students desired to rediscover the 'Bible evidence' which could definitively answer the burning question of the day: how does one know experientially that one has received the 'baptism of the Holy Spirit?'

According to Parham, the purpose of his communal bible school in Topeka, Kansas was to prepare evangelists for the end time harvest. The students were not there to learn things for the sole purpose of gaining theoretical doctrinal knowledge. They were there to gain a

---

[47] Frank Ewart, *The Phenomenon of Pentecost* (Hazelwood, MO: Word Aflame Press, 1947, rev. 1975), p. 60. He seems to be following Thistlethwaite's account of what happened at the Topeka Bible School, but this is uncertain because he does not cite sources. He may be relying on oral testimony (tradition). The theme under investigation was the baptism in the Holy Spirit, as assigned by C. Parham.

pietistic understanding of doctrine. As Sarah Parham, Charles' wife, explained, the purpose of the students' studies was to have 'each thing in the Scriptures wrought out in our hearts. And that every command that Jesus Christ gave be literally obeyed.'[48]

As Parham prepared to leave on a three-day trip, he gave his students this assignment:

> Having heard so many different religious bodies claim different proofs as evidence of their having a Pentecostal baptism, I set the students at work studying out diligently what was the Bible evidence of the baptism of the Holy Ghost, that we might go before the world with something that was indisputable because it tallied absolutely with the Word.[49]

On his return the students reported to him their stammering conclusion. According to the Spirit baptism accounts in Acts, the 'indisputable proof' was speaking in other (unlearned) foreign languages.[50]

---

[48] Mrs. (Sarah) Charles F. Parham, *The Life of Charles F. Parham: Founder of the Apostolic Faith Movement* (Joplin, MO: Hunter Printing Company, 1930), p. 51.

[49] S. Parham, *The Life of Charles F. Parham*, p. 52. See also R. Parham, *Selected Sermons of the Late Charles F. Parham, Sarah E. Parham*, p. 81. Parham was convinced that *HE* was the specifically chosen instrument of God to proclaim the 'restored' Apostolic faith message to the whole world.

[50] S. Parham, *The Life of Charles F. Parham*, p. 52. See also *Selected Sermons of the Late Charles F. Parham, Sarah E. Parham*, p. 83. Parham would always hold to the belief that speaking in an unlearned, yet existing foreign, language was the evidence for the baptism of the Holy Spirit. According to Parham, the purpose of the Pentecostal Spirit baptism was to enable missionaries to preach in a foreign language that they had not learned, thus hastening the second coming of Jesus and the spread of the Gospel. According to Sarah Parham, this was an important reason for Agnes N. Ozman's (LaBerge) (who was the first student and person to speak in tongues) desire to receive the Spirit baptism. 'She hoped to go to foreign fields' (in *The Life of Charles F. Parham*, p. 52). There are two somewhat conflicting accounts (Ozman's and Parham's) of the 'Topeka Revival'. See the 'Topeka Revival' in *DPCM*, pp. 850–52. Concerning Parham's doctrinal understanding of Spirit baptism see his sermon 'The Baptism of The Holy Spirit' in *Selected Sermons of the Late Charles F. Parham, Sarah E. Parham*, pp. 64–74, and especially pp. 71–72. He stated, 'I believe in tongues to be the *practical* means of reaching others that do not understand our language … I am looking for people that will come up with the languages and go to the ends of the earth, speaking the language of the nations' (emphasis added). Also see J.R Goff, Jr., *Fields White unto Harvest*, pp. 72–78. Goff explains their experience of tongues speech as a 'cryptomnesia' experience (p. 77). See also his essay 'Initial Tongues in the Theology of Charles Fox Parham' in Gary B. McGee (ed.), *Initial Evidence: Historical and Biblical Perspectives on the Pentecostal Doctrine of Spirit Baptism* (Peabody, MA: Hendrickson Publishers, 1991), pp. 57–71. For 'historical reports' of 'xenoglossa' (or 'xenolalia') in the Pentecostal movement see R.W. Harris, *Spoken*

How were the students able to discover the indisputable Bible evidence? According to one of Parham's Topeka Bible students, Lillian Thistlethwaite (Parham's sister), the only textbook they used was the Bible, the primary lecturer was Parham and the primary method used to study the Bible was

> to take a subject, learn the references on that subject, also where each quotation was found, and present it to the class in recitation as though they were seekers, praying for the anointing of the Holy Spirit to be upon the message in such a way as to bring conviction.[51]

In other words, they used the popular pietistic Bible Reading Method which incorporated both inductive and deductive reasoning skills in an attempt to arrive at a presently *livable demonstration and commonsensical understanding* of that particular topic.[52]

William Seymour

The Apostolic Faith (1.1, p. 2), which was edited by W.J. Seymour, provides a typical example of how early Pentecostals arrived at their doctrinal understanding of Spirit baptism.[53] The article entitled 'Tongues As A Sign' illustrates the Bible Reading Method:

> In Luke 24:49, Jesus told His disciples to 'Tarry ye in the city of Jerusalem, until ye be endued with power from on high.'

By the Spirit (Springfield, MO: Gospel Publishing House, 1973); W. Warner (ed.), *Touched By The Fire* (Plainfield, NJ: Logos International, 1978). However, other Pentecostal groups will not entirely affirm Parham's view and will modify their understanding of 'tongues' as speaking in heavenly ecstatic language (glossolalia). The reason for the modification was due to their experiential failure to match the tongues speaking with a foreign language. For an example of a direct refutation of Parham's understanding of the purpose of Spirit baptism see Lawrence, *The Apostolic Faith Restored*, p. 26. Lawrence stated, *'The gift of tongues was not given for the purpose of enabling the early ministry to evangelize the world'* (his italics).

[51] R. Parham, *Selected Sermons*, p. 82. For an excellent example, see Sarah Parham's sermon, 'Earnestly Contend for the Faith Once Delivered to the Saints' in *Selected Sermons*.

[52] Common Sense for the holiness folk simply meant that the ordinary Christian, preferably unschooled, with the aid of the Holy Spirit was able to understand the Bible. See Stephen J. Lennox, 'Biblical Interpretation In The American Holiness Movement, 1875–1920', ch. 2 and pp. 163–68.

[53] Both C. Parham and W.J. Seymour were Wesleyan Holiness Pentecostals who held that entire sanctification, subsequent to salvation, was an achievable and necessary prerequisite for the baptism in the Holy Spirit.

'And being assembled together with them, commanded them that they should not depart from Jerusalem, but wait for the Father, which, saith he, ye have heard of me. For John truly baptized with water, but ye shall be baptized with the Holy Ghost not many days hence. When they therefore were come together, they asked of him, saying, Lord, wilt thou at this time restore again the Kingdom to Israel? And he said unto them, It is not for you to know the times or the seasons which the Father hath put in his own power. But ye shall receive power after that the Holy Ghost is come upon you: and ye shall be witnesses unto me both in Jerusalem, and Judea, and in Samaria, and unto the uttermost part of the earth.' - Acts 1:4-8.

They obeyed this command, and Acts 2:4 states, 'And they were all filled with the Holy Ghost, and began to speak with other tongues, as the Spirit gave them utterance.' We see here that they all spoke in other tongues.

If you will now turn to Acts 10 and read the story of Peter and Cornelius, you will see that speaking in tongues was the sign or evidence to Peter that the Gentiles had received the Holy Ghost. Peter preached the Word, and they were cleansed through the Word, as the disciples before the Day of Pentecost. This was a hard dose for Peter to take, he being a Jew and having been taught that Gentiles were dogs and unclean. God had previously given Peter a vision of a great sheet let down from heaven, filled with all manner of animals, with the command, 'Rise Peter, slay and eat.' The preaching of Jesus to the Gentiles was part of the eating, but Peter obeyed, and Pentecostal signs followed (Acts 10:46): 'For they heard them speak with tongues and magnify God.' If you will now turn to Acts 19:1-6, you will find that about twenty-nine years after Pentecost, Paul found some deciples (sic) at Ephesus that had not received their Pentecost. He preached the Word and explained to them their great privileges in the gospel, 'And when Paul laid his hands upon them, the Holy Ghost came on them: they spake with tongues and prophesized.' -Acts 19:6.

How foolish so many of us have been in the clear light of God's Word. We have been running off with blessings and anointings with God's power, instead of tarrying until the Bible evidence of Pentecost came.[54]

Although I found no explanation of Seymour's interpretive method, an analysis of this biblical exposition makes it clear that Seymour was employing the familiar Bible Reading Method. As the reader can see, the author was tracing the theme of 'the baptism of the Holy Spirit' through Acts (chapters 2, 8 by implication, 10, and 19). Then the author synthesized the Biblical accounts into a doctrinal statement. The biblical evidence for the reception of Spirit baptism was speaking in tongues.[55] The result of the harmonization was to view Acts 2 as the normative and necessary experience for all Christians, with speaking in tongues as the specific experiential biblical sign for the reception of Spirit baptism. Another early Pentecostal leader, Joseph H. King explained:

> The Book of Acts is the only one in the Bible that presents to us the Pentecostal baptism from an historic standpoint; and it gives the standard by which to determine the reality and fullness of the Spirit's outpouring, since in every instance where the Spirit was poured out for the first time this miraculous utterance accompanied the same, so we infer that its connection with the baptism is to be regarded as an evidence of its reception.[56]

---

[54] They were tracing 'the baptism of the Holy Spirit' through Acts, and then deduced a general principle from the 'biblical facts'. The sentence, 'Peter preached the Word, and they were cleansed through the Word, as the disciples before the Day of Pentecost' is referring to Jn 15.3 and 13.10, where Jesus declares the disciples were clean by his word. Thus they argued that the disciples were already 'sanctified' Christians before the Pentecostal outpouring recorded in Acts 2. It is important to acknowledge that Seymour, by 1915, will no longer hold that 'tongues' is the only sign for Spirit baptism. He wrote in the preface to his *The Doctrines and Discipline of the Azusa Street Apostolic Faith Mission of Los Angeles, Cal.*, 'Wherever the doctrine of the Baptism in the Holy Spirit will only being known (sic) as the evidence of speaking in tongues, that work will be an open door for witches and spiritualists, and free loveism'. Seymour was responding to the ongoing racial rhetoric coming from some Pentecostal groups, especially Parham's (See Seymour's *The Apostolic Faith* 1.2, first story. Seymour disassociated himself from Parham). See Lawrence, *The Apostolic Faith Restored*, chs. 2 and 3, for a similar yet more sustained argument on the baptism in the Holy Spirit as evidenced with tongues.

[55] See the article 'Baptism in the Holy Spirit' in *DPCM*, pp. 40–48, for a brief overview.

[56] Joseph H. King, *From Passover To Pentecost* (Franklin Springs, GA: Advocate, 1976, 4th edn; originally published 1911), p. 183 as cited in G. McGee (ed.), *Initial*

Having biblical support for one's belief and practice was a very serious matter. 'For if it is not in the Bible Ye need not believe it, but if it is in the Word of God, Ye *must* receive it'.[57] Therefore, Bible doctrines are to be believed, experienced and practiced. Pentecostal interpretation of Scripture was always done with praxis being the goal.

How did one know if they had the right experience? The doctrine, which embraces experience and practice, must correspond to the biblically described account. Thus, Parham argued:

> all we claim is that if you get the baptism in the Holy Ghost it will correspond to the experience in the second chapter of Acts...We believe in having the Bible evidence, and the chief evidence if you get the same experience is, that 'they spake in tongues.'[58]

When someone would challenge the Pentecostal understanding that tongues was *the* evidence for the baptism in the Holy Spirit, they did so by arguing that there were biblical manifestations other than simply tongues which could be of equal experiential proof for Spirit baptism. The Pentecostals would tenaciously respond to the challenge with a similar response like that of George F. Taylor:

> Look up all the accounts given in Scripture of any receiving the Baptism, and you will find not any other manifestation mentioned without the manifestation of tongues...Show us any other Scriptural manifestation and we will accept it. Show us one account of an apostolic service of which the Book says, 'They were filled with the Holy Ghost, but did not speak with tongues.'[59]

Evidence: Historical and Biblical Perspectives on the Pentecostal Doctrine of Spirit Baptism, p. 109.

[57] R. Parham, *Selected Sermons*, p. 93, her emphasis.

[58] R. Parham, *Selected Sermons*, pp. 66, 70. For C. Parham, *The Everlasting Gospel* (Baxter Springs, KS: Apostolic Faith Bible College, nd, reprint of 1911), this Pentecostal baptism did not produce 'the chattering and jabbering, wind sucking, holy-dancing-rollerism going on over the country, which is a result of hypnotic, spiritualistic and fleshly controls, but a real sane reception of the Holy Spirit in baptismal power, filling you with glory unspeakable and causing you, without any effort, to speak freely in foreign languages' (p. 55).

[59] Taylor, *The Spirit and the Bride*, pp. 46–47. Taylor dedicated all of ch. 4, which is the longest segment in this book, to answering objections to the early Pentecostal understanding of Spirit baptism. See p. 41 for his concern 'not to defame his brethren ... but to point out the error of [their] teachings'.

The Pentecostals were arguing that they had 'rediscovered' the 'biblical evidence' for the baptism of the Holy Spirit.[60] For the early Pentecostals, the Bible evidence was speaking in tongues. This was understood not only as the correct understanding of Scripture, but was also thought to be a clear self-evident fact to those who honestly and humbly submitted themselves to the Spirit while reading the Scripture.[61] The Pentecostal plea was to 'accept all that is Scriptural; reject all that is erroneous'.[62] They were convinced of the Scriptural correctness of their doctrine and triumphantly proclaimed it as a *necessary* experience for every Christian. Those Christians who rejected their understanding of Spirit baptism were rejecting the 'Full Gospel' message and were in danger of experiencing the plagues of the great tribulation,[63] or even worse, losing their salvation.[64]

R.A. Torrey: A Holiness View of Spirit Baptism

The Keswickian R.A. Torrey published in 1895 a very popular work called *The Baptism with the Holy Spirit.*[65] Torrey's interpretive approach was the same popularistic Bible Reading Method that would later be used by the Pentecostals, yet he did not arrive at the same conclusion concerning the manifested evidence of Spirit baptism.[66] According to

---

[60] McGee (ed.), *Initial Evidence*. See especially chapters 4, 5, 6 and 7.

[61] The emphasis upon Scripture and its importance in establishing Pentecostal doctrine is constantly appealed to in early and contemporary Pentecostal literature. In the early literature, one will usually come across an invitation to the non-Pentecostal Christian to demonstrate from Scripture the inaccuracy of the Pentecostal interpretation. For an example, see Aimee Semple McPherson's sermon 'Death in the Pot' in *This Is That: Personal Experiences Sermons and Writings,* (Los Angeles, CA: Echo Park Evangelist Association, 1923), pp. 779–94.

[62] Taylor, *The Spirit and The Bride*, p. 6.

[63] Parham in *The Everlasting Gospel* wrote: 'Pentecost is given as a power to witness as well as to seal His people … The sealed ones will escape the plagues and wrath that are coming in the great tribulation. The Pentecostal endowment is the life insurance of the universe' (p. 66).

[64] Taylor's warning in *The Spirit and The Bride* is quite explicit: 'God holds both Calvary and Pentecost sacred … The soul that turns under the light of Divine truth away from Calvary or Pentecost turns from God's final offer of salvation and power, and turns to eternal woe' (p. 111). Taylor like Parham taught that Spirit baptism was the 'seal of the Spirit' and granted one 'entrance into the full enjoyment of being the Bride of Christ' which would assure one a place at 'the marriage supper of the Lamb' (pp. 8–9, 22, 121–2, 127–8).

[65] R.A. Torrey, *The Baptism with the Holy Spirit* (Chicago: The Bible Institute Colportage Association, Copyright 1895, by Fleming H. Revell).

[66] In the introduction of his *The Baptism with the Holy Spirit* Torrey wrote, 'it was a great turning point in my ministry when, after much thought and study and medi-

Torrey, the evidence of the baptism with the Holy Spirit was simply *power* for Christian service.[67]

When discussing the 'evidence' for Spirit baptism, Torrey wrote, 'In my early study of the Baptism with the Holy Spirit I noticed that in many instances those who were baptized "spoke with tongues"'. Yet he rejected tongues as the evidence for two reasons. First, he did not presently see Christians speaking in tongues. It seems that the supernatural gift had ceased with the early church, which of course would have been a notion reinforced by his more Reformed background. Second, and most importantly for Torrey's argument, was his understanding of the Apostle Paul's teaching on the gift of tongues, specifically, 1 Cor. 12.30. This verse posed the rhetorical question: Do all speak with tongues? The answer for Torrey was obviously no.[68]

Torrey rejected tongues-speech incidents in Acts as the definitive evidence for Spirit baptism by connecting it to the gift of tongues mentioned in 1 Corinthians. Torrey acknowledged that many New Testament Christians who were baptized in the Holy Spirit did speak in tongues, but not all of them spoke in tongues. He did encourage all Christians to seek the baptism in the Holy Spirit. He reminded them that not all would receive the gift of tongues. However, he did believe that one should have an experiential knowledge of Spirit baptism subsequent to one's salvation experience. The evidence of Spirit baptism was *power for service*, which was experientially manifested through the individual as the Holy Spirit desires.

Torrey used the same interpretive strategy as other Holiness groups in order to arrive at his doctrinal conclusion. The strategy was the Bible Reading Method which his book *The Baptism in the Holy Spirit* exemplified. He did not embrace tongues as the normative sign for Spirit baptism because he did not have first-hand knowledge of Holiness Christians presently speaking in tongues and he himself never spoke in tongues. Yet Torrey claimed to be Spirit baptized. He

---

tation, I became satisfied that the Baptism with the Holy Spirit was an experience for to-day and for me'.

[67] Torrey, *The Baptism with the Holy Spirit*, see pp. 10–16, 19. Torrey wrote, 'The Baptism of the Holy Spirit is not for the purpose of cleansing from sin, but for the purpose for service'. He maintained that one should know whether or not one had this second subsequent experience (p. 14).

[68] Torrey, *The Baptism with the Holy Spirit*, p. 16.

was able to claim a subsequent experience, without the evidence being tongues, through harmonizing all the biblical data concerning tongues-speech. For Torrey, Paul's discussion on the gifts of the Holy Spirit in 1 Corinthians 12–14 (which included tongues) was the important link. He used 1 Cor. 12.30 as the foundational verse for proper understanding of the Lukan narrative on Spirit baptism. In other words, the Spirit baptism accounts of Acts were interpreted through his contemporary Christian experience of a lack of tongues-speech among his Holiness communities. He then harmonized this with his understanding that tongues was one of the various gifts of the Holy Spirit, but it was not *the* sign of the baptism in the Holy Spirit. Paul's understanding of the gifts of the Spirit provided the context in which Torrey understood Luke's concept of Spirit baptism.

Torrey's work was clearly a Keswickian perspective on Spirit baptism. He saw Spirit baptism as a second experiential work of empowerment for service. This is different from the Wesleyan Holiness view of Spirit baptism which was understood to be the entire eradication of Adamic sin so that the heart is pure to love God fully.[69] When the Pentecostal movement emerged, Torrey was quick to denounce it. Torrey's works had influenced some Pentecostals. His works were widely read yet he would not embrace the Pentecostal understanding of Spirit baptism. For Frank Ewart (and others), this was troubling. Ewart wrote warmly:

> Dr. R.A. Torrey in his famous work: 'What The Bible Teaches,' said, 'If we had the normal faith and experience on earth, we would baptize repentant believers in the name of Jesus Christ, then lay hands on them and they would receive the Holy Spirit

---

[69] See Torrey's *First Course—Bible Doctrine*, (New York: Garland Publishing, 1988, a facsimile of 1901 publication with same title), pp. 271–80. See also his *The Person and Work of The Holy Spirit* (Grand Rapids, MI: Zondervan, 1974, a rev. edn of the original 1910 edn), pp. 172–76. By February 1978, this 1974 edition was in its eleventh printing, a testimony to the popularity of Torrey's long standing influence among the popularistic Christian communities. For an explanation of an early Wesleyan Holiness understanding see George D. Watson, *A Holiness Manual* (Jamestown, NC: Newby Book Room, 1882) and for a contemporary view see J. Kenneth Grider, *Entire Sanctification: The Distinct Doctrine of Wesleyanism* (Kansa City, MO: Beacon Hill Press of Kansas City, 1980).

baptism.' I told him that he was right, and that we had the normal faith in the Pentecostal Phenomenon.[70]

In sum, the 'Bible Reading Method' encouraged readers to trace out topics in Scripture and then synthesize the biblical data into a doctrine. The Bible Reading Method was the primary way in which Holiness communities developed their doctrines. It was also used by Pentecostals to develop their understanding of Spirit baptism. Even though these communities were using the same interpretive method, they were generating different theological understandings concerning both the purpose and evidence for the baptism in the Holy Spirit.[71]

With regard to Baptism in the Name of Jesus Only

The Bible Reading Method used from a Pentecostal point of view enabled Oneness Pentecostalism to come into existence. Oneness Pentecostalism came out of Trinitarian Pentecostalism; thus, this began as an in-house theological discussion or worse, a major crisis. This crisis could not be resolved by appealing to the correct or incorrect use of an interpretive method. The Bible Reading Method lent itself to create new theological mosaics.

Oneness Pentecostalism came into existence as a result of a 'new way of harmonizing' the Lukan baptismal formula (Acts 2.38) with the Matthean baptismal formula (Mt. 28.19).[72] This had a direct impact upon the traditional Trinitarian view of God and the early Pentecostal understanding of salvation. Oneness Pentecostals emphasized the singularity of God's identity and the singularity of God's name. Jesus was the divine name for God and the final revelation of God's identity. The new way of harmonizing resulted from their view of Acts 2.38, which was for them the 'Gospel in miniature'.

Salvation, from the Oneness understanding, was one progressive experience consisting of three distinct experiential phases as outlined in Acts 2.38. One was not a complete Christian until one successfully passed through the experiential stages. The threefold salvation experience as outlined in Acts 2.38 involved repentance, water baptism in

---

[70] *The Phenomenon of Pentecost* ... (1947), p. 134. Of course Ewart is speaking about Oneness Pentecostalism as the normative Apostolic Faith.

[71] Keswickians emphasized power for witnessing, Wesleyans emphasized holiness for living and the early Pentecostals emphasized the priority of holiness and then Spirit baptism with the biblical evidence of speaking in other tongues.

[72] Reed, *In Jesus' Name*, p. 174.

the name of Jesus, and Holy Spirit baptism with the evidence of tongues.[73] Hence, Oneness Pentecostals were insistent that one be re-baptized out of obedience to Apostolic teaching (Acts) and be baptized by immersion into the singular name of God—Jesus. Salvation was not complete until one successfully passed through these stages. Haywood's concluding remarks to his work called *The Birth of the Spirit in the Days of the Apostles* captures the intense concern of these Pentecostals:

> If you have never been baptized in the name JESUS CHRIST, you have never been immersed properly. This is the only name under heaven given among men whereby they must be saved. If you repent deeply enough in your heart, and be baptized in the name of Jesus Christ, I will guarantee that you shall receive the baptism of the Holy Ghost as you 'come up out of the water.'[74]

Oneness Pentecostalism came into existence by harmonizing the Lukan and Matthean baptismal formulas into a new coherent whole. This harmonization was done within the already acceptable common-sensical inductive and deductive methodological interpretive stance—the 'Bible Reading Method'. I shall now explain how Oneness Pentecostals justified their interpretation by drawing upon selected works of Oneness Pentecostals, namely Ewart and Haywood.[75]

Frank Ewart

Frank Ewart, on April 15, 1914, set up a tent just outside of Los Angeles and preached his first public sermon on Acts 2.38. He then, along with another evangelist, was rebaptized using the Acts formula. Reed states, 'this action credits Ewart as the first to chart a new direction within the early Pentecostal movement. It was he who formulated a theology of the name of Jesus to validate the new baptismal practice.'[76] Ewart's 'Theology of the Name' was rooted in the Jesus-centric Pietism of the late nineteenth century and was 'particularly

---

[73] Reed, 'Origins and Development of the Theology of Oneness', pp. 146, 167. See also, *In Jesus' Name*, pp. 313–23.

[74] Republished in *The Life and Writings of Elder G.T. Haywood* (Oregon: Apostolic Book Publishers, 4th printing, 1984), p. 40.

[75] Reed identifies these two men (Ewart and Haywood) as the most significant leaders of early Oneness Pentecostals. See 'Origins and Development of the Theology of Oneness' pp. 105–107, and *In Jesus' Name*, 141–46.

[76] Reed, 'Oneness Pentecostalism' in *DPCM*, p. 644.

concerned to defend the full deity of Jesus Christ and re-establish the presence and power of the Apostolic church'.[77]

In his work, *The Revelation of Jesus Christ*, Ewart defended his understanding of the Oneness of God. His argument was organized around two important themes: The essential oneness of God's nature and the singular name of God. Jesus is God and Jesus is 'the revealed name' of God. In this work he upheld both the deity and humanity of Jesus, yet he constantly attacked the orthodox understanding of Trinity. He explained that the Trinity implied the existence of three eternally separate Spirit beings.

Ewart understood Trinity to be a 'flagrant violation' of the essential unity of the Godhead because Trinitarians taught that God in heaven existed from eternity as three individual Spirit beings, not as separate corporal beings but nonetheless three individual beings.[78] He also felt that Mt. 28.19 was *the* proof-text for Trinitarian belief. Matthew 28.19 was used as a formula to baptize a person into three separate names which referred to three separate persons.[79]

He understood the doctrine of Trinity to teach a 'trinity of Gods' or to be Tritheistic.[80] He rejected both the word 'Trinity' and the word 'person' because neither were scriptural terms, and more specifically, the word 'person' meant a totally separate identity or individual Spirit being. This was his major problem with the Trinitarian view.[81] In fact the only place in the Bible that he could find the word 'persons' as having 'any relevancy to the deity' was Job 13.10 which

---

[77] Reed, 'Origins and Development of the Theology of Oneness', p. 84. Oneness Pentecostalism has always affirmed the evangelical doctrines of incarnation and deity of Jesus Christ (p. 46) while articulating a 'simultaneous modalism'. See, Reed, 'Oneness Pentecostalism' in *DPCM*, pp. 648–49. Although similar, oneness understanding of simultaneous modalism should not be confused with the heretical patristic doctrine called Monarchianism. Cf. *In Jesus' Name*, pp. 267–360, 343.

[78] Ewart, *The Revelation of Jesus Christ*, p. 19; see also pp. 4, 6. His definition of Trinity is based on Webster's Dictionary: 'Three persons in individuality; one in essence' (p. 14).

[79] Ewart, *The Revelation of Jesus Christ*, 'Every student of Trinitarianism knows that they base their entire reasoning on Matt. 28:19' (p. 7). He repeated this same comment on pp. 13 and 31. Ewart addressees the Matthean baptismal formula quite often in this work (see pp. 13, 15, 16, 19, 20 and 31) because for him Trinitarianism stands or falls with this verse.

[80] Ewart, *The Revelation of Jesus Christ*, p. 6.

[81] Ewart, *The Revelation of Jesus Christ*, pp. 22–23. Ewart stated 'It is admitted that the word "Person," or indeed "Persons" cannot be found in the Bible for defining either God or what people call the Godhead or Deity'.

reads 'He will surely reprove you, if you do secretly accept persons'.[82]
Ewart suggested that Pentecostals use the word 'Triunity instead of
Trinity' and 'substance' or 'entities' or 'manifestations' in place of
'person'.[83]

The initial problem of the Trinitarian view of God arose out of
the apparent contradiction between Matthew's baptismal formula and
the formula used in Acts. Ewart asked, 'Why is there no mention
made of Father, Son and Holy Ghost, in any formula of baptism
known and used by the Apostles?'[84] This is particularly troubling for
Ewart, who writes:

> if the Apostle Peter did not obey Christ's commandment (Mt
> 28:19) on the day of Pentecost (Acts 2), then it never has been
> obeyed. If the words of the Master were to be taken as a formula
> for Christian baptism, then the Acts of the Apostles present one
> of the most *colossal contradictions* of history. In that case, the church
> was built on a flagrant act of disobedience (emphasis and paren-
> thesis added).[85]

Ewart was convinced that the Apostles and therefore the entire Apostolic Church *never* baptized a person by the Matthean formula.[86]
Nor would he accept that the Apostles were disobedient to Christ's
command (an argument advanced by him to heighten the apparent
contradiction). The Apostles were expounding on the meaning of the
Matthean baptismal formula, which is to say; 'the Apostles knew how
to interpret Matthew 28:19'.[87] The interpretation of Mt. 28.19 was
Acts 2.38, because 'to say that Acts 2:38 is not the complete fulfill-

---

[82] Ewart, *The Revelation of Jesus Christ*, p. 25. He meant this as a warning from
God to those who would not accept his doctrinal position on the Godhead.

[83] Ewart, *The Revelation of Jesus Christ*, pp. 14 and 25. Ewart preferred the word
'substance' because he finds this to be a biblically sound word that reinforces the
solidarity and essential oneness of God. He translated both Heb. 1.3 and Col. 2.9
('Godhead bodily' or 'God's nature') as 'substance'. He believed every Greek
scholar would admit that Heb. 1.3 should be translated as 'the expression of his
substance', p. 25. He used the Weymouth translation for Col. 2.9 and Jas 2.19 to
further strengthen his argument.

[84] Ewart, *The Revelation of Jesus Christ*, p. 20.

[85] Ewart, *The Phenomenon of Pentecost*, p. 111 and also *The Revelation of Jesus Christ*,
p. 32.

[86] Ewart, *The Revelation of Jesus Christ*, p. 7. Ewart cited the work of William Phil-
lips Hall and others to support this claim.

[87] Ewart, *The Revelation of Jesus Christ*, p. 16 and p. 7.

ment of Matthew 28:19 is to assert that the Church of Jesus Christ was built on the most colossal contradiction of history'.[88] The Apostles, including Paul, had always 'baptized in the name of the Lord Jesus' which was the 'Apostolic' interpretation of Mt. 28.19.[89] Ewart read Matthew through Acts, hence, attesting to the priority (if not superiority) of Acts when interpreting other passages.

Ewart was able to resolve this 'colossal contradiction' with an innovative interpretation. He focused upon the *singular* form for the word 'name', which was found in both water baptismal accounts. Then, he reinterpreted the traditional Matthean account (three separate names of the Godhead) through the singular name Jesus used in the Acts accounts.[90] Hence the name for God is Jesus who is also described as the Father, Son and Holy Spirit. The singular form of the Greek word 'name' (ὄνομα) was the exegetical key to resolve the apparent contradiction between the formulas. He was able simultaneously to reinforce the deity of Jesus and the essential oneness of God.[91] However, Ewart's harmonization of these passages resulted in a theological revamping of the traditional Trinitarian view of God.

Ewart had a strong belief in the 'total deity' and 'complete humanity' of Jesus. He rejected the traditional Trinitarian view because it implied that *Jesus* was in a secondary (as the second person of the Trinity) and subordinate relationship with God, thus less than God. Furthermore, Trinitarianism implied that Jesus was not the totality of God which contradicted Ewart's understanding of John 1 and Col. 2.9.[92] He heard Jn 1.1, 14 and Col. 2.9 affirming that Jesus was the totality of God in human form, and he coupled this understanding to the 'Great Shema' (Deut. 6:4) and asserted that there was and is only one God.

Ewart, utilizing the insights of others, traces the word 'name' throughout the Bible. He comes to the conclusion that there is only *one* 'name' for God. In the Hebrew it is Yahweh and in the Greek it is

---

[88] Ewart, *The Revelation of Jesus Christ*, p. 32.

[89] Ewart, *The Revelation of Jesus Christ*, p. 39.

[90] Ewart, *The Revelation of Jesus Christ*, pp. 5, 11, 27–28, 32.

[91] Of course he would have found all the Holiness and non-oneness Pentecostal groups agreeing with him on the deity of Jesus and unity of the Godhead, but they would have understood these theological issues from the traditional Trinitarian view.

[92] Ewart, *The Revelation of Jesus Christ*, pp. 4, 7, 11.

Jesus.[93] He argued that the name Jesus was now the proper 'revealed' name of God (even though he saw Yahweh and Jesus as synonymous). This meant that the trilogy of names from Matthew (Father, Son and Holy Spirit) were not proper names for God, but descriptions or adjectives of the one God. Thus, Jesus is not just the second person of the Trinity; rather, he is the totality of God, and the complete incarnation of God. Jesus, then, was the Father and the Spirit.[94] This had to be so because Jesus said to baptize into the 'name' (Mt. 28.19), which is a singular noun in the Greek text.[95]

According to Ewart, if God had three names corresponding to the three persons of the Trinity, then Mt. 28.19 should have read, 'Baptizing them into the NAMES'.[96] Thus, Ewart was able to resolve the 'colossal contradiction' by appealing to the singular form of the word 'name' which along with the act of water baptism connected the two accounts together.

In sum, Ewart, by using the commonsensical inductive and deductive 'Bible Reading Method',[97] was able to link the many Old and New Testament passages together that reiterated the biblical theme that 'God was One'.[98] By appealing to John's Gospel and assumed Pauline passages, he asserted that Jesus was both the Father and the Spirit. The following song quoted by Ewart summarized his theological view:

If you're looking for the Father,

You will find him in the Son.

Much concern about the Spirit,

Don't you know the Three are One?

---

[93] Ewart, *The Revelation of Jesus Christ*, pp. 30, 40.

[94] Ewart, *The Revelation of Jesus Christ*, p. 18.

[95] Haywood's comment from his *Divine Names and Titles of Jehovah* is helpful, 'the Spirit and of the Father, the Spirit, and the Holy Spirit, and the Spirit of his Son, were different expressions of the one self-same spirit' (p. 12).

[96] Ewart, *The Revelation of Jesus Christ*, p. 15 (his emphasis).

[97] Ewart's repeated argument was that God is one. He understood 'one' as a numerical concept and he used a numerical argument to demonstrate the contradiction of the Trinitarian view—an example of commonsensical reasoning. See pp. 6, 11, 14 and 18.

[98] The OT verses used were Deut. 6.4, Isa. 45.5, 42.8; Exod. 3.15; Zech. 14.9; and the NT verses used were Col. 1.19, 2.9, Jn 1.1, 14.9, 11, 1 Tim. 3.16, Jas 2.19.

He's the resting place for sinners,

He is God in the form of man.

God, our Savior, wrought redemption's wondrous plan.

By appealing to the singular word 'name', Ewart was able to undermine the Trinitarian view (as implied by the English translation that God) existed in three persons, thus having three separate names. For Ewart, this implied that God existed as three separate beings (Tritheism). The one true God had one name and the English translation of that name was Jesus. Ewart believed the whole Trinitarian belief system hung upon one Scripture, Mt. 28.19. Hence, the word 'name' became the exegetical key that enabled Ewart to reaffirm the incarnation and deity of Jesus while undermining the traditional Trinitarian view.[99] However, it was his commitment to the 'only historical' account of Apostolic Christianity (Acts), which caused him to see the 'colossal contradiction' in the first place. His exegetical exercise was simply allowing 'Scripture to interpret Scripture'.[100] *Acts* was *the controlling narrative* through which all Scripture was read. If there were contradictions between Acts and other New Testament passages, then those contradictions would be harmonized with Acts. For all early Pentecostals, Acts was the historically inspired account of Apostolic teaching and practice. Thus, the popularistic commonsensical Bible Reading Method with its primary concern of developing and harmonizing biblical topics with the Book of Acts was the means to bring about this theological synthesis.

G.T. Haywood

Haywood, like all Pentecostals, believed that 'Scripture will interpret Scripture if we seek to rightly divide the word of truth'.[101] He also

---

[99] This writer agrees with Reed's suggestion that Ewart misunderstood the traditional (Latin and Greek) Trinitarian view because Ewart relied solely upon the English translation and focused in on the concept of 'person' which carries a stronger connotation of a separate and distinct identity than the Greek. For a thorough explanation of the Oneness Pentecostal argument see Reed, *In Jesus' Name*, chs. 12–14.

[100] A statement made often in early Pentecostal literature and other popularistic groups which refers to the proper way of interpreting the Bible (the Bible Reading Method).

[101] G.T. Haywood, *The Birth of the Spirit in the Days of the Apostles* (Indianapolis, IN: Christ Temple Book Store, nd), p. 5.

declared that 'if our experiences do not measure up to the word of God it is up to us to lay aside everything and seek God till we find Him'.[102] Many were claiming to have experienced God, but the Scriptures must validate one's experience. Thus, there must be scriptural evidence, even precedence, for the experience.

Haywood told a story about a man in Chicago who claimed to know the difference between the voices of the Father, the Son and the Holy Spirit. The man could tell if it was the Father speaking through him or whether it was the Son or the Holy Spirit. Haywood stated, 'This is very erroneous. Let us look at the Scriptures.'[103] Haywood urged his readers to look to the Scriptures for the proper understanding of the issues he would address so that they could see for themselves that he was presenting the scriptural (true) view. For example, in the forward of his *The Birth of the Spirit in the Days of the Apostles,* he wrote: 'We trust that no one will misunderstand the writings herein and lay the book aside before giving it a thorough examination with your Bible in hand to see whether these things are so'. Haywood, like all Pentecostals, urged opponents to turn to the Scriptures and see for themselves the truth of the message.

Haywood clearly stated his task for this published work:

> It is our purpose to take up the subject from a Bible point of view to see whether there is an experience in the New Testament Scriptures, called the birth of the Spirit, aside from the baptism of the Holy Ghost, according to the second chapter of the Acts of the Apostles. If we cleave to the Word of God we cannot fail.[104]

Haywood's primary goal was to explain the Oneness Pentecostal view of salvation from the perspective of the entire New Testament while affirming the book of Acts as the normative teaching and experience of Apostolic Christianity. He further felt this should be the

---

[102] Haywood, *The Birth of the Spirit in the Days of the Apostles*, forward.

[103] Haywood, *Divine Names and Titles of Jehovah* (Indianapolis, IN: Christ Temple Book Store, nd), p. 12. Haywood used this story to introduce the problem of the Trinitarian view and also as an introduction to the word 'speaking'. He then used verses from the Fourth Gospel (12.49, 50; 14.10, 24) to prove that when Jesus spoke it was the Spirit of the Father who spoke through him. Thus, the voice of God is the one self-same Spirit. Haywood did not give the context in which this event took place, but it most likely took place in a worship service and was seen as the operation of the gift of interpretation or prophecy.

[104] Haywood, *The Birth of the Spirit in the Days of the Apostles*, p. 2.

normative experience and belief of the present Christian communities. He, like Ewart, utilized the commonsensical Bible Reading
Method and then harmonized the passages concerning salvation-
redemption with his understanding of Acts, especially Acts 2.38.[105]

Haywood began his theological argument by first arguing that the
'rest' spoken of by Jesus in Mt. 11.28 ('Come unto me all ye that labor and are heavy laden, and I will give you rest') was a reference to
new birth (or full salvation). He was concerned that there was not a
direct connection (a repetition of the same phraseology) of Mt. 11.28
found in the book of Acts. Yet he was able to make a connection between the word 'rest' (salvation) spoken by Jesus and the baptism of
the Holy Spirit in Acts 2. The solution was the prophetic passage of
Isa. 28.11, 12.[106]
Haywood wrote:

> In turning to Isa. 28:11,12 we find these words 'For with stam-
> mering lips and *other tongues* will he speak to his people. To whom
> he said, this is the *rest* where with ye may cause the weary to *rest*.' It
> was on the day of Pentecost that God spake unto the people 'with
> stammering lips and *other tongues*' [Acts 2:4]. From the scriptures it
> can be plainly seen that '*rest*' and the *baptism of the Holy Ghost* are
> one and the same thing. Those who have really experienced the
> *full* baptism of the Holy Ghost and walked uncompromisingly be-
> fore God can truly testify to these things, that they have in truth
> 'found rest for their souls' (emphasis added).[107]

Haywood was able to make this argument plausible to some of his
targeted Pentecostal readers because he used an acceptable method.
The Bible Reading Method enabled him to link the passages together
by means of a key word or phrase (in this case 'rest') and/or similar
experiential phenomenon described in the passage (stammering lips
being similar to tongues). He also affirmed the accepted understanding of Mt. 11.28 as referring to salvation, and Isa. 28.11-12 as a pro-

---

[105] See Haywood, *The Birth of the Spirit in the Days of the Apostles*, pp. 2, 4. It is
painstakingly clear that Haywood is harmonizing the rest of the Bible with his understanding of Acts. Acts is the controlling narrative in the harmonization process.

[106] Haywood, *The Birth of the Spirit in the Days of the Apostles*, p. 2.

[107] Haywood, *The Birth of the Spirit in the Days of the Apostles*, pp. 2–3. The word
'full' before baptism is a reference to the three-phase salvation experience; thus it
could read 'real' or 'complete'.

phetic promise concerning the pouring out of the Holy Spirit, which finds fulfillment in Acts 2.4.[108] However, the 'new' twist to this common understanding was that salvation now involved three experiential phases, which he explained later in *The Birth of the Spirit in the Days of the Apostles*.

Next, Haywood examined Jesus' statement to Nicodemus that in order to enter the kingdom of God one had to be born again. Haywood argued that for Nicodemus to be born again, he indeed must be 'born of water and Spirit'.[109] Once again, Haywood was troubled because he could not find the exact phrase recorded in Acts. 'Not one place in the book of Acts can we find the words "born of water and the Spirit," or "born again," but we can find the words relating to "baptism" twenty seven times'.

Haywood resolved his concern by arguing that the phrase 'to be born of water and the Spirit' refers to the same event as being baptized with water and with the Holy Spirit in Acts 2.38. The words 'born' and 'baptized' were understood to be synonymous terms referring to the same experience. Haywood stated that if this was not true, then where is there any record in Acts of anyone being born again?[110] Therefore, 'to enter into the Kingdom of God one must be born of water and the Spirit, or, to enter into Christ, the Church, one must be baptized in water and the Holy Spirit', all of which referred to the *full* salvation experience. Hence, these two phrases simply meant the same thing—salvation.[111]

For Oneness Pentecostals there is no difference between being born of the Spirit and the baptism of the Spirit. This was a new challenge to the theological position of both Holiness groups (Wesleyan and Keswickian) and Trinitarian Pentecostals. For Oneness Pentecos-

---

[108] Many Pentecostals would view Isa. 28.11, 12 as a prophetic passage concerning Spirit baptism, which finds its first fulfillment in Acts 2.4. See Lawrence, *The Apostolic Faith Restored*, pp. 25, 29.

[109] Haywood, *The Birth of the Spirit in the Days of the Apostles*, p. 4.

[110] Haywood, *The Birth of the Spirit in the Days of the Apostles*, pp. 4–5. Later in this work, Haywood quoted a lengthy passage form Adam Clarke that supported his understanding of John 3 (p. 15). Under the heading 'What the Bible Teaches' (p. 8), he argued that Mk 16.1, Jn 10.9; Acts 2.38, Gal. 3.27 and Tit. 3.5 were all similar expressions meaning the same thing. For other examples of synonymous terminology, see pp. 5, 7 (the body of Christ and the Kingdom of God), pp. 8, 11 (circumcision of the heart is synonymous to new birth), pp. 28 and 29.

[111] Haywood, *The Birth of the Spirit in the Days of the Apostles*, p. 8.

tals, salvation was only complete when one experientially passed through the three phases. The three phases of the full salvation experience as outlined in Acts 2.38 included repentance, water baptism in the name of Jesus for the cleansing of sin, and Spirit baptism evidenced by speaking in other tongues (not necessarily an existing yet unlearned language: xenoglossa).[112]

Haywood desired more than anything else to continue in the teaching and practices commanded by Jesus. For him and all early Pentecostals, the book of Acts was the definitive record of the early Apostolic church's belief and practice. The book of Acts was always understood to be in harmony with Jesus' commands and practices as found in the Gospels. Thus, like Ewart, Pentecostals brought other biblical accounts into harmony with their understanding of Acts, specifically Acts 2.38.

Haywood demonstrated how Scriptures could use different words and phrases to refer to the same theological concept. Yet, he also took extended effort to demonstrate the converse; that is, just because the Scriptures used the same (or nearly the same) word or phrase did not mean they should be understood as synonymous or references to the same experiences. For example, he argued that there was a difference in meaning implied by the English words 'begotten' and 'born' even though they came from the same Greek word.[113] Haywood wrote, 'The word gennao, literally, means to bear, beget, be born, bring forth, conceive, be delivered of, gender, make, spring. And its translation depends upon what the sentences refers to in which it is used.'[114] Therefore, Haywood recognized the important

---

[112] Haywood, *The Birth of the Spirit in the Days of the Apostles*. Haywood offered Cornelius' household as a test case, p. 6. See also p. 10 where he refuted a Wesleyan understanding and p. 16 where he clearly delineates the three phases of salvation.

[113] Haywood, *The Birth of the Spirit in the Days of the Apostles*, p. 21, 'because the same Greek word, gennao is used in the original for both words, it does not necessarily imply that the words are the same meaning'.

[114] Haywood, *The Birth of the Spirit in the Days of the Apostles*, p. 23. Haywood differentiated between the meanings of 'born' and 'begotten', first by appealing to the English dictionary and then secondly by appealing to the original Greek word's definition which showed a wider range of meaning. (However, he did not cite his source, but I would say he is using an English concordance). He, like most early Pentecostals, relied first on the English translation and definition and then when the 'traditional' understanding was challenged, used the original language to prove his point. Haywood was both apologetic and humble about his use of the Greek. 'We do not do this to make a display of knowledge ... We do not profess to be a

role of the larger grammatical context when attempting to define the meaning of a word and would appeal to the larger grammatical context in order to clarify the meaning of a word, sentence or passage.

An important distinction made by Haywood was between the 'gifts of the Spirit' mentioned in 1 Corinthians 12 and 14 and the phenomenon of 'speaking as the Spirit gave utterance' mentioned in Acts 2.4. Haywood presented the typical Pentecostal position (both first generation and classical contemporary Pentecostals)[115] concerning the baptism of the Holy Spirit with the physical evidence of tongues as indicating a different purpose or experience than the gift of tongues mentioned by the Apostle Paul in Corinthians. The Acts 2.4 account was the sign of Spirit baptism and served as a *personal* prayer language. The gift of tongues mentioned in 1 Corinthians was just one of the gifts (emphasis on the plural) of the Holy Spirit that was to work in conjunction with the gift of interpretation in the *corporate* worship service.[116]

This of course was a reading of the collective 'tongues' passages that was different from the Keswickian and Wesleyan Holiness understanding. Torrey rejected tongues as the evidence for Spirit baptism because of the rhetorical question posed by Paul in 1 Cor. 12.30, 'Do all speak in tongues?' Thus Torrey viewed both Acts 2.4 (and other passages in Acts on Spirit baptism with tongues present) and 1 Corinthians 12 and 14 as the same phenomena. The Pentecostals, however, saw these as separate and different experiences[117] because

---

Greek student, but we desire to use a little Greek at this point, as we believe it will help some. ... We trust none of the children of God will stumble over these Greek words' (pp. 18–19).

[115] Trinitarian Pentecostal Lawrence wrote in his *The Apostolic Faith Restored* that 'The exercise of speaking in other tongues was intended primarily to edify or bless the speaker; in its secondary purpose it was when combined with interpretation, used to edify the church' (p. 26), and that 'There were many among us who do not have the gift of tongues as described in 1Cor. 12 and 14 who did speak in tongues as the people in Acts did' (p. 28). For a contemporary and classical re-presentation see R.H. Gause, *Living in the Spirit: The Way of Salvation* (Cleveland, TN: CPT Press, 2009), p. 164, n. 65.

[116] Haywood, *The Birth of the Spirit in the Days of the Apostles*, pp. 16–21.

[117] For the Oneness Pentecostals, Spirit baptism with tongues was the evidence of one's full salvation and for Trinitarian Pentecostals, it was the evidence of the Holy Spirit baptism. However both saw this as important to being a complete Christian. Yet, Trinitarian Pentecostals would have generally affirmed the salvation of holiness Christians, but these Christians would go through the great tribulation. As for the gifts in 1 Corinthians, these were given for the corporate church and

they served different purposes.[118] For Oneness Pentecostals, Spirit baptism with tongues was the final phase necessary for salvation, whereas for Trinitarian Pentecostals it was a separate and distinct work that came after regeneration thus not to be confused with salvation.

The Trinitarian Pentecostals and Holiness Christians understood salvation to involve the act of repentance and the experience of regeneration, which meant that one was to be born again or regenerated. Salvation was distinct from and prior to Spirit baptism. However, both Oneness and Trinitarian Pentecostal groups saw Acts 2.4 as a 'commanded promise' for all Christians—a special gift from God which was not to be confused with the gifts of the Spirit discussed in 1 Corinthians. The Pentecostal community knew who was Spirit baptized because the individual would speak in unlearned tongues as the Spirit gave utterance. Speaking in unlearned tongues provided empirical external evidence to confirm the presence of the Spirit.

Once again, the book of Acts became the controlling theological document through which the rest of the Bible was read. This was so because Acts was the definitive inspired historical account of Apostolic Christianity. The Gospels were extremely important, but they would be read through and in harmony with the Book of Acts. Consequently, in early Pentecostal communities the book of Acts and the Gospels were the primary narratives in the shaping of Pentecostal belief and practice. The Epistles played a secondary and supportive role. It was important to know, therefore, which biblical book or passage had the final word on any given topic when one 'interpreted Scripture in light of Scripture'.

In short, Ewart and Haywood's 'exegesis' of Scripture was similar to other Pentecostals and even other popularistic holiness traditions.[119] The Bible Reading Method was an inductive and deductive

---

thus one may have the prayer language tongues (Spirit baptism) and not have the gift of speaking in tongues. See Lawrence, *The Apostolic Faith Restored*, p. 28.

[118] Haywood, *The Birth of the Spirit in the Days of the Apostles*, p 17. Haywood explained that 'The speaking with other tongues as the Spirit gave utterance accompanied the "gift" of the Holy Ghost [Acts 2]; but the "divers kind of tongues" [1 Corinthians] is one of the "gifts" of the Holy Spirit, which He divides severally has (sic) he wills'. See also p. 19.

[119] Ewart and Haywood used typology and allegory, but not as the primary means to create a Biblical doctrine. Typology and allegory usually functioned to reinforce an already established doctrinal position. For examples, see Ewart's typo-

commonsensical method, which required all of the 'biblical data' on a particular topic to be gathered and then harmonized. Once this was accomplished, it could be formatted into a cohesive synthesis from a restorationist revivalistic perspective. From the Pentecostal perspective, they were being faithful to the whole council of God's word and attempted to remove human commentary on the subject under investigation. The book of Acts was understood to be a factual historical presentation of Apostolic belief and practice; therefore, all Scripture had to be harmonized with and interpreted through this account. Acts was the controlling narrative through which Scripture was read—their canon within the canon.

Summary

The Bible Reading Method encouraged a synchronic interpretive strategy that would extrapolate a verse from its larger context in its concern to string all the verses that relate to that word or topic together and lump it into one paragraph. However, the early Pentecostals (like the Holiness folk) were concerned in a limited sense about the historical cultural context from which the New Testament emerged as they attempted to understand a passage.[120] But the cultural and historical concerns were only analyzed when there was some sort of apparent difficulty in understanding a passage. They were also concerned about properly interpreting a passage according to the syntactical relationships of words and sentences. Hence they recognized the importance of reading Scripture within its cultural and grammatical contexts. This was a pre-critical commonsense approach. They rarely (but would on occasion) appeal to the original biblical languages in order to help clarify their theological positions. They did not attempt to interpret Scripture from the historical critical

---

logical (allegorical) interpretation of Mt. 13.33 (the parable of the leaven) in *The Revelation Of Jesus Christ*. The woman is the Roman Catholic Church, the leaven is the false doctrine of the Nicene Creed and three measures symbolized the Trinity (pp. 26–27). See also Haywood's allegorical reading of Job in *The Finest of Wheat* (Indianapolis, IN: Christ Temple Book Store, nd, pp. 8–11).

[120] Taylor in his exposition on the parable of the Ten Virgins found in *The Spirit and the Bride*, said, 'The best way to understand the parables spoken by our Lord, is to first note the facts from which he drew them'. Taylor then argued that Jesus drew this parable from the common Jewish custom of weddings, which was according to the customs of the East (pp. 112–13).

or scientific method. The Pentecostal reading was a popularistic precritical text centered approach from a restorationist biblicist perspective. From a modernisticly critical perspective (both liberal and conservative), the Pentecostals were blurring the boundaries of the past and present as they exegeted Scripture.

The Bible Reading Method lent itself to create new theological mosaics. It allowed the Pentecostals to push theological boundaries and make interpretive connections within the Scriptures that had not been previously noticed. Their innovative interpretations were considered to be heretical by other Christian communities[121] but for these Pentecostals, they were simply letting the Bible speak 'clearly' and 'plainly' for itself and thus recovering and practicing biblical truth that had been lost.

Lawrence wrote, 'We are sometimes condemned as heretical. *But we are the only body of Christians on Earth to whom the 12ᵗʰ and 14ᵗʰ chapters of 1ˢᵗ Cor. are applicable*'.[122] Haywood could not understand how one could not see the plain meaning of Jesus' statement as recorded in Jn 14.9 ('He who has seen me has seen the Father'): 'What could be more clearer then these words? Jesus is the Father as well as the Son.'[123] Jonathan Culler's comment about interpretation is revealing:

> interpretation is interesting only when it is extreme. Moderate interpretation, which articulates a consensus, though it may have

---

[121] For two typical and more vehement attacks upon early Pentecostals see Alma White [Wesleyan Holiness], *Demons and Tongues* (Zarephath, NJ: Pillar of Fire Publishers, 1936) and Jonathan E. Perkins, *Pentecostalism on the Washboard* (Fort Worth, Texas: Jonathan Elsworth Perkins, Publisher, no date but most likely published in the 1930's?). Alma White presented the typical Wesleyan holiness response that Pentecostals were simply deceived by Satan and tongues speech was a manifestation of demon possession. See also W.B. Godbey (who was a very influential person among the Wesleyan Holiness groups), *Tongue Movement, Satanic* (Zarephath, NJ: Pillar of Fire Publishers, 1918). Perkins, a Fundamentalist Baptist, had embraced Pentecostalism and worked for the Assemblies of God headquarters but later resigned. His work was an attack on Pentecostalism in general but particularly directed toward the Assemblies of God. He rejected Pentecostalism for a number of specific hermeneutical reasons all of which he believed violate the plain teaching of the Word of God, specifically for allowing women to be pastors and theologically for accepting an Arminian-Wesleyanism that jeopardized the Gospel. The concern of the Gospel being jeopardizing by Pentecostalism will be raised again when academic critiques of the movement by Reformed evangelicals appear in the 1960's.

[122] Lawrence, *The Apostolic Faith Restored*, p. 29.

[123] Lawrence, *The Victim Of The Flaming Sword* (Indianapolis, IN: Christ's Temple Book Store, nd), p. 17.

value in some circumstances, is of little interest…Many 'extreme' interpretations like many moderate interpretations, will no doubt have little impact, because they are judged unpersuasive or redundant or irrelevant or boring, but if they are extreme, they have a better chance, it seems to me, of bringing to light connections or implications not previously noticed or reflected on than if they strive to remain 'sound' or moderate.[124]

The Pentecostal doctrine of Spirit baptism and the Oneness view of God were 'extreme' from the non-Pentecostal perspective. But they were (and still are to some extent, if the growth of these movements are any indication of their persuasive presentation of Scripture) simply and strategically 'bringing to light connections or implications not previously noticed'. From the Pentecostals' perspective, they were simply following the standard procedure that 'every scripture must be interpreted by scripture, under the illumination of the Holy Spirit'.[125] In order to achieve this, one had to have 'an open heart' before God and 'ask God to help [them] to harmonize and understand the Scriptures'.[126] In other words, they used the Bible Reading Method with a desire both to believe and obey. Furthermore, the interpretive strategy was not unfamiliar to Pentecostals. They did not create a new method for interpreting an old Bible. However, the Bible Reading Method was used from a Pentecostal perspective, which made it a unique way of reading the Bible. The following chapter will explain this 'Pentecostal perspective' which served as the hermeneutical foil and filter for the Bible Reading Method.

---

[124] Umberto Eco *et al.*, *Interpretation and Overinterpretation*, p. 110.
[125] Myland, *The Latter Rain Covenant*, p. 107.
[126] Taylor, *The Spirit and The Bride*, p. 107.

4

PENTECOSTAL STORY:
THE HERMENEUTICAL FILTER

Devoted saints come from the HOLINESS church, bringing the message of Heart-Purity and the Coming of the Lord, and wonderfully blessed of God, as fruitage needing but one thing—the latter rain.[1]

Aimee Semple McPherson

Thus far I have identified the historical beginning of Pentecostalism which came as a result of the late nineteenth-century revivals, particularly the Wesleyan Holiness and Keswickian higher life movements. From this context of American restorationist non-cessationist revivalism came a distinct Pentecostal spirituality. 'It was the "black spirituality of former slaves in the United States" encountering the specific catholic spirituality of the movement's "grandfather", John Wesley'.[2]

What distinguished the early Pentecostal Bible Reading Method from the Holiness folk was not a different interpretive method but a 'distinct narrative' which held the similar methods together in a coherent and cohesive interpretive manner. The Pentecostal movement's continuation of Holiness praxis in confrontation with cessationist Fundamentalism and liberalism created a fertile context in which an authentic Pentecostal hermeneutical strategy emerged. The Pentecostal hermeneutical strategy at the foundational interpretive level was a unique story.

How Pentecostals or any community goes about doing 'exegesis' has as much to do with their social location and theological formation as it does with simply employing a so called neutral-scientific

---

[1] Aimee Semple McPherson, *This Is That* (Los Angeles, CA: Echo Park Evangelistic Association, 1923), p. 787.

[2] Land, *Pentecostal Spirituality*, p. 35. Land cites Walter J. Hollenweger, 'After Twenty Years' Research on Pentecostalism', *Theology* 87 (Nov. 1984), p. 404.

exegetical method. The role of the hermeneut in the interpretive process must also be considered. This touches upon the issue of community and identity.

One must take seriously the significant contemporary challenge that the use of any method is not objectively free from the social cultural location of the person utilizing it. Both the method and the person in community have been historically conditioned. One must also appreciate the contemporary challenge that for interpretation to take place the reader must participate. 'Reading involves using both the information that is present on the written page, as well as the information we already have in our minds'. The reader does not come as a blank slate.[3] Comprehension is both a discovery and the creation of meaningful understanding.[4]

The Community Story as the Influential Hermeneutical Filter

Harry Stout has demonstrated that there is an inescapable relationship between the community to which one belongs and how one explains past religious history.[5] In his essay 'Theological Commitment and American Religious History', Stout addresses the issue of the historian's commitment to a community and its influence upon the telling of American Christian history.

Stout examines two prominent non-Christian historians of Puritanism, Perry Miller and Edmund S. Morgan. Stout demonstrates that

---

[3] Jeff McQuillian, *The Literary Crisis: False Claims, Real Solutions* (Portsmouth, NH: Heinemann, 1998), p. 16.

[4] Bernard C. Lategan, 'Hermeneutics' in *ABD* (Doubleday, 1992), III, pp. 153–54. See also George Aichele *et al.*, *The Postmodern Bible: The Bible and Culture Collective* (New Haven: Yale University Press, 1995) who challenges both the notion of the Enlightenment's control of objectivity and stability of meaning (pp. 1–8). See also Anthony C. Thiselton's, *New Horizons in Hermeneutics* (Grand Rapids, MI: Zondervan, 1992) who argues for a contextualized hermeneutical approach that respects both the biblical horizon and the horizon of the reader (pp. 9–15). For a sustained response to Postmodernism see, Anthony Thiselton, *Interpreting God and the Postmodern Self: On Meaning, Manipulation and Promise* (Grand Rapids, MI: Eerdmans, 1995). In this monograph, Thiselton responds to the postmodern claim that all truth is manipulative interpretation. While recognizing that this claim has some validity, he presents a non-manipulative Christian response.

[5] Harry S. Stout, 'Theological Commitment and American Religious History', *Theological Education* 25 (Spring 1989), pp. 44–59.

one's theological or non-theological commitment does not affect
one's choice to pursue a religious subject nor one's ability to be em-
pathetic of the subjects being studied. Stout further demonstrates
that one's theological or non-theological commitment does not make
a difference in the selection and use of critical methods or critical
sources. Stout is convinced that 'on the level of method and sympa-
thy for the subject there is no connection between atheistic commitment and religious history writing'.[6] However, Stout does believe that
one's commitment to a particular community does shape the telling
of religious history in decisive ways because the view of the observer
is connected to the 'common memory' of the particular community
in which they are 'internally bound'.[7] He argues that it is at the deeper
level of philosophical commitment or the historian's 'point of view'
which 'directs the script and selects the themes in ways that invariably
point back to the ultimate values of the story-tellers' [historians].[8]

Stout, drawing upon the work of H. Richard Niebuhr, argues that
the storyteller's point of view allows for

> an existential relationship between the individual and his/her sub-
> ject that stays with writers throughout their work. Insofar as all
> history writing involves an ongoing dialectic between the sub-
> ject/actors and historian observer, the view of the observer does
> make a difference.[9]

The historian who observes is caught up in an existential dialectic
between subject/actors and being a historian/observer, hence 'history stories are neither past nor present, but both simultaneously
which results in a "participatory history"'.[10] One's point of view inevitably shapes the story and guides the methodological analysis being used along with the interpretation of the analysis.

One's 'point of view', as Stout calls it, is a result of participating in
a community. The historian's or biblical scholar's point of view
guides the methodological critical analysis and inevitably shapes the
present retelling of past history. The 'point of view' as discussed by

---

[6] Stout, 'Theological Commitment and American Religious History', pp. 45–46,
cited 47.

[7] Stout, 'Theological Commitment and American Religious History', p. 48.

[8] Stout, 'Theological Commitment and American Religious History', p. 52.

[9] Stout, 'Theological Commitment and American Religious History', pp. 47–48.

[10] Stout, 'Theological Commitment and American Religious History', p. 48.

Stout could also be understood as the narrative tradition of the community in which the historian is presently affiliated. Therefore, the narrative tradition of a community becomes an essential part of any hermeneutical strategy, for the making and explaining of meaning is inherently communal.

Pentecostal Story as a Hermeneutical Narrative Tradition

Alasdair MacIntyre, a philosophical ethicist, has had a major impact upon the understanding of moral reasoning.[11] He, as opposed to the 'Enlightenment Project', argues that all moral reasoning takes place from within a particular narrative tradition. He demonstrates that interpretive practices of a community are always dependent upon the community's narrative tradition. The narrative tradition provides the context in which moral reason, along with its interpretive practices can be understood.[12]

MacIntyre's concept of narrative as a descriptive category is difficult to grasp because of the different (and at times contradictory) ways he employs it.[13] But it nonetheless plays a central role in his understanding of moral reasoning. In fact, his argument concerning moral reasoning relies upon the interaction of four major concepts: narrative, tradition, virtue and practice.[14] However, for the purpose of this chapter, this writer is only concerned about narrative. One of MacIntyre's 'central theses' is that 'man is in his actions and practices, as well as in his fictions, essentially a story-telling animal'. Therefore, 'I can only answer the question "What am I to do?" if I can answer the prior question "of what story or stories do I find myself a

---

[11] See for example, Nancy Murphy, Brad Kallenberg and Mark Nation (eds.), *Virtues and Practices in the Christian Tradition: Christian Ethics after MacIntyre* (Harrisburg, PA: Trinity Press International, 1997).

[12] See Alasdair MacIntyre, *After Virtue: A Study in Moral Theory* (Notre Dame, IN: University of Notre Dame Press, 1984, 2d edn). Also see MacIntyre's sequel, *Whose Justice? Which Rationality* (Notre Dame, IN: University of Notre Dame Press, 1988).

[13] L. Gregory Jones, 'Alasdair MacIntyre on Narrative, Community, and the Moral Life', *Modern Theology* 4.1 (1987), p. 53.

[14] Brad J. Kallenberg, 'The Master Argument of MacIntyre's *After Virtue*' in Murphy, Kallenberg and Nation (eds.), *Virtues and Practices in the Christian Tradition*, p. 20.

part?'"[15] His primary concern has been to demonstrate that 'dramatic narrative is the crucial form for an understanding of human action' and moral reasoning.[16]

According to L. Gregory Jones there are two principles which underlie MacIntyre's diverse descriptions of narrative: historicity and human action.[17] Jones states, 'what MacIntyre is concerned to establish in all the uses of narrative is their historical character', and that 'MacIntyre believes that human action, in order to be intelligible, requires an account of a context which only a true dramatic narrative can provide'.[18] Therefore, any interpretive method with its epistemological system is 'inescapably historically and socially context bound' and is 'inseparable from the intellectual and social tradition in which it is embodied'.[19] Furthermore, the community's narrative envelops the tradition and makes the methodological argument understandable and meaningfully acceptable.[20] The 'community', then, 'is the bearer, interpreter and concert expression of its tradition'.[21]

Does this lead then to relative pluralism? No, it just emphasizes that all moral reasoning is dependent upon and takes place within a narrative tradition. Nancy Murphy writes: 'MacIntyre has complex and ingenious arguments to show that, despite the tradition-dependence of all specific moral arguments, it is nonetheless possible to make respectable public claims, showing one tradition of moral reasoning to be superior to its rivals'.[22] Trevor Hart further explains how MacIntyre's account of moral reasoning challenges relativism. MacIntyre is 'reminding us that traditions are rooted in communities, and thereby reinforcing the suggestion that rationality, far from being an isolated and uniquely personal or subjective thing, is in fact an in-

---

[15] MacIntyre, *After Virtue*, p. 216.

[16] Alasdair MacIntyre, 'Epistemological Crises, Dramatic Narrative, and the Philosophy of Science' in Stanley Hauerwas and L. Gregory Jones (eds.), *Why Narrative? Readings in Narrative Theology* (Grand Rapids, MI: Eerdmans, 1989), p. 150.

[17] Jones, 'Alasdair MacIntyre on Narrative, Community, and the Moral life', p. 57.

[18] Jones, 'Alasdair MacIntyre on Narrative, Community, and the Moral life', p. 57.

[19] MacIntyre, *Whose Justice? Which Rationality*, pp. 4, 8.

[20] Jones, 'Alasdair MacIntyre on Narrative, Community, and the Moral life.' Jones challenges MacIntyre for his lack of emphasis upon community (p. 59).

[21] Kallenberg, 'The Master Argument of MacIntyre's *After Virtue*', p. 64.

[22] Murphy, *Virtues and Practices in the Christian Tradition*, p. 2.

terpersonal matter as well'. Narrative traditions then 'are justified by
their supposed appropriateness as accounts of reality. They refer us
appropriately to the world, and facilitate a meaningful engagement
with it in its rich diversity.' MacIntyre 'is not a relativist but a realist'.[23]

At this point, I shall clarify how I understand the Pentecostal narrative tradition and its relationship to Christianity. The Pentecostal
community is a part of the larger Christian community and yet exists
as a distinct coherent narrative tradition within Christianity. The Pentecostal community or a collection of communities is bound together
by their 'shared charismatic experiences' and 'shared story'. The Pentecostal narrative tradition attempts to embody the Christian meta-
narrative.[24] Yet, because the Pentecostal community understands itself to be a restorationist movement, it has argued that it is the best
representation of Christianity in the world today. This may sound
triumphant, yet, the Pentecostals, like all restorationist narrative traditions of Christianity, desire to be both an authentic continuation of
New Testament Christianity and be a faithful representation of New
Testament Christianity in the present societies in which they exist. Of
course the understanding of what was and should be New Testament
Christianity is based upon a Pentecostal understanding, hence it reflects the narrative tradition of the community. Because Pentecostals
are also a part of the broader Christian community, they must be
concerned with the interpretation of its most authoritative text—the

---

[23] Trevor Hart, *Faith Thinking: The Dynamics of Christian Theology* (London: SPCK,
1995), p. 68. See also MacIntyre, *Whose Justice? Which Rationality*. 'Post-Enlight-
enment relativism and perspectivism are thus the negative counterpart of Enlightenment, its inverted mirror image' (p. 353).

[24] By meta-narrative, this writer is referring to a grand story by which human
societies and their individual members live and organize their lives in meaningful
ways. The Christian meta-narrative refers to the general Christian story about the
meaning of the world and the God who created it and humanity's place in it. A
story that begins with a good creation includes a fall into sin, redemption through
the Messiah, Christian Community and final restoration of all creation. The Christian meta-narrative is primarily dependent on the Bible for this general narrative.
See Gabriel Fackre, *The Christian Story: A Narrative of Basic Christian Doctrine* (Grand
Rapids, MI: Eerdmans, 3rd edn, 1996, I), for a basic outline of the 'Storyline' concerning the Christian meta-narrative. Fackre writes that 'Creation, Fall, Covenant,
Jesus Christ, Church, Salvation, Consummation … are acts in the Christian drama'
with the understanding 'That there is a God who creates, reconciles, and redeems
the word' as 'the "Storyline"' (pp. 8–9).

Bible. However, Pentecostals will engage Scripture and reality from their own community and narrative tradition.[25]

Pentecostal Story and the Making of Meaning

The Pentecostal story is synonymous with the Pentecostal narrative tradition. The Pentecostal story is the primary hermeneutical context for the reading of Scripture, hence providing the context for the production of meaning. The Pentecostal narrative tradition provides the Pentecostals with an experiential, conceptual hermeneutical narrative that enables them to interpret Scripture and their experience of reality. The Pentecostal narrative tradition is the horizon of the community and the means of articulating its identity. It is from this horizon that the Pentecostal community reads Scripture, thus producing meaning.

As Hart explains, 'Stories ... are very important to our identity as human beings in community. Every human community has a story which it tells both itself and others concerning its distinct origins and *raison d'être,* and about the sort of place this world in which it exists is'.[26] The Pentecostal narrative tradition is an eschatological Christian story of God's involvement in the restoration of the Christian community and God's dramatic involvement in reality and the Pentecostal community.[27]

The Pentecostal community's identity is forged from its reading of the Biblical narratives of Acts and the Gospels. Pentecostals desire to live as the eschatological people of God. They are caught up in the final drama of God's redemptive activity. The redemptive activity of God is channeled through Jesus and manifested in the community by the Holy Spirit. The Full Gospel is enthusiastically embraced and proclaimed. This places Jesus at the heart of God's dramatic story, which in turn emphasizes the missionary role of the community.

The Pentecostal community reads Scripture from a Pentecostal perspective. Thus like all readings there will be a transaction between the biblical text and the community which results in the production of meaning. Therefore there exists a dialectic encounter between two

---

[25] MacIntyre, *Whose Justice? Which Rationality,* p 354.
[26] Hart, *Faith Thinking,* p. 107.
[27] This will be presented later in this chapter.

poles, the biblical text and the community. This encounter is possible because within the biblical story and the Pentecostal community there is a working plot.

Dan Hawk speaks of plot as existing on a number of levels. He argues that plot functions on the surface level of the story and in this sense, it 'may refer to the framework of the story'.[28] Plot can also refer to the more detailed 'arrangement of incidents and patterns as they relate to each other' in a story.[29] These two functions of plot recognize that plot operates within the self-contained world of the text. Yet, Hawk also argues that there exist real yet abstract notions of plot operating within the mind of the reader. The reader, then also, 'exercises a tendency to organize and make connections between events'. Hawk argues that this function of plot in the mind of the reader is a 'dynamic phenomenon' which 'moves beyond the formal aspects of the text and addresses the interpretive processes that takes place between text and reader'.[30] This happens because a 'narrative … elicits a dynamic interpretative relationship between text and reader'.[31]

When the Pentecostal in community reads Scripture for the purpose of developing a praxis theology, s/he will place the biblical stories into the cohesive Pentecostal narrative tradition. This does not mean this employment is simply a linear process because Pentecostals will allow for the biblical stories to challenge and reshape their tradition. Therefore, there is a dialogical and dialectical encounter between the Bible and the community. However, this does imply that the making of meaning and the validation of that meaning will take place primarily within the community, thus meaning rests in the pragmatic decision of the community.[32] The community must discern what the text means and how that meaning is to be lived out in the commu-

---

[28] Hawk, *Every Promised Fulfilled*, p. 19.

[29] Hawk, *Every Promised Fulfilled*, p. 19.

[30] Hawk, *Every Promised Fulfilled*, p. 27.

[31] Hawk, *Every Promised Fulfilled*, p. 27.

[32] See Stanley Fish, *Is There a Text in This Class? The Authority of Interpretive Communities* (Cambridge: Harvard University Press, 1980). Fish left formalistic thinking about texts and here argues that communities write texts in the very act of reading. I do not totally agree with Fish's pragmatic view that communities dominate and use texts as they see fit but Fish is correct in his argument that interpretive communities do have the final decision in proclaiming what a text means and establish the hermeneutical ground rules for interpreting texts.

nity. This decision making process is imperative for Pentecostals because Pentecostal interpretation includes an act of willful obedient response to the Scripture's meaning.

The Pentecostal Story

The purpose of this section is to identify the Pentecostal story and demonstrate how it significantly influenced the Pentecostals' interpretation of Scripture. This will be accomplished by first demonstrating the impact that the Latter Rain motif had upon early Pentecostal identity and how that theological concept set the stage for the 'restoration' of the Full Gospel, hence the birth of the Pentecostal community.

The Latter Rain Motif

Faupel has demonstrated that the Latter Rain motif provides the primary organizational structure for the Pentecostal narrative tradition.[33] Thus the Pentecostal Bible Reading Method, although similar to the other budding popularistic evangelical traditions, differs because the Pentecostals held to a distinct narrative of which the 'Latter Rain' motif played a significant role in the construction of the Pentecostal story.[34] The Latter Rain motif also provided the early Pentecos-

---

[33] Faupel, *The Everlasting Gospel*, see ch. 2, pp. 19–43.

[34] The Biblical references used to develop the early and Latter Rain motif are Deut. 11.10-15; Job 29.29; Prov. 16.15; Jer. 3.3, 5.24; Hos. 6.3; Joel 2.23; Zech. 10.1 and Jas 5.7, with the more significant verses being Deut. 11.10-15:

For the land, whither thou goest in to possess it, is not as the land of Egypt, from whence ye came out, where thou sowedst thy seed, and wateredst it with thy foot, as a garden of herbs: But the land, whither ye go to possess it, is a land of hills and valleys, and drinketh water of the rain of heaven: A land which the LORD thy God careth for: the eyes of the LORD thy God are always upon it, from the beginning of the year even unto the end of the year. And it shall come to pass, if ye shall hearken diligently unto my commandments which I command you this day, to love the LORD your God, and to serve him with all your heart and with all your soul, That I will give you the rain of your land in his due season, *the first rain and the Latter Rain*, that thou mayest gather in thy corn, and thy wine, and thine oil. And I will send grass in thy fields for thy cattle, that thou mayest eat and be full' (KJV).

Joel 2.23: 'Be glad then, ye children of Zion, and rejoice in the LORD your God: for he hath given you the former rain moderately, and he will cause to come down for you the rain, *the former rain, and the Latter Rain* in the first month' (KJV).

tals with an important organization and relational role in the interpretive process. In other words, the Latter Rain motif enabled Pentecostals to relate and interpret the Old and New Testament according to a promise-fulfillment strategy. The promise-fulfillment strategy also allowed them to extend the promise into their present community thus enabling them to continue participation in the past promises. Taylor explained the significance of the Latter Rain motif:

> God fashioned the land of Palestine to be the model land of all lands, to contain the produces of all zones and climes, to be a miniature world in itself, and so He arranged the coming and going of its rain clouds on a spiritual pattern, to beautifully adumbrate the movements of the Holy Spirit. So just what the rain is to the earth, the Holy Spirit is to the soul. God arranged the showers of rain in the land of Canaan, as a type of the operations of grace. Many Scriptures allude to the early and Latter Rain, and these are used as types of the Holy Spirit.[35]

The 'Latter Rain' motif is based upon the typical weather cycle in Palestine and the biblical promise that God would provide the necessary rain for a plentiful harvest (the former and latter rains) if Israel remained faithful to their covenant with Yahweh.[36] The 'Latter Rain' motif provided the Pentecostal community with a stable conceptual framework through which they interpreted God's involvement with the whole of human history and 'provided the broad framework in which the Pentecostal world-view could be constructed'.[37] Therefore,

---

Jas 5.7: 'Be patient therefore, brethren, unto the coming of the Lord. Behold, the husbandman waiteth for the precious fruit of the earth, and hath long patience for it, until he receive the *early* and *Latter Rain'* (KJV) (emphasis added to all above).

[35] Taylor, *The Spirit and The Bride*, p. 90. He dedicated ch. 9 of this work to the explanation of the early and Latter Rain (pp. 90–99).

[36] See A.H. Joy, 'Rain' in J. Orr (ed.), *The International Standard Bible Encyclopedia* (Chicago: Howard Severance Company, 1915), pp. 2525–26. Faupel, *The Everlasting Gospel*, points out that the Pentecostals misunderstood the Palestinian weather cycle. They thought that the early and latter Rain pattern took place between the hot dry summer, thus a spring and then fall rain, when in actuality it takes place during the winter rainy season between October (early rain) and April (the latter Rain) (p. 30).

[37] See Faupel, *The Everlasting Gospel*, pp. 32–36, citing 35–36, for an important discussion on the significance of the 'Latter Rain' motif contribution to the structure of the Pentecostal message. See also Blumhofer's discussion of the importance

the Latter Rain motif played a prominent role in the construction of
the narrative tradition of the early Pentecostal hermeneutic by providing the basic structure for the Pentecostal story.

'Latter Rain' terminology was common among the various Holiness groups.[38] People were praying for and expecting a great outpouring of God's Spirit at the turn of the twentieth century. They longed
for the promised 'Latter Rain' which would bring in the end-time
harvest. A.B. Simpson, founder of the Christian and Missionary Alliance (CMA), wrote in his denominational magazine:

> We may ... conclude that we are to expect a great outpouring of
> the Holy Spirit in connection with the second coming of Christ
> and one as much greater than the Pentecostal effusion (Acts 2) as
> the rains of autumn were greater than the showers of spring ...
> We are in the time ... when we may expect this Latter Rain (par-
> enthetical added).[39]

Simpson, like many at the turn of the century, were praying and long-
ing for the eschatological fulfillment of Joel's prophecy which they

---

of the Latter Rain concept upon the lifestyle of the early Pentecostals (*Restoring The Faith*, pp. 93–97).

[38] Blumhofer, *Restoring the Faith*, p. 96, argues that 'proto-fundamentalists' [her term] like A.T. Pierson, prayed for the Latter Rain outpouring and 'diligently' charted the rainfall patterns of Palestine, yet unlike the Pentecostals, 'they [proto-fundamentalists] did not expect the full recurrence of apostolic "signs"'. I disagree with Blumhofer's statement because there existed within the 'proto-fundamentalist' coalition those traditions and people who were cessationist like Keswickian dispen-sationalist A.T. Pierson; but there were also Keswickian folk like A.B. Simpson who were not cessationist. Thus, it depends upon whether or not one was a cessa-tionist as to whether or not one expected miracles to be restored to the Church. Also, the Wesleyan Holiness, Pentecostal and proto-fundamentalists (cessationist and Keswickian) will predominately embrace the Scofieldian dispensational herme-neutic (all Baptistic fundamentalists had already done so), yet those non-cessationists like the Pentecostals will modify it in light of the 'Latter Rain' narra-tive. Therefore, not all proto-fundamentalists were cessationist, and some like A.B. Simpson were praying for the restoration of the supernatural gifts to the Church. Thus the application of the term proto-fundamentalist to these early revivalistic groups creates more confusion than clarity.

[39] Cited in Blumhofer, *The Assemblies of God*, p. 151. For a very important pres-entation of A.B. Simpson's relationship with Pentecostalism, see Charles W. Nienkrichen, *A.B. Simpson and the Pentecostal Movement: A Study In Continuity, Crisis, and Change* (Peabody, MA: Hendrickson Publishers, 1992). Nienkrichen argues that the contemporary attitude of the current Christian Missionary Alliance denomina-tion was primarily shaped more by the later revisionist interpretation of Simpson's writings by A.W. Tozer than by Simpson himself.

believed was beginning to take place because they had already experienced a sprinkling of the 'Latter Rain' showers (sanctification, divine healing and premillennialism). Because the 'early rain' (Acts 2) empowered the early Church with supernatural gifts, Simpson and those who did not embrace a cessationist view, expected a full and greater restoration of all the gifts during the 'Latter Rain' just prior to the second coming of Christ.[40]

Pentecostals, however, seized the 'Latter Rain' motif and utilized it as an apologetic explanation for the importance of their movement. The early rain was the outpouring of the Holy Spirit upon the first-century Christians at Pentecost as recorded in Acts 2. The latter rain was the outpouring of the Holy Spirit upon saved and sanctified Christians at the turn of the twentieth century. The time between the early and latter rain was a time of drought caused by the 'great apostasy' of the Roman Catholic Church.

The biblical 'Latter Rain' motif became an important contribution to the Pentecostal story. The 'Latter Rain' motif enabled the Pentecostals to hold together the 'Full Gospel message' because it provided a coherent explanation for the restoration of the gifts, while also providing the primary organizational structure for their story. The Pentecostals became the people of the prophetically promised 'Latter Rain', which meant that they had fully recovered not only the Apostolic faith, but also the Apostolic power, authority and practice.[41] Pentecostals often appealed to the manifestation of miracles as validation of their message. Thus, 'signs and wonders' became an important 'proof' for validating the Pentecostal story, and with this came the development of a 'Signs Theology'. For example, in *The Apostolic Faith* under the banner 'Signs Follow', one reads:

> The signs are following in Los Angeles. The eyes of the blind have been opened, the lame have been made to walk, and those who

---

[40] For Simpson's understanding of the 'Latter Rain' motif see Nienkrichen, *A.B. Simpson and the Pentecostal Movement*, pp. 65–68. Nienkrichen correctly points out that there is a logical corollary of Simpson's doctrine of 'Latter Rain' and his emphasis upon the restoration of New Testament miracles, which 'was his categorical rejection of cessationism' (p. 66). Simpson would not embrace the normative argument of the Pentecostals concerning Spirit baptism as being evidenced by speaking in tongues, even though he was sympathetic to the movement and supportive of the manifestation of supernatural gifts (p. 129).

[41] Faupel, *The Everlasting Gospel*, p. 39.

have accidentally drunk poison have been healed. One came suffering from poison and was healed instantly. Devils are cast out, and many speak in new tongues. All the signs in Mark 16:16-18 have followed except the raising of the dead, and we believe God will have someone to receive that power. We want all the signs that it may prove that God is true. It will result in the salvation of many souls.[42]

The Early and Latter Rain Motif According to Myland, Taylor and Lawrence

D. Wesley Myland (1858–1943) was the featured speaker at a Pentecostal convention held at the Stone Church in Chicago in May through June of 1909. At this convention, Myland presented a series of lectures on the 'Latter Rain' and the Pentecostal outpouring. This series of homiletical lectures, which was a sweeping and lengthy exposition of the Old and New Testaments, was first published in *The Latter Rain Evangel*, which was edited by William Hammer Piper, the pastor of the influential Stone Church. These lectures were then published in book form in 1910 with the title *The Latter Rain Covenant and Pentecostal Power: With Testimony of Healings and Baptism*. This book became the classical definitive apologetic for the validation of the Pentecostal outpouring as the fulfillment of the expected 'Latter Rain'.[43]

Myland spent four years training to be a Methodist minister and maintained his credentials with the Methodist Church throughout his ministry career. He was also affiliated with the CMA from 1890 to 1912. After leaving the CMA, he became a prominent independent leader among the Pentecostals.[44] Myland was a talented songwriter, evangelist and Bible school teacher and was respected in various Christian circles.

---

[42] *Apostolic Faith*, 1.3 (October 1906), p. 4.

[43] See Donald Dayton's prefatory introduction to *Three Early Pentecostal Tracts* (New York: Garland Press, 1985). Also see Faupel, *The Everlasting Gospel*, p. 34.

[44] See E.B. Robinson's essay 'Myland, David Wesley' in *DPCM*, pp. 632–33. According to Robinson, Myland served in two leadership positions with the CMA (Ohio District Secretary, 1894, and then as Superintendent from 1898 to 1904), but he broke his affiliation with the CMA in 1912, due to their rejection of tongues as the evidence of Spirit baptism. Myland affiliated with the CMA because of his strong belief in divine healing. See Myland's brief comment on how his healing ministry caused some problems with his relationship with the Methodist Church in his *The Latter Rain Covenant and Pentecostal Power*, pp. 159–60.

The publication of his influential Pentecostal theological apologetic received the warm recommendation of Vicar Alexander A. Boddy of Sunderland, England. Boddy wrote in the introduction for Myland's *The Latter Rain Covenant and Pentecostal Power:*

> There has been much literature issued of late in connection with the Baptism in the Holy Spirit, but nothing more scriptural or more satisfying has been printed than this remarkable book by Pastor D. Wesley Myland, which I now warmly commend to God's people every where.

Boddy went on to write that Myland's book should 'be found in *every* Pentecostal home' because 'it is an invaluable work of reference on the all-important subject of the Baptism in the Holy Spirit' [emphasis added]. William Piper wrote in the preface that 'No man could have *thought* these lectures out; they bear the imprint of heaven's teaching'. He was convinced of the scriptural and spiritual soundness of Myland's exegesis of Scripture. He triumphantly declared, 'Our studies in Exegesis have revealed nothing which in uniqueness and originality equals this exposition of the Blessed Latter Rain truths'. Myland's book was promoted as an authoritative 'exposition of the Word' which 'ought to be a required part of the curriculum of every really Pentecostal School'.[45] Blumhofer writes that Myland's lectures 'commanded wide respect among Pentecostals' because they 'generally considered them profound in their scholarship'.[46] No doubt his homiletical lectures influenced much of Pentecostal thinking and generally represented the Pentecostal understanding of the Latter Rain's connection with Spirit baptism, restoration of the gifts, and the imminence of Jesus' Second Coming.[47]

Myland clearly stated his interpretive approach to Scripture. But before he stated his exegetical method, he invited his listeners to evaluate his teaching by the Word of God. 'If I preach anything but the Word of God, God bless the man or woman that will help me get

---

[45] D. Wesley Myland, *The Latter Rain Covenant*; Boddy's citation is found after Piper's prefatory remarks (no page numbers).

[46] Blumhofer, *Restoring the Faith*, p. 95. She states that much of Myland's language was duplicated in other publications, some of which were not 'classical' Pentecostal but yet open to the supernatural manifestations such as the CMA.

[47] Also ch. 9, 'The Early and Latter Rain' in Taylor's *The Spirit and The Bride*. Taylor also makes this connection.

it right'.[48] Myland argued that Scripture ought to be interpreted in a dual manner. First, Scripture should always be interpreted historically or literally, and then secondly Scripture should be applied to the Christian Church spiritually or typologically. Hence, he, unlike the academic Fundamentalists, affirmed the long-standing tradition of the patristic period that Scripture had two senses—a historical and a spiritual.

Yet, he also argued that there were some portions of Scripture that require a threefold interpretive approach. This threefold approach moves from a literal or historical understanding through the typological or spiritual application and into the prophetic or dispensational understanding of God's redemptive plan. The 'Latter Rain covenant', which he ranked third among the seven great covenants of God, was the central covenant to achieving God's purpose for this Gospel age. But in order to understand the Latter Rain covenant required one to use a threefold interpretative approach to Scripture. Myland stated,

> There are many Scriptures that are not only double-barreled, but triple-barreled; they are literal, typical and prophetical; or putting it in another words, historical, spiritual and dispensational. A large portion of Scripture, of course, is double-barreled, and we ought always to consider it that way; first, as a matter of history, an account of literal things and literal people, and also that it has a spiritual significance for us; but some Scripture like the Latter Rain Covenant have a third aspect—dispensational.[49]

Myland utilized this threefold interpretive strategy to articulate his theological understanding of the Latter Rain.

Myland relied upon his Hebrew and Greek concordances in attempting to understand the importance of the early and latter rain terminology. He said that as far as he knew God had not revealed this important covenant to any other 'man', but he was privileged to receive this revelation when he was baptized in the 'Holy Ghost and

---

[48] Myland, *The Latter Rain Covenant*, p. 3.

[49] Myland, *The Latter Rain Covenant*, p. 32. This quotation came at the end of the first paragraph of the second chapter (lecture), and Myland stated something very similar to this at the outset of his first chapter (p. 6). Myland weaves together this literal or historical, typological and prophetic understanding of the Latter Rain throughout his lectures.

Fire' on November 3, 1906. He said, 'I then took up the Hebrew and Greek and found the word which stands for "Latter Rain" appears just seven times in addition to its appearance in the Latter Rain Covenant'.[50] Thus, Myland, like all early Pentecostals, employed the inductive-deductive commonsense Bible Reading Method as the primary means for the interpretation of Scripture. In this particular case the theme or topic under investigation was 'Latter Rain'.[51] Myland's seven lectures, which are the first five chapters of the published book, utilized the 'triple-barreled' method to construct his theological doctrine on the 'Latter Rain'.[52]

His emphasis upon revelation did not diminish the importance of studying Scripture, yet his understanding of it did mean more than the traditional understanding of illumination. Revelation, when used by these early Pentecostals, meant an experiential redemptive knowledge that one comes to comprehend through one's experience with

---

[50] Myland, *The Latter Rain Covenant*, p. 33, and see pp. 6–7 were he first introduces the Latter Rain Covenant and states his reliance on the concordance. The first place the word 'Latter Rain' was used was Deut. 11.14, but Myland argued that this was the establishment of the Latter Rain Covenant with Israel which was found in Deut. 11.10-26 (p. 2). Thus the word appears seven times besides the covenant establishment. Myland stated the word appears 'Seven; no more or no less' (p. 6). Numerology played an important role in shaping his theological interpretation of the Latter Rain and shaped the very structure in which he presented his lectures and book. The two important biblical numbers were seven and three. Seven means perfection while three refers to Trinity. He stated 'You cannot find perfection without trinity, and where you find trinity you find perfection', and 'trinity runs through this sevenfold or complete "Latter Rain covenant"' (p. 16). His book contained seven chapters, with chs. 1, 2, 6 and 7 containing seven subsections and some subsections have three more subsections. Ch. 1 is the explanation of the 'Latter Rain Covenant' which was an exposition of Deut. 11.10-21, a total of twelve verses. Myland was quick to point out that twelve was 'typical [or typological] ... of the twelve tribes of Israel, to whom it was first given, and also of the twelve patriarchs and the twelve apostles of the Lamb that form the great foundations of the city of God' (p. 2). In ch. 2 he dealt with 'restoring' the covenant, while ch. 5 was an exposition on the 29th Psalm—the Seven voices of God. Ch. 7 was a testimonial of seven of his miraculous healings. Chs. 3 and 5 both have 5 subsections and ch. 5 contains 10 subsections. Myland, like other Pentecostals, will mimic biblical themes (persecution of the righteous), numbers (3, 7, 12, 40) and episodes in explaining the important of a doctrine and life experience. This attests to their emersion into biblical narrative.

[51] Myland, *The Latter Rain Covenant*, p. 6. Myland defined the Hebrew and Greek word for 'Latter Rain', but did not cite his source.

[52] His understanding of the significance of the number three, even though he did not explicitly say it, probably reinforces his triple-barreled method.

the Holy Spirit. However, Scripture must validate one's experiential redemptive knowledge. There must be an obvious correlation between a person's experience and a similar experience narrated in Scripture. Thus there is this dialogical interaction between Pentecostal experience and the Scripture. For a Pentecostal like Myland, this was a very important part of the interpretive process. 'Every Scripture must be interpreted by Scripture, under the illumination of the Holy Spirit, to get its deeper sense'.[53]

This, of course, is what Myland and others set out to do when they interpreted Scripture. Yet, it is important to remember that the early Pentecostals shaped their theological views within the confines of the sanctuary not the library. In the very posture of Pentecostal prayer (on one's knees) and with an eagerness not only to believe, but also to obey the truth of Scripture, and with the full concern of the *present* problems facing the Pentecostal community, they read Scripture. The altar became the place to experience the Holy Spirit and the pulpit became the primary means to proclaim these redemptive experiences.

The Pentecostal communities have always been highly 'oral' in the transmission of their teachings, with the primary setting being a worship service. Myland's homiletical lectures are an example of how the oral presentation of a message shapes the written presentation of a message. His lectures were well thought out, creative sermons for an audience who appreciated the oral presentation of the Scripture in the setting of the sanctuary.[54] This did not mean that the study of Scripture was unimportant but it did mean that all doctrinal reflection and articulation should have as its primary concern the experiential redemptive knowledge, which could be experientially grasped by the listener.[55] This experiential knowledge must be *revealed* by the Holy

---

[53] Myland, *The Latter Rain Covenant*, p. 107.

[54] I am not suggesting that Pentecostals did not write for publications that would be widely circulated. Pentecostals seized every opportunity to get the Full Gospel message out into the world and Pentecostal papers, pamphlets and magazines flowed steady into the farthest corners of the world. The information was put into the form of testimonials, sermons, Bible studies and question and answers, not formal theological defenses. Myland's 'scholarly' lectures presented with homiletical structure, alliteration and illustration, reflect his audience and his creative ability.

[55] The Pentecostals argued one should experientially or tangibly know they are saved, sanctified, and Spirit filled, see Seymour, 'Bible Salvation', *The Apostolic Faith* 1.3 (October, 1906), p. 4.

Spirit, *validated* by Scripture, and *confirmed* by the community. Hence Myland warned his listeners:

> It will not do to take the extreme position of relying upon spiritual revelation alone. There must be an earnest study of the Word of God also, and to be a teacher I must have the understanding as well as the revelation. If one is to lead others to God he must know the Word and be apt to teach it. Therein we need to wait on God with our Bibles open.[56]

Myland wrote, 'the Latter Rain Covenant not only has a literal bearing upon the land, but it applies typically to God's people, and also prophetically to God's plan of the ages'.[57] By literal, Myland meant that Scripture has a straightforward historical account of what happened to real people at actual places. This historical or literal level of Scripture was an already established and accepted way to interpret Scripture. Myland saw the Latter Rain Covenant as being given to the people of Israel, and connected to the land. His differentiation between a literal people (Israel) and a spiritual people (the Christian community) was a typical premillennial dispensational distinction.

The 'Latter Rain covenant' also had a spiritual or typological sense. 'For just as the literal early and Latter Rain was poured out upon Palestine, so upon the First century was poured out the early rain, and upon us the Latter Rain'.[58] The people and land of Israel were the type, and the people of God [not to be confused with traditional mainline Christianity or churches] were the anti-type.[59] Myland maintained and reiterated throughout his book this typological distinction between the literal OT people of God and the spiritual people of God who were grafted into the literal people of God by means of the cross. The spiritual people were the authentic Christians of the Church age (New Testament Christians and those Christians who

---

[56] Myland, *The Latter Rain Covenant*, pp. 15–16, 107. However, the study of Scripture should not be equated with formal academic study of Scripture, see pp. 70–71.

[57] Myland, *The Latter Rain Covenant*, p. 32.

[58] Myland, *The Latter Rain Covenant*, p. 1.

[59] Myland, *The Latter Rain Covenant*, p. 48. Myland utilized this typological interpretive approach throughout the whole book.

were authentically saved and sanctified). Thus typology played a significant role in reapplying Scripture to the Christian community.[60]

Typological interpretation can be found in most Pentecostal literature, but their typological understanding will correspond to their theological positions. Hence, the importance of the overarching interpretive role of the 'Latter Rain Story' and the theological grid of the Full Gospel message provided a firm interpretive lens for the fluid Pentecostal community and their reading of Scripture.

The actual weather pattern of early and latter rain upon the land of Israel paralleled the early and Latter Rains on the people of God. Myland wrote:

> The Latter Rain was once literally restored to Israel's land after the seventy years of captivity, but that rain largely ceased. God is bringing it back the second time to the land which he had shown by the reports from the weather bureau in Jerusalem ... The official record of rainfall which was not kept until 1860, divides the time into ten-year periods, and the facts are that forty-three per cent more rain fell between years 1890 and 1900 then fell from 1860 to 1870.

> Spiritually the Latter Rain is coming to the church of God at the same time it is coming literally upon the land, and it will never be taken away from her, but will be upon her to unite and empower her, to cause her to aid in God's last work for this dispensation, to bring about the unity of the body, the consummation of the age, and the catching away of the spiritual Israel, the bride of Christ.[61]

For the early Pentecostals, the early rain was the first Holy Spirit outpouring (Acts 2), and the Latter Rain came as a result of the restoration of the doctrine of Spirit baptism, which brought about the great

---

[60] Myland finds types in almost every Old Testament passage related to the 'Latter Rain'. For one example, see pp. 16–17, 22–23 where the promise of the Latter Rain is threefold and typologically understood according to the roles of the Trinity. See also Taylor, who wrote 'Doctor Seiss says, "There is a sacred significance in numbers"... Three represents the Trinity ... Four represents humanity. Seven is the union of three and four, hence it represents salvation ... [and] it also signifies dispensational fulness' (sic), p. 17.

[61] Myland, *The Latter Rain Covenant*, pp. 78–79. Myland included at the end of his book a copy of the rainfall charts issued by The American Colony, Jerusalem which offered verifiable proof for his claim (pp. 178–79).

Pentecostal revival. With the 'Latter Rain' outpouring, God was bringing to a close the Church age dispensation and thus preparing the people for the second coming of Christ. Myland wrote that 'the first Pentecost *started* the Church, the second Pentecost, *unites* and *perfects* the Church unto the coming of the Lord'.[62]

This 'early and Latter Rain' motif brought together the restoration of the charismatic gifts with the imminence of the second coming. Evangelist Mrs. T.M. Rist expressed it this way:

> I cannot describe the experience [her Pentecost] ... It was revealed to me that this 'Latter Rain' was getting people ready for the 'Marriage supper of the Lamb' ... I know Jesus is coming soon. He said, 'When the Bride begins to put on the wedding garments, it is not long until the wedding takes place.'[63]

The dispensational understanding of the 'Latter Rain' motif meant that this covenant of promise was the key to understanding God's involvement presently in human history. The dispensational or prophetic understanding allowed one to grasp and participate in God's great redemptive plan. In fact, the 'Latter Rain' motif placed the Pentecostals at the very center of God's redemptive plan and at the climax of human history.

The first generation of Pentecostals used dispensational terminology but did not interpret according to the Fundamentalists' dispensational rules. They were not cessationists, nor did they shy away from typological interpretive strategies, which the Fundamentalists argued was a form of spiritualizing the passage. In the Old Testament they found prefigurations of the Church. They also believed that the supernatural gifts and ministry gifts (apostles, prophets, teachers, evangelists and pastors) were for the contemporary Church and not just for the New Testament age. Their understanding of God's involvement within human history was that it was the same today as it was in Bible times. This was a different understanding than that of Fundamentalism or dispensationalism.[64] Furthermore, the Pentecostal 'prophetic' understanding of the 'Latter Rain' helped make sense of the

---

[62] Myland, *The Latter Rain Covenant*, pp. 84–85. Myland like many early Pentecostals was a pretribulational premillennialist, see pp. 109, 115–16.

[63] *The Apostolic Faith*, 1.3 (October 1906), p. 4.

[64] See chapter two of this study for an explanation of Fundamentalist Dispensationalism.

lack of spiritual gifts that occurred between the early Church and the present manifestations of the gifts. It was a result of the Church's disobedience and corruption.[65]

Myland argued that when the literal aspects of the 'Latter Rain covenant' (literal 'Latter Rains' were beginning to fall again on the Land of Israel, along with the returning of the literal Jews back to the land) and the spiritual aspect (God was pouring his Spirit out again upon the spiritual people) come together at the same time, you have the inauguration of the dispensational phase, which meant that the coming of Jesus was imminent.[66] Myland, like other Pentecostals, saw God working in history in a particular way. God works in circles, that is, he begins and ends the Gospel dispensation in a similar fashion.[67] They also expected that the 'Latter Rain' outpouring would be even greater than the 'Early Rain'.

Joel's prophecy played a key role in extending this literal promise of the early and 'Latter Rains' to the Christians, both first century and then at the turn of the century, while also emphasizing the immediate coming of Jesus.[68] According to Myland, Peter's quotation of Joel's prophecy 'particularly refers to the *beginning* and *end* of this Gospel

---

[65] Lawrence, *The Apostolic Faith Restored*, p. 15, wrote '*Professed believers may not allow God to do these things.* And here you have the real reason. "These signs shall follow them that believe." When men will not believe, signs have no one to follow'. The Pentecostals emphasized the condition of the covenant. This view was different from the Fundamentalist dispensationalist, who argued that the gifts had ceased with the apostles according to God's sovereign plan. The Pentecostals placed the blame upon the corruption of the Church, thus God removed his gifts, yet there always existed a remnant who had the gifts. Faupel, *The Everlasting Gospel*, p. 37, states that the early Pentecostals searched the earliest Church writings in order to

> discover evidence that New Testament Christianity was taught and experienced by a faithful remnant in every century. This 'evidence' was compiled into litanies which have been included in virtually every historical account of the movement ... The intent of these litanies was to demonstrate that a faithful remnant bore testimony to the fact that God had intended the Pentecostal emphasis to be normative in the Church.

[66] Myland, *The Latter Rain Covenant*, p. 107.

[67] The Pentecostal understanding of the gospel dispensation was significantly different from the cessationist dispensationalism of C.I. Scofield. The Scofieldian understanding of a dispensation was that God introduced a new law at the beginning of the dispensation and then ended the dispensation with divine judgment because humanity failed to keep the law.

[68] Myland, *The Latter Rain Covenant*, p. 80.

dispensation'.[69] In addition, Joel's prophecy, as used by Peter in Acts, enabled the Pentecostals to make a connection between the pouring out of the Spirit with the 'early and Latter Rain' motif. Hence they understood the great prophetic promise, 'I will pour out my Spirit' according to a triple-barrel understanding of the Latter Rain covenant. This meant literally on 'Israel' and typologically upon the 'Church' with signs and wonders and 'dispensationally to bring in the consummation of the ages and open the millennium'.[70] No wonder Myland saw the Latter Rain covenant as the most significant covenant for today, because the Latter Rain covenant was 'the basis and condition of all man's supply from God'.[71] Moreover, it was a sign that a new age was coming—the millennial reign of Christ.

The purpose of the 'Latter Rain' Pentecostal outpouring was to bring the true Church to perfection and unity, while empowering the individual Christian with supernatural power in order to be a witness in these last days.[72] Thus, Myland said, 'No matter how often you said, "saved, sanctified, and healed," you still need Pentecost'.[73] The Latter Rain outpouring was 'the fullness of the Spirit and the power of the Gospel of Christ restored'.[74]

The primary candidates for the Latter Rain outpouring were the financially poor and outcast of society. Myland wrote,

> 'Thou, O God, hast prepared of Thy goodness for the poor'… I don't know what the poor can do, the church has little use for them; but God sent this Latter Rain to gather up all the poor and outcast, and make us love everybody: feeble ones, base ones, those that have just been cast out of human society; no one wants them,

---

[69] Myland, *The Latter Rain Covenant*, p. 80. Myland also saw a literal and spiritual type in how Joel's prophecy was worked out in the beginning of the Church age—thus Acts traces four outpourings upon literal Jews and upon a Gentile group. Myland's modification of dispensationalism created irreconcilable tension, which he did not resolve.

[70] Myland, *The Latter Rain Covenant*, p. 87.

[71] Myland, *The Latter Rain Covenant*, p. 23.

[72] Myland, *The Latter Rain Covenant*, see pp. 29, 52, 88, 96, and 99.

[73] Myland, *The Latter Rain Covenant*, p. 61.

[74] Myland, *The Latter Rain Covenant*, p. 54.

all the outcasts of India and China; these are what God sent the Latter Rain people to pick up.[75]

The Pentecostals were marginalized people who heeded the call to empty themselves of 'self-love' and 'self-will' and embraced the 'Latter Rain' story, which was the restoration of the Gospel of Christ for the preparation and participation of the end time harvest.[76]

In sum, the 'Latter Rain' motif provided the Pentecostals with a persuasive apologetic account for the existence of their community. The 'Latter Rain' motif provided the basic structure for the Pentecostal story. The Pentecostal story brought together the Full Gospel message and extended the past biblical 'Latter Rain' covenant of promise into the present Pentecostal movement. The Pentecostals, then, understood themselves as the prophetically promised eschatological movement that would bring about the unity of Christianity and usher in the second coming of Christ.

Primitivistic Impulse

In this section, I will explain the influences that motivated Pentecostals to read Scripture in a restorationist manner. This is also directly related to the importance and priority of the biblical book of Acts when Scripture was harmonized. Their community concerns were important in causing the Pentecostals to ask specific questions whose answers had to be found in Scripture.

Mark Noll has stated that the typical attitude of nineteenth-century conservatives toward Scripture was that 'the Bible was a book to be studied *with* the history of the Church, not *against* it'.[77] Pentecostals knew that past Church history lacked a consistent attestation of the supernatural gifts operating throughout Christianity. Yet this did

---

[75] Myland, *The Latter Rain Covenant*, p. 53. See p. 84 where he argued that all who wanted to be used by God must become servants and handmaidens. See pp. 113–14 where he condemns the wealthy non-Christian and on p. 87 where he rebukes the Christian who has money. Myland proclaimed 'If the Lord should burst through the air with the sound of the trump and voice of the archangel, many who profess to believe these truths could not go up to meet him because they are bound down by bank stocks, bonds, and real estate—these are weights upon them.'

[76] Myland, *The Latter Rain Covenant*, p. 52. The Azusa Street revival was often compared to the humble surroundings of Christ's birth.

[77] Mark Noll, 'Primitivism in Fundamentalism and American Biblical Scholarship: A Response' in Richard T. Hughes (ed.), *The American Quest for the Primitive Church* (Urbana, IL: University of Illinois, 1988), p. 125.

not dissuade them, instead it reinforced the veracity of their claim. Pentecostals were convinced that they were simply returning to primitive Christianity, and that they had restored the Full Gospel; namely, 'the restoration of the faith once delivered unto the saints'.[78]

Pentecostal culture had wholeheartedly embraced the pronouncements made by the influential Wesleyan Holiness leader, John P. Brooks, who was the chief architect of 'Come-outism'. Brooks denounced all denominational churches as sects and declared that the true Church was to be found among the local holiness churches.[79] Brooks was convinced that the true Church was made up of visible, local congregations, whose members were all 'regenerated' and 'going on to perfection'. He rejected hierarchical ecclesiastical governmental structure and argued that local churches were to be independent and governed by local elders and deacons who were called by Christ from among the congregation.

Brooks made some important arguments that were echoed throughout early Pentecostal literature and reflected the mindset of those who circulated among the Holiness groups. Brooks believed that the New Testament contained all the necessary information for Christian belief and polity. He was also convinced that the sanctified Christian lifestyle rooted in love would eradicate all selfish and sinful interests, which created sectarianism, denominationalism and creeds. The power of the Holy Spirit enabled one to live a sanctified life and this would allow for true unity among all Christians.

He argued that the whole 'New Testament' was 'the statute book of the Church'. Thus, no new polity was needed, only a return to the God-inspired account.[80] The Reformation brought about a restoration of doctrine, but failed to recover 'the primitive polity and order of the Church which had been hidden, since the creation of hierarchy, in the oblivion of centuries'.[81] Brooks advocated that the real

---

[78] Lawrence, *The Apostolic Faith Restored*, p. 12.

[79] John P. Brooks, *The Divine Church* (Columbia, MO: Herald Publishing House, 1891), p. 283. Brooks was convinced that authentic salvation with a desire to pursue holiness and that a return to the New Testament doctrine and polity was all that was needed to bring unity and perfection among all true Christians. The Pentecostals believed that unity and perfection would be the result of the Pentecostal outpouring.

[80] Brooks, *The Divine Church*, pp. 26–28.

[81] Brooks, *The Divine Church*, p. 39.

Christians must withdraw from all forms of organized Christianity and band together in local congregations in order to form the authentic Church. The authentic Church must be patterned after the true Church as revealed in the New Testament. The primitive Church of Scripture was intended by God to be 'permanent and perpetual'. He stated:

> It [the Church of the New Covenant] must continue the same, in oneness of faith, of order, of sacraments, of polity, till Christ should come again. These must abide unchanged, to preserve the identity of the Church. To change the one faith of the Church, or its order, or its sacraments, or its polity would be an innovation on its constitution, and it would no longer be the Church that Christ founded.[82]

Brooks was a 'primitivist'.[83] Like all primitivists, he desired to return to the pure Church of the New Testament. The present Church was perverted and apostate. Like other restorationists, he had to transcend at least eighteen hundred years of Christian history in order discover the pure, authentic, primitive or true Church. The Wesleyan Holiness traditions resonate with primitivistic concepts of the Church.[84]

Primitivists were keenly aware of the differences between the primitive Church of Scripture and the Church of history. Brooks simply argued that the great 'dissimilarity' was due to the apostasy of the patristic Church, which was epitomized by the Roman Catholic Church. It was seen as the mother of all sectarian churches that had fallen into complete apostasy through the Emperor Constantine. As a result, 'the true Church dropped out of sight, and what remained was apostate ecclesiasticism'.[85] The true Church began to resurface again

---

[82] Brooks, *The Divine Church*, p. 17.

[83] Richard T. Hughes states that 'the common thread that bound all primitivists together was a mutual striving to live and move in a perfect Church, patterned after an apostolic model' ('Christian Primitivism as Perfectionism: From Anabaptists to Pentecostals' in Stanley Burgess (ed.), *Reaching Beyond: Chapters in the History of Perfectionism* [Peabody, MA: Hendrickson Publishers, 1986], pp. 214–15).

[84] See Steven L. Ware, 'Restoring the New Testament Church: Varieties of Restorationism in the Radical Holiness Movement of the Late Nineteenth and Early Twentieth Centuries', *Pneuma* 21.2 (Fall 1999), pp. 238–47.

[85] Brooks, *The Divine Church*, pp. 219, 225.

as a result of the Reformation and could clearly be seen among the independent holiness churches.

Brooks argued that the apostasy of the early Church caused the cessation of divine miracles. He did not believe that God desired to have the miracles cease with the death of the Apostles. He argued instead that the divine power of God will be manifested within the true Church and that one should not expect to see miracles in the apostate Church. Since the Church had become the 'apostate church', the divine approval of God was withdrawn from it, but not permanently. Thus, one should not expect to find miracles in the 'apostate church', but one should find miracles in the true Church.

> The truth is that the marks of supernaturalism with which the church was originally clothed were intended to abide with it, and to accredit its doctrine as Divine, just as Christ's own doctrine was accredited as Divine; because as already observed, the ministry of the church was to be a continuation of the ministry of Christ, and in his design, no doubt, was to be accompanied with the same phenomena of supernaturalism that verified his own ministry ... And as in the future that Church (the true Church) shall more and more emerge into notice from amidst the confusions and carnalities of sectarian Christendom, it cannot be doubted that there will be a reassertion of all the original gifts of which it was in the beginning made the possessor by its divine Lord, the gift of miracle included.[86]

Brooks (like other prominent non-cessationist holiness/Keswick proponents—notably A.B. Simpson) was providing the Pentecostals with a powerful argument for the acceptance and validity of their movement. The manifestation of the gifts among the Pentecostals should be understood as a divine sign of the movement's legitimacy. The Pentecostals claimed that their movement ushered in the 'Latter Rain' era, which the Holiness/Keswick movements were anticipating. Hence, the 'Latter Rain' narrative became the Pentecostals' story, as the following quotation from Lawrence testifies:

> The honest-hearted thinking men and women of this great movement, have made it their endeavor to return to the faith and

---

[86] Brooks, *The Divine Church*, p. 21.

practice of our brethren who serve God prior to the apostasy. They have made the New Testament their rule of life. This effort, which is so general throughout the movement, has had a particular effect upon those who were exercised thereby ... The Pentecostal movement has no such history; it leaps the intervening years crying, '*Back to Pentecost*'. In the minds of these honest-hearted, thinking men and women, this work of God is immediately connected with the work of God in the New Testament days. Built by the same hand, upon the same foundation of the apostles and prophets, after the same pattern, according to the same covenant, they too are a habitation of God through the Spirit. They do not recognize a doctrine or custom as authoritative unless it can be traced to that primal source of church instructions, the Lord and his apostles.[87]

Hence the validity of the Pentecostal interpretation of Scripture, from their perspective, was not only biblically supported but it was also experientially demonstrated. God was confirming to the world that the Pentecostal Christians were the pure churches because they had the testimony of miracles.

The Apostolic Faith, under the bold heading, 'The Promised Latter Rain Now Being Poured Out on God's Humble People', stated:

All along the ages men have been preaching a partial Gospel. A part of the Gospel remained when the world went into the dark ages. God has from time to time raised up men to bring back the truth to the church. He raised up Luther to bring back to the world the doctrine of justification by faith. He raised up another reformer in John Wesley to establish Bible holiness in the church. Then he raised up Dr. Cullis who brought back the wonderful doctrine of divine healing. Now He is bringing back the Pentecostal Baptism to the church.[88]

The focal point of the 'Latter Rain' was the 'restoration of the Gospel' but the primary character of the story was Jesus. The doctrines

---

[87] Lawrence, *The Apostolic Faith Restored*, pp. 11–12.
[88] *Apostolic Faith*, 1.2 (October 1906), p. 1, lead article). See also D. William Faupel, *The Everlasting Gospel*, p. 38, n. 52, who argues that this pattern is found repeatedly in Pentecostal literature and presents a partial listing.

being restored, the five or four–fold Gospel, all have to do with one's relational understanding of the work of Jesus.

In sum, the Pentecostals, who had been shaped by the Christian culture of 'Come-outism', read Scripture without the need to appeal to the development of tradition. The unadulterated Christian history was recorded in the Book of the Acts of the Apostles, so there was little need to trace a historical account of the supernatural gifts being active throughout Church history. They, however, needed to present a plausible reason for the lack of the supernatural manifestations. They simply adopted and re-presented an already acceptable solution. The gifts had generally ceased due to the great apostasy; however, they would return to those holiness Christian communities that sought the empowerment of the Holy Spirit.[89] This understanding was woven into the 'Latter Rain' motif and helped to create the Pentecostal story.

Mark Noll writes, 'when studying biblical primitivism, it does seem important to ask which part of the Bible functions as the standard, for it is rarely the entire text'.[90] For Pentecostals, the standard was the book of Acts. The Pentecostals read the Bible as though they were the Roman god Janus, seeing frontward and backward simultaneously. They read the Old Testament through Acts and read the New Testament through Acts. Therefore, Acts served as their beginning and ending point. Donald Dayton's comment correctly captures this reality concerning Pentecostals. He notes that they read Scripture 'through Lukan eyes especially with the lens of Acts'.[91]

Acts was the authentically inspired historical record of the 'primitive church'. The Pentecostals compared their contemporary Christianity with the original 'Apostolic' pattern in Acts, and found contemporary Christianity lacking in both power and purity. They sought to continue the restoration of doctrine and practice started by the Pro-

---

[89] Richard Hughes aptly explains the primitivistic quest of the Pentecostals. '[T]he Holiness tradition emphasized an *ethical primitivism*, concerned with a sanctified way of life, the Pentecostals sought an *experiential primitivism* directed toward recovery of the apostolic gifts of the Spirit, especially glossolalia and healing. Indeed, Pentecostals sought nothing less than a restoration of the Jerusalem Pentecost' ('Christian Primitivism as Perfectionism: From Anabaptists to Pentecostals', p. 243).

[90] Noll, 'Primitivism in Fundamentalism and American Biblical Scholarship: A Response' in *The American Quest for the Primitive Church*, p. 121.

[91] Dayton, *Theological Roots of Pentecostalism*, p. 23.

testant Reformers. The Pentecostals, unlike the protestant Reformers but similar to the Holiness folk, sought for the restoration of miracles. The Pentecostals, along with the Wesleyan Holiness community, embraced the book of Acts as the normative expression of authentic Christianity. The Pentecostals began and ended their Bible Reading Method with the Book of Acts. Thus, the harmonization of Scripture was always from a primitivist impulse with Acts in view. This is the way they preferred to use the very words and phrases of Acts.[92]

The Pentecostal Story as the Central Narrative Convictions of the Community

The purpose of this section is to identify the Central Narrative Convictions of the first generation of Pentecostals.[93] By Central Narrative Convictions (hereafter identified as CNCs), I mean the primary story used to explain why the Pentecostal community existed, who they were as a community, how they fit into the larger scheme of Christian history and what responsibilities should be bear. The CNCs shaded perceptions that colored and made meaningful the reading of Scripture as well as experienced reality. These convictions are more than a rational cognitive grid which can be taken off or laid aside. The CNCs cannot be reduced to presuppositions or preunderstandings. The CNCs may be modified or changed, but cannot be set aside.

---

[92] Donald Dayton, 'Asa Mahan and The Development of American Holiness Theology', *The Wesleyan Theological Journal* 9 (Spring, 1974), pp. 60–69, shows how the Book of Acts became very important in the latter period of the holiness movements. This was due to the influence of Asa Mahan, especially his book titled 'The baptism of the Holy Spirit' which signaled an important shift in the language and theological emphasis of this time.

[93] For a helpful discussion concerning 'Foundational Narrative Convictions' as they relate to hermeneutical communities see Douglas Jacobsen's 'Pentecostal Hermeneutics in Comparative Perspective', a paper presented to the Annual Meeting of the Society for Pentecostal Studies, March 13–15, 1997 (Oakland, CA) and Kenneth J. Archer's 'Pentecostal Response' to Jacobsen's paper also presented at the SPS meeting in Oakland. The central thrust of his argument is that Christian communities will have different FNCs, which describe 'who they are as a community and where they fit in [the] larger scheme of Christian and human history'. These FNCs serve to explain why the group exists, who they are as a community and what responsibilities they should perform. This writer has modified his term FNCs to Central Narrative Conviction, while retaining the basic concept.

Every Christian tradition has CNCs that shape, influence, and at some points, determine the 'meaning' of the biblical interpretation.

Douglas Jacobsen hints at this dialectical interactive epistemological process of the interpreter rooted in a hermeneutical community and the reading of Scripture. He writes:

> our communally different readings of the Bible have largely been derived from the text [Scripture]. Our different experiences have shaped the way we see the text and situate the text in relation to ourselves and the world, but our readings of the Bible have also helped form those very experiences, helped form our foundational views of life.[94]

Central Narrative Convictions function in a similar manner within the community's worldview.[95] The CNCs operate within the socio-cultural Pentecostal 'worldview' and hold its central assumptions and beliefs in a coherent and cohesive story. The CNCs were and are the primary filter used to sift the Scriptures for meaning. Furthermore, the Pentecostal story is the hermeneutical matrix in which meaning is produced.

J. Richard Middleton and Brian Walsh suggest that 'worldviews give faith answers to a set of ultimate grounding questions'.[96] They argue that such questions could be framed as:

> (1) *Where are we?* or What is the nature of the reality in which we find ourselves? (2) *Who are we?* or What is the nature and task of human beings? (3) *What's wrong?* or How do we understand and

---

[94] Jacobsen, 'Pentecostal Hermeneutics in Comparative Perspective', p. 5. Jacobsen lists and briefly describes 10 distinguishable elements that he believes apply to all Biblical hermeneuts. They are: Experience, Inherited Interpretive Schemes, Intuition, Systematic Analysis, Communal Corroboration, Reader-Response 'Expansion' of the Text, Ritual Response, Desired Result, Academic Analysis and a Second Naïveté (see pp. 2–4, for a fuller discussion). Hermeneutics is much more then adopting a certain exegetical approach.

[95] Charles Kraft, *Anthropology for Christian Witness* (Maryknoll, NY: Orbis Books, 1996), p. 52. Kraft defines a worldview as 'the culturally structured assumptions, and commitments/allegiances underlining a people's perception of reality and their response to those perceptions'.

[96] J. Richard Middleton and Brian Walsh, *The Transforming Vision: Shaping A Christian World View* (Downers Grove, IL: InterVarsity Press, 1984), ch. 2.

account for the evil and brokenness? (4) *What's the remedy?* or How do we find a path through our brokenness to wholeness?[97]

The CNCs of the Pentecostals perform a similar function. The CNCs also serve as the Pentecostal version of Christianity. Hence, by identifying the CNCs, I expose the Pentecostal cultural worldview and simultaneously recognize the important contribution of the social location of the reader and *her* community in the hermeneutical process.[98] Hermeneutics is concerned with the historical horizon of the Scripture, but it is also concerned with the equally challenging horizon of the contemporary reader.

As I have already demonstrated, the first generation of Pentecostals interpreted Scripture with similar methods used by both the noncessationist Holiness community and to some extent the cessationist dispensational fundamentalist community. Pentecostals used typology, inductive reasoning and even dispensational schemes. Yet, what distinguished the early Pentecostal hermeneutic from their Holiness sisters was the *distinct narrative* that held these similar methods together. This distinct story encouraged them to interpret Scripture from a new angle: they were the marginalized people of the 'Latter Rain'.

The 'Latter Rain' motif provided the early Pentecostals with an experiential conceptual framework. It also enabled them to offer a persuasive explanation for their movement. It provided the hermeneutical lens for the interpretation of Scripture and their present experience of reality.

> The early rain came at Pentecost, and immediately the seed which Jesus and His disciples had sown sprang up. This early rain continued for more than a hundred years, during which time the Church was kept inundated with mighty floods of salvation. But

---

[97] J. Richard Middleton and Brian Walsh, *Truth Is Stranger Than It Used To Be: Biblical Faith In A Postmodern Age* (Downers Grove, IL: InterVarsity Press, 1995), p. 11.

[98] I am purposefully using 'her' in order to remind the reader that it was a woman who first spoke in tongues at Parham's Bible school in Topeka Kansas and that women played a significant role in carrying the Pentecostal message throughout the world. Also, it was black sanctified women who made significant contributions to the Azusa Street revival and Pentecostalism in general, see Cheryl J. Sanders, *Saints In Exile: The Holiness-Pentecostal Experience in African American Religion and Culture* (New York: Oxford University Press, 1996).

when the Church became popular and was formed into a great hierarchy, the long drought began, interspersed with a local shower of gracious revival now and then through the middle ages. Under the reformations, the Latter Rain began to be foreshadowed. The holiness revivals which have been going on in our land for the last few years are the preliminary showers of this rain. They have been glorious and wonderful: so much so that many have taken them for the Latter Rain itself. But we know that these revivals, though gracious, have fallen short of the apostolic revivals—the early rain. The Scriptures seem to teach that the Latter Rain is to be far greater than the former … The early rain began on the Day of Pentecost, and the first manifestation was speaking with other tongues as the Spirit gave utterance, and then followed the healing of the sick, casting out devils, etc. So it would only be natural that the Latter Rain Pentecost should be repeated and followed by the same manifestation. It seems [the Latter Rain] to have its starting point in the year 1906 in Los Angeles, Cal.[99]

The Pentecostal story was transmitted orally and by publications. Taylor's explanation of the 'Latter Rain' is typical and can represent the traditional Pentecostal understanding of the 'Latter Rain', which serves also as the CNCs of the Pentecostal community.

The Pentecostal CNCs have three key transitional points. In the beginning, God poured his Spirit out on a saved and sanctified Christian community with the biblical sign of speaking in tongues (Acts 2). The Church started out pure and unified. However, after the death of the Apostles, the early Church would become the apostate Church. This was a result of wandering from the truth and practice of Jesus and the Apostles. The second transitional point was the complete apostasy that came when the Church embraced the Roman Empire with the conversion of Constantine. The result was that God withdrew his Spirit from the apostate *hierarchical* Roman Church. This was viewed as the beginning of the Dark Ages. During the long drought of the Middle Ages, however, God always had a faithful *'persecuted'* remnant. The Reformers, through John Wesley, brought the middle section of the story to a close and prepared the Church for the Latter Rain. The 'Latter Rain' outpouring or Pentecostal outpouring was the

---

[99] Taylor, *The Spirit and the Bride*, pp. 90–91.

beginning of the end of the all-encompassing story. Jesus was coming very soon—before this generation would die. Only the ones who were 'Baptized in the Holy Ghost' with the biblical evidence of *tongues* and *divine love* would escape the great day of judgment coming upon the world. Thus, one needed to experience Pentecost in order to be included among the 'sealed bride of Jesus'.

The Pentecostal story was a teleological reading—bringing the beginning and end of the Church age together. This enabled Pentecostals to eclipse modernity and return to a pre-modern era where the supernatural was normal rather than abnormal. The Pentecostal story brought together the restoration of charismatic gifts with the imminence of the second coming of Jesus. This narrative was central to Pentecostal identity and spirituality and not only served as the primary filter through which Scripture was sifted for meaning, but it also was used to interpret their experience of reality and their understanding of Church history. Therefore, the interpretive methods employed by Pentecostals were subservient to their story from which the interpretation of Scripture took place.

A spider's web makes for a good analogy and may present a better picture of how the CNCs hold together as a cohesive interpretive narrative. At the center of the web is Jesus, with emphasis placed upon the restoration of the supernatural gifts to the pure Church. Coming out of the center of the web are five stabilizing theological strands identified as the Five-fold Gospel or the Full Gospel. The outer circumference of the web is the 'Latter Rain' story, which was the common frame of reference of early Pentecostalism. Woven into this web are testimonies, experiences, and scriptural passages, all of which serve to strengthen the whole web (which are the CNCs).[100]

When Pentecostals read Scripture, they did so from within their cultural worldview. They read Scripture as the marginalized people of the 'Latter Rain'. At the center of the story stood Jesus. Their Jesus was the God-human messiah. Jesus was a mighty miracle worker because he was a holy man empowered by the Holy Spirit, not necessarily because he was God. The Five-fold Gospel, then, was the experientially and relationally understood extension of one's participatory salvific relationship with the living God. The Pentecostal salvific rela-

---

[100] See Faupel, *The Everlasting Gospel* ch. 2, for a thorough overview of the early Pentecostal message.

tionship with Jesus was the controlling theological center, not the doctrine of Trinity. Thus, the 'Latter Rain' motif was concerned about the restoration of the Full Gospel message and reinforced the significance of the signs and wonders within the Pentecostal community. Hence, the Pentecostals were concerned to be like the past 'apostolic Christians' and behave as the present 'eschatological bride of Christ'.

This narrated hermeneutical approach had a cohesive theological structure and centered upon the restorative dramatic Pentecostal story of God. The Pentecostal story contributed to and placed constraints upon their interpretive creativity. Hence, some Pentecostals were Oneness but most remained Trinitarian; some were finished work while others held to a third blessing. Importantly, all embraced the Pentecostal story. Their various theological differences, no doubt, added a distinct accent to the general Pentecostal story, but it did not substantially change the structure of their story. They were the marginalized people of the Latter Rain.

Pentecostals and Their Oral-Aural Relationship with Scripture

Pentecostals love their Bible. Biblical themes, stories, and significant biblical numbers (3, 7, 12, 40) permeated Pentecostal literature. More importantly, these things saturate Pentecostal oral testimonies. In their narrated testimonies, one can clearly hear echoes of biblical stories, themes, and phrases. Pentecostals assimilated scriptural stories, verses and concepts into their interpretation of reality.

Pentecostals had an intuitive ability to grasp narrative features of the Bible, such as repetitive themes, aspects of narrated time, plot development, and characterization. Pentecostals were comfortable with narrative. This was due to their primary reliance upon oral means of communication.[101]

---

[101] Hollenweger argues that the narrativity and orality of early Pentecostalism comes from the African-American contribution to Pentecostalism. See his 'After Twenty Years' Research on Pentecostalism', *International Review of Mission* 75 (January 1986), pp. 3–12. This writer would also suggest that it also has to do with Pentecostalism's connection to the cultural conditions of living in the southern mountainous regions.

According to Hollenweger, the early Pentecostal oral means of communication involves the following:

> Orality of liturgy; narrative theology and witness; maximum participation at levels of reflection, prayer, and decision making, and therefore a reconciliatory form of community; inclusion of dreams and visions into personal and public forms of worship that function as a kind of 'oral icon' for the individual and the community; an understanding of the body-mind relationship that is informed by experiences of correspondence between body and mind as, for example, in liturgical dance and prayer for the sick.[102]

In fact, Hollenweger goes on to say that 'the Pentecostal poor are oral nonconceptual peoples who are often masters of story. Their religion resembles more that of early disciples than religion taught in our schools and universities.'[103]

Deborah McCauley's important work reinforces Hollenweger's emphasis on the primacy of oral communication.[104] McCauley's book fills a gaping hole in American Christian history because it deals with 'Mountain Religion'—a group often overlooked because it is an oral culture.[105] McCauley's work touches on various Christian traditions in Appalachian America and so deals with Pentecostalism. Why is this important? Because Pentecostalism's roots are entrenched both in the slave Christianity of the South and in the Appalachian mountainous regions of the United States. Furthermore, all the major early Pentecostal denominations have their headquarters in the Appalachian and Ozark regions.[106]

---

[102] W. Hollenweger, 'The Pentecostal Elites and the Pentecostal Poor: A Missed Dialogue?' in Karla Poewe (ed.), *Charismatic Christianity as a Global Culture* (Columbia, SC: University of South Carolina, 1994), p. 201.

[103] Hollenweger, 'The Pentecostal Elites and the Pentecostal Poor: A Missed Dialogue?', p. 213. The first generation would be included in his understanding of the 'poor' which he contrasts with the contemporary elite Pentecostals. The Elites are those who are 'literary conceptual peoples who pride themselves on speaking the language of science and technology' (p. 213).

[104] Deborah McCauley, *Appalachian Mountain Religion: A History* (Urbana and Chicago: University of Illinois Press, 1995).

[105] McCauley, *Appalachian Mountain Religion*, p. 195.

[106] McCauley, *Appalachian Mountain Religion*, see pp. 481–82 n. 38. For an explanation of the interaction of Holiness Pentecostal intermixing with mountain Christian religious culture, see p. 273.

McCauley explains that most Christian mountainous people know the Bible primarily as oral literature and they know it very well, even if they cannot read (and this would include Pentecostals).[107] They prefer the narratives of Scripture (the stories of the Old Testament, Gospels and Acts) to the Law of the Old Testament and the Epistles of the New Testament. They interpret the Bible 'more concretely, more midrashic, allowing texts to interpret each other, following the lead of text by listening deep within to its own embedded literary structure [which is possible only through a comprehensive oral memory of the Bible]'.[108] Early Pentecostals were keenly acquainted with the KJV Bible and interpreted their Bibles in a similar fashion.

Pentecostals interpreted their contemporary events through the stories of Scripture; their testimonies echoed and were patterned after biblical stories. Yet they also interpreted Scripture through their life experiences. From modernity's perspective, Pentecostals constantly blurred the exegetical boundaries of what the text meant to its original readers and what the text meant to contemporary readers.

Topeka Kansas Outpouring

Parham wrote an account (which became ch. 7 of *Selected Sermons*) about the first outpouring of the baptism of the Holy Spirit at his Bethel 'Bible School' in Topeka, Kansas. The chapter was entitled 'The Latter Rain'.[109] His retelling of the Pentecostal outpouring not only replicates the first biblical account found in Acts 2, but it also included significant numbers repeated throughout biblical narrative, such as 3, 12 and 40.

Parham's communal Bible School opened in October 1900.[110] He wrote that he gave his '40' students an assignment prior to leaving on

---

[107] McCauley, *Appalachian Mountain Religion*, pp. 61–62, 76. McCauley finds that the Christian folk who desire to learn to read do so in order to read the Bible (see p. 167). As a result of being primarily illiterate, they have 'highly developed listening skills ... compensating extremely well for whatever lapses in literacy ...' (p. 382).

[108] McCauley, *Appalachian Mountain Religion*, pp. 76–77. She contrasts this with 'clergy' of Evangelical Fundamentalism who prefer the legal portions and the epistles as they present a tightly structured blueprint for living. Mountainous preachers live with ambiguity and contradiction.

[109] Robert L. Parham, compiler, *Selected Sermons of the Late Charles F. Parham, Sarah E. Parham: Co-Founders of the Original Apostolic Faith Movement* (Baxter Springs, KS: np, 1941).

[110] For a critical historical presentation of this phase of Parham's ministry see James R. Goff, Jr., *Fields White Unto Harvest: Charles F. Parham and the Missionary Ori-*

a 'three day' preaching trip to Kansas City. The assignment, in his words, was to 'set the students at work studying out diligently what was the Bible evidence of the Baptism of the Holy Ghost'.[111] Parham returned on the third day, to find the students 'united' in their conclusion 'that the indisputable proof on each occasion was, that they spake with other tongues'. He had the entire school community (about 75) gather for the watch night prayer service on New Year's Eve. Only one student received the baptism of the Holy Spirit. Agnes Ozman (LaBerge) received the baptism after Parham laid hands on her and prayed in 'the Name of Jesus'. Parham wrote, 'a halo seemed to surround her head and face and she began speaking in the Chinese language and was unable to speak English for three days'.[112] Even more astonishing was that she could not even write in English during this time, only Chinese. Parham kept this piece of writing as tangible evidence of the miracle. Just three months after the school opened and on the dawn of the new millennium, God poured out his Spirit upon a group of people who were living communally, united in their faith and practice, and praying in the designated 'upper room' of the school. The 'Latter Rain' began to fall.

Parham and 'twelve' ministers all from 'different' denominations, would receive their baptism on January 3rd 1901, 3 days after Agnes Ozman and after three days of prayer-filled tarrying. Not only did the twelve ministers speak in tongues 'in at least six different languages', but also an elderly saint testified that she saw 'tongues of fire … sitting upon their heads'. Parham's baptism followed but only after he was willing to submit to God's will for his life (an important and recurring theme in early Pentecostal testimonial literature). Parham

---

gins of Pentecostalism (Fayetteville: University of Arkansas Press, 1988), ch. 3, entitled 'The Gospel of the Latter Rain'.

[111] *Selected Sermons*, p. 76. Parham wrote that prior to the Topeka outpouring, he had always believed 'a missionary should be able to preach in the language of the natives' (p. 75). Parham may have come to this conclusion from his reading of the conservative biblical commentator, Adam Clarke, because Parham cited Clarke as saying 'They will speak in a language with which they are not formerly familiar' as a supporter of his idea (p. 70).

[112] *Selected Sermons*, pp. 76–77. There is a bit of confusion concerning the exact time Agnes Ozman spoke in tongues. According to this account it would appear to have happened on New Year's Eve, but immediately following Parham's account there is a picture of the Bethel Bible School with this caption, 'Where the baptism of the holy Ghost first fell January 1st, 1901, in this Latter Rain' (p. 81).

wrote, 'He [God] made it clear to me that He raised me up and trained me to declare this mighty truth to the world, and if I was willing to stand for it, with all the persecutions, hardships and trials, slander, scandal that it would entail, He would give me the blessing'. Parham received his blessing that day and spoke in various languages throughout the night.[113]

Parham's narration of the Topeka, Kansas outpouring contained identical parallels to the biblical account in Acts. He highlighted the importance of unity even with different denominations being represented. He stated that 'a mighty spiritual power filled the entire school'.[114] All of them were praying in an 'upper room' as they awaited the baptism. They spoke in languages unlearned to them, yet according to Parham, these were real foreign languages which were verified by 'reporters' who were supposedly 'professors of languages'. Parham stated that the phenomenon attracted 'Government officials' who came to investigate all the noise.[115] There appeared to some 'tongues of fire' dancing above their heads. For Parham, this experience was none other 'then the restoration of Pentecostal power',[116] and he was 'convinced' that 'he personally stood at the center of the Creator's plan for eschatological salvation'.[117] He articulated this event as the 'restoration' of Pentecost and himself as the founder and spiritual leader of the movement.[118]

The Azusa Street Revival

The Azusa Street Revival serves as another example of how Pentecostals incorporated scriptural themes and stories into their testimonies and explanations of the significance of their experienced events. The Azusa Street Revival has often been compared to the humble origins and birth of none other than Jesus of Nazareth.

---

[113] *Selected Sermons*, p. 78.

[114] *Selected Sermons*, p. 78.

[115] Parham wrote that these investigators 'all agree that the students of the college were speaking languages of the world, and that with proper accent and intonation' (p. 79).

[116] *Selected Sermons*, p. 78.

[117] Goff, *Fields White unto Harvest*, p. 166.

[118] It is hard to miss the significance that there were 12 ministers (in similarity to the 12 apostles) of which he was the leader of the 'real' or 'original' Apostolic Faith movement. Parham rejected the Azusa Street Revival and later Pentecostal movements that were not under his leadership.

When Christ was born, it was in a barn at Bethlehem; and when He began sending the 'Latter Rain' about two years ago, the outpouring of the Holy Spirit, it was in a barn in Los Angeles; for the old Mission is like a barn in its humility and plainness.[119]

Frank Bartleman, an eyewitness and participant at the Azusa Street Revival emphasized the humbleness of the mission in his accounts of the Revival.[120] He argued that all the great movements of God require a people who are humble and repentant. He illustrated this point by writing that the Reformation began by Martin Luther 'in a tumbled down building'.[121] Why? Because God willed his glory to be restored in 'the humblest surroundings'. The Azusa Mission was a perfect place for God to choose to pour out his Spirit because it was 'outside ecclesiastical establishments' and was a 'humble "stable"'.[122] One Methodist layman rejoiced in the humbleness of the Azusa Mission and the wisdom of God for not starting the revival in a church building. He stated,

> I bless God that it did not start in any church in this city, but in a barn, so that we might all come and take part in it. If it had started in a fine church, poor colored people and Spanish people would have not got it, but praise God it started here.[123]

Humility, persecution and God's preference for the poor were important biblical themes that Pentecostals could easily identify. Their marginal status contributed to their attentive reading of 'marginal and humble voices' embedded in Scripture, which were ignored by mainline and academic readings of that time.

Pentecostals found biblical parallels with their life experiences and would incorporate these into their testimonies. This reinforced the Pentecostal story. Hence, Pentecostals did not see a difference be-

---

[119] 'From Azusa Mission', *The Apostolic Faith* 1.12 (January, 1908), p. 1, col. 3.

[120] Frank Bartleman, forward by Vinson Synan, *Azusa Street* (S. Plainfield, NJ: Bridge Publishing, 1980). This is a complete and unabridged reprint of Frank Bartleman's 1925 history entitled, *How "Pentecost" Came to Los Angeles—How it was in the Beginning*.

[121] Bartleman, *Azusa Street*, p. 43.

[122] Bartleman, *Azusa Street*, p. 43.

[123] 'Bible Pentecost', *The Apostolic Faith*, 1.3 (November, 1906), p. 1, col. 1. The Azusa street mission was located at 312 Azusa Street in Los Angeles and the building was formerly an African Methodist Episcopal Church building. Prior to it becoming the Azusa Mission it was used as a stable.

tween how God worked in biblical times and how God worked in the present. In addition, they did not recognize any difference in perceived reality due to the changing of time or culture. People have always had similar experiences. Thus, they saw their experiences as similar to those of Bible times. This outlook reiterated the easy accessibility and immediacy of the meaning of Scripture for their Pentecostal community.

Early Pentecostals did not place the emphasis on explaining the historical context of Scripture, nor were they concerned with the author's original intention. They used Scripture in such a way as to allow for slippage between what it meant and what it means. They read the Bible as the Word of God and attempted to understand it presently. The horizons of past and present were fused, or from a critical perspective, confused.

The interpretation of Scripture without any concern for the historical distance allowed Pentecostal preachers to emphasize the immediate meaning of Scripture for their communities. Joseph Byrd, after researching the first decade of Pentecostal preaching, draws the following four descriptive conclusions about Pentecostal sermons:

1. Preaching was spontaneous and *not* relegated to professional clergy.

2. Preaching participated in the overall trajectory of worship services, and it was *not* necessarily the climax of the service.

3. The *congregation participated* in the sermon in terms of responding, but the sermon also allowed for participation of the congregation more fully in the 'altar call'.

4. The sermon reached for an *immediate experience* for the listeners and was not characterized by a hermeneutic that spent its time exegeting a text in a historical-critical manner. Put simply, the preacher focused on the immediate meaning of a text and not upon what a text meant [emphasis added].[124]

The Holy Scripture, for early Pentecostals, was not viewed as a past 'static deposit of truth' but as the present and 'primary source book for living the Pentecostal life'. The Pentecostal expected all the supernatural manifestations of the Scriptures to be realized during the

---

[124] Joseph Byrd, 'Paul Ricoeur's Hermeneutical Theory and Pentecostal Proclamation', *Pneuma* 15.2 (Fall 1993), pp. 204–205.

present era.[125] This 're-experiencing' of the biblical text was further emphasized in the worship service by testimonies. These testimonies offered by laity provided evidence that God was continuing to work miracles in the present. The testimony not only served to provide evidence of God's miraculous power, but it also aided in the process of interpreting Scripture. The testimonies presented by the community helped shape the understanding of those who were attending the worship service. Therefore, the Pentecostal community participated in the hermeneutical process.[126]

Pentecostal denominations (such as the Assemblies of God) readily accepted the Fundamentalist-dispensational hermeneutic with some important modifications.[127] Some have argued that this is a sign of the Pentecostals' desire to find acceptance by the Fundamentalists.[128] Yet others argue that this adoption was a result of the Pentecostal self-identity as God's eschatological community.[129] The integration of a Pentecostal reading with a Fundamentalist dispensational hermeneutic has been complicated. Pentecostals who used a dispensational interpretive method had to modify it in order to preserve their emphasis upon the miraculous in this church age.[130] As Gerald Sheppard points out, those Pentecostals who used dispensationalism violated its hermeneutical rules. A Pentecostal would read 'both the Old Testament and the Gospels as a literal address to the Christian Church and to the contemporary arena in which Pentecostals did their theology'.[131] The dispensational cessationist hermeneutic of popularistic premillennial Fundamentalism would be recast into the narrative of the 'Latter Rain'.

---

[125] Arrington, 'Hermeneutics' in *DPCM*, p. 383.

[126] G. Wacker, 'The Functions of Faith', *Harvard Theological Review* 77 (1984), p. 362, writes that the Pentecostal movement was 'profoundly communal' and that testimonies could take up thirty minutes of a service.

[127] Arrington, 'Dispensationalism' in *DPCM*, pp. 247–48.

[128] Gerald T. Sheppard, 'Word and Spirit: Scripture in the Pentecostal Tradition, Part II', *Agora* (Summer 1978), p. 5.

[129] Arrington, 'Hermeneutics', p. 385.

[130] Sheppard, 'Word and Spirit', pp. 5–33.

[131] Sheppard, 'Word and Spirit', p. 16. See also his 'Pentecostals and the Hermeneutics of Dispensationalism: The Anatomy of an Uneasy Relationship', *Pneuma* 6.2 (Fall, 1984) pp. 5–33. In this article Sheppard demonstrates how early Pentecostals were not united on their understanding and usage of the dispensational hermeneutic and how their later adoption of the dispensational hermeneutic created problems for Pentecostal identity.

Summary

What distinguished the early Pentecostal Bible Reading Method from the Holiness folk was not a different interpretive method but a *distinct narrative* which held the similar method together in a coherent and cohesive interpretive manner. The Pentecostal movement's continuation of Holiness praxis in confrontation with cessationist Fundamentalism and liberalism created a fertile context in which an authentic Pentecostal hermeneutical strategy emerged. The Pentecostal hermeneutical strategy at the foundational interpretive level was a unique story (which was a new twist on the Christian story). The primitive impulse and Bible Reading Method shaped and were shaped by the Pentecostal story.

The 'Bible Reading Method' was a commonsense method that relied upon inductive and deductive interpretative reasoning. Once the 'biblical data' were analyzed, they were then synthesized into a biblical doctrine. Harmonization was an acceptable and necessary way to synthesize all the 'biblical data' on a particular subject. The early Pentecostals developed their doctrinal understanding by utilizing the 'Bible Reading Method' from a Pentecostal point of view. In other words, the Bible Reading Method functioned within the Pentecostal story, which was the primary arena for the production of meaning.

The Pentecostal Bible Reading Method was thoroughly pietistic and popularistic. Thus, it was a pre-critical, text centered, synchronic approach from a revivalistic restorationist Pentecostal perspective.[132] The early Pentecostals used the inductive and deductive commonsense method to develop their understanding of the baptism of the Holy Spirit as *physically evidenced* with speaking in other tongues. The Oneness Pentecostals also used this method to formulate their doctrinal understanding that salvation was an experience that passed through three phases. Oneness Pentecostals also rejected the terminology of Trinity in favor of a Triunity understanding of God without reducing Jesus to merely a human. The 'Bible Reading Method' functioned within the Pentecostal story.

---

[132] They were canonical only in the sense that they stayed within the Protestant canon and interpreted the Old Testament in light of the New Testament as they developed their doctrine. They were text centered in the sense that they favored 'world of the text' over 'the world behind the text'.

The biblical 'Latter Rain' motif became an important contribution to the Pentecostal story. The 'Latter Rain' motif enabled the Pentecostals to hold together the 'Full Gospel' message because it provided a coherent explanation for the restoration of the gifts while providing the primary organizational infrastructure for their story. The Pentecostals became the people of the prophetically promised 'Latter Rain', which meant that they had fully recovered not only the Apostolic faith, but also the Apostolic power, authority, and practice. Pentecostals often appealed to the manifestation of miracles as validation of their message. Thus, 'signs and wonders' became an important 'proof' for validating the Pentecostal story, and with this came the development of a 'Signs Theology'.

The Central Narrative Convictions of the Pentecostals served as the hermeneutical context in which Scripture and their experience of reality was interpreted. Pentecostalism is one of many restorationist Christian discourses competing to be *the* Christian story. The first generation of Pentecostals understood themselves to be the people of the Latter Rain. These Pentecostals were not academically trained 'critics' of Scripture. They were pietistic 'readers'. As readers they honored and revered the Scriptures.[133] Yet they were critical of aspects of modernity and mainline Christianity.

The Pentecostal movement was an alternative hermeneutical path forged in opposition to modernity and mainline Christianity at the turn of the century. The liberals and Fundamentalists built upon the same philosophical foundation and yet remained antithetical to each other. The Modernist-Fundamentalist debates exemplify that these communities were addressing the same issues and responding with the same philosophical reasoning. The Pentecostals, in continuation with the non-cessationist Wesleyan Holiness folk, were concerned with living the biblical truth, more so than cognitively defending the truth. The Wesleyan Holiness emphasis was 'on regeneration more than justification, on impartation of grace and virtue rather than its imputation'.[134] This understanding encouraged a 'therapeutic' view of grace which was 'restoring the ability to love in regeneration and

---

[133] George Stiener, 'Critic/ Reader', *New Literary History* 10 (1979), pp. 423–52.

[134] Donald Dayton, 'The Use of Scripture in the Wesleyan Tradition' in Robert Johnston (ed.), *The Use of the Bible in Theology: Evangelical Options* (Atlanta: John Knox Press, 1985), p. 128.

sanctification'. Dayton argues that 'this is a significant shift of axis and a movement away from "forensic" categories of the Reformation['s understanding of the work of justification] to the "organic" and "biological" categories of Pietism'.[135]

This is not to suggest that they were not concerned about defending their doctrinal views, but it is to suggest that they went about it differently than the modernistically nurtured academic Fundamentalists such as B.B. Warfield. The Pentecostals were people of praxis and piety. They were concerned about truth, but truth rooted in piety. They shared some concerns with the Fundamentalists, but were never included among them or invited to participate in their debates. They were kept on the margins.

Pentecostals were convinced that God was breaking into their world, and so they babbled.[136] In their babbling they protested modernity along with cessationist Christianity and were able to create an intense experiential eschatological counter-culture Christian community. Interestingly, their narrated hermeneutical approach, which emphasized the importance of a controlling story and the immediacy of experiential meaningfulness, has much more in common with the (pre-modern) New Testament writers' approaches than the historical critical approaches of modernity.[137]

---

[135] Dayton, 'The Use of Scripture in the Wesleyan Tradition', p. 127. Dayton explains the result of this shift. 'It may be overstating a significant truth to notice that, in part because of the emphasis on faith, the generations after the Reformation were devoted to the clarification of the faith and they left us the legacy of great creeds and doctrinal systems. The Wesleyan tradition, on the other hand, has left us a legacy of works of love—the crusades against slavery, concern for the poor, campaigns for the reform of society, and so on—in its efforts to "spread scriptural holiness across the land and to reform a nation"' (p. 128).

[136] Luke T. Johnson, *Religious Experience in the Earliest Christianity: A Missing Dimension in New Testament Studies* (Minneapolis, MN: Augsburg Fortress Press, 1998), p. 116, suggests that tongues speech or glossolalia 'is a verbal expression of a powerful emotional state. It is not a real language but a kind of structured or ordered babbling.'

[137] For an insightful look at the Apostle Paul's hermeneutic, which supports my observation, see Richard B. Hays, *Echoes Of Scripture In The Letters Of Paul* (New Haven: Yale University Press, 1989).

5

CURRENT PENTECOSTAL HERMENEUTICAL CONCERNS

A strict adherence to traditional evangelical/fundamentalist hermeneutic principles leads to a position which, in its most positive forms, suggests the distinctives of the twentieth century Pentecostal movement are perhaps nice but not necessary; important but not vital to the life of the Church in the twentieth century. In its more negative forms, it leads to a total rejection of Pentecostal phenomena.[1]

Mark McLean

The purpose of this chapter is to enter into the contemporary debate concerning Pentecostals and hermeneutical concerns. The debates focus primarily upon the historical critical methods, specifically exegesis and redaction criticism. The emphasis falls upon the proper use of methods. This is an important concern, but limited.[2] Hermeneutics involves more than exegetical methods.

What is at stake in the present hermeneutical debate is *not* whether Pentecostals have correctly exegeted the Lukan corpus according to the traditional historical critical methodologies (source, form, and redaction). Rather what is at the heart of the debate is the Pentecostal community's identity and how this affects interpretive methodology and understanding. Interpretation never takes place within a neutral

---

[1] Mark McLean, 'Toward A Pentecostal Hermeneutic', *Pneuma* 6.2 (Fall 1984), p. 37.

[2] For a notable exception see Arden C. Autry, 'Dimensions of Hermeneutics in Pentecostal Focus', *JPT* 3 (October 1993), pp. 29–50. Autry's stated purpose is 'to identify and describe briefly the basic hermeneutical concerns or dimensions which should shape our approach to biblical interpretation ... What is being proposed is not a methodology as such but a theory of hermeneutics' (pp. 30–31). Autry discusses five dimensions (history, language, existence in time, transcendence and community) and their important contribution to biblical hermeneutics.

vacuum but instead always takes place from within the contextual horizon of the reading community.

People from outside and inside the Pentecostal community have argued that early Pentecostal theological doctrine was based upon an uncritical, nineteenth-century holiness exegetical method, thus both their theological position (especially Spirit baptism) and interpretive practice was incorrect. In short, they argue that Pentecostals need to perform exegesis correctly.[3]

Today, one must take seriously the significant contemporary challenge that the use of any method is not objectively free from the social cultural location of the person utilizing it. Both the method and the person in community have been historically conditioned.[4] Also one must appreciate the contemporary challenge that for interpretation to take place, the reader must participate. 'Reading involves using both the information that is present on the written page, as well as the information we already have in our minds'. A reader cannot come to the written text as a blank slate.[5] Comprehension is both a discovery and the creation of meaningful understanding.[6] Meaning is the result of a dialectic transaction between the readers' contributions and a text's contribution.[7]

How Pentecostals or any community goes about doing 'exegesis' has as much to do with their social location and theological formation as it does with simply employing a so-called neutral-scientific exegetical method. The role of the hermeneut in the interpretive process must also be considered. This touches upon the issue of community and identity.

---

[3] See the conversational exchange between Max Turner and John Christopher Thomas in *JPT* 12 (April 1998), pp. 3–38.

[4] John Goldingay, *Models For Interpretation Of Scripture* (Grand Rapids, MI: Eerdmans, 1995), p. 45.

[5] Jeff McQuillian, *The Literary Crisis: False Claims, Real Solutions* (Portsmouth, NH: Heinemann, 1998), p. 16.

[6] Bernard C. Lategan, 'Hermeneutics' in *ABD*, III, pp. 153–54. See also George Aichele *et al.*, *The Postmodern Bible: The Bible and Culture Collective* (New Haven: Yale University Press, 1995), pp. 1–8, which challenges both the notion of the Enlightenment's control of objectivity and stability of meaning. See also Anthony C. Thiselton, *New Horizons in Hermeneutics* (Grand Rapids: Zondervan, 1992), p. 9, who argues for a contextualized hermeneutical approach that respects both the biblical horizon and the horizon of the reader.

[7] Hart, *Faith Thinking*, p. 121.

In the following section, I shall briefly review the essential themes of the Pentecostal community's identity. This will place the contemporary debates concerning Pentecostals and hermeneutical issues into their appropriate context. Then the modernization of Pentecostal hermeneutical concerns will be explained with an analysis of the current debate among Pentecostals concerning hermeneutics. Finally, this writer will offer a critique and suggest that a contemporary and critical Pentecostal hermeneutical strategy that desires to be informed by the first-generation hermeneutical approach can do so by embracing some contemporary critical concerns and methodological approaches.

Essential Themes of the Pentecostal Community

Thus far I have identified the historical beginning of Pentecostalism, which came as a result of the revivals of the late nineteenth century, particularly the Wesleyan Holiness and Keswickian higher life movements. Emerging from this context of American restorationist, noncessationist revivalism came a distinct Pentecostal spirituality: 'It was the "black spirituality of former slaves in the United States" encountering the specific catholic spirituality of the movement's "grandfather", John Wesley'.[8] Pentecostals were people who lived on the margins of society.

Pentecostalism's unique doctrine was the merger of the holiness concept of baptism in the Holy Spirit with the 'Bible evidence' of speaking in other tongues. Thus, 'Pentecostals succeeded in doing what the Holiness Movement could not do in that it offered the believer a repeatable and unmistakable motor-expression which in effect, guaranteed his possession of the Spirit'.[9] Yet, this writer argued that Pentecostalism is much more than ecstatic tongues speech.

The Pentecostal movement was rooted in a shared cultural worldview that transformed them into the people of the 'Latter Rain'. The 'Latter Rain' narrative provided a stable structured story for their interpretive methods and empowered them to protest modernity and superficial Christianity. In other words, Pentecostalism, was a way of

---

[8] Land, *Pentecostal Spirituality*, p. 35. Land cites Hollenweger, 'After Twenty Years' Research on Pentecostalism', p. 404.

[9] Synan, *The Holiness-Pentecostal Movement in the United States*, p. 122.

life, and the 'Latter Rain' narrative was the means to explain and order their way of life.

Pentecostalism's dramatic narrative constantly emphasizes the supernatural manifestations within the worshiping community. Grant
Wacker, in his penetrating article 'The Functions of Faith in Primitive
Pentecostalism', argues that the framework in which speaking in
tongues should be analyzed is the thoroughly experiential supernaturalistic conceptual horizon.[10] In fact, Pentecostalism came into existence as a result of this 'thoroughly experiential supernaturalistic'
worldview. This worldview arose as a result of attempting to mimic
the biblical stories, especially those found in Acts and the Gospels.
Pentecostal identity was shaped from the beginning by an 'eschatological intensity and an existential identification with "the Full Gospel" of the New Testament Apostolic Christianity'.[11]

The Pentecostals lived under the eschatological outpouring of the
'Latter Rain', which permeated every aspect of their lives and transformed them into 'the sealed bride of Christ'. They viewed this outpouring of the Holy Spirit as the sign that the final act in the dramatic
story of human salvation had indeed begun. They were convinced
that the second coming of Jesus was going to happen very soon—
within their lifetime. Thus, this experiential and supernaturalistic horizon of Pentecostalism was 'marked by living in and from the
eschatological presence of God'.[12]

Pentecostalism with its manifestation of the charismatic gifts
(tongues, prophecy and healing) and interracial worship services 'offered invincible certitude that the supernatural claims of the gospel
were really true'.[13] Pentecostalism perceived itself as a revival movement that called the Church to re-live the Apostolic experiences that
are related in the New Testament.[14] Pentecostals, like other restorationist groups, were certain they had rediscovered the essential fea-

---

[10] Grant Wacker, 'The Functions of Faith in Primitive Pentecostalism', *Harvard
Theological Review* 77.3–4 (1984), p. 360.

[11] M. Dempster, 'The Search for Pentecostal Identity', *Pneuma* 15.1 (1993), p. 1.

[12] Land, *Pentecostal Spirituality*, p. 184.

[13] Wacker, 'The Functions of Faith in Primitive Pentecostalism', p. 361. For the
importance of an integrated Church services as a sign, see Seymour (ed.) *The Apostolic Faith* 1.6 (Feb.-Mar., 1907), p. 7, column 4.

[14] Arrington, 'Hermeneutics' in *DPCM* (1988), p. 381.

tures of the New Testament Church.[15] These features included the gifts of the Holy Spirit, which were once again available to all Christians. Their message was 'Back to Pentecost' which enabled them to eclipse the death grip of modernity.[16]

Steven Land concisely and accurately explains the Pentecostal worldview:

> The faith, worldview, experience and practice of Pentecostals was thoroughly eschatological. They lived both in the tension of the already but not yet consummated Kingdom … Time and space were fused and transcended in the Spirit, and at the heart of testimony, expectation and worship was Jesus, the Savior, Sanctifier, Healer, Baptizer with the Spirit, and Coming King.[17]

This biblically inspired and eschatologically oriented worldview was and still is antithetical to modernity's conception of reality, and challenges the basic premise of the so-called 'scientific exegesis' of Enlightened modernity—the notion of detached neutral objectivity.[18]

In presenting a review of some of the essential themes of Pentecostalism, this writer hopes to reiterate that the essence of the movement was the belief in and encounter with the supernatural Jesus in the Christian life, which was articulated by the 'Latter Rain' story. This experiential worldview accepted the 'supernatural' events

---

[15] Wacker, 'The Functions of Faith in Primitive Pentecostalism', p. 364.

[16] Wacker argues that early Pentecostalism exemplified a 'conceptual ahistoricism' of folk religion which made them 'exempt from adverse judgments drawn from the history of the Church, insulated (them) from the rational refutation based on relativistic cultural premises, and protected (them) from empirical disconfirmation by a future that did not yet exist' ('The Functions of Faith in Primitive Pentecostalism' p. 374; see also pp. 363–64).

[17] Land, *Pentecostal Spirituality*, pp. 55–56.

[18] For critiques of historical critical method see, Peter Stuhlmacher, *Historical Criticism and Theological Interpretation Of Scripture: Towards A Hermeneutic of Consent* (Philadelphia: Fortress Press, 1977); Robert Morgan with John Barton, *Biblical Interpretation* (New York: Oxford University Press, 1988); Edgar V. McKnight, *Post-Modern Use of The Bible: The Emergence of Reader-Oriented Criticism* (Nashville: Abingdon Press, 1988); Eta Linnemann, *Historical Criticism of The Bible: Methodology or Ideology* (Grand Rapids, MI: Baker Book House, 1990); Ulrich Luz, *Matthew In History: Interpretation, Influence, and Effects* (Minneapolis, MN: Fortress Press, 1994). For a sustained argument against redaction and audience criticism by a notable historical theologian and biblical scholar, who favors 'historical' analysis, see Richard Bauckham (ed.), *The Gospels For All Christians: Rethinking The Gospel Audiences* (Grand Rapids, MI: Eerdmans, 1998).

of the Bible as normative experiences and placed emphasis primarily upon the present meaningfulness of Scripture for the community. It also encouraged active participation of the community in the interpretive process. Additionally, the Pentecostals argued that they had rediscovered normative New Testament Christianity. Since they felt that they had restored New Testament Christianity, they saw themselves as the closest representation of Christianity existing today. In fact, they argued that they were New Testament Christianity restored. This was and still is a challenge to other Christian communities' identity, especially those who were children of the Reformation.

All of these concerns smack modernity head on, and it is easy to see why concern about the proper use of the historical critical methods became a recurring issue for Pentecostals who entered into the academic community. It was only a natural result of the education process that Pentecostals utilized the academically acceptable hermeneutical methods. In doing so, Pentecostals became increasingly more modern. Therefore, the proper exegetical method—an objective and scientific method—would be called upon to become the arbitrating judge to resolve the conflicting interpretations.

The Modernization of the Early Pentecostal Hermeneutic

As Pentecostals entered the universities and academic seminaries, they abandoned the early Pentecostal 'Bible Reading Method' and adopted the historical critical approaches of modernity. The historical critical method was the approved and practiced 'scientific' hermeneutic of the academy. Pentecostals used these approaches while maintaining traditional Pentecostal and conservative conclusions.[19] They accepted the basic principles of historical criticism while rejecting the naturalistic worldview of modernity; hence they accepted a modified and evangelical approach to historical criticism. The modified approach had already been articulated from the Reformed wing of early academic Fundamentalism and was called the critical historical-

---

[19] Gerald Bray, *Biblical Interpretation: Past And Present* (Downers Grove, IL: InterVarsity Press, 1996), states that 'by 1945, virtually all professional biblical scholars had accepted its [historical criticism's] principles, though some still continued to draw conservative conclusions from them' (p. 223).

grammatical exegetical method.[20] Furthermore, the historical-grammatical method became the primary method used by many Pentecostals.[21] Even today, the historical-grammatical method (exegesis), along with emphasis upon authorial intent is the favored means to biblical interpretation.[22] The Pentecostals moved from the margins into mainstream, from the paramodern into the modern. They embraced the modernistic foundations poured by the Enlightenment.

Gordon Anderson, a contemporary and classical Pentecostal, is representative of the majority of academically trained Pentecostals.[23] He is concerned that some contemporary Pentecostals (primarily pastors) have embraced heretical beliefs and practices because they do not use the proper exegetical method. According to Anderson, the proper exegetical method is the historical-grammatical method, which is the same method used by conservative Evangelicals.[24] Anderson writes, 'The intended meaning of the original author is still considered primary, and meanings gained through historical/grammatical study are seen as objective and universally authoritative'.[25] The original intent is objective because the 'Bible is objective and it speaks a clear and uniform message to all peoples, at all times and in all cultures' but it may have many applications of 'the fixed and objective meaning'.[26] Anderson's exegetical method attempts to embrace Kris-

---

[20] See Bray, *Biblical Interpretation: Past and Present*, pp. 354–55. Bray refers to this as the most conservative form of biblical study, and observes that it relied heavily on exegetical principles.

[21] Gordon L. Anderson, 'Pentecostal Hermeneutics: Part 2', *Paraclete* 28.2 (Spring 1994), states that 'at the level of exegetical method, Pentecostals follow the same basic historical-grammatical method as do other conservative evangelical interpreters ... I contend that at this basic level of exegetical method (discovering what the text meant), all interpreters take the same approach when they do their work correctly' (p. 13).

[22] Anderson, 'Pentecostal Hermeneutics: Part 2' and also see (Pentecostal scholar) Gordon Fee, *New Testament Exegesis: A Handbook for Students and Pastors* (Louisville, KY: Westminster/ John Knox Press, rev. edn, 1993), p. 27. Fee writes, 'exegesis is primarily concerned with intentionally: What did the author *intend* his original readers to understand?' For an Evangelical perspective see William Klein's 'Evangelical Hermeneutics' in Simon Maimela and Adrio König's (eds.) *Initiation into Theology: The Rich Variety of Theology and Hermeneutics* (Pretoria: J.L. van Schaik Publishers, 1988).

[23] There are many academically trained Pentecostals who do not fit this generalization, but they are in the minority.

[24] Anderson, 'Pentecostal Hermeneutics: Part 2', p. 13.

[25] Anderson, 'Pentecostal Hermeneutics: Part 2', p. 22.

[26] Anderson, 'Pentecostal Hermeneutics: Part 2', p. 14.

ter Stendahl's distinction between 'what a text meant' and 'what the texts means'. Anderson, like most Evangelicals, relies heavily upon the literary theory of E.D. Hirsch who makes a distinction between the single objective meaning of a text as identified with authorial intention and then its significance/application for the present reader.[27] As can be seen, Pentecostals have firmly embraced conservative yet modernistic concerns about texts.

At the Society for Pentecostal Studies, Anderson addressed the contemporary moral crisis in Pentecostalism. Anderson argued that, 'the moral crisis for pentecostals lies, in part, in the tendency to use poor exegetical methods and taking an existential approach to the interpretation of Scripture and the construction of doctrine'.[28] He identifies the 'poor' and 'inappropriate exegetical methods' as 'allegorizing the text and creating typologies which the Bible never intended'. According to Anderson this 'constitutes a fundamental disavowal of the commitment to ground doctrine in the plain meaning of scripture'.[29] Although this author is sympathetic to Anderson's concerns about moral integrity and the misuse of Scripture, this writer emphatically disagrees with Anderson's implicit assertion that a uniformly applied correct standard of principles of exegesis (the historical-grammatical method) would resolve all the theological prob-

---

[27] Anderson, 'Pentecostal Hermeneutics: Part 2' (p. 22). Anderson cites a paragraph from Krister Stendahl's article 'Biblical Theology, Contemporary' in *Interpreter's Bible Dictionary* (New York: Abingdon Press), I, p. 42, in support of his statement. He also embraces E.D. Hirsch's distinction between meaning and significance as explained in Hirsch's *Validity and Interpretation* (New Haven, CT: Yale University Press, 1967). This issue between what a text meant, the intended meaning of the author and what the texts means to the reader (the significance or application) is a central issue in Evangelical hermeneutical theory. But most contemporary Pentecostals, like most Evangelicals embrace this dichotomy and find it helpful. For Evangelical usage of Hirsch see Millard J. Erickson's, *Evangelical Interpretation: Perspectives on Hermeneutical Issues* (Grand Rapids, MI: Baker Books, 1993) and Grant R. Osborne, *The Hermeneutical Spiral: A Comprehensive Introduction to Biblical Interpretation* (Downers Grove, IL: InterVarsity Press, 1991).

[28] Gordon Anderson, 'The Changing Nature of The Moral Crisis of American Christianity', a paper presented to the Annual Meeting of the Society for Pentecostal Studies, November 1990. p. 18.

[29] Anderson, 'The Changing Nature of The Moral Crisis of American Christianity', p. 11. He lists three characteristics of Pentecostal existentialism. The first is 'subjective feelings and personal experience often take precedence over the effort to establish the objective facts of doctrine on any given issue' (p. 10). The second is improper exegesis and the third is that Pentecostals are prone to accept 'new revelations of the "meaning" of the Bible' (p. 12).

lems.[30] Interpretation of Scripture is also dependent upon spiritual discernment because most doctrinal and ethical concerns cannot be resolved by exegetical method alone.[31] Thus, a Christian community cannot rely upon exegetical method alone to validate its interpretation; even though understanding the methodological approach may help to distinguish between competing interpretations, it still may not be able to resolve them.

A Pentecostal hermeneutic or any hermeneutic cannot be reduced to a static, distinctive exegetical methodology[32] but must include the important element of the social location of the readers and their narrative tradition. This is why the word hermeneutics needs a qualifier before it. Different communities often derive different and at times contradictory doctrinal positions, even when they utilize the same exegetical principles.[33] Hermeneutics is concerned with the historical horizon of Scripture and the equally challenging horizon of the reader in community.[34]

Contemporary Pentecostal Hermeneutical Debates

Walter J. Hollenweger's early monumental study of Pentecostalism opens with this dedication: 'To my friends and teachers in the Pentecostal movement who taught me to love the Bible and to my teachers

---

[30] I agree with Richard Bauckham, 'the Bible's meaning for today cannot result automatically from the correct use of a set of hermeneutical principles' in his *The Bible in Politics: How to Read the Bible Politically* (Louisville, KY: Westminster/John Knox Press, 1989), p. 19. See Anderson, 'Pentecostal Hermeneutics', pp. 13–22, for his explanation and understanding of a Pentecostal hermeneutic. For an argument supporting the superiority of allegorical interpretation see David C. Steinmetz, 'The Superiority of the Pre-Critical Exegesis', *Ex Auditu* 1 (1985), pp. 75–82. This is a reprint from *Theology Today* 37 (1980), pp. 27–38.

[31] See Luke Timothy Johnson's *Scripture and Discernment: Decision Making In the Church*, especially chapter 6.

[32] Douglas Jacobsen's 'Pentecostal Hermeneutics in Comparative Perspective', p. 4, and pp. 2, 5, 7. For contra arguments see Robert P. Menzies, *Empowered for Witness: The Spirit in Luke–Acts* (JPTSup, 6; Sheffield: Sheffield Academic Press, 1994), pp. 239–43. Menzies' monograph uses redaction criticism in his analysis and is an interesting contribution from a Pentecostal perspective to Lukan pneumatology.

[33] A helpful introduction to some of the more current and important hermeneutical positions can be found in Maimela and König (eds.), *Initiation Into Theology: The Rich Variety of Theology and Hermeneutics*.

[34] See Thiselton, *New Horizons in Hermeneutics*, (pp. 33–36, 44–46).

and friends in the Presbyterian Church who taught me to understand it'.[35] Hollenweger's chiding remark no doubt reflects the simplistic and 'uncritical' work among early Pentecostals, even though there were a few educated readers. It also implies that the Reformed tradition has provided him with a better intellectual approach to understanding the Scripture than has the Pentecostal tradition. This is no longer the case, however, as Hollenweger acknowledges in his 1992 article. He states that today 'one finds scores of first-class Pentecostal scholars', and these scholars 'deserve to be taken seriously'.[36] He concludes the article by saying

> Pentecostalism has come of age. It is now possible to be filled with the Spirit, to enjoy the specific Pentecostal charismata and Pentecostal spirituality, to believe in Pentecostal mission, and at the same time to use one's critical faculties to develop them and to use them—as any other charisma for the Kingdom of God.[37]

Pentecostal scholarship has reached new levels of sophistication as the Fall 1993 issue of *Pneuma: The Journal of the Society for Pentecostal Studies* demonstrates. This issue contained essays on the topic of Pentecostal hermeneutics. 'Here we see social scientific research coupled with postmodern methodologies of interpretation and an ability to appeal to the most recent trends in biblical and theological studies'.[38] These Pentecostal scholars are utilizing the latest methods in order to re-present valuable aspects of Pentecostal experience and tradition. However, these Pentecostals are few in numbers.

The focus of this section will be upon the contemporary Pentecostal discussion of hermeneutics. The topic of hermeneutics has generated a lively debate among Pentecostal scholars. This can be attested by examining the current contents of two prominent Pentecostal journals, namely, *Pneuma* and the *Journal of Pentecostal Theology*. This writer will show how some Pentecostal scholars are responding to a general call to develop a hermeneutic with which to construct a

---

[35] Walter J. Hollenweger, *The Pentecostals* (London: SCM Press, 1972), preface.
[36] Walter Hollenweger, 'The Critical Tradition of Pentecostalism', *JPT* 1 (October 1992), p. 7.
[37] Hollenweger, 'The Critical Tradition of Pentecostalism', p. 17.
[38] G. Sheppard, 'Biblical Interpretation after Gadamer', *Pneuma* (Spring 1994), p. 127.

theology worthy of the name Pentecostal.[39] Yet other scholars are asserting that a Pentecostal hermeneutic is really the same as an Evangelical hermeneutic in general. Hence, there exist two predominate voices in the Anglo-Pentecostal academic community.

The majority voice comes from the group of scholars who understand Pentecostalism to be a subgroup of Evangelicalism. Faupel argues that 'this view can only be sustained through a selective reading of Pentecostal history and through an abandonment of many of the initial Pentecostal assumptions'.[40] The less popular voice desires to explain Pentecostalism as an authentic social cultural expression of authentic Christianity that is distinct and different from Evangelicalism, even though they share many things in common. This view, according to Faupel, is still emerging but has a particular concern to recover the initial impulses that gave rise to the Pentecostal movement. This mission of recovery is similar to Paul Ricoeur's concept of the 'second naïveté'.[41] The minority voice understands Pentecostalism to have 'its own mission, its own hermeneutic, and its own agenda'.[42] In the following analysis of the current hermeneutical discussions among Pentecostals and non-Pentecostal scholars, both voices will be heard.

Pentecostals have a distinct way of reading and harmonizing the Scriptures. They read the Scriptures 'through Lukan eyes, especially with the lenses provided by the book of Acts'.[43] The reading of the entire New Testament through Acts has led Pentecostals to the conclusion that the believer should have not only a salvation-regeneration experience but also a second or third subsequent Spirit baptismal experience. This experience of Spirit baptism should be normative for all believers and result in the empowerment of the community for evangelistic and missional purposes. The initial biblical sign of the baptism of the Holy Spirit is 'speaking in tongues'.

---

[39] Land, *Pentecostal Spirituality*, p. 38.

[40] D. William Faupel, 'Wither Pentecostalism? 22nd Presidential Address Society for Pentecostal Studies', *Pneuma* 15.1 (Spring 1993), p. 26.

[41] Paul Ricoeur, *Freud and Philosophy: An Essay on Interpretation* (trans. Denis Savage; New Haven, CT: Yale University Press, 1970), p. 496.

[42] Faupel, 'Wither Pentecostalism?', p. 26.

[43] Dayton, *Theological Roots of Pentecostalism*, p. 23. Dayton points out how the Pentecostal usage of Acts in reading the New Testament is 'In contrast to magisterial Protestantism, which tends to read the New Testament through Pauline eyes' (p. 23).

Outsiders do not share these assumptions. Rather they insist that such an understanding could only be developed through inadequate hermeneutical methods or through the misuse of exegetical methodological procedure.[44] Thus, the outsiders first drew attention to what they believed was the inadequate hermeneutical practices of Pentecostals as they examined the Pentecostal understanding of 'Spirit baptism'.

The Lukan narrative perspective not only encouraged Pentecostals to embrace 'Spirit baptism', but it also gave early Pentecostals a biblical narrative account of women participating in ministry. Thus, the reading of Luke–Acts motivated Pentecostal women (and some men) to challenge the predominant view that women were not to be preachers or ordained ministers. This view relied heavily on one passage in Scripture: 'Let the woman learn in silence with all subjection. But I suffer not a women to teach, nor usurp authority over the man, but to be in silence' (KJV).[45] Pentecostals, like some Wesleyan Holiness communities, appealed to the sovereignty of the Holy Spirit in calling women and men into ministry, hence gender was not a prerequisite for ministry leadership in the Church.[46]

---

[44] James D.G. Dunn, *Baptism In The Holy Spirit: A Re-examination of the New Testament Teaching on the Gift of the Spirit In Relation to Pentecostalism Today* (Philadelphia: Westminster Press, 1970). Dunn argues that early Pentecostals (like Catholics and Wesleyan Holiness) read Acts 2 as an experience that is subsequent to salvation only by asserting that the Acts 2 account assumes that people were already regenerated. He points out that this notion was based on the Gospel of John which he then argues is an exegetical methodological mistake because one cannot start the exegetical process of Acts 2 by relating it to Jn 20.22, see pp. 38–40.

[45] See 1 Tim. 2.11-12, also 1 Cor. 14.34, 'Let your women keep silence in the churches: for it is not permitted unto them to speak' (KJV).

[46] For a contemporary Pentecostal statement on the role of Women in ministry that is consistent with but moves beyond early Pentecostalism by affirming full gender equality, see 'The Role of Women in Ministry as Described in Holy Scripture'. This is an official position paper of the General Council of the Assemblies of God adopted by the General Presbytery, August 1990. See also, Kimberly Ervin Alexander and R. Hollis Gause, *Women in Leadership: A Pentecostal Perspective* (Cleveland, TN: Church of God Theological Seminary's Center for Pentecostal Leadership and Care, 2006). The issue of a woman pastoring a Pentecostal Church was a reoccurring question that appeared frequently in the question and answer section of the Assembly of God publication, *The Weekly Evangel* edited by E.N. Bell. Women were affirmed in the ministry gifts of preaching, teaching and pastoring, but they also were required to be submissive to men. Most, but not all, Pentecostal churches allowed for full involvement in the preaching ministry but did not grant women an equal and authoritative standing with men. For examples, see *The Weekly Evangel*,

The Hermeneutical Debate Initiated from Outside the Pentecostal Community

F.D. Bruner and James D.G. Dunn have provided important critiques of Pentecostal exegetical readings of Scripture. They both set out to evaluate the claim made by classical Pentecostals that the baptism in the Holy Spirit is a second and subsequent normative experience for all Christians.[47] Both scholars employ the historical critical exegetical methodologies to recover the author's original intent.[48] Both scholars find no exegetical support for a subsequent Spirit baptism experience. Dunn, however, is more sympathetic in his evaluations than Bruner.

Bruner believes that the heart of the Gospel is under attack because the Reformation doctrine of justification by faith alone has been impaired.[49] Bruner's comments reveal this concern:

A principal error of Pentecostalism, shared by some of Pentecostalism's parents and relatives in conservative evangelicalism, is the conviction that the gospel is sufficient for the beginning but not

---

January 29 and February 5, 1916, p. 8 question 20; July 22, 1916, p. 8 question 79; September 2, 1916, p. 8 question 91, March 10, 1917, p. 9, question 151; May 26, 1917, p. 9 question 203; January 25, 1919, p. 5 question 603; May 17, 1919, p. 5 question 677 (Bell's response makes women subject to male leadership and here he states that a woman may pastor a church, but if there is a qualified man then he should be the pastor because men are to be the leaders); June 14, 1919, p. 5 question 687; November 29, 1919, p. 5 question 780; March 6, 1920, p. 5 question 806 (here Bell explains the difference between ordained men and women in the Assemblies of God which subjects women to male leadership and does not allow women to perform ministry acts of an official nature nor perform marriage services); June 11, 1921, p. 10 question 1031.

[47] James D.G. Dunn, 'Baptism in the Spirit: A Response to Pentecostal Scholarship on Luke–Acts', *JPT* 3 (1993), p. 5. See also his *Baptism in the Holy Spirit*. F.D. Bruner, *A Theology of the Holy Spirit: The Pentecostal Experience and the New Testament Witness* (London: Hodder and Stoughton, 1970), p. 78, 'Is the Pentecostal teaching on the experience of the Spirit in conformity with New Testament teaching ... should Christians seek a second ... experience subsequent to their Christian initiation ... should I have the Pentecostal experience?'

[48] Dunn, *Baptism in the Holy Spirit*, pp. 39–40. Dunn makes clear that the author's thought and intent is limited to the written text. Cf. Bruner, *A Theology of the Holy Spirit: The Pentecostal Experience*, p. 153: 'The final question at stake in our confrontation with Pentecostalism is not: was Luke right or wrong ... but: does Pentecostalism rightly or wrongly understand Luke ...?'

[49] H. Lederle, 'Pre-Charismatic Interpretations of Spirit-Baptism' in *A Reader on the Holy Spirit: Anointing, Equipping and Empowering for Service* (Los Angeles, CA: International Church of the Foursquare Gospel, 1993), p. 33.

for the continuing of the Christian life, for bringing the Holy Spirit initially but not fully … Christians not only once-and-for-all receive the Spirit through the message of faith apart from the fulfilling of conditions (Gal. 3:2) but they continue to be supplied fully with the Spirit and ministered miracles through the very same message without additional techniques or deeper messages or secret means (3:5) … The consequence for the Pentecostal doctrine of fullness must be the abandonment of any condition for the fullness of the Holy Spirit other than the one, initiating, sustaining, and powerful message of faith in Jesus Christ. There is for Christians no fuller, no more fulfilling gospel than the gospel that makes a man a Christian; to assert that there is, is to fall under Paul's severest censure (Gal. 1:6-9; 5:2-12).[50]

Two observations can be drawn from Bruner's work. First, he believes he has correctly interpreted Luke–Acts by utilizing the historical-grammatical method. Second, he reflects the general attitude of the Reformed tradition that Pentecostalism jeopardizes the Gospel.[51] This second observation touches upon the issue of Pentecostal identity and the larger issue of how Pentecostals understand 'gospel'.

Mainline Reformed Protestantism has generally viewed Pentecostalism and the Holiness movement as an Evangelical subculture—those scandalous cousins.[52] But, one must remember that Pentecostalism and the Holiness movements did not come out of old-school Presbyterianism. They are products of Wesleyan thought. The structures of Wesleyan thought are not characteristically those of the tradition of 'Protestant orthodoxy' and so 'these movements are not classical Protestantism but protests against it'.[53] Thus, there is more involved in Pentecostal theology and identity than the exegesis of Acts. Pentecostal experiential participatory spirituality along with how Pen-

---

[50] Bruner, *A Theology of the Holy Spirit*, p. 240.
[51] See also Donald G. Bloesch, *Essentials of Evangelical Theology* (San Francisco: HarperCollins, 1978), II, p. 236.
[52] See Mark Noll, *The Scandal of the Evangelical Mind*, p. 24. The Wesleyan Theological Society made this book by Noll a topic for discussion at its annual meeting in 1996 and three of the papers presented were later published in the *Wesleyan Theological Journal* 32.1 (Spring 1997), pp. 157–86.
[53] Donald W. Dayton, 'Yet another Layer of the Onion or Opening the Ecumenical Door to let the Riffraff in', pp. 98–99.

tecostals interpret 'Scripture in light of Scripture' are also important contributions to hermeneutical inquiry.

Dunn, according to the editors of the *Journal of Pentecostal Theology*, has been the most 'provocative and stimulating' dialogue partner for Pentecostal biblical scholars.[54] Dunn's *Baptism in the Holy Spirit*, in particular, and his *Jesus and the Spirit*, in general, challenged the classical Pentecostal understanding of Spirit baptism while at the same time affirming the charismatic character of the early Church.[55] In response to Dunn's challenging work, a number of Pentecostals set out to overturn his conclusions.[56] This author will focus on one Pentecostal scholar in particular, namely, Robert Menzies, Assemblies of God missionary and Seminary educator.

The debate between Dunn and Menzies has been carried out in the *Journal of Pentecostal Theology*. Both R. Menzies and Dunn use the historical critical exegetical method. Moreover, Menzies argues that he is following the methodology outlined by Dunn.[57] The charge made by R. Menzies and other Pentecostals is that Dunn does not give Luke enough credence for a view of pneumatology that is dis-

---

[54] This comment made by the editors appears in Dunn's article, 'Baptism in the Spirit', *JPT* 3, (1993), p. 3, editorial note.

[55] R. Menzies, 'Luke and the Spirit: A Reply to James Dunn', *JPT* 4, (1994), p. 115.

[56] Dunn cites the following in his article 'Baptism in the Spirit: A Response to Pentecostal Scholarship on Luke–Acts', *JPT* 3, p. 4. H.D. Hunter, *Spirit-Baptism: A Pentecostal Alternative* (Lanham, MD: University Press of America, 1983); H. Ervin, *Conversion-Initiation and the Baptism in the Holy Spirit: An Engaging Critique of James D.G. Dunn's Baptism in the Holy Spirit* (Peabody, MA: Hendrickson, 1984); R. Stronstad, *The Charismatic Theology of St. Luke* (Peabody, MA: Hendrickson, 1984); F.L. Arrington, *The Acts of the Apostles* (Peabody, MA: Hendrickson, 1988); J.B. Shelton, *Mighty in Word and Deed: The Role of the Holy Spirit in Luke–Acts* (Peabody, MA: Hendrickson, 1991); R.P. Menzies, *The Development of Early Christian Pneumatology with Special Reference to Luke–Acts* (JSNTSup, 54; Sheffield: Sheffield Academic Press, 1991). Other scholars who have also recognized a distinctive character to Luke's pneumatology include H. Gunkel, *The Influence of the Holy Spirit* (trans. Roy A. Harrisville and Philip A. Quanbeck II; Philadelphia: Fortress Press, 1979; original German ed., 1888); E. Schweizer, 'Πνευμα', in *TDNT*, VI, pp. 389–455; D. Hill, *Greek Words and Hebrew Meanings* (Cambridge: Cambridge University Press, 1967), and M.M.B. Turner, *Luke and the Spirit: Studies in the Significance of Receiving the Spirit in Luke–Acts* (PhD thesis, University of Cambridge, 1980).

[57] R. Menzies, 'Luke and the Spirit: A Reply to James Dunn', pp. 115–16. Menzies' believes that Dunn's work 'demonstrated that Pentecostals could no longer continue to rely on the interpretive methods of the nineteenth-century holiness movement and speak to the contemporary church world', p. 115.

tinctly different from Paul. Specifically, R. Menzies argues that 'Luke describes the gift of the Spirit exclusively in charismatic terms as the source of power for effective witness', and it was Paul who was the first to attribute soteriological functions to the Spirit.[58] Therefore, the central issue concerning the debate between Dunn and Menzies is: 'Does Luke separate the outpouring of the Spirit on individuals from conversion initiation and see it as an empowering gift rather than a soteriological gift?'[59] Dunn argues 'no' and Menzies argues 'yes'.

The debates about what the author (Luke) intended his readers to understand will probably not be resolved.[60] Yet as a result of this debate, Pentecostal scholarship has demonstrated the ability to defend its doctrinal distinctive with scholastic sophistication. Pentecostal scholarship has also aided in elevating Acts from a purely historical narrative to a historical-theological narrative. This gives Acts the same doctrinal clout as Paul and John.[61] This would be consistent with the understanding of early Pentecostals that the genre of narrative has the same authoritative role in the formulation of praxis belief as the epistolary genre.[62]

R. Menzies (and other Pentecostals) argues for a distinct Lukan pneumatology, yet he also believes that it is complementary *not* con-

---

[58] R. Menzies, 'Luke and the Spirit', p. 117.

[59] Dunn, 'Baptism in the Spirit', p. 6 and R. Menzies, 'Luke and the Spirit', p. 117.

[60] See also R.P. Menzies, 'Spirit and Power in Luke–Acts: A Response to Max Turner', *JSNT* 49 (1993), pp. 11–20, which is a critical response to Max Turner's 'The Spirit and the Power of Jesus' Miracles in Lucan Conception', *NovT* 33 (1991), pp. 125–52. Menzies argues here that Turner, like Dunn, has missed Luke's continuity with first-century Jewish thought (the Spirit is presented exclusively as the source of esoteric wisdom and inspired speech and not with healings, exorcisms or feats of strength) and this is discontinuous with Paul (who attributes soteriological and healing functions to the Spirit) and the non-Pauline primitive Christian communities, (Mark, Matthew, Q, and Jesus—wh0 attribute exorcisms and healings to the Spirit) (p. 12).

[61] I. Howard Marshall's *Luke: Historian and Theologian* (Grand Rapids, MI: Zondervan, 1971) marked an important shift in evangelical thinking by recognizing Luke both as historian *and* theologian.

[62] See Taylor, *The Spirit And The Bride*, pp. 47–48, where he responds to the dispensational argument that the epistles were more authoritative than the other portions of Scripture because they were given to guide the Church in this dispensation of grace. Taylor sarcastically responded, 'I never knew it before that it would not do for the Church to follow any Scripture unless it could be found in the Epistles'.

tradictory to Paul and/or the rest of the New Testament.[63] The importance of homogenous application of the diversity of biblical understanding concerning a subject will be worked out. Moreover, this harmonization will be worked out from a Pentecostal perspective. Menzies works out a harmonious understanding of Spirit baptism by granting Luke–Acts equality to the Pauline corpus. When it comes to Spirit baptism, most Pentecostals will grant Luke–Acts an equal if not superior position (even though it is narrative) to the Letters in the harmonization process. First generation Pentecostal exegesis did not distinguish between a Lukan and Pauline pneumatology, but read Paul in light of Acts. Menzies, while affirming different pneumatological views in the New Testament, is able to harmonize the Lukan and Pauline perspectives into a workable 'two-stage' classical Pentecostal understanding—conversion then Spirit baptism. Menzies writes:

> I would suggest that a high view of Scripture demands, not that Luke and Paul have the same pneumatological perspective, but rather that Luke's distinctive pneumatology is ultimately reconcilable with that of Paul, and that both perspectives can be seen as contributing to a process of harmonious development.[64]

---

[63] R. Menzies, 'The Essence of Pentecostalism', *Paraclete* 26.3 (Summer 1992), p. 1; *idem*, 'Coming to Terms with an Evangelical Heritage', *Paraclete* 28.3 (Summer 1994), p. 22: 'Luke's pneumatology is *different* from—although complementary to—that of Paul'. Menzies acknowledges in 'The Essence of Pentecostalism', that D.A. Carson cannot accept two different pneumatological views in Scripture because it would create problems for an evangelical doctrine of inspiration (p. 7). What is different and yet complimentary for Menzies and Pentecostals is different, contradictory and destructive for Carson and the evangelical Reformed tradition.

[64] R.P. Menzies, *Empowered For Witness: The Spirit In Luke–Acts*, p. 240 and pp. 240–43. For an important analysis and response to Menzies' understanding and harmonization, see Max Turner, *The Holy Spirit and Spiritual Gifts: In the New Testament Church and Today* (Peabody, MA: Hendrickson, 1998), ch. 10. Turner writes,

> Menzies' argument would probably only work if what Luke envisaged by the 'gift of the Spirit' involved quite *distinct* activities of the Spirit from those implied in Paul's understanding of the gift of the Spirit at conversion. What Luke meant by the 'gift of the Spirit' could then be 'added' to the believer who had already experience what Paul meant by receiving the gift of the Spirit ... The fact is, however, that Paul's conception of the gift of the Spirit is simply *broader* then Luke's, *while nevertheless containing everything that Luke implies* ... Paul's comprehensive understanding of the gift of the Spirit granted to Christians at conversion does not leave anything for Luke's to 'add' (pp. 153–55, his emphasis).

Hollenweger was correct when he wrote, 'When we look for the biblical roots of the Baptism of the Spirit, we discover that the Pentecostals and their predecessors based their views almost exclusively on the Gospel of Luke and the Acts of the Apostles'.[65]

What these particular scholars hold in common is the notion that 'meaning' is embedded into a text by an author. These scholars understand a text a stable entity with determinate meaning. The task, then, of the biblical scholar is to extrapolate or discover the text's objective single meaning (which is generally synonymous with discovering the author's intended meaning) and explain it to the contemporary person. The determinate meaning can be discovered by the proper usage of the historical critical methods. Stephen Fowl writes that the notion of determinate meaning attempts to make the meaning of the biblical text clear and coherent to all reasonable people. The aim of determinate interpretation is to end all interpretation because it 'views the biblical text as a problem to be mastered'.[66]

The Hermeneutical Debate within the Pentecostal Community

The Dunn–Menzies debate touches upon and raises an important question: Have Pentecostals created a unique method? Do Pentecostals need a unique hermeneutic in order to establish their beliefs and practice in Scripture? Robert Menzies declared, 'The hermeneutic of evangelicalism has become our hermeneutic'.[67] Robert's father, William Menzies, also made a similar argument. W. Menzies regarded redaction criticism's emphasis upon the author/editor's original intention as a positive development within the historical critical hermeneutical method. He believed that redaction criticism is the important exegetical key for 'the kind of hermeneutic required for a Pentecostal theology of Spirit-baptism initiation accompanied by tongues'.[68]

---

[65] Hollenweger, *The Pentecostals*, p. 336. Even Hollenweger believes that James Dunn's *Baptism in the Holy Spirit* interprets Luke through 'Pauline' eyes, and Hollenweger himself believes that Catholics and Pentecostals have some justification in Luke but not in Paul for their beliefs (p. 350).

[66] Stephen Fowl, *Engaging Scripture: A Model for Theological Interpretation* (Malden, MA: Blackwell Publishers, 1998) p. 32, see pp. 33–40 for Fowl's explanation and critique of this view.

[67] Menzies, 'The Essence of Pentecostalism', p. 1.

[68] W. Menzies, 'The Methodology of Pentecostal Theology: An Essay on Hermeneutics' in *Essays on Apostolic Themes* (ed., Paul Elbert; Peabody, MA: Hendrickson, 1985), p. 8.

Robert Menzies utilized redaction criticism in an attempt to demonstrate a Lukan pneumatology that is *different* and *ignorant* of a Pauline pneumatology,[69] and yet he remains supportive of a classical Pentecostal understanding of the baptism in the Holy Spirit with the initial evidence of speaking in tongues.[70] Yet Evangelicals do not support his final affirmation of a two-stage New Testament pneumatology.[71] They do all agree, however, that the use of historical critical methods can clearly produce the most probable intent of the author.

W. and R. Menzies and prior to them, Gordon Fee,[72] represent the predominant attitude within Anglo-Pentecostal scholarship. These scholars constitute a group who have turned to the Evangelical wing of the Church in order to find 'particular hermeneutical assistance'.[73] They understand Pentecostalism to be a subgroup of Evangelicalism. Timothy Cargal correctly recognizes that North American Pentecostal scholars (such as Fee and Menzies) 'have tended to align themselves with evangelicals in their move toward adopting the methods of historical criticism'.[74] For R. Menzies, this 'assimilation of the

---

[69] Menzies, *Empowered for Witness: The Spirit in Luke–Acts*, 'I have argued that unlike Paul, who frequently speaks of the soteriological dimension of the Spirit's work, Luke never attributes soteriological functions to the Spirit. Furthermore, his narrative presupposes a pneumatology which excludes this dimension' (p. 237). Menzies believes that Luke was not aware of Paul's soteriological perspective. He suggests that 'Luke was not acquainted with any of Paul's epistles' and Luke knew Paul's theology only through limited conversation or secondary oral sources (pp. 241–42).

[70] See his *Empowered for Witness*, chs. 12–14, especially, pp. 254–55.

[71] Specifically, James Dunn and Max Turner.

[72] See Fee's reprint of lectures and essays, which span about 20 years, in his *Gospel and Spirit: Issues In New Testament Hermeneutics* (Peabody, MA: Hendrickson, 1991). Fee does not adhere to the classical two-stage understanding, yet he believes that there is a 'basic rightness of Pentecostalism's emphasis on the experienced, empowered work of the Spirit, including the ongoing manifestations of the various spiritual gifts' (p. x). For Pentecostal responses to Fee's book see: Roger Stronstad, 'Pentecostal Hermeneutics: A Review of Gordon D. Fee', *Pneuma* 15.2 (Fall 1993), pp. 215–22; William Menzies' review of 'Gospel and Spirit', *Paraclete* (Winter 1993), pp. 29–32; and Robert Menzies, *Empowered for Witness: The Spirit in Luke–Acts*, pp. 233–40.

[73] R. Johnston, 'Pentecostalism and Theological Hermeneutics: Evangelical Options', *Pneuma* 6.1 (Spring 1984), p. 55. He recommends that the Pentecostal community should look to Evangelicals for help in developing an Evangelical hermeneutic with some Pentecostal aspects.

[74] Timothy Cargal, 'Beyond the Fundamentalist-Modernist Controversy: Pentecostals and Hermeneutics in a Postmodern Age', *Pneuma* 15.2 (1993), p. 163. Over against Menzies, Cargal argues: 'Any hermeneutic which cannot account for its loci

modern Pentecostal movement into the broader evangelical world is an exciting and positive event'.[75] The Menzies' hope that through this assimilation Pentecostalism will bring the Church back to 'a fuller understanding of the theology of the Spirit, not an essentially different understanding'.[76] These Pentecostal scholars believe that the historical critical method does not undermine Pentecostal doctrinal positions but rather legitimizes them. However, other scholars have correctly pointed out the inherent weakness and philosophical biases of the historical critical method for theological interpretation.[77] The historical critical method used by Evangelicals places the method into a context different than the one it emerged from, thus modifying it. Furthermore, when Pentecostals use the historical critical method, they are not using it within the context of an Evangelical community but within the Pentecostal community. There is much in common between these communities (Evangelical and Pentecostal), but there also exists significant differences that affect the understanding of what a text meant or means.

Pentecostals who use redaction criticism and the historical-grammatical method are primarily concerned with historical analysis in order to discover the author's intended meaning. They seek to unlock the passage's meaning by elucidating what cultural influences and beliefs lie behind the text.[78] The primary focus, then, is the world behind the text and not the text itself. The importance of the horizon of the present reader has been ignored and furthermore the world of the text becomes secondary to the historically reconstructed world behind the text which is used to interpret the 'world of the text'. Hence, the majority of academically trained Pentecostals who embrace historical criticism have moved away from the early Pentecostals emphasis upon the text and readers. They have embraced mod-

---

of meaning within a postmodern paradigm will become nonsensical and irrelevant' (p. 187).

[75] R. Menzies, 'Jumping off the Postmodern Bandwagon', *Pneuma* 16.1 (1994), p. 119.

[76] W. Menzies, 'The Methodology of Pentecostal Theology: An Essay on Hermeneutics', p. 1. Notice the restorationist theme in his statement.

[77] Morgan and Barton, *Biblical Interpretation*, pp. 172-77.

[78] As Lategan explains in his essay, 'Hermeneutics', 'The basis for all these methods [those methods associated with historical criticism] is the genetic principle: the idea that insight into the origins and development of a phenomenon contains the key to its understanding' (p. 151).

ernity's critical approaches that have always been primarily concerned with the world behind the text.[79] Thus, they have moved away from the early pre-critical paramodern approach of early Pentecostals to the acceptable critical modern approaches, and in doing so aligned themselves with conservative North American Evangelicalism whose roots are Reformed and modernistic.[80]

The minority voice within the Pentecostal community, however, views this assimilation of Pentecostalism into Evangelicalism as destructive to Pentecostal experiential identity and doctrine. Mark McLean highlights this concern:

> A strict adherence to traditional evangelical/fundamentalist hermeneutic principles leads to a position which, in its most positive forms, suggests the distinctives of the twentieth century Pentecostal movement are perhaps nice but not necessary; important but not vital to the life of the Church in the twentieth century. In its more negative forms, it leads to a total rejection of Pentecostal phenomena.[81]

An exegetical approach that focuses only upon what the original inspired author meant and/or intended his first readers to understand will not completely satisfy the requirements of a Pentecostal hermeneutical strategy. Pentecostals need a hermeneutical approach that not only elucidates the original meaning of the biblical text (the *supposed* function of the historical critical methodologies) but also answers the question of what the text means today. In other words, the Pentecostal hermeneutic will want to comprehend the biblical passage in such a way that the illusive dichotomy of what a text meant and what a text means is overcome. Pentecostals see the full purpose of biblical interpretation as not only to uncover or discover truth, but also to apply Scripture to one's own life and to the community of faith.[82] The heart of Pentecostalism asserts that 'the spiritual and ex-

---

[79] W. Randolph Tate, *Biblical Interpretation*, pp. xxi-xxii.

[80] Alister McGrath, *Evangelicalism and the Future of Christianity*, pp. 23, 27–36. McGrath writes, 'The Reformation remains a focus and defining point of reference for evangelicalism today'.

[81] McLean, 'Toward A Pentecostal Hermeneutic', p. 37.

[82] F.L. Arrington, 'The Use of the Bible by Pentecostals', *Pneuma* 16.1 (Spring 1994), p. 107. Cf. Larry R. McQueen, *Joel and the Spirit: The Cry of a Prophetic Hermeneutic* (JPTSup, 8; Sheffield: Sheffield Academic Press, 1995), who argues that the biblical text speaks a present word to the believing community, thus manifesting

traordinary supernatural experiences of the biblical characters are possible for contemporary believers'.[83]

This concern has led some scholars to articulate a hermeneutic that is more representative of the early tradition and ethos of Pentecostalism. These scholars desire to move away from a hermeneutical system that is heavily slanted toward rationalism that tends to downplay experience and/or the role of the Holy Spirit.[84] These scholars are attempting to present a *holistic* Pentecostal hermeneutical strategy. French Arrington reflects this desire:

> The real issue in Pentecostalism has become hermeneutics, that is, the distinctive nature and function of Scripture and the roles of the Holy Spirit, the Christian community, grammatical-historical research, and personal experience in the interpretive process.[85]

The important role of the Holy Spirit and the impact of personal experience upon hermeneutics are the most frequently discussed dimensions.

A common complaint about Pentecostals is that they insert their experiences into the text; thus, they experience something and then find it in Scripture.[86] Roger Stronstad challenged this charge by building upon the suggestions of MacDonald[87] and W. Menzies[88] who ar-

---

the prophetic element in Pentecostal hermeneutics. See also Lee Roy Martin, *The Unheard Voice of God: A Pentecostal Hearing of the Book of Judges* (JPTSup, 32; Blandford Forum, UK: Deo Publishing, 2008), pp. 52–79, who uses the terminology of 'hearing' the text as a way of describing the goal of Pentecostal hermeneutics.

[83] Joseph Byrd, 'Paul Ricoeur's Hermeneutical Theory and Pentecostal Proclamation', *Pneuma* 15.2 (Fall 1993), p. 205.

[84] E.g., J.C. Thomas, 'Women, Pentecostals and the Bible', *JPT* 5 (1994), p. 41; Robby Waddell, *The Spirit of the Book of Revelation* (JPTSup, 30; Blandford Forum, UK: Deo Publishing, 2006), pp. 39–96; Martin, *The Unheard Voice of God*, pp. 52–79.

[85] Arrington, 'The Use of The Bible by Pentecostals', p. 101.

[86] Gordon Fee, 'Hermeneutics and the Historical Precedent: A Major Problem in Pentecostal Hermeneutics' in R. P. Spittler (ed.), *Perspectives on the New Pentecostalism* (Grand Rapids, MI: Baker Book House, 1976), p. 122.

[87] William McDonald, 'A Classical Viewpoint' in Spittler (ed.), *Perspectives on the New Pentecostalism*, p. 6. He describes Pentecostal theology as a 'Christ centered experience certified theology'.

[88] W. Menzies, 'The Methodology of Pentecostal Theology: An Essay on Hermeneutics', pp. 12–13: 'Personal experience should not be given priority in establishing theology' yet 'testimony and exposition are equally handmaidens to truth' thus 'if a biblical truth is to be promulgated, then it ought to be demonstrable in life'. For Menzies, personal experience should verify the theological truth or dem-

gue that personal experience should be assigned to a certification or verification function at the end of the hermeneutic process. Yet, Stronstad correctly contends that 'experience enters the hermeneutical enterprise at the beginning of the hermeneutical process'.[89] His article sets out to demonstrate that 'charismatic experience in particular and spiritual experience in general give the interpreter of relevant biblical texts an experiential presupposition which transcends the rational or cognitive presuppositions of scientific exegesis'.[90] Stronstad contends that a Pentecostal hermeneutic will have a variety of cognitive (Protestant grammatico-historico exegesis) and experiential elements (salvation and charismatic experience or at least openness to the reality of contemporary charismatic experience).[91] Stronstad recognizes that charismatic experience in itself will not enable one to become 'an infallible interpreter' of Scripture; yet, charismatic experience provides an important pre-understanding to the Scripture.[92] By experiential verification, Stronstad recognizes that normative doctrinal positions cannot be validated by exegesis alone. The doctrinal positions must be livable and demonstrable within the Pentecostal community. In this manner, the community validates the understanding of Scripture. He, like all Pentecostals, desires to incorporate the theological truths into contemporary Christian experience. This testifies to the New Testament presentation of Scripture as ethical-spiritual experiential theology.

John McKay argues that Charismatic theology is a theology of 'shared experience'. Shared experience expresses the Charismatic-Pentecostal 'awareness of the similarity between their own experience and that of the prophets, apostles and Jesus, and also their awareness of being active participants in the same drama in which the biblical personages were involved'.[93] These shared experiences enable Charismatics and Pentecostals to grasp the central theme of Scripture—

---

onstrate the continuity between the biblical concept and experiential reality, thus it comes at the end of his hermeneutical procedure.

89 Stronstad, 'Pentecostal Experience and Hermeneutics', p. 16.
90 Stronstad, 'Pentecostal Experience and Hermeneutics', p. 17.
91 Stronstad, 'Pentecostal Experience and Hermeneutics', p. 25.
92 Stronstad, 'Pentecostal Experience and Hermeneutics', pp. 25–26.
93 John McKay, 'When the Veil is Taken Away', *JPT* 5 (1994), p. 26.

God restoring humanity to a right relationship with him and inviting the person to participate in God's restoration of his creation.[94]

This emphasis on 'shared charismatic experience' emanates from the Pentecostal/Charismatic understanding of God's presence in creation and among God's people. Pentecostals recognize not only the fruit of the Spirit as vital to the community's identity but also the gifts of the Spirit being just as vital because the manifestation of God's presence has been continuous from creation down to this very day.[95] Thus the supernatural experiential worldview of Scripture, which helped to create Pentecostalism, helps also to sustain the Pentecostal view of God. That is, an understanding of God who is greater than and beyond creation yet in and among his people. Signs and wonders provide evidence for this understanding. Therefore, the Pentecostal/Charismatic experiences help people to identify with the charismatic experiences of biblical characters creating an existential bond of 'shared experience', which reinforces the community's identity as the eschatological people of God.

The role of the Holy Spirit is continually referred to by Pentecostals as an important element in hermeneutics. A fundamental principle is that 'Scripture given by the Holy Spirit must be mediated interpretively by the Holy Spirit'.[96] The Holy Spirit is viewed as both the one who inspires Scripture as well as the one who illuminates Scripture; therefore, the Holy Spirit plays a vital part in elucidating the contemporary meaning of the Scripture.[97]

Pentecostals argue for a prominent role of the Holy Spirit in the interpretive process. French Arrington suggests four ways in which the interpreter relies on the Holy Spirit:

(1) submission of the mind to God so that the critical and analytical abilities are exercised under the guidance of the Holy Spirit;

---

[94] See McKay, 'When the Veil is Taken Away', pp. 17–40. McKay reveals his identity with the Pentecostal story and restorationist motif. Notice the strong emphasis upon this present era as God's final act in the drama of salvation.

[95] McLean, 'Pentecostal Hermeneutic', p. 38.

[96] Arrington, 'The Use of The Bible by Pentecostals', p. 104.

[97] Arrington, 'The Use of The Bible by Pentecostals', p. 104. Arrington appears to be drawing upon an earlier article by Rick D. Moore, 'A Pentecostal Approach to Scripture', *Seminary Viewpoint* 8 (November 1987), pp. 4–5, 11. See also H. Ervin who said, 'There is no hermeneutic unless and until the divine hermeneutes (the Holy Spirit) mediates an understanding' in his 'Hermeneutics: A Pentecostal Option' in *Essays on Apostolic Themes*, p. 27.

(2) a genuine openness to the witness of the Spirit as the text is examined; (3) the personal experience of faith as part of the entire interpretative process; and, (4) response to the transforming call of God's Word.[98]

The Holy Spirit enables the interpreter to bridge the historical and cultural gulf between the ancient authors of the Scriptures and the present interpreter.[99] This concern for the Holy Spirit's involvement in interpretation comes from the Scriptures, which emphasize the role of the Holy Spirit as revealing God and God's will to his people (1 Cor. 2.9-10a). Arrington's suggestions further imply that the Scriptures are able to transform the reader, thus the reader is not to master the biblical text but let the biblical text master her.

These two dimensions (experiential and pneumatic) can lead to a selective interpretive process of what is meaningful now. However, it must be pointed out that Scripture has always stood as the standard to which Pentecostal experience and belief must submit or replicate. If it does not then it should be repudiated. Thus Bruner, whose work is sharply critical of Pentecostalism, recognizes that 'Pentecostalism quite openly declares that unless it can support its case biblically it has no final compelling reason to exist'.[100]

John Christopher Thomas has suggested a holistic Pentecostal hermeneutical paradigm which incorporates Arrington's concern for a pneumatic illumination and a dialogical role between Scripture and experience.[101] He deduces his paradigm from the Jerusalem council as recorded in Acts 15. Thomas points out that Acts 15 grants an important role to the community and to the Holy Spirit in the interpretive process of dealing with Gentile Christians. Thomas makes several observations concerning this passage before proposing his Pentecostal hermeneutic. These are worth mentioning because in them we hear the concerns of some Pentecostals who find the historical critical methodology to be oppressive and alienating to the common laity. The danger is that the historical critical methodology takes the Bible out of the hands of the Christian community, out of the hands of the

---

98 Arrington, 'The Use of The Bible by Pentecostals', p. 105.
99 Arrington, 'The Use of The Bible by Pentecostals', p. 104.
100 Bruner, *A Theology of the Holy Spirit*, p. 63.
101 Thomas, 'Women, Pentecostals, and the Bible', pp. 41–56.

ordinary person, and puts it in the laboratory of the expert who alone has the proper tools and training to interpret Scripture.

First, Thomas argues that the interpretive methodological approach of the Jerusalem Council (Acts 15) is one in which the interpretive process moves from their present context to the past biblical text. This particular biblical move is in reverse order of the historical critical method that starts with the historical context of the biblical text and then moves to the present context of the reader. Secondly, the Holy Spirit in the community is seen to enable or illuminate the Christian community to overcome the difficulty of receiving Gentiles as Christians. Plenty of Old Testament passages existed that proclaimed the impossibility of Gentiles becoming full-fledged members of God's covenant community. Thirdly, Scripture was used in this process, yet, as applied to the matter of rules for table fellowship, it generated only a temporary resolution.[102] This reveals that the text's authority is not unrelated to its relevance to the community or its own diversity of teaching on a given topic.[103]

Thomas' hermeneutic contains three primary components: the community, the activity of the Holy Spirit and the Scripture. These components are not static but in dialogue with each other. The community testifies to the experiences attributed to the Holy Spirit and then engages Scripture (from a formalistic literary perspective) to validate or repudiate the experience or issue.[104]

Thomas applies this paradigm to the contemporary issue of women in ministry, and in so doing, he demonstrates how the paradigm can both work and help to resolve an issue which Scripture in and of itself cannot resolve. Scripture, with the aid of personal testimony through the inspirational guidance of the Holy Spirit, can resolve this issue. His hermeneutical strategy regards Scripture as authoritative and central for the rule and conduct of the Church, because

> ultimately the experience of the church must be measured against the biblical text and in that light, practices or views for which there is no biblical support would be illegitimate … this includes

---

[102] Thomas, 'Women, Pentecostals and the Bible', p. 50.
[103] Thomas, 'Women, Pentecostals and the Bible', p. 50.
[104] Thomas, 'Women, Pentecostals and the Bible', pp. 51–56.

respect for the text's literary genre and diversity as well as the unity of Scripture.[105]

Thomas has thus far presented a hermeneutical approach that attempts to be consistent with early Pentecostal ethos and resists the complete adoption of an Evangelical and modernistic historical critical method. The traditional Evangelical historical critical methods could be utilized in the hermeneutical dialogical process but must not monopolize the process. Contemporary Christian experience must also be included in the hermeneutical process. Moreover, Thomas' concern for literary analysis would take precedent over the historical critical approaches.[106] Hence, the world of the text and not the world behind the text would be the central concern. However, the meaning of the passage will be negotiated in the present interaction of the community of Pentecostal readers (both laity and scholarly), the working of the Holy Spirit and the testimony of Scripture.[107] Therefore, in his Pentecostal hermeneutical process, Thomas recognizes the important role of spiritual discernment in negotiating the meaning of a passage. The present meaning of the text becomes the determinate meaning, which of course may be renegotiated at a later time.

In sum, Pentecostalism began among the poor and racially marginalized people in society. Even today Pentecostalism's greatest growth is in the majority world. Pentecostalism in its early beginning should not be viewed as premodern or modern but as paramodern. Pentecostals were never invited to be equal partners in the modernist debate, but they still ate from the crumbs that fell from the table of modernity. They demonstrated modernist influences by arguing that they had scriptural empirical verification of their spiritual experience (Spirit baptism resulting in speaking in tongues).

Today, some Pentecostals attempt to express themselves with an Evangelical and modernistic hermeneutic (the historical critical methods). Yet if Pentecostalism desires to continue in its missionary

---

[105] Thomas, 'Women, Pentecostals and the Bible', p. 55.

[106] See his 'Max Turner's *The Holy Spirit and Spiritual Gifts: Then and Now* an Appreciation and Critique', *JPT* 12 (April 1998), pp. 13–14, 17–19.

[107] See John Christopher Thomas, 'Reading the Bible from within Our Traditions: A Pentecostal Hermeneutic as Test Case' in Joel Green and Max Turner (eds.), *Between Two Horizons: Spanning New Testament Studies and Systematic Theology* (Grand Rapids, MI: Eerdmans, 2000), pp. 108–22.

objective while keeping in tune with its early ethos, it must move beyond modernity. Pentecostalism is both a protest against modernity
as well as a proclamation to move beyond modernity.[108] This does
not imply that Pentecostals should embrace postmodernity uncritically but it does imply that the concerns of modernity are less helpful
than some post-critical concerns.[109] For Pentecostal scholars a satisfying hermeneutic cannot be uncritical or even remain paramodern. But
I would argue that our hermeneutic must move beyond the historical
critical methodology, which has gradually transformed biblical writings into museum pieces without contemporary relevance.[110] In moving beyond modernity the Pentecostal community should attempt
always to remain faithful to Pentecostal Christianity first and foremost as a counter culture movement, which in turn encourages them
to live on the margins in opposition to the world.

Pentecostals believe that the Holy Spirit still speaks today, and
when the Spirit speaks, the Holy Spirit has more to say than just
Scripture,[111] even though the Spirit will echo and cite Scripture. This
results from the Holy Spirit being present in creation and among the
community. Thus the Spirit will speak horizontally with a human
voice or through human dreams. This is possible because humanity is
created in God's image, and God took upon God's self humanity.
There exists, then, an essential relatedness that makes communication
possible.[112] In other words, a Pentecostal hermeneutical strategy is
needed which rejects the quest for a past determinate meaning of the
author and embraces the reality that interpretation involves both the
discovery of meaning and the creation of meaning. Thus, texts are by
their very nature, indeterminate.

---

[108] Bryan Turner (ed.), *Theories of Modernity and Postmodernity* (London: Sage Publications, 1990), pp. 1–12.

[109] James P. Martine, 'Toward a Post-Critical Paradigm', *New Testament Studies* 33
(1987), pp. 370–85.

[110] Edgar V. McKnight, *Postmodern Use of the Bible: The Emergence of the Reader-
Oriented Criticism* (Nashville: Abingdon Press, 1988), p. 14.

[111] Clark Pinnock, 'The Work of the Holy Spirit in Hermeneutics', *JPT* 2 (1993)
pp. 3–23. Pinnock is not a Pentecostal, but he argues for the same idea in this article. 'The Spirit helps us understand what was meant by the biblical authors with a
view to our understanding what God wants to say to us today' (p. 9).

[112] Francis Watson, *Text, Church and World*, (Edinburgh: T. & T. Clark, 1994),
pp. 107–23.

Thomas' hermeneutical paradigm captures both the dialogical and dialectical essence of Pentecostalism. He also includes the community in the hermeneutical process. This author agrees with Thomas that there exists interdependence between the Scripture, Spirit, and reader/readers. 'There must be a constant dialogue between the interpreter and the text' because 'God's Word is not a dead letter to be observed coldly but a word which speaks to my situation'. Therefore, 'the hermeneutical circle is not only unavoidable but desirable'.[113] There exists a Pentecostal hermeneutical strategy that can be revisioned from the early spiritual ethos of Pentecostalism. This hermeneutical strategy will speak with a liberating voice accented by postmodernity.

A 'Pentecostal Hermeneutical Strategy' can be recovered from the earliest phases of the Pentecostal movement and then critically reappropriated. The concern here is how identity shapes interpretive methods, and in turn how interpretive methods can reshape community identity. Methods are not neutral tools; instead, they have emerged from specific worldviews as *arbitrators of truth*. These methods are connected to epistemological systems that contain within themselves hints as to what is or is not a valid interpretation. Thus, interpretive methods are part of the communal narratives that evolved within a social cultural location.[114] In order for any Christian scholar to use the traditional historical critical methods, they must be reconfigured so as to be acceptable to his/her Christian worldview.[115]

Critique of the Evangelical Historical Critical Method

In general, Pentecostals have adopted the Evangelical historical critical methods along with its emphasis upon discovering the determi-

---

[113] G. Stanton, 'Presuppositions in New Testament Criticism' in I. Howard Marshall (ed.), *New Testament Interpretation* (Carlisle: Paternoster Press, rev. edn, 1985), p. 66.

[114] MacIntyre has demonstrated that all moral reasoning takes place from within a particular narrative tradition. See his *After Virtue: A Study In Moral Theory*, which is especially concerned to show how the 'Enlightenment project' of modernity has failed in providing an account of ahistorical reasoning and also his sequel *Whose Justice? Which Rationality?*, pp. 3–4.

[115] For example, Harrisville and Sundberg in their *The Bible in Modern Culture* are concerned to present a 'confessionally critical' historical critical methodology that can be 'responsible to the church and its dogmatic tradition' (p. 3).

nate meaning of a text by identifying the author's intended meaning. In doing so, Pentecostal biblical scholars have aligned themselves with the concerns associated with conservative modernism. This has affected North American Pentecostal community identity—an identity that becomes less Pentecostal and more acceptable to mainstream rationalistic and politically Republican Evangelicalism.

The great irony is that both the Fundamentalists and the liberals based their arguments on the same modernistic epistemological conviction. The conviction was based on the notion that only that which could be shown to be historically, scientifically, and objectively verifiable could be true, thus meaningful. As Thomas Oden has shown, 'liberal historicism and fundamentalist historicism remain to this day very much alike'.[116] Fortunately, the foundation of modernity has been crumbling, along with its view of historicism and objectivism. Unfortunately, those Christian traditions that have embraced modernity are also toppling.

This has become particularly challenging for much of Evangelical and Pentecostal biblical scholarship, because most Pentecostal scholars have totally adopted the concerns of the modernistic historical paradigm as the defining arbitrator of truth.[117] Thus, they are convinced that one can and must objectively capture the biblical author's intent by setting aside their own assumptions and understandings,[118] a view based on 'the naive Romantic intentionalism of Hirsch'.[119] Once the authorial intention is uncovered, which is then argued to be the true meaning of the text, one may apply it to the contemporary Church. This application of the past meaning, however, would be the *significance* of the text for the contemporary reader. The significance of the text should not be confused with the intended *meaning* of the author. The significance of the text will become the different applications based on the intended meaning, but the meaning always re-

---

[116] Oden, *After Modernity … What?*, p. 68.

[117] See Cargal, 'Beyond the Fundamentalist-Modernist Controversy: Pentecostals and Hermeneutics in a Postmodern Age', pp. 163–87.

[118] Hart, *Faith Thinking*, p. 116.

[119] Roger Lundin, *Disciplining Hermeneutics: Interpretation in Christian Perspective* (Grand Rapids, MI: Eerdmans, 1997), p. 21. For another sustained critique of Hirsch's theory see T.K. Seung, *Semiotics and Thematics in Hermeneutics* (New York: Columbia University Press, 1982), pp. 10–45.

mains fixed and determined.[120] Hart summarizes the primary task of the Evangelical exegete using the historical critical method. He states, 'the task of the biblical interpreter, therefore, is to decode the text, and thereby to retrieve the hidden inspired meaning of its human author'.[121] Hart points out how historical reconstruction is actually interpretation. His comment says it all: 'The distinction between "what a text means" and "what the text means to me" is to this extent a wholly misleading one'.[122] In other words, the division between what a text meant and what it means is a false illusion.

This aspect of the historical critical strategy is deceptive and insufficient for two reasons.[123] First, the method 'denies the necessary contribution of the reader and the reader's community in the act of interpretation … texts have meaning only as they are read and used by communities of readers.'[124] Pentecostals must accept the reality that the contemporary interpreter helps create meaning.[125] 'Meaning is actualized not by the author at the point of the text's conception but by the reader at the point of the text's reception'.[126] The interpreter

---

[120] Klein, Blomberg, and Hubbard, *Introduction to Biblical Interpretation*, p 401.

[121] Hart, *Faith Thinking*, p. 116.

[122] Hart, *Faith Thinking*, p. 126.

[123] Of course, this approach is susceptible to those critiques of Hirsch's theory. See Hart's, *Faith Thinking*, pp. 115–29. See also Stephan E. Fowl, *Engaging Scripture: A Model for Theological Interpretation*, pp. 33–40. Fowl challenges both determinate and anti-determinate approaches of interpretation and argues for an underdetermined approach to interpretation. He writes,

> Underdetermined interpretation recognizes a plurality of interpretive practices and results without necessarily granting epistemological priority to any one of these. An underdetermined biblical interpretation allows space for Christian theological convictions, practices, and concerns to shape and be shaped by biblical interpretation without being ruled by a determinate (or anti-determinate) theory of meaning' (p. 33, parenthetical added).

[124] Hayes, *Echoes of Scripture in the Letters of Paul*, p. 189. Hayes is *not* arguing for interpretive freedom without constraints. He writes, 'If there are no such constraints, Scripture will lose its power to form the identity of the community: it will become a lump of clay to be shaped according to the whim of the reader' (p. 190). The Scripture as written literature contains constraints.

[125] Umberto Eco, *The Role of the Reader: Explorations in the Semiotics of Texts* (London: Hutchinson, 1981); Wolfgang Iser, *The Act of Reading: A Theory of Aesthetic-Response* (London: Routledge, 1978). For an introduction and critique of 'Reader-Response' approaches, see Thiselton, *New Horizons*, ch. 13.

[126] Kevin J. Vanhoozer, 'The Reader in the New Testament Interpretation' in Joel Green (ed.) *Hearing The New Testament: Strategies For Interpretation* (Grand Rapids, MI: Eerdmans, 1995), p. 301.

cannot escape her historical-cultural-linguistic context or its impact on the interpretive process. Meaning is created in the very process of dialogue with a text. Meaning (understanding) is located in this very act of communication, which recognizes that misunderstanding can and does take place.[127]

Second, the extension, application or contemporization of the text's meaning is very important to all Christians. The concern of Evangelicals to hear and obey the Scripture has led them to emphasize the importance of applying God's word to their daily lives.[128] But their method of intention, based on Hirsch's literary theory, has encouraged them to seek an objective normative moral principle hidden in the text by the author.[129] This has led Evangelicals to find general principles in very culturally particular passages that then could be embodied in contemporary acceptable practices.

Evangelical hermeneut Klein writes, 'recent evangelical analysis has come to a consensus that the key to legitimate application involves what is usually called "principlizing"'.[130] Principlizing is the attempt to remove the cultural husk of the text in order to reveal its hidden kernel, the moral principle. The moral principle is a general and broad theological concept which becomes a timeless truth and often slips into the eternal ahistorical realm.[131] From this perspective, the discovered principle (which now is the author's intended meaning) functions as an immutable propositional truth claim set free from the prison of cultural particularity. Bauckham points out that, 'the dilemma with which cultural relativity presents us is that the more specific the biblical material is in its application to its own historical context, the less relevant it seems to be in our context'. Yet Bauckham resists looking for general principles. He asks,

---

[127] See Green (ed.), *Hearing The New Testament*, pp. 1–10. I agree with Green's comment that 'Today, no one interpretive method can claim to provide the one authentic understanding of any given NT text' (p. 9).

[128] Klein, *Introduction to Biblical Interpretation*, chapter 10; cf. Milliard J. Erickson, *Evangelical Interpretation: Perspectives on Hermeneutical Issues* (Grand Rapids, MI: Baker Books, 1993), ch. 3.

[129] Klein, *Introduction to Biblical Interpretation*, p. 401.

[130] Klein, *Introduction to Biblical Interpretation*, p. 407.

[131] Erickson, *Evangelical Interpretation*, pp. 62–72. He is attempting to avoid slipping into the ahistorical realm and at the same time avoid the relativistic nature of principlizing.

Must we then look in the Bible only for permanent norms of a highly generalized character? This would be foreign to the nature of the Bible and would leave a great deal of it unusable, since the Bible is God's message in, to and through very particular historical situations. Its universality must be found in and through its particularity, not by peeling its particularity away until only a hard core of universality remains.[132]

If the goal of biblical interpretation is to isolate the hidden principle, then Scripture ceases to function as an address to the community in and of itself. One is left with a disembodied principle(s) which become the authoritative word of God. However, as a Pentecostal I would affirm that the Scripture is inspired and not the extracted 'principle'.[133]

A related concern for this present writer is that the quest for these principles (aka foundational propositional truths) has caused some Evangelicals and Pentecostals to place certain biblical genres over others when developing their doctrinal positions, such as epistle and law over narrative.[134] McGrath argues that Evangelicalism has followed the Enlightenment in the gradual rejection of narrative. For Evangelicals, 'The narrative character of Scripture has been subtly marginalized, in order to facilitate its analysis purely as a repository of propositional statements, capable of withstanding the epistemological criteria of the Enlightenment'.[135] Evangelicalism has placed the genres of law and epistle in an authoritative position over narrative (Gospels and Acts). Evangelicals, especially from the Reformed tradition reread Gospels and Acts through their own reconstructive

---

[132] Bauckham, *The Bible in Politics: How to Read the Bible Politically*, p. 12.

[133] I suggest this dualistic concept that Scripture contains both inner principle and outer practice demonstrates the reliance of Evangelicalism upon a certain epistemological philosophical tradition which favors cognitive or theory over practice. For a helpful critique and explanation of overcoming this Western dualistic practice see Cheryl Bridges Johns, *Pentecostal Formation: A Pedagogy among the Oppressed* (JPTSup, 2; Sheffield: Sheffield Academic Press, 1993).

[134] See for example Stanley Grenz, *Theology for The Community of God*. Grenz cites Pauline passages frequently and at one place states 'historical narrative (Gospels and Acts) alone is not necessarily a sure foundation for doctrine'. For Grenz, Paul is more important for the construction of his theology (p. 421). Thus 'Narrative' in and of itself is an insufficient form of theological discourse as compared to 'Epistle'.

[135] Alister McGrath, *A Passion for Truth: The Intellectual Coherence of Evangelicalism* (Downers Grove, IL: InterVarsity Press, 1996), p. 106.

Pauline eyes, a practice that would be foreign to the earliest Christians (including Paul). Pentecostals on the other hand have had to argue for the narrative genre (Acts and Gospels) to be an authoritative doctrinal source, an acceptable not inferior form of theological discourse.[136]

Principlizing then, can be disastrous for the primary literary genre of Scripture—narrative. Narrative is story and as a story it creates a world in which the reader may dwell. Narrative invites the reader to create meaning. Reducing the story to some moral principle seems to imply that the narrative portions of Scripture are not effective means in and of themselves by which a community's identity can be shaped or challenged. Thus, principlizing emphasizes the notion that 'narrative is a relatively unimportant moral category' which sees '"stories" as illustrations of some deeper truth that we can and should learn to articulate in a non-narrative mode'.[137]

In Scripture, narrative is the chosen genre for theological discourse. However, this move to place law and epistle over narrative is even more disastrous to the Bible when one recognizes that the 'Bible is not primarily a book of timeless doctrines or a book of moral law. It is primarily a story ... Story is the overarching category in which others (genres) are contextualized.'[138]

Willard Swartley's *Slavery, Sabbath, War and Women*[139] clearly demonstrates that the understanding of scriptural truth took on different and even contradictory meanings in different Christian social-historical contexts. Thus, the idea that one can grasp the ahistorical timeless principle is an elusive endeavor. One cannot simply peel off the cultural husk (the relative particularity of a passage) and arrive at the kernel of truth (an ahistorical timeless principle) because meaning is communicated in and through the culturally conditioned passage.

---

[136] See Roger Stronstad, *The Charismatic Theology of St. Luke*.

[137] Stanley Hauerwas, *The Peaceable Kingdom: A Primer in Christian Ethics*, p. 25. Hauerwas is not discussing Evangelical principlizing but his concern for narrative to shape identity and practice over against propositional rules is germane to this discussion, see especially ch. 2, 'A Qualified Ethic: The Narrative Character Of Christian Ethics', pp. 17–34.

[138] Richard Bauckham, *Scripture and Authority Today* (Cambridge: Grove Books, 1999), p. 10 (parenthetical added). A shorter version of this essay was published as 'Scripture and Authority', *Transformation* 15/2 (1998), pp. 5–11.

[139] Willard Swartley, *Slavery, Sabbath, War and Women* (Scottsdale, PA: Herald Press, 1983).

Meaning can only be found in the confines of a particular social location.[140] According to Swartley's case studies, the meaning (understanding) of the biblical text changed, yet the written text has stayed
the same. Therefore, the Spirit of God must be involved in the communicative process, thus making meaningful a past document for a
contemporary Christian community. Furthermore, the meaning of
the biblical passage must be presently negotiated in a community
marred by sin. The Holy Spirit, along with the community's ability to
discern, is a necessary participant in the hermeneutical process. This
process of negotiating meaning takes place in the arena of the narrative tradition of the community.

A Pentecostal hermeneutical strategy that desires to be a part of
the ethos of the first generation of the Pentecostal movement and be
critically concerned must take seriously the challenge that meaning
exists in the social-linguistic-cultural location in which a community
reads. Even an understanding of its past meaning is also dependent
upon the contemporary reader. Hence, what it meant and what it
means is a false dichotomy. In this sense meaning is what happens as
a result of reading.[141] However, Pentecostals would want to grant
Scripture a superior position in the communicative event. The Scripture, as the meta-narrative, must master the reader based on the narrative's terms. The reader should not dominate and subjugate the passage to her own horizon without attempting to hear the narrative
from its horizon.[142] The Bible's normative praxis interpretation is created and lived out in the contemporary social-location of the readers
in community.[143]

I am not suggesting that the biblical passage can mean just anything, because 'a Bible that can mean anything means nothing'.[144] Nor

---

[140] See Bauckham, *The Bible in Politics*, pp. 12–19.

[141] Hart, *Faith Thinking*, p. 127.

[142] See John Goldingay, *Models For Interpretation of Scripture*, pp. 46–55, see p. 53,
n. 73.

[143] I am purposefully reworking a now accepted notion that meaning is located
in three contextual worlds: the world behind the text, in the text, and in front of the
text. See Lategan, 'Hermeneutics', p. 152 and Tate, *Biblical Interpretation*.

[144] Morgan, *Biblical Interpretation*, p. 13. This is an important volume on the history of modernistic biblical interpretation. Morgan's concern is to demonstrate the
value of a theological literary approach to the interpretation of Scripture.

am I embracing relativism by rejecting objectivism.[145] Neither am I arguing for a total rejection of the historical investigation of a text. What I am posing is that the historical critical method leads the community in the wrong direction. The historical critical concern is historical reconstruction; thus, the emphasis is on the world behind the text and not the text itself. This emphasis has led to the eclipse of biblical narrative.[146]

Additionally, the historical critical method looks for the determinate meaning, but can this theory of meaning satisfy the ongoing needs of Christian communities? The Scriptures require an open-ended (indeterminate) approach to interpretation[147] which allows for the possibilities of future meaning.[148] The Bible speaks to the Christian community's present real life situations which supersede its past. Therefore, future meaning is possible and desirable because Scripture is a 'grand meta-narrative'[149] which engages the reader.

It is obvious to most that the first generations of Pentecostal interpreters have more in common with the so-called naive approaches of popularistic Christianity than with the modernisticly nurtured historical critical approach of the Fundamentalists and liberals. Timothy Cargal was correct to point out that most contemporary Pentecostal scholars have more in common with the Fundamentalist, yet the Pentecostal in the congregation has more in common with postmodern concerns.[150]

---

[145] See Hart, *Faith Thinking*, which is an attempt to steer a course between objectivism and relativistic pluralism. This author agrees with Hart's creative approach to this current dilemma.

[146] See Hans Frei, *The Eclipse of Biblical Narrative: A Study in Eighteenth and Nineteenth Century Hermeneutics* (New Haven: Yale University Press, 1974).

[147] Stephan E. Fowl and L. Gregory Jones, *Reading in Communion: Scripture And Ethics in The Christian Life* (Grand Rapids, MI: Eerdmans, 1991), pp. 30–34, give four reasons why this is so. Two important ones are that the very nature of all interpretation in general is indeterminate, and influences of sin have affected people's practical reasoning abilities. Their concern is to show that Christian interpretation of Scripture requires wise and virtuous readers, which is an exercise in practical reasoning with the goal of embodying the interpretation.

[148] See Clark Pinnock, 'Biblical Texts: Past And Future Meanings', *Wesleyan Theological Journal* 34/2 (Fall 1999), pp. 136–51.

[149] Pinnock, 'Biblical Texts', p. 141. Pinnock lists four factors which give evidence for the future 'potentiality of meaning that is waiting in the biblical text to be realized' (p. 140). The Bible as a grand meta-narrative is his second factor.

[150] Cargal, 'Beyond the Fundamentalist-Modernist Controversy: Pentecostals and Hermeneutics in a Postmodern Age', pp. 163–87.

Some have suggested that we need to 'jump off' this postmodern bandwagon.[151] Yet, it appears that we are in the midst of another paradigm shift from modernity to postmodernity.[152] If one should jump off the wagon, where should one land? Pentecostals cannot return to the modernistic cessationist worldview, nor can they be numbered among the Neo-Fundamentalist or Non-Charismatic Evangelical Reformed traditions (which are still very much modernistic cessationists and hostile towards Pentecostalism).[153] This worldview is what the Pentecostal/Charismatic Christians have helped to undermine. A Pentecostal hermeneutical strategy should attempt to continue to forge an alternative path that neither entirely accepts the pluralistic relativism of postmodernism nor entirely affirms the objectivism of modernism—a pathway that began to be forged in early Pentecostalism.

Do Pentecostals need a unique method? This is an inappropriate question to ask. Pentecostals have used methods similar to and common among other interpretive communities. What makes the reading or interpretation distinct is that it is being generated within a Pentecostal community.[154] Thus, the concern should focus upon the Pentecostal narrative tradition—its story. It was the Pentecostal community's usage of the 'Bible Reading Method' from the 'Latter Rain' perspective and not an isolated exegetical method that shaped the readers and placed constraints upon the possible readings. Meaning is not something we discover then appropriate. Meaning is something we construct.

---

[151] See Menzies, 'Jumping off The Postmodern Bandwagon', pp. 115-20. I would suggest that his sentiments reflect that of those Pentecostal scholars who have seen themselves as academic 'Fundamentalist with a difference' and who belief that redaction criticism is the method for discovering the author's intention.

[152] See Turner (ed.), *Theories of Modernity and Postmodernity.*

[153] See Millard J. Erickson, *The Evangelical Heart and Mind: Perspectives on Theological Issues* (Grand Rapids, MI: Baker Book House, 1993) especially ch. 8 where he clearly reveals his more modernistic worldview.

[154] Gordon Fee exemplifies this. Although he no longer affirms a distinct and subsequent Spirit baptism, he is still a Pentecostal and biblical scholar who generates Pentecostal readings even though he relies upon a modified (due to his Pentecostal perspective) historical critical method. See his magnus opus, *God's Empowering Presence: The Holy Spirit in the Letters of Paul* (Peabody, MA: Hendrickson, 1994). This work reiterates an important point. Fee, because he is Pentecostal, writes a work like this and in doing so demonstrates that a Pentecostal community concerns affect his exegetical method.

Summary

This chapter set out to bring the reader(s) into the contemporary debate concerning Pentecostals and hermeneutical concerns. The first section introduced Pentecostalism as a movement in the margins, which set itself apart from the larger Christian community with the distinct doctrine of 'Spirit baptism' and 'speaking in tongues'. This doctrine stands at the core of Pentecostal identity, thus acting as the foundation of the contemporary challenges facing this movement. Additionally, this first section discussed essential themes of the Pentecostal community that arise in this hermeneutical debate. These themes include demonstrating the basis of Pentecostalism's movement from the primitive 'Bible Reading Method' to the modernist 'historical critical method'. This author established that academic Pentecostals were drawn to the acceptable Protestant hermeneutical methodologies in order to avoid the so-called 'inappropriate exegetical methods'. They sought to solve the hermeneutical problems by solely replacing the primitive 'Bible Reading Method' with that of the Reformed Protestant methodology. This, however, created another sizable dilemma, namely one of identity. The supporters of this failed to realize the importance of the Pentecostal community's role in the hermeneutical process. This first section explains how these themes moved Pentecostalism to begin relying upon the modernistic hermeneutic to solve the exegetical discrepancies arising in exegesis.

The second section of chapter five is primarily concerned with the modernization of the Pentecostal hermeneutic. Here this author shows that as Pentecostals entered the academic arena they began abandoning the 'Bible Reading Method' and embracing the 'historical critical method' of modernity. Yet while embracing modernity, the Pentecostals simultaneously retained and maintained their traditional Pentecostal and conservative conclusions. The primary conclusion of this section was that through the modernization of the Pentecostal hermeneutical concerns the role of the community had been forgotten. The hermeneut must be concerned with more than only the horizon of the text. This author asserts that any hermeneutical strategy must negotiate the tension between the two horizons (the horizon of the text and the horizon of the reader in community).

The third section deals specifically with the ongoing current hermeneutical debate taking place within Pentecostalism. At the outset of this chapter, this author stated that two voices within Pentecostalism would be heard. In this section the two voices are defined and explained. The first voice is heard from those Pentecostals who embrace the modernistic hermeneutical methods. The second voice is heard from those who see this modernization as a threat to Pentecostal identity, and thus seek to recover the initial impulses that gave rise to the Pentecostal movement.

Following this explanation, another voice is added to the debate. This fourth section introduces a voice from outside the Pentecostal community, namely that of F.D. Bruner and James D.G. Dunn. Their emergence into the debate raises important issues that face the Pentecostal tradition. The specific conclusion drawn from their involvement is the source or location of 'meaning'. This author demonstrates that both Bruner and Dunn commonly hold to the idea that meaning in endued in the text by the author. Consequently, the task of the biblical scholar is to extrapolate the text's objective single meaning, which is synonymous with discovering the author's intended meaning. This in turn makes the interpretation process the end all of hermeneutics.

Next, the focus moves from the debate with outside sources to the hermeneutical debate within Pentecostalism. The primary questions this section wrestles with are, 'Have Pentecostals created a unique method?' And do they need a unique method firmly to establish their beliefs and practice in Scripture? As demonstrated in this section of chapter five, the initial movement of Pentecostalism was a response against both liberalism and Fundamentalism. This author has shown how Pentecostalism has attempted to forge a third path. Along the way it has used some of the modernistic methods while attempting to retain the Pentecostal worldview. In retrospect, Pentecostalism has survived the onslaught of modernity. The conclusions drawn here are that though the movement has utilized the modernistic methodologies, the result has not ended with a modernistic Pentecostal. On the contrary, I have shown that the Pentecostal movement has more in common with certain post-critical concerns even though the Pentecostal movement is not 'postmodern'.

Finally, the central purpose of this chapter is achieved by setting up the key thesis of this study. I draw the conclusion from the hermeneutical debate that a Pentecostal hermeneutical strategy should attempt to continue to forge an alternative or third path that neither entirely accepts the pluralistic relativism of postmodernism nor entirely affirms the objectivism of modernism. The distinguishing feature of the Pentecostal hermeneutic is that it lies within the Pentecostal community and is an extension of the community's Central Narrative Convictions. Therefore the focus of the hermeneutic should be upon the Pentecostal narrative—its story. After all, it was the Pentecostal community's usage of the 'Bible Reading Method' and the 'Latter Rain' perspective that placed constraints upon the possible readings. This, therefore, sets the stage for the final chapter that will propose a post-critical hermeneutical strategy that is committed to narrative interpretation.

6

A CONTEMPORARY PENTECOSTAL HERMENEUTICAL STRATEGY

Pentecostals ... would want to approach interpretation as a matter of the text, the community, and also the ongoing voice of the Holy Spirit.[1]

Rickie Moore

In this chapter, I will outline a critical contemporary Pentecostal hermeneutical strategy. This contemporary Pentecostal hermeneutical strategy will be critical and yet remain faithful to the Pentecostal community and the Pentecostal narrative tradition that shapes its identity and makes meaning possible. This hermeneutical strategy desires to be faithful to the Pentecostal community's ethos and yet sensitive to current academic methodological perspectives concerning the interpretation of Scripture.[2] In doing so, I will present a Pentecostal hermeneutical strategy which will take seriously the Pentecostal community and its Central Narrative Convictions. The hermeneutical strategy must emphasize the importance of praxis and of retaining the early perspective of what it meant to live on the margins. In doing so, this strategy will be concerned with the multicultural and interracial dimensions of the community. The poor (both economically and spiritually) will be given a voice as they participate in the making of meaning.

---

[1] Rick D. Moore, 'Canon and Charisma in the Book of Deuteronomy', *JPT* 1 (October 1992), pp. 75–92.

[2] This does not imply a blind allegiance to any one classical Pentecostal tradition, nor complete approval of all the Pentecostal beliefs and practices, but this does imply that the hermeneut is involved in and concerned about the Pentecostal community.

A Narrative Strategy that Embraces a Tridactic Negotiation for Meaning

The strategy recognizes the important contributions that the Pentecostal community brings to the interpretive process. This will shift the emphasis away from the individual hermeneut and her commitment to an acceptable and correctly applied method and place primary emphasis upon the community as the spiritual cultural context in which interpretation takes place. The primary filter for interpretation will be the Pentecostal narrative tradition. Yet the Pentecostal strategy will resist positioning the community over and against Scripture. This writer will show that a promising hermeneutical strategy can be extrapolated from the spiritual ethos and the narrative tradition of early Pentecostals and woven into a critical contemporary hermeneutical strategy that could be beneficial for Pentecostals (and other Christians traditions).

This strategy does not pretend to be a full-blown theory of interpretation, nor will it desire to become a static method. Nevertheless, the strategy will be a product of the community and based upon a biblical model from Acts.[3] The hermeneutical strategy will be a narrative approach that embraces a tridactic negotiation for meaning between the biblical text, the Holy Spirit and the Pentecostal community. Meaning then is arrived at through a dialectical process based upon an interdependent dialogical relationship between Scripture, Spirit and community.

In the previous chapter this writer argued that a Pentecostal hermeneutical strategy should be concerned with both a discovery of meaning as well as with the creation of meaning. This is necessary because all written communication is indeterminate or, better, underdeterminate. Written communication is underdeterminate in the sense that a reader is needed to complete the communicative event, hence producing meaning.[4] This does not imply that the biblical pas-

---

[3] The reader will recall that the hermeneutical model narrated in Acts 15 as understood by the Pentecostal scholar J.C. Thomas was discussed in ch. 5 of this work, therefore there is no need to restate the information. Thomas' hermeneutical model based upon Acts 15 comprises three primary components: the believing community, the activity of the Holy Spirit and Scripture.

[4] J. Severino Croatto, *Biblical Hermeneutics: Toward a Theory of Reading as the Production of Meaning* (Maryknoll, NY: Orbis Books, 1987), p. 10.

sage can mean whatever a community wants or desires it to mean. There is a dialectical interdependent relationship between the written text and the community of readers. Thus, there exists an actual communication event that takes place as the text is read. The text, which in this case is a biblical passage, desires to be understood by the readers in a Christian community.[5] The biblical passage is at the mercy of the community. However, a Pentecostal Christian community will want to give the biblical passage the opportunity to interact with the readers in such a way that the passage fulfills its dialogical role in the communicative event. This is so because the Pentecostal community recognizes the Bible as sacred revelation—the inspired, authoritative word of God. Furthermore, the community believes that the Scripture can speak clearly and creatively as the word of God to the contemporary Pentecostal community's situations and needs. Hence, the Pentecostal community will read the Bible as 'Sacred Scripture' which speaks to its culturally specific needs and concerns enabling the community to live faithfully before and with the living God.

The strategy will be self-consciously a *narrative* approach to the understanding and the making of theological meaning. Furthermore, the Pentecostal strategy will incorporate a text centered and reader oriented interpretive method.[6] Knowledge as meaningful understanding will be rooted in and related to human life because 'the only sort of (theological and theoretical) knowledge that really counts is knowledge grounded in life'.[7] 'Meaning, therefore, is no longer seen in terms of an original "cause" or ultimate "effect" but in terms of relationship'.[8] Meaning then is arrived at through a dialectical process

---

[5] Fowl and Jones, *Reading in Communion*, p. 8.

[6] Edgar V. McKnight, *Post-Modern Use of the Bible: The Emergence of Reader-Oriented Criticism* (Nashville, TN: Abingdon Press, 1988). According to McKnight,

The postmodern perspective which allows readers to use the Bible today is that of a radical reader-oriented literary criticism, a criticism which views literature in terms of readers and their values, attitudes, and responses ... A *radical* reader-oriented criticism is postmodern in that it challenges the critical assumption that a disinterested reader can approach a text objectively and obtain verifiable knowledge by applying certain scientific strategies. A radical reader-oriented approach sees the strategies, the criteria for criticism and verification, the 'information' obtained by the process, and the use of such 'information' in light of the reader (pp. 14–15).

[7] McKnight, *Post-Modern Use of the Bible*, p. 19 (parenthetical statement added).

[8] McKnight, *Post-Modern Use of the Bible*, pp. 22–23.

based upon an interdependent dialogical relationship between Scripture, Spirit and community. Pentecostals in general and this Pentecostal writer in particular takes very seriously Goldingay's warning that 'those who pretend to be objective and critical and then find their own (Enlightenment or existential or feminist) concerns in the texts they study need to take a dose of self-suspicion'.[9] Hence, this strategy will embrace a 'hermeneutic of suspicion' and a 'hermeneutic of retrieval'[10] as it negotiates creative and constructive meaningful readings of Scripture grounded in the Pentecostal community's desire to live faithfully with God. In the remainder of this chapter I will outline a Pentecostal contemporary hermeneutical strategy that embraces a tridactic negotiation for meaning between the biblical text, the Holy Spirit and the Pentecostal community.

The Contribution of the Biblical Text

In order for a communicative event to take place there must be space between the text, a stable but underdeterminate entity, and a reader in community. The reader in community reads/listens interpretively to the written text in an attempt to understand the text, thereby completing the communicative act. Semiotics is a theory that emphasizes both the space between the reader and a text and the necessary dialectical link between the reader and the text in the production of meaning.

Semiotics
Semiotics and semiology have become interchangeable labels for the systematic study of signs.[11] Semiotics is concerned with signs as conveyers of meaning. Signs are not limited to a written language but

---

[9] John Goldingay, *Models for Interpretation of Scripture*, p. 45.

[10] See Ricoeur, *Freud and Philosophy*, p. 27, who argues that 'Hermeneutics seems to me to be animated by this double motivation: willingness to suspect, willingness to listen; *vow of rigor, vow of obedience*'.

[11] Terence Hawkes, *Structuralism and Semiotics* (Berkeley and Los Angeles, CA: University of California Press, 1977), p. 124. Hawkes points out that Europeans prefer semiology with regard to Saussure's coinage of the term, whereas English speakers prefer semiotics because of Peirce. See Ferdinand de Saussure, *Course in General Linguistics* (New York: Philosophical Library, 1959), pp. 15–17; and Charles Sanders Peirce, *Collected papers of Charles Sanders Peirce* ; 6 vols. (eds. Charles Hartshorne and Paul Weiss; Cambridge: Harvard University Press, 1931–35).

include a great diversity of human (and animal) activities.[12] The focus here, however, is with written communication. Semiotics is concerned with linguistics, and linguistics is the science of language.[13] Semiotics as it relates to linguistics is concerned with both the 'speech-act', whether written or spoken, and the 'language' in which the speech act functions. Abrams writes that the aim of semiotics 'is to regard the *parole* (a single verbal utterance or particular use of a sign or set of signs) as only a manifestation of the *langue* (that is, the general system of implicit differentiations and rules of combination which underlie and make possible a particular use of signs)'.[14] In other words the language (*langue*) 'is a system of signs and laws regulating grammar and syntax—a sort of "canon" establishing guidelines for meaning'.[15] Meaning, in the sense of what a 'speech-act' is saying grammatically, is not viewed as a referential sign about what it is referring to historically.[16] Speech (*parole*) 'is the *act* executing the given possibilities residing within a system of signs'.[17] In order for communication to transpire, both the writer/speaker and the reader/listener must have some competency in the language (*langue*). Therefore, semiotics emphasizes the transaction of meaning between texts and readers, thus involving the reader in the production of meaning in order to complete the communication event.

Biblical hermeneutics is concerned with the interpretation of the Bible. The Bible is a collection of written speech acts. Semiotics, therefore, can provide helpful insights and guidance for a hermeneutical strategy. This writer does not want to confuse semiotics with biblical hermeneutics but instead desires to approach a Pentecostal hermeneutical strategy through semiotics.[18] Semiotics recognizes the distance between the reader and the text by emphasizing the impor-

---

[12] See Hawkes, *Structuralism and Semiotics* ch. 4 for an introduction, explanation and the diversity of semiotics.

[13] M.H. Abrams, *A Glossary of Literary Terms: Seventh Edition* (Orlando, FL: Harcourt Brace College Publishers, 1999), p. 280.

[14] Abrams, *A Glossary of Literary Terms*, p. 280.

[15] Croatto, *Biblical Hermeneutics*, p. 13.

[16] Paul Ricoeur, 'Biblical Hermeneutics', *Semeia* 4 (1975), p. 81.

[17] Croatto, *Biblical Hermeneutics*, p. 14. See also Abrams, *A Glossary of Literary Terms*, p. 141. This distinction between the language (a system of signs) and the speech act was introduced by Saussure.

[18] In doing so this author is following Croatto's argument in *Biblical Hermeneutics*, p. 10.

tant contributions of both the text and reader in the making of meaning. The following information will not provide an extensive explanation of semiotic theory; rather, it will attempt to glean helpful guidance from one practitioner of semiotics, Umberto Eco.

Eco presents a critical interpretive semiotic strategy that takes seriously the 'dialectical link' between the written text and the reader.[19] He, in a series of published lectures, attempts to limit the possible interpretations a text can generate for the reader.[20] He recognizes that a reader can 'overinterpret' a text.[21] Eco does not reduce a text to one correct interpretation but allows for valid multiple interpretations.[22] In order for the interpretation to be valid, it must be latent within the text. The reader then is challenged to actualize the underdeterminate meaning.[23] Eco explains:

> I tried to show that the notion of unlimited semiosis does not lead to the conclusion that interpretation has no criteria. To say that interpretation (as the basic feature of semiosis) is potentially unlimited does not mean that interpretation has no object and that it 'riverruns' merely for its own sake.[24]

Eco argues that there are criteria for limiting interpretation.[25] In order to avoid overinterpretation (an improper interpretation of the text), he argues that the reader must be sensitive to the intention of the text (*intentio operis*).[26] The work, then, contains the basic criteria for limiting the possible meanings. However, the work itself cannot prove that there is only one correct interpretation nor 'that there must be

---

[19] Eco *et al.*, *Interpretation and Overinterpretation*, p. 64. For a helpful overview of Eco's semiotic theory see Thiselton, *New Horizons*, pp. 524–29.

[20] Collini in *Interpretation and Overinterpretation* writes, 'Eco's lectures in this volume explore ways of limiting the range of admissible interpretations and hence of identifying certain readings as "overinterpretation"' (p. 8).

[21] Eco, *Interpretation and Overinterpretation*, pp. 23–24. See also Umberto Eco, *The Limits of Interpretation* (Bloomington and Indianapolis: Indiana University Press, 1990).

[22] Eco writes that a reader 'would not be entitled to say that the message can mean *everything*. It can mean many things, but there are senses that it would be preposterous to suggest ... No reader-oriented theory can avoid' the constraints presented by the message (*Interpretation and Overinterpretation*, p. 43).

[23] Eco, *Interpretation and Overinterpretation*, p. 23.

[24] Eco, *Interpretation and Overinterpretation*, pp. 23–24.

[25] Eco, *Interpretation and Overinterpretation*, p. 40.

[26] Eco, *Interpretation and Overinterpretation*, p. 25.

one right reading'.[27] The intention of the text does, however, limit the possible interpretations and helps to suggest which interpretations are unacceptable.[28] The intention of the text 'operates as a constraint upon the free play of the *intentio lectoris*' (intention of the reader).[29]

Eco does not collapse the intention of the text back into the intention of the author (*intentio auctoris*). He argues that the intention of the author is 'very difficult to find out and frequently irrelevant for the interpretation of a text'.[30] His emphasis upon textual interpretation 'makes the notion of an empirical author's intention radically useless'.[31] His understanding of the function of the intention of the text makes the text, rather than the author of the text, the source for meaning.[32] This is an important contribution to the Pentecostal hermeneutical strategy because Pentecostals would not want simply to produce meaning in a manner that places the community over and against the text but instead allow the text to be a full fledged participant in the making of meaning. Hence the biblical text is respected as an interdependent dialogical participant in the making of meaning.

Eco argues that the intention of the text is part of (his) semiotic strategy which always keeps 'a dialectic link between *intentio operis* and *intentio lectoris*'.[33] The empirical reader is necessary because the reader 'has to decide to see it' (the intention of the text). The intention of the text is a transparent reality that requires the reader to see it.[34] Eco explains:

> The text's intention is not displayed by the textual surface. Or, if it is displayed, it is so in the sense of the purloined letter. One has to

---

[27] Eco, *Interpretation and Overinterpretation*, p. 9.

[28] Eco leaves upon the door for multiple acceptable meanings of a text but the work does set limits to the possible range of legitimate meanings, see *Interpretation and Overinterpretation*, p. 52.

[29] Eco, *Interpretation and Overinterpretation*, p. 9.

[30] Eco, *Interpretation and Overinterpretation*, p. 25.

[31] Eco, *Interpretation and Overinterpretation*, p. 66. Collini writes, 'Eco accepts the doctrine, enshrined by the New Critics several decades ago, that the author's pre-textual intention—the purposes that may have lead to the attempt to write a particular work—cannot furnish the touchstone of interpretation, and may be even irrelevant or misleading as guides to a text's meaning or meanings' (p. 10).

[32] Eco, *Interpretation and Overinterpretation*, p. 9, see also ch. 3. Eco writes 'I hope my listeners will agree that I have introduced the empirical author in this game only in order to stress his irrelevance and to reassert the rights of the text' (p. 84).

[33] Eco, *Interpretation and Overinterpretation*, p. 64.

[34] Eco, *Interpretation and Overinterpretation*, p. 64.

decide to 'see' it. Thus it is possible to speak of the text's intention only as a result of a conjecture on the part of the reader. The initiative of the reader basically consists in making a conjecture about the text's intention.

A text is a device conceived in order to produce its model reader. I repeat that this reader is not the one who makes the 'only right' conjecture. A text can foresee a model reader entitled to try infinite conjectures. The empirical reader is only an actor who makes conjectures about the kind of model reader postulated by the text. Since the intention of the text is basically to produce a model reader able to make conjectures about it, the initiative of the model reader consists in figuring out a model author that is not the empirical one and that, in the end coincides with the intention of the text. Thus, more than a parameter to use in order to validate the interpretation, the text is an object that interpretation builds up in the course of the circular effort of validating itself on the basis of what it makes up as its result. I am not ashamed to admit that I am so defining the old and still valid 'hermeneutic circle'.[35]

Eco's argument is that the text must be given the opportunity to construct the model reader. The model reader is one who reads the text in the way in which the text was designed to be read.[36] This once again emphasizes that the text is a stable entity that significantly contributes to the making of meaning.

The actual or empirical reader then must take into account the cultural and linguistic context (*langue*) in which the text was generated (*parole*) when postulating the intention of the text. In other words, the reader must be both sensitive and responsible to the cultural and linguistic aspects of the text when interpreting the text.[37] Hence, meaning here carries a dual sense in that it acts as both referential meaning, what the signs are referring to and, as linguistic meaning, how the sentence grammatically conveys meaning. In other words, meaning refers to both how a sentence conveys meaning according to the rules of the language of which it belongs and to the word/sign's so-

---

[35] Eco, *Interpretation and Overinterpretation*, p. 64.
[36] Eco, *Interpretation and Overinterpretation*, p. 10.
[37] Eco, *Interpretation and Overinterpretation*, pp. 68–69.

cial-historical-cultural reference. For Eco, the empirical reader is to be concerned about the text's intention, which a reader 'is able to recognize in terms of textual strategy'.[38]

But this is not an easy task. Eco warns:

> The act of reading must evidently take into account all these elements, (the elements belonging to language as a social treasury) even though it is improbable that a single reader can master all of them. Thus every act of reading is a difficult transaction between the competence of the reader (the reader's world knowledge) and the kind of competence that a given text postulates in order to be read in an economic way[39] (the first parenthetical statement added).

Thus the empirical reader must prove her conjecture about the intention of the text from the text itself. This of course requires a competence in the lexical system of the language at the time of the text's production and an acceptance of the text as a coherent whole. The text or literary work is self-sufficient and requires careful analysis. Hence the only way to prove the conjecture about the intention of the text

> is to check it upon the text as a coherent whole ... any portion of a text can be accepted if it is confirmed by, and must be rejected if it is challenged by, another portion of the same text. In this sense the internal textual coherence controls the otherwise uncontrollable drives of the reader.[40]

Eco believes that this semiotic procedure is the best way to go about interpreting texts and ruling out unacceptable interpretations of a text. 'Between the unattainable intention of the author and the arguable intention of the reader there is the transparent intention of the text, which disproves an untenable interpretation'.[41]

---

[38] Eco, *Interpretation and Overinterpretation*, p. 69. See also Umberto Eco, *The Role of the Reader: Explorations in the Semiotics of Texts* (Bloomington, IN: Indiana University Press, 1979), pp. 7–11.

[39] Eco, *Interpretation and Overinterpretation*, p. 68.

[40] Eco, *Interpretation and Overinterpretation*, p. 65.

[41] Eco, *Interpretation and Overinterpretation*, p. 78. Eco embraces some notions of the school of thought called 'New Criticism' specifically the emphasis upon the text as the source for meaning.

My Pentecostal hermeneutical strategy will adopt Eco's concern to keep a dialectical link between the reader and the text. His notion of the 'model reader' needs to be displaced by the reality that no actual reader is or can become the model reader. It is important to recognize that in the communicative event the speaker/writer will have a general or even specific audience in mind when communicating. Hence, the genre of the written text will be an important aspect to take into consideration. The genre will aid the readers in community in the interpretive process. However, Eco's recognition that a literary text has textual constraints that limits the possible meanings that can be generated within the imagination of the readers in community is very helpful.

The early Pentecostals attempted to interpret 'Scripture in light of Scripture', hence emphasizing the world of the text as the means to understanding Scripture. They appreciated the cultural context in which a text was generated, thus they would look to commentaries to inform their understanding, but this was not the historical critical method. Because of this, a text centered approach from a semiotic perspective is not only congenial to early Pentecostals, but it also reinforces the contemporary hermeneutical concern for a critical interpretive strategy that allows for the participation of the reader in the making of meaning. Therefore a semiotic interpretive strategy will be the most conducive for Pentecostals because it allows for an open interdependent dialectic interaction between the text and the reading community in the making of meaning. However, the Holy Scripture in its final canonical form, provides the primary arena in which the Pentecostal community desires to understand God.[42]

The text provides textual clues as to how it desires to be read and understood. The early Pentecostals primarily relied upon the Bible Reading Method, which emphasized the world of the text, and thus they attempted to hear the text without immediately absorbing it into

---

[42] See J. Barton, *Reading the Old Testament* (Philadelphia: Westminster, 1984), pp. 140–57, who argues that Brevard Childs' 'Canonical Criticism' resembles the principles of New Criticism. For a helpful explanation and critique of Brevard Childs' canonical approach see Charles J. Scalise, *Hermeneutics As Theological Prolegomena: A Canonical Approach* (Macon, GA: Mercer University Press, 1994). Scalise modifies Childs' approach by addressing Childs' inadequate account of tradition and canonical intentionality, and the need to include within the canonical approach newer sociological and literary approaches.

the mind of the community. In other words, they did attempt to allow the text to speak to the community as another voice, which from the Pentecostal perspective was perceived as the voice of God. Furthermore, Pentecostals affirm that the biblical text can challenge them, as well as offer resistance against forcing an understanding upon the text which could not be substantiated by the text.

From a semiotic viewpoint the text contains latent but nonetheless potent cues as to how it desires to be understood. The way to 'see' and 'hear' these cues is through a close (formalistic) analysis of the text illuminated by social cultural context in which it was written. The Pentecostal contemporary strategy would affirm the importance of the text's genre along with the grammatical rules of the language to which the specific speech-act belongs. The text would be analyzed, however, from a formalistic perspective while affirming the importance of the social cultural context in which the text came into existence. Meaning is negotiated through the conversation between the text, community and Spirit, with the world behind the text informing not controlling the conversation.[43]

Inner Texture and the Bible Reading Method

The early Pentecostals utilized the Bible Reading Method as they interpreted the Bible. This popularistic method paid close attention to the repetition of phrases and words within a passage and even within the whole canon of Scripture. This contemporary Pentecostal strategy would affirm the importance of the Bible Reading Method (without affirming its paramodern philosophical context) but would also desire to move beyond it. The Bible Reading Method's concern to capture the inner texture of the text and interpret Scripture with Scripture is valuable contributions to this contemporary strategy.

A primary way of analyzing a text would be to pay close attention to the inner texture of the text. Inner textual analysis pays close attention to the verbal signs and their relationship to each other in the passage. 'The purpose of this analysis is to gain an intimate knowledge of words, word patterns, voices, structures, devices, and modes in the text, which are the context for meanings and meaning-effects that an interpreter analyzes'.[44] Inner textual analysis then would be an

---

[43] See Tate, *Biblical Interpretation*, p. xxv.

[44] Vernon K. Robbins, *Exploring the Texture of Texts: A Guide to Socio-Rhetorical Interpretation* (Valley Forge, PA: Trinity Press International, 1996), p. 7.

important way to get to the intention of the text and at how the text cues the interpreter in the making of meaning.

In short, semiotics affirms that a dialectical interdependent link exists between the text and the reader. Semiotics also views the text as an underdeterminate yet stable entity that affirms the reader as a necessary component in the communicative event and the making of meaning. The text is to be respected as a dialogical partner in the communicative event. This Pentecostal hermeneutical strategy affirms the semiotic concern that a text can be misunderstood and finds semiotic theory to be a helpful critical aspect of the hermeneutical strategy.

The Contribution of the Pentecostal Community

In chapters 2 through 4 this writer has demonstrated that interpretative methods and readings are dependent upon a hermeneutical community. Moral reasoning is always rooted in a particular narrative tradition which offers its version of reality to other communities. In the negotiating of meaning, one's community is an important and necessary component of the hermeneutical strategy. In order to produce a 'Pentecostal' reading of Scripture, one needs to identify with the Pentecostal community.

This hermeneutical strategy recognizes that all interpretive readings are culturally dependent and inherently contain the ideological perspective(s) of the community. Furthermore both the interpretive method and the community readings are ideologically biased. Hermeneutical strategies reflect the bias of those using them. This strategy affirms this reality hence the importance of practicing a hermeneutic of suspicion and retrieval.[45] Also this strategy affirms a praxis oriented hermeneutical stance because the interpretive activity is generated in the present concrete experience of living in the Pentecostal community. The community moves towards the biblical text with

---

[45] Schneiders, 'Feminist Hermeneutics' in Green (ed.), *Hearing The New Testament: Strategies For Interpretation*, p. 349–69. Schneiders writes, 'Those who continue to hope that the biblical text is susceptible of a liberating hermeneutic must pass by the way of suspicion to retrieval. Suspicion leads to ideology criticism. But ideology criticism is then in the service of advocacy and reconstruction' (p. 352).

specific concerns and needs and looks to the Scripture to speak to its present situations.

The Pentecostal Hermeneutical Community: The Context

The Pentecostal hermeneut must be entrenched within a Pentecostal community and in tune with the concrete needs and aspirations of the Pentecostal community.[46] This strategy affirms the necessity of the hermeneut living among the Pentecostal community. Therefore, the hermeneutical emphasis will fall upon a semiotic and narrative approach with the context of the reader in community providing the hermeneutical filter and the matrix for understanding and completing the communicative event.

The Pentecostal hermeneut who is educated by the academy must also be a participant within the Pentecostal community; that is, she should understand her Christian identity to be Pentecostal.[47] In order to be included as part of the Pentecostal community, she must embrace the Central Narrative Convictions of Pentecostalism. The Pentecostal story must be interwoven into her personal story. This does not imply that one cannot be concerned about the larger Christian community or attempt to understand the Scripture from a different perspective or interpretive strategy, but it does mean that one's identity is shaped and formed by participating in a Pentecostal community.

In order for one to be a Pentecostal hermeneut (whether lay, clergy, educated or non-educated), one needs to be recognized as a Pentecostal. The hermeneut must share her story (testimony) and receive the important 'amen' of affirmation from the community. Thus, one will need to have a clear and convincing testimony concerning his/her experiential relationship with the Lord Jesus Christ. The 'Full Gospel' must be embraced and experienced, including especially Spirit baptism. This does not mean a Pentecostal hermeneut must have experienced every dimension of the Full Gospel, but she must be willing to participate in the Pentecostal story.[48] In this way,

---

[46] See Thomas, 'Reading the Bible from within our Traditions: A Pentecostal Hermeneutic as Test Case', pp. 120–22.

[47] This may include those who are neo-pentecostal.

[48] This writer is not saying that the community requires the hermeneut to have experienced divine healing or entire sanctification but to be Pentecostal is to embrace the 'Full Gospel' perspective which encourages one to be saved, sanctified, healed, Spirit baptized and eagerly awaiting the soon return of Jesus. The point is

the reader is an extension and participant of the community not an isolated individual.

The sharing of testimonies always involves and requires discernment from within the community. Therefore, one is not a Pentecostal hermeneut because one uses a Pentecostal method; rather, one is a Pentecostal hermeneut because one is recognized as being a part of the community. The community, along with its concerns and needs, is the primary arena in which a Pentecostal hermeneut participates. The community actively participates in the Pentecostal hermeneutical strategy not passively but actively through discussion, testimony, and charismatic gifts.

Generally, the academic hermeneut will always have an active leadership role in the Pentecostal community, whether it is as a pastor, teacher or lay leader. One needs to appreciate that most Pentecostals who are a part of academic educational communities were and many times remain credential-holding ministers of Pentecostal communities.

The Pentecostal hermeneutical strategy argues that the place to hear the present Word of God is the current context in which one lives. The past Word of God (Scripture) then speaks a present Word of God, which is to be believed and obeyed. The point of view of the reader/interpreter is not to be dismissed but embraced. This does not mean that Scripture cannot resist the reader's point of view. It does mean that the readers' community plays a significant role in what is found in Scripture. Because Pentecostals recognize that Scripture is authoritative and able to transform lives, they would want to hear the Scripture on its own terms, first and foremost. Yet, the hearing of Scripture is filtered through the Pentecostal narrative tradition. As a result of this, there is an interdependent dialogical and dialectical link between the community and the Scripture with the goal being personal and social transformation.

Narrative Criticism: The Method

The readers (hermeneuts) in community select certain methods which they use in order to interpret texts. One of the important contributions of the hermeneut is the interpretive method. The method is not

---

that one has a particular participatory relationship with Jesus that is experiential, which is defined by the 'Full Gospel' message and rooted in a Pentecostal community. The hermeneut is never alone in the interpretive process.

isolated from the person but becomes a tool that the hermeneut uses in the creative negotiation of meaning. The most helpful contemporary literary method that could be woven into a strategy for Pentecostals is a narrative critical approach. A narrative method allows for the dialectic interaction of the text and reader in the negotiation of meaning. Pentecostals by their very nature are inherently storytellers. They primarily transmit their theology through oral means.[49] They have been conditioned to engage Scripture as story. Thus a narrative critical approach with a bent towards reader response would enable the Pentecostal community not only to interpret Scripture critically but also to let Scripture critically interpret them.

Why choose narrative criticism when there are a plethora of interpretive methods available to biblical exegetes? There are a number of important reasons for this choice.

First and foremost is that the traditional historical critical methods have not paid enough attention to the primary literary genre of Scripture which is narrative. Hans Frei demonstrated how the traditional historical critical methodologies eclipsed the primary genre of Scripture, which is narrative.[50] Instead of focusing attention upon the biblical text as a piece of coherent literature with specific genres, historical criticism has turned its attention to the world behind the text. Powell summarizes the goals of the various methods associated with the historical critical analysis quite succinctly as it pertains to the Gospels:

> this method seeks to reconstruct the life and thought of biblical times through an objective, scientific analysis of biblical material. Source criticism, for example attempts to delineate the sources that the evangelists used in the composition of their Gospels. Form criticism concentrates on defining the *Sitz im Leben* (setting in life) that individual units of tradition may have had before they came to be incorporated into the Gospels. Redaction criticism seeks to discern the theologies and intentions of the evangelists themselves by observing the manner in which they edited their

---

[49] W.J. Hollenweger, 'The Pentecostal Elites and the Pentecostal Poor: A Missed Dialogue?' in Karla Poewe (ed.), *Charismatic Christianity as a Global Culture* (Columbia, SC: University of South Carolina Press, 1994), p. 201.

[50] Hans W. Frei, *The Eclipse of Biblical Narrative: A Study in Eighteenth and Nineteenth Century Hermeneutics* (New Haven, CT: Yale University Press, 1974).

sources and arranged the individual units of tradition. These disciplines share a common desire to shed light upon significant periods in the transmission of the Gospels: the period of the historical Jesus, the period of oral tradition in the early church, or the period of the final shaping of the Gospels by the evangelists.... In focusing on the documentary status of these books, the historical-critical method attempted to interpret not the stories themselves but the historical circumstances behind them.[51]

Powell and other biblical scholars who welcome literary approaches to the interpretation of Scripture recognize the value of the historical critical method but also emphasize its limitation in reading narrative as a sustained coherent story.[52] Therefore, narrative criticism's primary concern is to read the biblical narratives as story and 'attempts to read these stories with insights drawn from the secular field of modern literary criticism'.[53]

The metaphors of a window and a mirror help to describe the differences between the historical critical approaches and literary approaches. Historical criticism treats the biblical text as a window. Biblical scholars analyze the text for its historical referential function. The goal is to reconstruct the historical past but not necessarily interpret the text itself as a narrative. The biblical scholar who uses a literary approach views the biblical passage as a mirror. In this manner the narrative is analyzed according to its poetic function. The poetic aspect is concerned with the elements that make up the story and how the story affects the reader.[54] Powell writes: 'Granted that the Gospels may function referentially as records of significant history, might they not also function poetically as stories that fire the imagination, provoke repentance, inspire worship and so on?'[55] Narrative criticism reads the story as a coherent piece of literature that invites the reader's participation in the creation of meaning while also recog-

---

[51] Mark Allan Powell, *What Is Narrative Criticism?* (Minneapolis, MN: Fortress Press, 1990), p. 2.

[52] Powell, *What Is Narrative Criticism?*, pp. 2–3. 'The prevailing sense was not that historical criticism had failed or that its goals were invalid, but that something else should also be done' (p. 3).

[53] Mark Allen Powell, 'Narrative Criticism' in Green (ed.), *Hearing the New Testament: Strategies for Interpretation*, p. 239.

[54] Powell, *What Is Narrative Criticism?*, p. 8.

[55] Powell, 'Narrative Criticism', p. 240.

nizing that narratives can shape the perception of the reader. In this way, a story may shape 'the way readers understand themselves and their own present circumstances'.[56]

This first reason to interpret the biblical text from a literary perspective that embraces its poetic function leads directly into the second reason for using a narrative approach. Narrative criticism is a text centered approach that attempts to understand the biblical text on its own terms. Therefore, the emphasis does not fall upon the world behind the biblical text even though an understanding of the social and cultural setting that the narrative assumes is beneficial to the contemporary reader's understanding of the text. The emphasis of narrative criticism is on the story world of the text itself.[57]

The Pentecostal community desires to understand the biblical text in its final form. The final canonical form of the biblical narrative is what shapes the reader and enables the reader to develop a praxis-oriented understanding of life. By embracing the final form of the narrative and analyzing the formal features of a narrative text, narrative criticism marks an important shift away from the fragmentation of the biblical text to restoring the coherent wholeness of the narrative.[58] Narrative criticism, unlike the historical critical methods that fragment the text, will bracket historical referential concerns and examine the text as a closed universe of the story world.[59] The reader following a narrative approach is deeply 'absorbed in the world of the text'.[60] The story world serves as its own context in which people, places, and events are understood.[61] Hence, the reader spends most of her time reading and re-reading the passage in light of the larger narrative in which it is found. Therefore, the Pentecostal community could critically enhance its understanding of the story world of biblical narrative by embracing narrative criticism. The Biblical narrative could challenge and shape them as a community as they locate their

---

[56] Powell, 'Narrative Criticism', p. 240.

[57] Powell, *What is Narrative Criticism?*, p. 5.

[58] George Aichele, *The Postmodern Bible: The Bible and Culture Collective* (New Haven: Yale University Press, 1995), pp. 85–86.

[59] David Rhoads, Joanna Dewey and Donald Michie, *Mark As Story: An Introduction to the Narrative of a Gospel* (Minneapolis, MN: Fortress Press, 2nd edn, 1999), pp. 3–5. Also Powell, *What is Narrative Criticism?*, pp. 6–8.

[60] Powell, *What is Narrative Criticism?*, p. 86.

[61] Rhoads, *Mark as Story*, p. 5.

story within the biblical narrative, specifically the Gospels and Acts. In this way, the contemporary Pentecostal hermeneut could move away from the fragmented process of the historical critical method and critically retrieve from early Pentecostals an interpretive approach that embraces the text as a coherent world with the necessary potential for providing meaning.

A third reason to employ a narrative critical approach is the benefit it brings to the Christian communities' understanding and use of the Bible as Holy Scripture. The Bible functions as a meta-narrative and is the foundational story for belief and practice. Christians have read Scripture or heard Scripture read as coherent stories; therefore, narrative criticism is a means by which scholars and nonprofessional Christian readers can be brought together.[62]

Narrative criticism, which is concerned with story telling, provides a natural bridge for the Pentecostal community. The Bible is not reduced to propositions but instead functions as it was intended to—as stories that grip and shape the readers while challenging them to infer from the narrative, a praxis oriented theology. To read Scripture as a set of propositional premises is to misunderstand the primary literary genre of Scripture-narrative. Narrative critical theory, then, can also become the means to produce a Pentecostal narrative praxis theology.[63] Thus, narrative theory is not an end in itself but spills over and intersects other Christian disciplines such as theology, ethics and practical theology (preaching, teaching and counseling) as well as narrative critical exegesis.[64]

A fourth reason for using a narrative approach is that narrative insists on the role of the reader in the creative transaction of meaning.[65] Narrative theory like 'all theories of literature' will 'understand the

---

[62] Powell, *What is Narrative Criticism?*, p. 87.

[63] See Alister E. McGrath, *The Genesis Of Doctrine: A Study in the Foundation of Doctrinal Criticism* (Grand Rapids, MI: Eerdmans, 1997), pp. 52–67. McGrath argues that 'scripture recounts a narrative, a set of particularities, (therefore) a process of inferential, rather than deductive, analysis is clearly indicated' (p. 62).

[64] Stephen D. Moore, *Literary Criticism and the Gospels: The Theoretical Challenge* (New Haven, CT: Yale University Press, 1989), p. xviii.

[65] Seymour Chatman, *Story and Discourse: Narrative Structure in Fiction and Film* (Ithaca, NY: Cornell University Press, 1978). Chatman writes, 'Whether the narrative is experienced through a performance or through a text, the members of the audience must respond with an interpretation: they cannot avoid participating in the transaction' (p. 28).

text as a form of communication through which a message is passed from the author to the reader'.[66] In order for the communicative event to transpire, there must be someone who can read and understand the message.[67]

Narrative critics recognize that narratives such as John's Gospel or the book of Judges can be understood by various and diverse audiences for whom they were not originally intended. Historical critical approaches would interpret what a passage meant by its original author for a specific community at a particular time and place. Narrative criticism, conversely, is concerned with 'discerning the anticipated effects that this narrative may have on readers in any place or time who follow the guidance of the narrator'.[68] Furthermore, the goal of narrative criticism is not to interpret the text from the perspective of its original, actual audience or solely from the perspective of the contemporary reader. Rather, narrative criticism has as its goal to read the narrative from the perspective of its implied reader.[69]

The implied reader is a hypothetical 'imaginary person who always responds to the story "with whatever emotion, understanding, or knowledge the text ideally calls for"'.[70] The implied, ideal reader or model reader 'is presupposed by and constructed by the text itself'.[71] This imaginary reader is the one who has 'all the ideal responses *implied by* the narrative itself'.[72] Rhoads, Dewey and Michie argue that there are responses implied for readers in every line of the narrative. These responses elicited by the narrative may include:

> filling gaps, identifying with characters, being held in suspense, anticipating later parts of the story, recalling earlier parts of the story,

---

[66] Powell, *What is Narrative Criticism?*, p. 9.

[67] See Wolfgang Iser, *The Act of Reading: A Theory of Aesthetic Response* (Baltimore, MD: Johns Hopkins University Press, 1978), p. 107.

[68] Mark Allen Powell, 'Toward a Narrative-Critical Understanding of Matthew' in Jack Dean Kingsbury (ed.), *Gospel Interpretation: Narrative-Critical and Social-Scientific Approaches* (Harrisburg, PA: Trinity Press International, 1997), p. 12.

[69] Powell, *What is Narrative Criticism?*, p. 20. See also Chatman, *Story and Discourse*, pp. 149–50. Chatman defines the implied reader as the counter part to the implied author. The implied reader is 'the audience presupposed by the narrative itself'. Thus the implied readers are the audience 'immanent to the narrative' whereas the real readers are 'extrinsic and accidental to the narrative' (p. 150).

[70] Kingsbury, *Gospel Interpretation*, p. 11.

[71] Powell, *What is Narrative Criticism?*, p. 15.

[72] Rhoads, *Mark as Story*, p. 138.

being drawn by the narrator asides and irony, having emotions aroused, having expectations raised and revised, experiencing resolution (or lack of it), and so on.[73]

The reader's responses are shaped and limited by the story.[74] Thus, the implied reader is the counterpart to the implied author, both of whom are imbedded in the text itself.[75]

Powell argues that narrative critics tend to view the written message as a complete communication event in the sense that a message contains within itself a implied author (sender) and implied reader (receiver), and so it is complete in itself.[76] This does not mean that the actual reader is not necessary, but that actual readers are to look for 'clues in the narrative that indicate an anticipated response from the reader'.[77] The responses of the actual reader must be checked against the text itself. In this way, narrative criticism does allow for the dynamic production of meaning by the reader's interaction with the text.[78]

Narrative criticism's concern is similar to Eco's semiotic concern to keep a dialectic link between the reader and the text. This dialectic link between the narrative text and the reader insists on the reader responding to the text in ways that are signaled by the text for the production of meaning. Therefore, the empirical contemporary reader in community is an active participant in the production of meaning. The meaning(s) of the text is not simply found in the text, nor is it simply found in the reader but comes into existence in the *dialectic interaction* of the reader *with* the text.[79]

This dialectic interpretive tension is not simply a linear move of meaning from text to reader, as if in the classical literary interpretive sense that meaning is inherently and entirely found *in* the text. Nor is the reader given freedom to construe meaning in the way that meets her creative concerns, which from that perspective allows the reader

---

[73] Rhoads, *Mark as Story*, p. 138.
[74] Powell, *What is Narrative Criticism?*, pp. 11–22.
[75] Chatman, *Story and Discourse*, p. 148.
[76] Powell *What is Narrative Criticism?*, pp. 19–20.
[77] Powell *What is Narrative Criticism?*, p. 19.
[78] Powell *What is Narrative Criticism?*, p. 18, Iser, *The Act of Reading*, pp. 18–21, argues that there can be no meaning unless this interaction takes place thus the text elicits responses from the reader.
[79] Powell, *What is Narrative Criticism?*, pp. 17–18.

to stand *over* and *against* the text.[80] Once again, meaning is produced through the on-going interdependent dialectical interaction of the text and reader, both of which are necessary for there to be a creative transaction of meaning. Hence, neither the reader nor the text is to dominate the negotiation of meaning. The reader and text must work together in actualizing the potential meaning(s) of the text through the process of reading.[81] The reader in community and the text make different kinds of contributions to the production of meaning, which allows the communicative event to succeed. This interdependent dialectical and dialogical interactive process is reinforced by narrative criticism's concern to follow the unfolding plot and its interaction with characters, settings and events in the story world of the narrative. This also allows for narrative criticism to spill over into reader response criticism.[82]

In sum, narrative criticism offers a text centered interpretive approach that allows for the social-cultural context in which the text was generated to inform the contemporary reader, but in no way does it allow for it to dominate or control the interpretation of the text. Instead, the text is appreciated for what it is—a narrative; thus, the interpreter is concerned with the poetic features and structure of the story as a world in itself. The text invites the reader to produce meaning through a dialectical process of reading. Narrative critics are concerned to follow the responsive clues of the narrative from the perspective of its implied reader. Yet, the implied reader, whether a hypothetical construct of the text[83] or a hypothetical construct in the mind of the empirical reader,[84] necessitates the involvement of the

---

[80] Powell, *What is Narrative Criticism?*, pp. 16–21. Powell places reader response criticism into three categories: the reader *over* the text, the reader *with* the text and, the reader *in* the text. He argues that narrative criticism falls into the third category, hence a more 'objective' interpretive theory. This present author is arguing that there is much more overlap between reader response and narrative criticism than Powell would want to acknowledge.

[81] Iser, *The Act of Reading*, pp. 34–35.

[82] Moore, *Literary Criticism and the Gospels*, p. 73. Moore correctly points out that reader response criticism is not 'a conceptually unified criticism; rather it is a spectrum of contrasting and conflicting positions' (p. 72). Cf. Powell, *What is Narrative Criticism?*, p. 21, who writes, 'narrative criticism and dialectic modes ("with the text") of reader response are most similar and they may eventually become indistinguishable'.

[83] Narrative critics like Powell, Kingsbury, and Rhoads.

[84] Iser and Chatman.

empirical reader in the production of meaning. This opens the door for reader response criticism, which is 'a spectrum of contrasting and conflicting positions'.[85] This writer will now address narrative criticism's relationship with reader response criticism.

Reader Response Criticism: A Necessary Contribution

Stephen Moore defines narrative criticism as a story-preoccupied criticism. 'Being preoccupied with story means, most of all, being preoccupied with *plot* and *character*'.[86] Plot refers to 'a sequence of events that are related in terms of their causes and consequences'.[87] Plot plays a key role in following the unfolding message of the story. The connections of settings, events and characters as well as interaction of the narrator create the plot of the story. To know the plot is to understand how a story begins, how the story progressively moves forward, and how conflicts arise, develop, and are resolved. By becoming familiar with the plot of the narrative, one is able to grasp better the significance of the positioning of each episode within the overall story, and the role the episode plays in the story.[88]

As this writer has already argued, plot functions on three levels. The plot functions on the surface level of the story. In this way, plot refers to how the whole story is fabricated. Plot as the forward action of a story has a beginning, middle and end. Yet the plot can also refer to the more detailed 'arrangement of incidents and patterns as they relate to each other' in a story.[89] These two functions of plot recognize that plot operates within the world of the text. However, there exists a real yet abstract third notion of plot that operates within the mind of the reader. The reader also exercises a tendency to organize and make connections between events within the narrative.

Chatman argues that the mind of the reader 'inevitably seeks structure' and will provide the causative connection of events in a narrative, and 'even the most divergent events' will be connected. This is so because the sequenced structure of the narrative 'is not simply linear but causative'. The events within the narrative 'are radi-

---

[85] Moore, *Literary Criticism and the Gospels*, p. 72.

[86] Moore, *Literary Criticism and the Gospels*, p. 14.

[87] Richard G. Bowman, 'Narrative Criticism of Judges' in Gale A. Yee (ed.), *Judges and Method: New Approaches in Biblical Studies* (Minneapolis, MN: Fortress Press, 1995), p. 26.

[88] Kingsbury, *Gospel Interpretation*, p. 3.

[89] Hawk, *Every Promised Fulfilled*, p. 19.

cally correlative, enchaining, entailing' and the causative sequence of the events 'may be overt, that is explicit, or covert, implicit'.[90] The reader then supplies or fills in the gaps of the imagined details of the events that are not expressly presented in the narrative. These imagined details, drawn from the reader's repertoire of knowledge and experience, will fill out the narrative, thus making it complete.[91]

Hawk argues that this function of plot in the mind of the reader is a 'dynamic phenomenon', which 'moves beyond the formal aspects of the text and addresses the interpretive processes that takes place between text and reader'.[92] This happens because a 'narrative ... elicits a dynamic interpretative relationship between text and reader'.[93] Therefore the reader is involved in the negotiation of the potential meaning a narrative elicits because a narrative 'evokes a world of potential plot details. Many of these details go unmentioned but can be supplied' by the reader.[94] The reader then is involved in the creative transaction of meaning by bringing the communicative event of the text to completion.

Kevin Vanhoozer presents an overview of the various reader response criticisms in his essay titled 'The Reader in New Testament Interpretation'.[95] Vanhoozer points out that for literary theorists 'reading is not merely a matter of perception but also of production; the reader does not discover so much as create meaning ... What is in the text is only a potential of meaning'. The reader at the point of the text's reception produces meaning. She does not simply *re*produce meaning or discover meaning in the text.[96] Reader response criticism is concerned primarily with how readers produce meaning and how this meaning is related to the text and reader (or readers in community).[97] 'For Reader Response critics, meaning is not a content in the text which the historian simply discovers; meaning is an experience which occurs during the reading process'.[98]

---

[90] Chatman, *Story and Discourse*, pp. 45–47.

[91] Chatman *Story and Discourse*, p. 30.

[92] Hawk, *Every Promised Fulfilled*, p. 27.

[93] Hawk, *Every Promised Fulfilled*, p. 27.

[94] Chatman, *Story and Discourse*, p. 29.

[95] In Green (ed.), *Hearing the New Testament*, pp. 301–28.

[96] Vanhoozer, 'The Reader in New Testament Interpretation', p. 301.

[97] Vanhoozer, 'The Reader in New Testament Interpretation', p. 304.

[98] Aichele, *The Postmodern Bible*, p. 42.

Reader response critics, like semioticians (and to a certain extent narrative critics) embrace the notion that meaning results from the experience of reading. They reject the notion that meaning is a stable and determinate reality of the text. Reader response shares the conviction that meaning is indeterminate and is the production of the interaction of the text and reader.[99] However, there are two predominant ways of understanding and applying the concept of indeterminate meaning which requires the reader to make meaning. These two different ways reinforce and correspond to Vanhoozer's argument that there are two primary approaches of reading: a conservative reader response approach which he calls 'Reader-Respect' and a radical reader response approach which he identifies as 'Reader-Resistance'.[100]

According to Vanhoozer, the conservative 'Reader-Respect' views the text's indeterminacy as an invitation for the reader to make meaning by completing the narrative through filling in the gaps of the text. This understanding of indeterminacy then 'refers to an unfinished meaning that the reader completes by following authorial instructions and textual indications'.[101] Texts are 'unfinished objects whose "gaps" and indeterminacies call out for completion by the reader'.[102] The conservative approach of reading emphasizes a dynamic interdependent dialectic interaction between the text and the reader, but the reader is to follow the cues offered by the implied author to the implied reader. By following the latent clues within the text, the real reader brings completion to the text in various ways that are acceptable to the implied reader. Therefore, the conservative reader affirms both the openness of the text as well as the constraints of the text.[103]

---

[99] Vanhoozer, 'The Reader in New Testament Interpretation', p. 305.

[100] Vanhoozer, 'The Reader in New Testament Interpretation', pp. 305–306, 308–12.

[101] Vanhoozer, 'The Reader in New Testament Interpretation', p. 306.

[102] Vanhoozer, 'The Reader in New Testament Interpretation', p. 308.

[103] Vanhoozer, 'The Reader in New Testament Interpretation', p. 309, Vanhoozer sites both Iser and Ricoeur as those who practice a Reader-Respect approach for the reading of texts. He quotes Iser's often cited analogy of readers and stargazers: the stargazers 'may both be looking at the same collection of stars, but one will see the image of a plough, and the other will make out a dipper … The "stars" in a literary text are fixed; the lines that join them are variable' (p. 308), citing Wolfgang Iser, *The Implied Reader: Patterns of Communication in Prose Fiction from Bunyan to Beckett* (Baltimore, MD: John Hopkins University, 1974), p. 282.

The constraints of the text, however, are given primacy over the imagination of the reader. That is, the reader is to fill in the gaps in ways that are consistent to the worldview of the implied reader of the text. In this way, the text allows for more than one correct interpretation but limits the range of possible interpretations.[104] Thus, the conservative reader shares Umberto Eco's concern that the real or empirical reader can overinterpret texts. The act of reading requires the reader to cooperate *with* the text in the actualization of potential meaning.

Vanhoozer's radical reader, which he labels as 'Reader-Resistance', understands a text's indeterminacy as an opportunity which invites 'the reader to determine what to make of the text' and its meaning.[105] Meaning resides entirely within the world of the actual flesh and blood reader. Similar to the conservative reader's understanding, meaning is not fixed in the text, but unlike the conservative reader's approach, the text has unlimited potential for meaning. The reader comes to the text and positions herself *over* the text creating a meaningful text that is consistent with her ideological viewpoint. Texts, then, are to be used. Some texts are to be resisted if the text is attempting to convey an ideological viewpoint that is not acceptable to the reader.[106] 'Meaning is rather a function of a reading strategy brought to the text' by the community to which the reader belongs. Therefore, the community provides the constraints for the reader, not the text itself or a literary canon.[107]

Vanhoozer's analysis of reader response criticism is really an attempt at locating who or what should play the most significant role in the production of meaning. In other words, Vanhoozer is trying to identify who or what dominates the reading experience—the text or the reader. The conservative reader attempts to hear the text on its

---

[104] Vanhoozer, 'The Reader in New Testament Interpretation', p. 309.

[105] Vanhoozer, 'The Reader in New Testament Interpretation', p. 306, Vanhoozer further divides the Reader-Resistance into two groups that he labels post-structuralists (deconstruction) and neo-pragmatics. The neo-pragmatics are represented by the later writings of Stanley Fish. Vanhoozer cites Fish, 'The interpretation constrains the facts rather than the other way around and also constrains the kinds of meanings that one can assign to those facts' (Stanley Fish, *Is There a Text in This Class? The Authority of Interpretive Communities* [Cambridge: Harvard University, 1980], p. 293).

[106] Vanhoozer, 'The Reader in New Testament Interpretation', p. 307.

[107] Vanhoozer, 'The Reader in New Testament Interpretation', p. 311.

own terms, following the guidance of the text in the production of meaning. The conservative approach to reading encourages the text and the reader to cooperate with each other by fulfilling their perspective roles in the communicative event. The radical reader, on the other hand, recognizes that the community or individual is the sole arena in which meaning is produced. This does not mean that the community can do whatever it wants with the text, but that the reading constraints are part of the ideological perspective of the reader's community. The reading conventions themselves become another text to be read.[108] The conservative reader, however, must take seriously the radical reader's concern that reading inherently involves the experience of the empirical reader. Thus as Fowler notes, the reader's experience of reading and making meaning is already shaped by her community. The reader cannot escape her historical-cultural-ideological context and this context shapes, but may not necessarily pre-determine, what she finds as meaning when reading a text.[109]

Although Vanhoozer's review and assessments are very helpful, he seems to limit the location of meaning to either the text (the conservative approach) or to the reader (the radical approach). He correctly argues that the radical reader approach denies meaning as existing, even in a limited manner, in the text; thus, this approach is, philosophically speaking, anti-realist.[110] In the game of making meaning, there are no rules *per se*, just creatively attractive readings.

This writer agrees with Vanhoozer's argument that 'without a certain "realism of reading," where meaning is independent of the interpretive process, reading would cease to be a dangerous, world shattering project'.[111] If a text does not have some limited potential ability to convey meaning, then a text could never inform, transform or challenge the reader. A coherently written text in some real sense desires to be understandable to a reader thus presenting potential meaning. Thus, meaning is potentially latent (underdeterminate) within the text, but it cannot be produced apart from a real reader who brings the necessary imagination based on her life experiences to the text.[112]

---

[108] Aichele, *The Postmodern Bible*, p. 55.
[109] Robert Fowler, 'Reader Response Criticism' in *Mark and Method: New Approaches in Biblical Studies* (Minneapolis, MN: Fortress Press, 1992), p. 53.
[110] Vanhoozer, 'The Reader in New Testament Interpretation', p. 317.
[111] Vanhoozer, 'The Reader in New Testament Interpretation', p. 317.
[112] Tate, *Biblical Interpretation*, p. 172.

Narrative theory is based upon and is an extension of communication theory. Narrative criticism gravitates to and is primarily made up of 'conservative readers' because the text is viewed as desiring to communicate meaning.[113] Meaning is an interactive negotiated construct that is produced by means of the reading process. The reader in community and the text produced by an author in community engage each other in a dialogical dialectic interactive process. This should be an interdependent relationship with the goal being to understand the message of the text. However, 'Reading is dynamic, open-ended, always subject to modification, change, evaluation, and rereading'.[114] Reading is a dialogical process in which the text and reader engage in an ongoing interdependent dialogue. Reading is not a monological process where the text simply speaks to a passive reader.[115] Hence, it is better to view the text as *underdeterminate*. The text is underdeterminate in the sense that it requires a reader while resisting the reader to read it any which way.

The empirical reader, even though she may desire faithfully to follow the clues offered in the text to the implied reader, is never free from her social-cultural community's influence. When the narrative critic searches the narrative for the clues of how the implied reader should respond, she is really searching for how the empirical reader should respond.[116] Thus, reading is never neutral. The production of meaning is always ideologically biased. Both text and the reader are ideologically biased. However, if the reader recognizes that all readings, texts and readers have and/or maintain socio-political-ideological preferences and practices, then the reader may be open to scrutinize both the text and herself during and after the reading. Therefore, reading simultaneously involves a hermeneutic of suspi-

---

[113] See Aichele, *The Postmodern Bible*. These authors argue that reader response criticism is a sibling of redaction criticism's union with narrative criticism. According to the authors, biblical reader response critics embrace Iser's phenomenological reception theory which 'has left unaltered the fundamental concepts of historical criticism, especially the notion of a stable text with determinate meanings' (p. 39). The authors present a helpful overview of 'Reader Response' (ch. 1, pp. 20–69). However, see Powell who clearly presents important differences between the historical critical method and literary approaches; also see Morgan, *Biblical Interpretation*, pp. 172-77.

[114] Tate, *Biblical Interpretation*, p. 160.

[115] Tate, *Biblical Interpretation*, p. 160.

[116] Aichele, *The Postmodern Bible*, p. 67.

cion and a hermeneutic of retrieval; thus, there must be some limited autonomy (space) between readers and texts.

This writer has argued that Eco's semiotic approach, along with narrative theory which contains reader response concerns, provides a reading interpretive strategy in which both the text and the reader are seen as necessary interdependent dialogical partners participating in the communicative event. A real reader should attempt to understand a text as it desires to be understood, and this requires the reader and the text to be in a dialectic dialogical engagement. Thus, there exists an interdependent relationship between the text and the reader. Meaning is the production of the transaction between the reader in community and the underderterminate text.

Iser's phenomenological understanding of reading helps to clarify how meaning is produced through an interdependent and interactive dialectic engagement of the text and reader. Iser writes,

> If interpretation has set itself the task of conveying the meaning of a literary text, obviously the text itself cannot have already formulated that meaning. How can the meaning possibly be experienced if—as is always assumed by classical norm of interpretation—it is already there, merely waiting for a referential exposition? As meaning arises out of the process of actualization, the interpreter should perhaps pay more attention to the process than the product … Far more instructive will be an analysis of what actually happens when one is reading a text, for that is when the text begins to unfold its potential; it is in the reader that the text comes to life, and this is true even when the 'meaning' has become so historical that it is no longer relevant to us. In reading we are able to experience things that no longer exist and to understand things that are totally unfamiliar to us.[117]

Iser desires to explain the reading process as an aesthetic response in which there exists a dialectic relationship between the reader and the text.[118] The dialectic relationship between the poles of the text and

---

[117] Iser, *The Act of Reading*, pp. 18–19.

[118] Iser, *The Act of Reading*, writes,

response is therefore to be analyzed in terms of a dialectic relationship between text, reader and their interaction. It is called aesthetic response because, although brought about by the text, it brings into play the imaginative and per-reader interact in order for the potential meaning to be actualized.[119] The dialectic relationship takes place 'as the reader passes through the various perspectives offered by the text and relates the different views and patterns to one another he sets the work in motion, and so sets himself in motion, too'.[120] Furthermore, 'any description of the interaction between the two must therefore incorporate both the structure of effects [text] and that of response [of the reader]'.[121]

Iser views a text as a literary communicative object that contains textual structures which allow for the latent potential meaning of the text to be actualized by the reader. The text 'offers guidance' to the readers 'as what can be produced, and therefore cannot itself be the product'.[122] The text initiates the reader's imaginative ability of perceiving and processing the text but it in no way determines the meaning.[123] The meaning of the text comes out in the gradual unfolding of the text as the reader interacts with the text. The reader listens to the structural clues of the text, the different perspectives represented in the text [narrator, characters, plot and the fictitious implied reader], and then from the reader's vantage point, actualizes the meaning of the text, thus completing the communicative event.[124] Actualization of meaning is the final convergence of the textual structures and the reader's responses. Therefore, the text does provide guidelines for potential meanings, but the actualization of the meaning is the result of the dialectic interaction of the reader and the text.[125]

Iser argues that communication is made possible because all texts have 'gaps' or 'blanks' that must be 'filled' in by the reader.[126] The reader encounters these indeterminacies as she reads the text and by

---

ceptive faculties of the reader, in order to make him adjust and even differentiate his own focus (p. x).

[119] Iser, *The Act of Reading*, pp. x, 20–21.
[120] Iser, *The Act of Reading*, p. 21.
[121] Iser, *The Act of Reading*, p. 21.
[122] Iser, *The Act of Reading*, p. 107.
[123] Iser, *The Act of Reading*, p. 107.
[124] Iser, *The Act of Reading*, pp. 35–36.
[125] Iser, *The Act of Reading*, p. 21. He writes 'we can safely say that the relative indeterminacy of a text allows for a spectrum of actualizations' (p. 24 and pp. 37–39).
[126] Iser, *The Act of Reading*, pp. 168–70. 'Whenever a reader bridges the gaps, communication begins. The gaps function as a kind of pivot on which the whole text-reader relationship revolves' (p. 169).

necessity, fills in these gaps. Iser writes, 'It is the elements of indeterminacy that enable the text to "communicate" with the reader, in the sense that they induce him to participate both in the production and comprehension of the work's intention'.[127] The text contains clues and offers guidance on how these gaps are to be filled. In this way, the text offers limitations as to what may be appropriate for filling in the gaps. The text cannot determine the filling of gaps. This is left to the reader.[128] As Fowler notes,

> Reading is not only a matter of making sense of what is there in the narrative but also what is not there … The gaps that appear in the path we walk through the reading experience must be negotiated somehow, but readers often have considerable freedom to handle them as they see fit. Many arguments between readers are over how best to deal with the gaps in texts we read. As long as there are gaps (which is forever), readers will argue about how to handle them.[129]

An important aspect of Iser's theory is the filling in of the gaps by the implied reader. Iser's implied reader is one of the structures of the text which offers guidance to the empirical reader in how the gaps should be filled. He writes,

> If, then, we are to try and understand the effects caused and the responses elicited by a literary work, we must allow for the reader's presence without in any way predetermining his character or his historical situation. We may call him, for lack of a better term, the implied reader. He embodies all those predispositions necessary for a literary work to exercise its effect—predispositions necessarily laid down, not by an empirical outside reality, but by the text itself. Consequently, the implied reader as a concept has his roots firmly planted in the structure of the text; he is a construct and in no way to be identified with any real reader … The concept of the implied reader is therefore a textual structure an-

---

[127] Iser, *The Act of Reading*, p. 24.

[128] Iser, *The Act of Reading*, pp. 38, 67, 167–72. 'If communication between the text and reader is to be successful, clearly, the reader's activity must be controlled in some way by the text'. The control of the text is 'exercised *by* the text, it is not *in* the text' (pp. 167–68). See also Iser, *The Implied Reader*, pp. 278–79.

[129] Fowler, 'Reader-Response Criticism: Figuring Mark's Reader', p. 61.

ticipating the presence of a recipient without necessarily defining him: this concept prestructures the role to be assumed by each recipient, and this holds true even when texts deliberately appear to ignore their possible recipient or actively exclude him. Thus the concept of the implied reader designates a network of response-inviting structures, which impel the reader to grasp the text.[130]

The implied reader is a prestructured reading role offered to the real reader of the work. The implied reader 'is a product of the encounter *between* the text and the reader, a realization of potentials *in* the text but produced *by* a real reader'.[131] Therefore, the implied reader is a creation of the real reader's imagination, yet the implied reader is dependent upon the text even though she is not exactly in the text nor entirely outside the text.[132] In Iser's words, 'the concept of the implied reader is a transcendental model which makes it possible for the structured effects of literary texts to be described'.[133] The implied reader as a transcendental model is created in the dialectic activity of reading and offers guidance to the real reader as to how the real reader should fill in the gaps.[134]

Another important aspect of Iser's theory is that the reading experience is temporal. That is, the reading experience is time bound with the unfolding time flow of the text, a linear phase by phase encounter with the text. The reader can never fully perceive the text as a whole object at any one time.[135] 'The "object" of the text can only be imagined by way of different consecutive phases of reading' which 'are situated inside the literary text'. According to Iser, this 'mode of grasping an object is unique to literature' because 'there is a moving viewpoint which travels along *inside* the text' which the reader has to follow in order to apprehend it.[136]

> The reader's wandering viewpoint is, at one and the same time, caught up in and transcended by the object it is to apprehend.

---

[130] Iser, *The Act of Reading*, p. 34, see also pp. 107–13.
[131] Aichele, *The Postmodern Bible*, p. 31. See also Iser, *The Act of Reading*, p. 38.
[132] Aichele, *The Postmodern Bible*, p. 31.
[133] Iser, *The Act of Reading*, p. 38.
[134] Narrative critics have latched on to Iser's concept of the implied reader in order to control the possible meanings generated by the text during the reading experience.
[135] Iser, *The Act of Reading*, p. 108.
[136] Iser, *The Act of Reading*, p. 109. Iser views this as an advantage, see p. 112.

Apperception can only take place in phases, each of which contains aspects of the object to be constituted, but none of which claim to be representative of it ... The incompleteness of each manifestation necessitates syntheses, which in turn bring about the transfer of the text to the reader's consciousness. The synthesizing process, however, is not sporadic—it continues throughout every phase of the journey of the wandering viewpoint.[137]

Iser's wandering viewpoint is his attempt to 'describe the intersubjective structure of the process through which a text is transferred and translated' to the reader.[138] It is the implied reader, and not necessarily the real reader, who is time-bound to the unfolding narrative, even though the real reader is also restricted to the time flow of the text as she reads.[139]

The wandering viewpoint encounter in the text by the reader during the reading process exists because

each sentence correlate [or phase] contains what one might call a hollow section, which looks forward to the next correlate, and a retrospective section, which answers the expectations of the preceding section ... Thus every moment of reading is a dialectic of protension and retention.[140]

In other words, the reader, during the reading process, is constantly reevaluating what she has just read and anticipating what is to come in the next phase. Iser explains: 'We look forward, we look back, we decide, we change our decisions, we form expectations, we are shocked by their non fulfillment, we question, we muse, we accept, we reject; this is the dynamic process of recreation'.[141] The wandering viewpoint allows the reader to become entangled as she travels throughout the text. It also enables her to make connections between the different phases by helping her to fill in the blanks in a cohesive fashion, hence enabling her to grasp the potential meaning of the text and come to experience a different perspective than her own.[142] In

---

[137] Iser, *The Act of Reading*, p. 109.
[138] Iser, *The Act of Reading*, p. 108, see pp. 108–18.
[139] Iser, *The Act of Reading*, pp. 148–50.
[140] Iser, *The Act of Reading*, p. 112.
[141] Iser, *The Implied Reader*, p. 288, cited in *The Postmodern Bible*, p. 31.
[142] Iser, *The Act of Reading*, pp. 118.

this way, the reader completes the communicative event because she is able to grasp the work that is more than the written text. 'The text only takes on life when it is realized ... The convergence of text and reader bring the literary work into existence'.[143]

Iser's theory of the reader's response emphasizes the necessary participation of the reader's imagination in the reading process. Neither the reader nor the text is to dominate the process, but they are to cooperate in coming to grips with the meaning of the text. Iser's theory views the text more from a formalist perspective, thus allowing the text to have an important role in the communicative process of eliciting a response from the reader. Iser's reader response approach has made him 'by far the most influential figure in the appropriation of reader-response criticism by biblical scholars'.[144]

In sum, a Pentecostal hermeneutical strategy would embrace the narrative theory of Chatman while appropriating the phenomenological theory of Iser in such a way that an interdependent interactive dialectic link between the reader and the text is maintained. Narrative criticism, which was really a term coined by gospel critics, provides a helpful methodology for the interpretation of narrative texts.[145]

Narrative critics like Powell will place more constraints on the real reader by redefining Iser's concept of the implied reader. From Powell's perspective, the implied reader is in the text. This is different from Iser's notion of the implied reader being the product of the reader that is created through a dialectic encounter of the reader with the text.[146] Powell, like most narrative critics, argues that 'the goal of Narrative Criticism is to read the text as the implied reader'.[147] Therefore, the hermeneutical methodology of narrative criticism provides an important means to interpreting the biblical narrative.

Pentecostals could easily embrace the narrative method, yet resist to some extent, the narrative critic's notion of implied reader. This would allow the text to give formative guidance without determining the actual response. The imagination of the real reader that both Chatman and Iser discuss is vital to the reader's ability to compre-

---

143 Iser, *The Implied Reader*, pp. 274–75.
144 Aichele, *The Postmodern Bible*, p. 31, see also pp. 41–51.
145 As Moore points out, *Literary Criticism and the Gospels*, p. xxii.
146 Powell, *What is Narrative Criticism*, p. 19.
147 Powell, *What is Narrative Criticism*, p. 20.

hend the text. In this way, a Pentecostal would read the Bible as she would any other text or experience, through the utilization of her imagination,[148] which is shaped and formed in the Pentecostal community by means of its narrative tradition.

One must ask if the notion of the implied or model reader is as helpful as it is claimed to be. In considering biblical texts of the New Testament, would not a community of readers and hearers be the targeted audience of the writers? As Richard Bauckham points out, 'in historical terms to talk about the implied reader of Romans is misleading. It [Romans] would be read aloud by one [person], heard by a group, and discussed and understood in a participatory hearing'.[149] In other words, the individualism of an 'implied (singular) reader' needs to be discarded for the concept of an 'implied community of readers and hearers'. This especially pertains to the Bible. Scripture was read in community and discussed by the community. The community, along with its potential multiple understandings, becomes the necessary participant in the ongoing interpretive process. The notion of an implied or model reader is discarded for the reality that the readers of this strategy are the Pentecostal community. The community engages the biblical text and so produces meaningful readings in ways that attempt to maintain the interdependent interactive dialogical relationship between the text and the community. The community, not an isolated real reader, will negotiate the meaning through discussion. In doing so, it will remain more faithful to the interpretive process of the first century Christian community (from a narrative perspective, as a direct address to the present Christian community and primarily in the service of preaching).[150] As Richard Hays demonstrates through examining the Apostle Paul's writings,

---

[148] This writer recognizes that the Bible contains many forms of genre with narrative being the most prevalent. However, a few Bible critics recognize the value of narrative as it is a necessary backdrop to the non-narrative portions of Scripture. See for example Norman R. Petersen, *Rediscovering Paul: Philemon and the Sociology of Paul's Narrative World* (Philadelphia: Fortress Press, 1985) and Ben Witherington III, *Paul's Narrative Thought World: The Tapestry of Tragedy and Triumph* (Louisville, KY: Westminster/John Knox Press, 1994).

[149] This concern was brought to my attention in email correspondence with my Professor Richard Bauckham.

[150] See Richard B. Hays, *Echoes of Scripture in the Letters of Paul* (New Haven, CT: Yale University Press, 1989), pp. 161, 183–85. Hays argues that '*if we learned from Paul how to read Scripture, we would read it primarily as a narrative of promise and election* ...

Our account of Paul's interpretive activity has discovered no systematic exegetical procedures at work in his reading of Scripture
... his [Paul's] comments characteristically emphasize the immediacy of the text's word to the community rather then providing
specific rules of reading ... Paul reads the text as bearing direct
reference to his own circumstances ... [and] that Scripture is
rightly read as a word of address to the [present] eschatological
community of God's people.[151]

In short, this Pentecostal hermeneutical strategy will embrace a
modified narrative critical methodology while simultaneously affirming the Pentecostal community as the arena for the making of meaning. Interpretation is the result of a creative transaction of meaning,
and this meaning is always done from the particular context of an
actual reader in community. Croatto argues that the Bible is a present
living word for the believing community. 'As a result, what is genu-
inely relevant is not the "behind" of a text, but its "ahead", its "forward"—what it suggests as a pertinent message for the life of the one
who seeks it out'.[152] Hence, it is the reading of the Scripture from a
new praxis and in community that opens up valid yet multiple meanings of biblical texts.[153] Therefore, a Pentecostal reading would not
only pay attention to the poetic features and the structure of the text,
but would also fully affirm the importance of the contemporary
Christian community's participation in the making of meaning. The
Pentecostal strategy would desire to keep the making of meaning in
creative interdependent dialectic tension between the text and the
community, which is always moving into new and different contexts.
In this manner, the making of meaning is a constructive ongoing cooperation between the text and community of faith. The Pentecostal
community's theological conviction that the word of God speaks to
the present eschatological community collapses the distance between

---

ecclesiocentrically ... *in the service of proclamation* ... *as participants in the eschatological drama
of redemption'.* As this writer has demonstrated the Pentecostal community has al-
ways read the Scripture 'as the people of the endtime', from a narrative prospective
of promise and from within the community as a word for the present which requires the interaction of the Holy Spirit.

[151] Hayes, *Echoes of Scripture*, pp. 160, 166. See also McGrath, *The Genesis of Doctrine*, p. 56.

[152] Croatto, *Biblical Hermeneutics*, pp. 50–53.

[153] For Croatto the new context of praxis is the fight against oppression.

the past and present allowing for creative freedom in the community's acts of interpretation.

The primary constraint that contemporary Pentecostals employ in order to limit their interpretive freedom is their narrative tradition. This constraint is a theological rather than a methodological constraint. Pentecostals would shout a hearty 'amen' to Hays' argument that all of Scripture must be interpreted in light of and as a witness to the Gospel of Jesus. 'Scripture must be read as a witness to the gospel of Jesus Christ. No reading of Scripture can be legitimate if it fails to acknowledge the death and resurrection of Jesus as the climatic manifestation of God's righteousness.'[154]

The contemporary Pentecostal community needs to recapture the promise of God and what it means to live on the margins in relationship to Jesus as expressed through the Full Gospel. This is a praxis-oriented approach that encourages a pragmatic constraint on the interpretation. If the interpretation does not encourage or motivate the listeners to experience transformation through participating in God's eschatological community then it should be rejected. The reading will desire to echo an Acts-Gospels praxis context within the contemporary situation. This is not to suggest that the past and present are static, nor is truth static, but it is to suggest that the contemporary community maintains an intertextual dialectic with Acts-Gospels and the rest of canonical Scripture.

The Contribution of the Holy Spirit

The Pentecostal hermeneutical strategy is a tridactic negotiation for meaning. I have discussed the contributions of the biblical text and community. The contributions of the Holy Spirit to the hermeneutical process will now be addressed.

Explaining the contribution of the Holy Spirit is more difficult due to the realization that the Holy Spirit, although affirmed as being present and active participant in the interpretive process, is nonetheless dependent upon the community and Scripture. The Holy Spirit does have a voice, but the Spirit's voice is heard 'horizontally' in and through the individuals in community and in and through Scripture.

---

[154] See Hays, *Echoes of Scripture*, p. 191.

The Spirit's voice is not reduced to or simply equated with the Biblical text or the community, but is connected to and dependent upon these as a necessary means for expressing the concern(s) of the Godhead (Trinity).

The role of the Holy Spirit in the hermeneutical process is to lead and guide the community in understanding the present meaningfulness of Scripture. This ministry of the Holy Spirit is an extension of the ministry of the incarnate, crucified, ascended, and glorified Christ.[155] Therefore human society, in general, and the Christian community, in particular, have not been abandoned by the living presence of God as a result of the ascension of Christ Jesus. The Holy Spirit, believed to be a real participant in the life of the Christian, enables the Christian in community to live faithfully with the living God as the community continues the mission of Jesus.[156] Hence the Spirit does speak and has more to say than just Scripture. This requires the community to discern the Spirit in the process of negotiating the meaning of the biblical texts as the community faithfully carries on the mission of Jesus into new, different and future contexts. 'The Spirit's intervention and interpretive work is crucial if the followers of Jesus are faithfully to carry on the mission Jesus gives them'.[157] For this reason, the voice of the Spirit cannot be reduced to simple recitation of Scripture, nonetheless it will be connected to and concerned with Scripture.

The Spirit's Voice Heard in and through the Pentecostal Community

Pentecostals desire the Holy Spirit to lead and empower them in fulfilling the missionary task Jesus mandated to his followers. Pentecostals seek the Spirit's guidance in understanding Scripture and reality in order to live obediently with God.

The Spirit's Voice in the Community

The community provides the context in which the Spirit's manifestation takes place. Personal testimonies, charismatic gifts, preaching, teaching, witnessing, serving the poor, praying, (all acts of ministry)

---

[155] See John 13–17, in Jesus' farewell discourse, where he speaks of the importance of the Holy Spirit's ministry to the Christian community and human society.

[156] Fowl, *Engaging Scripture*, p. 99.

[157] Fowl, *Engaging Scripture*, p. 98.

provide opportunities for the manifestation of the Holy Spirit. The community is involved in discerning the authenticity of these manifestations and activities. The activities of the Pentecostal community's participants are 'assessed and accepted or rejected'.[158] Many times something (belief and activity) will be tolerated until more witness from the Spirit by means of Scripture and/or personal testimony can be given. The community provides the context for the manifestation/voice of the Spirit to be heard.

Pentecostals will invite the Holy Spirit to manifest in various ways in the community. The purpose of these manifestations and community activities is to empower, guide, and transform, the individuals in community so that the Pentecostal community can faithfully follow the Lord Jesus Christ. This requires the community to discern the Holy Spirit in the midst of the community activities and manifestations and follow the Spirit's guidance. More will be said about 'discerning' the Spirit in the following section—'Validating the Meaning'. Here, however, this author is reiterating the important interdependent relationship between the community, Scripture and the Holy Spirit. The Christian community provides the dynamic context in which the Spirit is actively invited to participate because without the Holy Spirit's participation there is no authentic Christian community. The individual's claim of being led by or speaking in behalf of the Spirit will be weighed in light of Scripture and other individual testimonies. Thus the community must interpret the manifestations of the Spirit.[159] 'Experience of the Spirit shapes the reading of scripture, but scripture most often provides the lenses through which the Spirit's work is perceived and acted upon'.[160]

---

[158] Thomas, 'Reading the Bible from within our Traditions', p. 119.

[159] Fowl, *Engaging Scripture*, correctly points out that 'it is important to recognize that the presence of miraculous signs is not a straightforward event' (p. 104). The community must discern if the miraculous sign is of the Holy Spirit and what the sign is signifying to the community.

[160] Fowl, *Engaging Scripture*, p. 114. This writer agrees with Fowl who argues that it is impossible in practice 'to separate and determine clearly whether a community's scriptural interpretation is prior to or dependent upon a community's experience of the Spirit' (p. 114).

The Spirit's Voice Coming From Outside Yet Back through the Community.

The Pentecostal narrative tradition has placed missionary outreach at the heart of the Pentecostal community. Pentecostals have and continue to embrace with great vigor the missionary task of reaching all people with the Gospel. They proclaim the 'Full Gospel' to all who will listen in prayerful hope that non-Christians will respond to God's gracious salvific invitation to embrace Jesus and join the Pentecostal community. This passion for expanding God's Kingdom has encouraged Pentecostals to take the Gospel to the ends of the earth and thereby spreading the 'Full Gospel' into regions outside of their cultural context and geographical locations. Pentecostals (especially those discerned to have the 'missionary call' but also, in a limited sense the local layperson) evangelistically engage and confront other individuals in community. Pentecostals do not stand from a distance (as was seen in the early chapters) but get involved in the life of other people while retaining their allegiance to their Pentecostal community. The engagement with other communal stories allows for openness to the voice of the Spirit to come to them from outside the community.

Pentecostals will not limit the work of the Spirit to their community but recognize that God's prevenient grace has been bestowed upon all of humanity. Furthermore, they fully expect the Holy Spirit to be actively working upon the lives of non-Christians and in the lives of all Christians. This activity does not imply that people who have not had an opportunity to respond to the Gospel are Christian. But it does underscore the importance and necessity of the Holy Spirit's involvement and the importance of the Holy Spirit being active upon the lives of those before the Pentecostal missionaries arrive. Pentecostals, through their hospitable missionary outreach, have developed relationships with people outside their community and have 'discerned' the presence of the Spirit.[161] As a result, the Pentecostals will discern what the Spirit is saying to them from outside their community, which may be both typical and yet surprising for the Pentecostal community. In this way the Spirit may speak from

---

[161] This would include not only officially recognized missionaries but also local Christian communities made up of both laity and clergy. Every Pentecostal is to be a witness for Jesus Christ.

outside the Pentecostal community by means of speaking through Pentecostal missionaries, evangelists and recent converts. Once again the community, Scripture and Spirit are all necessary participants in the making of meaning with the community energized by the Spirit being the arena in which the Scripture and the Spirit converge.

The Spirit's Voice Comes In and Through the Scripture
Pentecostals hold to a 'high view' of Scripture. The Bible is understood to be an authoritative and trustworthy testimony about the living God produced by humans that were inspired by the Holy Spirit. Scripture is affirmed as the sacred account of the living God's revelation to humanity and specifically to the Christian community. Because of this belief, 'Pentecostals regard the Scripture as normative and seek to live their lives in light of its teaching'.[162] Pentecostals read Scripture for more then just information; they read with a desire to know and do the will of God, thus experiencing redemptive transformation. Therefore Pentecostals, both laity and academicians, actively invite the Holy Spirit to guide and reveal meaningful understanding of Scripture.

How does the Spirit speak in and through the Scripture? The community must discern the Holy Spirit's voice, and the Holy Spirit must be granted an opportunity to be actively involved in the hermeneutical process. As Thomas argues, the Holy Spirit's involvement in the interpretive process as narrated in Acts 15, 'heavily influenced the choice and use of Scripture' in resolving the thorny issues concerning the Gentiles' inclusion into the early Jewish Christian community.[163] This indicates that the Holy Spirit's presence was not passive but active in guiding and directing the community's engagement with Scripture. The participants in the 'Jerusalem Council' could offer much Scriptural support concerning God's rejection of Gentiles, but not all of the Old Testament Scripture supports such a notion. Hence, when Scripture (both Old and New Testaments) offers diverse and even contradictory information concerning a particular practice or concern, the Spirit can direct the congregation through experience, visions, gifts, and testimonies to a new understanding. This new understanding will still be rooted in Scripture yet will move beyond it. The

---

162 Thomas, 'Reading the Bible from within our Traditions', p. 110.
163 Thomas, 'Reading the Bible from within our Traditions', p. 118.

community, then, must discern the Holy Spirit's involvement in the present context of the Christian community.[164] The Spirit then is creating a concert environment in which and through which he speaks to the church.

Inviting the Holy Spirit into the Hermeneutical Process

French Arrington suggests that the interpreter of Scripture should submit his or her 'mind to God so that the critical and analytical abilities are exercised under the guidance of the Holy Spirit'. This allows the interpreter to have a conscious and 'genuine openness to the witness of the Spirit'. The hermeneut positions him or herself in a favorable disposition of responding to the transforming call of the Spirit's voice coming through the Scripture.[165] Hence the personal faith in Jesus Christ is affirmed as a necessary aspect of the entire interpretative process.

Pentecostals believe that it is in the context of the believing community that Scripture should be interpreted. The Scripture is not subordinate to the community. The Scripture is a precious gift of God's grace to the community, God's words to them, which is Spirit and truth. The goal of the community is to come to an understanding of what the Spirit is saying presently to the community in and through the biblical text(s) and in and through their cooperate experiences of the Holy Spirit.

In review, the hermeneutical model being advocated encourages a tridactic dialectical and dialogical interdependent relationship between Scripture, Spirit and Community for the negotiation of meaning. The model finds biblical support in Acts 15 and is consistent with both early and contemporary popularistic Pentecostal hermeneutical practice. The particular method will be a narrative approach from a semiotic understanding of language.

Validating the Meaning

In this final section, I will address the testing process for the validation of the negotiated constructive meaning of the biblical text(s),

---

[164] See Kenyon, 'An Analysis of Ethical Issues in the History of The Assemblies of God', p. 408.

[165] Arrington, 'The Use of the Bible by Pentecostals', p. 105.

which becomes the normative meaning. Before delineating the process of validation, it is important to acknowledge that hermeneutical strategy will operate at two levels. At the primary level, the hermeneutical strategy will function within the pre-established Pentecostal story along with its doctrinal beliefs, practices and experiences. Thus, Pentecostal preachers and teachers as well as laity will use Scripture allegorically, typologically and exegetically in ways that confirm and motivate people to embrace and practice the Pentecostal way of life. At the secondary level, the hermeneutical strategy can be subjected to critical reflection that may include the critical scrutiny of the Pentecostal narrative tradition, interpretive methods and specific interpretations. Hence both the hermeneutical strategy and the particular interpretations and readings could be critically reflected upon (at both levels), thus maintaining the importance of a praxis oriented hermeneutical strategy. It is at the secondary level that the validation of meaning is of greatest concern because once a belief becomes a normative doctrinal practice, it will be included within the hermeneutical story. The hermeneutical story will be the primary filter by which Scripture will be understood. The validating process will be primarily concerned with the secondary level but not limited to it. The validation process should also be utilized in the reexamining of established normative interpretation of particular passages and doctrines. Additionally, the validation of meaning within the Pentecostal community will always favor theological constraints over interpretive methodological constraints; thus the discernment of the community in relationship to the Holy Spirit is always necessary.[166] It is not formal methodological constraints that limit and validate the readings of Scripture, but instead the constraints and validation will be relationally construed by the community's theological narrative tradition. Furthermore, there will always be an interdependent relationship between the community, Scripture, and the Holy Spirit. Nevertheless, I will offer a relational and dialogical way to validate meaningful readings of Scripture.

---

[166] It is interesting to note that Richard Hays argues that Paul's interpretive constraints are 'primarily from material (i.e., theological) concerns rather than from formal methodological considerations' (*Echoes of Scripture*, p. 161).

Willard Swartley contends that the validation of the meaning must address some important factors.[167] The first factor is to examine and understand the hermeneutical methodology being used by the hermeneut. The method should be explained in a clear and coherent manner 'so that another person can follow the logic and development of thought'. For this to be accomplished, the method of study which led to the interpretation must be clearly demonstrated and be able to be repeatable.[168]

As I have shown through the previous chapters, Pentecostals desire to show from Scripture how they have arrived at their theological positions. Early Pentecostals used the 'Bible Reading Method' to arrive at the conclusion that Spirit baptism evidenced by speaking in tongues is rooted in Scripture, albeit a reading of Scripture from a Pentecostal perspective. Later on, Pentecostals sought to demonstrate the validity of this doctrine by embracing more academically acceptable methods of interpretation.[169] To some extent this was a result of modernity's pervasive influence upon the academic Pentecostals to attempt to demonstrate the claim of modernity that interpretation must be objectively and scientifically verifiable.[170]

All Pentecostals recognize that it is important for other interpreters to be able to follow the Pentecostals' interpretive methodological approach used to arrive at their understanding of the passage. Thus, Pentecostals concur with Swartley that the validation of the meaning must include a method that can be followed and be both logical and coherent to those outside the community. Pentecostals reject the notion that the validation of meaning or the creation of meaning rests solely upon some 'individual' esoteric experience that cannot be communicated to those both inside and outside of its narrative tradition.

---

[167] Swartley, *Slavery, Sabbath, War and Women*, pp. 222–24. Swartley lists five that will be retained but presented slightly differently.

[168] Swartley, *Slavery, Sabbath, War and Women*, p. 222.

[169] The methods argument has been a two edged sword because some Pentecostals would no longer embrace Spirit baptism because they believed modern exegetical practice could not support it while others argued it could.

[170] Walter Brueggemann, *Texts Under Negotiation: The Bible and the Postmodern Imagination* (Minneapolis, MN: Fortress Press, 1993), see preface and ch. 1. This writer agrees with Brueggemann that historical criticism is the particular practice of modernity with objectivity being its elusive foundation.

Those testing the interpretation need to ask if both the method and the meaning have a sense of spiritual rightness. Swartley identifies this as 'the testimony of the Holy Spirit as it bears witness in our spirits'.[171] The Holy Spirit plays a significant role in leading and guiding the community in 'both determining and validating' the meaning.[172] Swartley cautions the reader as to the difficulty of ascertaining the Holy Spirit's guidance, but he recognizes the significant role the Spirit plays in helping the community come to a decision on the validation of the meaning.

The important and often negated influence of the Holy Spirit's involvement in the making and validation of meaning has been addressed by Luke Timothy Johnson in his *Scripture and Discernment: Decision Making In The Church*. Johnson argues that the first use of discernment is the believer's responsibility as she searches out of a response of faith for God's will and direction in her life. However, the whole community must also discern God's will when the acceptance of meaning will affect the whole community. In order for the church community to discern, it must first hear and then test the narrative experience of the individual or individuals. Johnson writes:

> As we have seen in the Acts account how multiple individual narratives enabled the community narrative to develop. As that happened the church was able to exercise discernment concerning the work of the Spirit within it, and decide for God. The narrative of experience is the prerequisite for the kind of discernment required for the church to reach decision as an articulation of faith.[173]

Because the narrated testimony is an expression of the individual's personal religious experience, it is offered to the congregation as a form of witness of what God is doing in her life and in the world. The community does not have to accept or validate it as an authentic Christian experience, but it must decide if it is or is not an appropri-

---

[171] Swartley, *Slavery, Sabbath, War and Women*, p. 222. This is Swartley's second step but it seems as though it should be part of the first. This writer has collapsed them into one stage.

[172] Swartley, *Slavery, Sabbath, War and Women*, p. 223.

[173] Luke Timothy Johnson, *Scripture and Discernment: Decision Making In The Church* (Nashville, TN: Abingdon Press, revised 1996), p. 135. Johnson employs the word 'narrative' as the ordered expression of personal religious experiential memory, which is offered to the church community as one's personal faith story or as an extension as the community story (p. 137).

ate Christian experience. The experience may be an appropriate experience but that does not mean it should be a normative experience. Sometimes the Church must say no, but it must first be willing to hear the 'narrative of faith' offered by the individual.

> The meaning, adequacy, and implications of personal religious experience and history call forth the community's discernment as it seeks to decipher God's Word to it in the present moment. Not every spirit is the Holy Spirit, not every word is God's Word. Not every 'turning' a conversion. Not every Kingdom is the Kingdom of God. There are 'religious experiences' that are not encounters with the true God.[174]

Johnson writes that the process of discernment is obviously 'hazardous' but 'when the church proceeds on the assumption that there is no work to *be* tested … it won't be a community of faith in the Spirit'.[175]

Pentecostals have always sought and encouraged the involvement of the Holy Spirit in the community. Pentecostalism encourages high levels of community participation. The testimonies or narratives of faith offered by individual members were and are encouraged and sensitively listened to in order to bear witness that it was and is the Holy Spirit involved in the person's experience. The sharing of personal testimonies plays an important role in the Pentecostal communities' discernment of the spirits and allows for the validation of meaning to include the whole community and not just the professionally trained clergy. Thus, a passage of Scripture may function in such a way as to motivate the community to live in a way (orthopraxy) that it may not have meant to its implied community of readers and hearers. The validation of the passage, however, will be discerned within the community and reflect its Central Narrative Convictions. Swartley argues correctly that 'the community of faith is

---

[174] Johnson, *Scripture and Discernment*, pp. 137–38.

[175] Johnson, *Scripture and Discernment*, p. 138. Johnson explains how the sharing of stories could be carried out in a church service and the necessary attitudes required for discernment to function properly with in the community see pp. 138–39, 158–65). See also Fowl, *Engaging Scripture: A Model for Theological Interpretation*, who also is concerned about the important role of discernment and the virtues necessary for Christians to discern properly.

the proper context in which Scripture is to be understood'.[176] Thus, like Johnson, he affirms that the community plays a significant role in validating the meaning.

Swartley offers some important advice about the role of the community in validating the meaning. He observes that

> The Bible arose out of human historical and existential experiences ... The Bible testifies to God's initiative among, and self-disclosure to, specific groups of people who understand themselves to be people of God. Because these testimonies to divine revelation encompass well over a thousand years in time in written form, the interpreter must pay attention to the vertical axis of communication (God-humanity, humanity-God) but also to the horizontal movement from earlier to later testimony, especially because scripture dialogues and critiques itself.[177]

In other words, the community recognizes that the Bible unfolds a revelation concerning God over time and that within the canon there are stories or passages which may offer a critique to earlier understanding. This of course is addressing the importance of the relationship of New Testament to the Old Testament when interpreting Scripture. For Swartley (and to some extent early Pentecostals), it is the Gospels which take the primary position of authority within the canon. Yet this would also extend past the canon to the Church's understanding of Scripture through time. The community must take into consideration the wider church body and the history of doctrinal development as it assesses the validation of the meaning.

Here is where the Pentecostal doctrine of 'Oneness theology' comes under greater scrutiny than the Pentecostal affirmation of the continuation of the charismatic gifts for today's Christians. Oneness Pentecostals cannot find historical orthodox Christianity embracing the Oneness' understanding of the Godhead entirely. Oneness Pentecostals clearly affirm the incarnation and deity of Jesus (thus in a very important sense they do hold to a central historical orthodox doctrine), yet they reject the Trinity. When Trinitarian Pentecostals challenged Oneness Pentecostals, they did not reject their view based upon their interpretive method; rather, they appealed to historic

---

[176] Swartley, *Slavery, Sabbath, War and Women*, p. 215.
[177] Swartley, *Slavery, Sabbath, War and Women*, p. 216.

Christianity's understanding of God as Triune. In validating the meaning, Trinitarian (and Oneness) Pentecostals recognized the value of historic orthodox belief, and this is why they searched the chronicles of church history to find ecstatic gifts operating in the Church. However, when Oneness Pentecostals rejected the doctrine of the Trinity, they argued more stringently that they were recovering Apostolic doctrine that was lost due to the early apostasy of Christianity. Hence, Oneness Pentecostals attempted to defend their belief more so on Scripture alone. Therefore, the concern to submit the meaning of Scripture to the community is helpful in ascertaining the validity of the interpretation, especially when the meaning of the passage challenges already established beliefs and practices.

The second factor concerning the validation of meaning is that meaning must be validated through the 'praxis of faith'.[178] Here the concern is whether the meaning can be embraced and lived out in the community. Swartley cautions that just because it is livable does not necessarily make it correct. However, if meaning is not livable then it probably is not correct.

Early and contemporary Pentecostals view Christianity as a way of life. Thus, the praxis of faith is the primary context in which interpretation takes place. The community not only wants to be recognized as orthodox, but it is also concerned with orthopraxy and orthopathy. As this writer has shown in the previous chapter, this is a primary concern of Pentecostal Roger Stronstad. He argued that the validity of the interpretation cannot stand on an exegetical method alone but must be verified by being livable within the community of Faith. Stronstad's concern is consistent with current academic Pentecostals like Cheryl Bridges Johns who would argue that knowledge is rooted in the context of Pentecostal experience and that truth concerning ultimate reality must be connected to life experience.[179] 'Experience and interpretation are mutually informing and correcting elements in any community'.[180]

---

[178] Swartley, *Slavery, Sabbath, War and Women*, p. 223.

[179] Bridges Johns, *Pentecostal Formation*, p. 100.

[180] Amos Yong, *Discerning The Spirit(s): A Pentecostal-Charismatic Contribution to Christian Theology of Religions* (JPTSup, 20; Sheffield: Sheffield Academic Press 2000), p. 181.

Thirdly, the validity of interpretation must be subjected to cross-cultural validation.[181] This is one of the more important tests because it crosses cultural and economic boundaries:

> Because the church in its essential nature must be missionary in its thought and action, its understandings can never be, or remain, provincial. When particular insights are affirmed by people in various cultural settings, they gain validity. They stand as something more that personal insights or cultural biases.[182]

This is especially important because Christianity makes historically revealed permanently binding truth claims for faith and practice, regardless of one's cultural location.

The Pentecostals of North America need to take into consideration their Pentecostal brothers and sisters who reside in different cultural communities as they validate the meaning of their interpretations. This becomes especially crucial when they are attempting to understand Scripture as it speaks directly to political and social issues and impose these views upon their brothers and sisters. Pentecostal missionaries have affirmed the importance of indigenous Pentecostal communities (usually in the form of sister denominations). They have built in networks that they can use as a means to engage these issues. Therefore, the validation of meaning should take very seriously the cross-cultural dialogue.

Fourthly, the validation of meaning should be open to the scrutiny of academic communities both non-Christian and Christian. This keeps the Pentecostal community from 'placing a protective hedge' around the Bible.[183] The Christian community understands the Bible to be making historically revealed permanent truth claims. Thus, it must be open to public scrutiny. This does not mean that these communities have the final say; rather, it means that their understanding should be considered. The final 'credibility and applicability' of the meaning of Scripture must be tested in the believing community who desires to embody the message because 'the *ultimate goal* in

---

[181] Swartley, *Slavery, Sabbath, War and Women*, p 223.

[182] Swartley, *Slavery, Sabbath, War and Women*, p 223.

[183] Swartley, *Slavery, Sabbath, War and Women*, p. 217. This is not one of Swartley's numerated tests, but he does talk about it and so this writer included it as an important test, but not the conclusive test for validating meaning.

interpretation is to allow the bible to speak its own message with a view to worship and obedience'.[184]

In sum, the Pentecostal community should embrace these various tests for validating the meaning of Scripture. In the past, the primary test has been based upon correct methodology. Method alone cannot validate the meaning, but it can help to discern if it is appropriate. Having drawn from Swartley, this writer suggests that the Pentecostal global community could come together to share their testimonies and discern a proper way of living as an authentic counter cultural community whose life and power comes from the Spirit.

The Pentecostal community must take a praxis oriented dialogical and dialectical approach to validating the meaning of Scripture. The community must allow for cross-cultural dialogue to discern meaning. The community, the Scripture, and the Spirit must negotiate the meaning in the context of faithful praxis. In doing so, some interpretations will not be embraced; others will be shelved and later re-addressed; still others will be embraced only to die out over time.[185] In this way, doctrine does not become static but remains open to the revision of the Spirit and Scripture in light of the testimony of Pentecostal Christian experience.

Summary

As was shown in chapter five, Pentecostals require a hermeneutical strategy that involves an interdependent tridactic dialogue between Scripture, the Spirit and community resulting in a creative negotiated meaning. Chapter six sets forth this strategy in a way that suggests that the hermeneutical strategy is a product of the Pentecostal identity. All three participants of the strategy make contributions in the hermeneutical processes. This author has outlined a critical contemporary Pentecostal hermeneutical strategy that takes place through the interdependent dialogical and dialectic process. The readers in community, the story world of the text, and the leading of the Holy Spirit are participants in the tridactic negotiation for meaning.

---

184 Swartley, *Slavery, Sabbath, War and Women*, p. 240.
185 Swartley, *Slavery, Sabbath, War and Women*, p. 223.

7

CONCLUSIONS AND CONTRIBUTIONS

The purpose of this study was to present a Pentecostal hermeneutical strategy that was informed by early Pentecostal identity. This strategy would have to recognize the role of the Spirit, Scripture and community in the interpretation process. In this particular case, the Pentecostal community is the primary arena in which the Scripture and Spirit interact in a dialogical process. The goal for Pentecostal interpretation has always been praxis-oriented. The purpose of interpretation of Scripture is to hear God's voice through the Scripture guided by the Spirit in order to obey the will of God in the present context.

To accomplish the task, it was necessary first to define Pentecostalism. Through an investigation of the primary historical literature, this study demonstrated that Pentecostalism emerged from the Wesleyan/Keswickian Holiness movements and restorationist revivalistic concerns. Early Pentecostalism was held together by a common doctrinal commitment to the Full Gospel message and a passionate emphasis upon an ecstatic religious experience with the Holy Spirit. This author argued that the Pentecostal movement should be understood as a paramodern movement in opposition to modernity and mainline Protestant orthodoxy. This chapter concluded that while Pentecostalism was influenced by modernity, it could never accept the modernistic worldview and in fact was in opposition to the central ideologies of modernity.

Having defined Pentecostalism and identified its worldview, chapter two set out to place the early Pentecostal movement within its hermeneutical context. First, this chapter showed that the dominant hermeneutical context of the early 19th century was Common Sense Realism. Following the dramatic effects that German higher criticism and the 'new science' had upon biblical scholarship, a rift occurred generating the Fundamentalist/liberal debate. This debate was a paradigm shift within the academic community. The Fundamentalists relied upon the older yet modern scientific thinking that was based upon common sense realism and the Baconian model. Conversely, the liberals were embracing the newer but still modern scientific model. The question arises as to where Pentecostalism is in relationship to this debate. The conclusion of this chapter shows that Pentecostals attempted to forge an alternative path that lies outside the modernistic controversy, thus concluding that Pentecostalism is a 'paramodern' movement with a hermeneutical strategy that is distinct from both the liberal and Fundamentalists methodologies.

The argument of chapter three set out to demonstrate that there existed an early Pentecostal method that was used by the first generation of Pentecostals. The early interpretive method was the 'Bible Reading Method'. This was a precritical common sense interpretive approach. It relied upon inductive and deductive reasoning and required that all the biblical data available on a particular topic be harmonized into a cohesive synthesis from a restorationist revivalistic perspective. In other words, the 'Bible Reading Method' encouraged a synchronic interpretive strategy that would extrapolate a verse from its larger context (in its concern to string all the verses that relate to that word or topic together) and lump it into one paragraph. However, what distinguished this method from the other Holiness groups was that it was used from a Pentecostal perspective.

Having identified the Pentecostal interpretive method, it then was necessary to distinguish its method from that of other Holiness traditions. Chapter four argued that all moral reasoning takes place from within a particular community. The community shares a common narrative tradition (story). The primary distinguishing factor for the Pentecostal hermeneutical strategy was not the method itself but the Central Narrative Convictions (CNCs) of the Pentecostal community. Hence, it was the dramatic story that provided the Pentecostals with an experiential conceptual interpretive framework. The Pentecostal story was a teleological reading—bringing the beginning and end of the church age together. This enabled Pentecostals to eclipse modernity and return to a premodern era where the supernatural was normal rather than abnormal. The Pentecostal story synthesized the restoration of charismatic gifts with the imminence of the second coming of Jesus. This narrative was central to Pentecostal identity and spirituality and not only served as the primary filter through which Scripture was sifted for meaning, but it also was used to interpret their experience of reality and their understanding of church history. Therefore, the interpretive methods employed by Pentecostals were subservient to their story from which the interpretation of Scripture took place. Having concluded this, it became apparent that a more suitable hermeneutical strategy for the contemporary Pentecostal community would be a combination of some methods rooted within a narrative critical strategy.

However, before I could present a Pentecostal hermeneutical strategy, there were some contemporary Pentecostal hermeneutical concerns that first needed to be addressed. These concerns lie in the methodological shift from the 'Bible Reading Method' to the historical critical method of modernity. This shift occurred as Pentecostals entered the academic arena and conformed to the acceptable modernistic hermeneutical approach. In doing so, Pentecostals increasingly became more modern. They accepted the basic principles of historical criticism, yet rejected the naturalistic worldview of modernity. They used an Evangelical adaptation of historical criticism called the historical grammatical method. This method became the primary method used by many Pentecostals. By embracing the modernistic foundations poured by the Enlightenment, Pentecostals moved from the paramodern into the modern. This chapter showed that the danger of embracing the Evangelical method is that the interpretive emphasis now lies in the world behind the text rather than the biblical text and the present context. A by-product of this has been a reconfiguring of the Pentecostal identity, which has caused it to lose sight of its roots. Therefore, this chapter demonstrates the need for a contemporary Pentecostal hermeneutical strategy that rejects the notion of a past determinate meaning of the author's intent and embraces the reality that interpretation involves both the discovery and creation of meaning for the present.

Chapters four and five established the need for a contemporary Pentecostal hermeneutical strategy. Chapter six presented a strategy that incorporates a tridactic dialogical interpretive process that consists of the Spirit, Scripture and community. This strategy is both fluid and eclectic but remains fundamentally a narrative approach anchored in the Pentecostal community. The strategy presented is one concerned with both the discovery and creation of meaning, which constrains the meaning through a tridactic relationship between the Spirit, text and the readers in community.

The contribution of the linguistically stable text was that it presents to the reader underdeterminate meaning. Semiotic theory provides the necessary space for authentic dialogue to take place between the text and readers. Semiotics encourages a dialectic link between the reader and the text. Meaning is the transaction of this dialectical and dialogical encounter. Semiotics underscores a text-centered and reader-response approach to interpretation that affirms the text as a contributing dialogical partner in the hermeneutical conversation.

The readers/listeners come anticipating the text to communicate with them. Readers will interpret texts according to their Central Narrative Convictions. Narrative with reader-response provides a critical and contemporary methodology which consistent with Pentecostal identity and the tridactic negotiation for meaning.

The Holy Spirit was affirmed as a real participant in the hermeneutical conversation. The Holy Spirit speaks in, through, to the community and also speaks through Scripture. The Spirit of God has more to say to the community then just Scripture yet it will be scripturally seasoned. Having sketched out the strategy, I then centered on the validity of meaning.

The validating of meaning will occur through the process of four stages: discerning the spiritual rightness of both meaning and method, applicability of the meaning, cross-cultural validity of the meaning, and scrutiny of secular and academic communities concerning the meaning with the recognition that the Pentecostal community will be the primary deciding factor.

Finally, this Pentecostal reading strategy embraces a modified narrative critical methodology while simultaneously affirming the contribution of the community. This results in the recognition that all reading is a production of meaning, and this meaning is always done from the particular context of an actual reader. It is the reading of the Scripture from a new praxis and in community that opens up valid yet multiple meanings of biblical texts. Therefore, a Pentecostal reading not only pays attention to the poetic and structural features of the text, but also fully affirms the importance of the contemporary Christian community's participation in the making of meaning. The Pentecostal reading strategy desires to keep the making of meaning in creative interdependent dialectic tension between the text and the community, which is always moving into new and different contexts. In this manner, the making of meaning is a constructive ongoing cooperation between the Spirit, text and community of faith. The Pentecostal community's theological conviction that the word of God speaks to the present eschatological community collapses the distance between the past and present allowing for creative freedom by the community's acts of interpretation. The Pentecostal story is the predominant hermeneutical filter in the making of meaning.

This investigation has demonstrated that there existed a distinct hermeneutical strategy that was used by the Pentecostal community. Moreover, it has shown that the majority of academic Pentecostals have moved away from the early paramodern approach to the Evangelical modernistic approach. Therefore this writer has presented a revised post-critical hermeneutical strategy that is informed by early Pentecostal ethos and facilitates the missional objectives of the contemporary Pentecostal community in relation to a post-critical context. By doing so, I hope to avoid the epistemological foundationalism of modernity and reappropriate the active participation of the community and Holy Spirit in the interpretive process.

Contributions of this Monograph

This study makes significant contributions to the Pentecostal and hermeneutical debates in the following ways. First, the study argues that the early Pentecostals where a paramodern movement that existed on the margins of modernity which affected their reading of Scripture. The classification of Pentecostalism as 'paramodern'[1] is an important contribution in understanding Pentecostalism as a movement. The term had not been utilized in publication when I penned the section in chapter one defining Pentecostals as a paramodern movement. Second, the study readdresses the interpretive method of early Pentecostals. As was demonstrated, early Pentecostals did not simply use a literalistic fundamentalist interpretive method but instead used the more dynamic 'Bible Reading Method'. The Bible Reading Method overcomes current misguided notions of how early Pentecostals interpreted Scripture. The study also demonstrated that

---

[1] I picked up the term 'paramodern' from a conversation with Cheryl Bridges Johns at a conference of the Society for Pentecostal Studies. She attributed it to her husband, Jackie Johns. I am using it in ways that are slightly different than them.

theological interpretations generated by the 'Bible Reading Method' were acceptable only if one had embraced the Pentecostal story, which held the method together. In other words, the Pentecostal story was the primary hermeneutical filter and served as the matrix for the Bible reading Method.

The third significant contribution this study makes has to do with the important role of the community in the hermeneutical process. The 'Central Narrative Convictions' attempt to convey the community as an embodiment of its convictions free from foundationalist language. The narrative convictions of the community place constraints upon the interpretive process and provide the context in which both the hermeneutical process and results make sense. Hermeneutical investigation never takes place in a vacuum, thus the notion of an ahistorical neutral interpretive method functioning as the sole arbitrating judge in the validation of an interpretation was rejected in favor of the tridactic negotiation of meaning.

Fourthly, this study painted a picture of early Pentecostal identity. The role of the Pentecostal community has not been dealt with sufficiently in the hermeneutical debates relating to the Pentecostals' usage of Scripture. Hence this study uncovers the Central Narrative Convictions of the early Pentecostal community. These convictions have to do with the importance of Pentecostal identity and how it impacts the hermeneutical process.

Finally, I presented a contemporary and post-critical hermeneutical strategy which attempts to move the Pentecostal academic community beyond the present impasse created by modernity. The strategy presented was a creative approach that desired to remain faithful to the Pentecostal story yet sensitive to contemporary concerns. The strategy was a revision of early Pentecostal ethos for the contemporary Pentecostal community. Hence the strategy was not attempting to simply find contemporary interpretive methods that would reinforce Pentecostal interpretations, but instead the strategy can serve as a creative and critical hermeneutical strategy, which if practiced can also challenge and shape present Pentecostal identity.

Implications and New Questions Raised by the Study

This work presents a theoretical Pentecostal hermeneutical strategy. The strategy needs to be utilized in the process of the interpretation of Scripture in order to see if it is practical. This writer presented portions of this study to the Society for Pentecostal Studies in order to receive both academic Pentecostal and non-Pentecostal feedback. The feedback received has been taken into consideration, thus demonstrating the importance of community dialogue. It is hoped that the contemporary theoretical strategy of the study will also be discussed. But the important test will be whether or not the strategy (not to be confused with any one method) will be successful in the meaningful interpretation of Scripture for the Pentecostal community. This application of the strategy needs to be applied to biblical passages. In doing so, it will help to show both the usefulness and practicality of the strategy. It also remains to be determined if the strategy can shed new light that may challenge other communities' understanding of Scripture as well as open new avenues of dialogue with other Christian and non-Christian communities.

Another issue that arises is how early North American Pentecostal identity compares to contemporary Majority World Pentecostalism. Pentecostalism adapts and reconfigures according to its surroundings. This begs the question of how much overlap exists between the early Pentecostal story and contemporary Majority World Pentecostalism? This writer would suggest that there is significant overlap, which means that contemporary European Pentecostals could learn anew what it means to live life on the margins of society, thus enhancing the contemporary interpretive strategy.

GLOSSARY: DEFINITION OF KEY TERMS AND CONCEPTS

Bible Reading Method: A synchronic commonsensical interpretive method that relied upon commonsense inductive and deductive reasoning. The method was used to trace key themes and topics throughout Scripture and then synthesize this biblical information into a doctrine. The Bible Reading Method was the primary exegetical method used by early Pentecostals in its formation of doctrine.

Central Narrative Convictions: A concept that refers to the primary story of the community. It holds together the community's central beliefs, practices and assumptions in a coherent communal narrative that explains who the community is, why the community exists and how the community is to live within society.

Culture: A system of patterned values, meanings, and beliefs that give cognitive structure to the world, provide a basis for coordinating and controlling human interactions, and constitute a link as the system is transmitted from one generation to the next.

Enlightenment: The seventeenth and eighteen-century western movement that emphasized individual autonomy and critical philosophical reasoning. Rationalism, skepticism and empiricism characterized this intellectual period. Science made significant technical progress during this time. Because it replaced human reasoning with external authorities as a source of knowledge it aroused great suspicion concerning the claims of traditional Christianity. The Enlightenment provides the womb for the conception of historical criticism. Nineteenth-century Academic Fundamentalism was dependent upon certain Enlightenment thinkers and concepts as it attempted to academically resist modernism.

Hermeneutics: Traditionally understood as the art and science of interpretation. In this monograph it is used to refer specifically to Biblical interpretation and all the elements involved in the interpretive process such as the interpretive method and the persons in community who are involved in interpretation. In this way hermeneutics is concerned with both the horizon of the biblical text and the horizon of the reader/listener.

Modernity (Modernism): A nineteenth and twentieth-century western cultural worldview that was an intensive extension of Enlightenment beliefs. It is characterized by strong belief in human progress through scientific, rationalistic reasoning from the perspective that a person can be neutral and objective. Scientific and historical verification were the means of validating all truth claims. Modernism was the attempt of some Christians to bring Christianity into harmony with the beliefs of modernity. The reconfiguration of traditional Christian thought into acceptable modernistic concepts produced liberalism and Fundamentalism.

Paramodern: A concept applied to the early Pentecostalism that characterizes the movement socially as existing on the margins of mainstream society and Christian denominations. This concept emphasizes that early Pentecostals exhibited aspects of premodern, modern and postmodern concerns while being in opposition to modernity, mainline Christianity and 'the World'.

Pentecostalism: A Christian restorationist revivalistic movement that emphasizes the continuing work of Jesus Christ through the personal agency of the Holy Spirit, proclaiming Jesus as Savior, Sanctifier, Spirit Baptizer, Healer and Soon Coming King. Pentecostals envision themselves as a restoration of New Testament Christianity living in the 'lasts days'.

Praxis: A concept that affirms both experience and theory as mutually informing and correcting each other in the epistemological process. Theory and practice are not separated but united dialectically through experience. Theory comes out of reflective experience and yields further praxis. A Pentecostal praxis oriented hermeneutic understands theological truth to be grounded in life experience which flows out of a covenant relationship with God through Jesus Christ.

Pre-critical: This concept is not to be understood from a historical developmental perspective such as the pre-critical, critical and post-critical era, but instead is an approach to Bible reading that assumes the Bible can be read in a straightforward manner without taking into account the social linguistic reality of language.

BIBLIOGRAPHY

Abrams, M.H., *A Glossary of Literary Terms* (Orlando, FL: Harcourt Brace College Publishers, 7th edn, 1999).

Adam, A.K.M., *What is Postmodern Biblical Criticism?* (Minneapolis, MN: Fortress Press, 1995).

Ahlstrom, S., 'The Scottish Philosophy', *Church History* 24 (September 1955), pp. 257–72.

Aichele, George *et al.*, *The Postmodern Bible: The Bible and Culture Collective* (New Haven, CT: Yale University Press, 1995).

Anderson, Gordon L., 'The Changing Nature of the Moral Crisis of American Christianity' (Paper presented to the Annual Meeting of the Society for Pentecostal Studies, November 1990).

—'Pentecostal Hermeneutics: Part 2', *Paraclete* 28.2 (Spring 1994), pp. 13–22.

Anderson, Janice Capel and Stephen D. Moore (eds.), *Mark and Method: New Approaches in Biblical Studies* (Minneapolis, MN: Fortress Press, 1992).

Anderson, Robert M., *Vision of the Disinherited: The Making of American Pentecostalism* (Peabody, MA: Hendrickson Publishers, 1979).

Archer, Kenneth J. 'A Pentecostal Way of Doing Theology: Method and Manner', *International Journal of Systematic Theology* 9.3 (July 2007).

—'The Spirit and Theological Interpretation: A Pentecostal Strategy', *Cyberjournal for Pentecostal/Charismatic Research* 16 (2007). http://www.pctii.org/cyber/table.html

—'Pentecostal Story: The Hermeneutical Filter for the Making of Meaning', *Pneuma* 26.1 (Fall 2004), 36-59.

—'Nourishment for our Journey: The Pentecostal Via Salutis and Sacramental Ordinances', *Journal of Pentecostal Theology* 13.1 (October 2004), pp. 79-96.

—'Early Pentecostal Biblical Interpretation', *Journal of Pentecostal Theology* 18 (April 2001), pp. 32–70.

—'Pentecostal Story as the Hermeneutical Filter' (Collected Paper presented to the Society for Pentecostal Studies, Tulsa, Oklahoma, March 8–10, 2001).

—'Early Pentecostal Biblical Interpretation: Blurring the Boundaries' (Collected Paper presented to the Society for Pentecostal Studies, Seattle, Washington, March 16–18, 2000).

—'Pentecostal Babbling: The Narrative Hermeneutic of the Marginalized' (Collected Paper presented to the joint conference of the Society for Pentecostal Studies and the Wesleyan Theological Society, Cleveland, Tennessee, March 12–14, 1998).

—'Pentecostal Hermeneutics: Retrospect and Prospect', *Journal of Pentecostal Theology* 8 (April 1996), pp. 63–81.

—'Pentecostal Response' (A response paper presented to the Annual Meeting for the Society for Pentecostal Studies, Oakland, CA, March 13–15, 1997).

Arrington, F.L., 'Hermeneutics' in Stanley M. Burgess and Gary B. McGee (eds.), *Dictionary of Pentecostal and Charismatic Movements* (Grand Rapids, MI: Zondervan, 1988), pp. 376-89.

—'The Use of the Bible by Pentecostals', *Pneuma* 16.1 (1994), pp. 101–107

Audi, Robert (ed.), *The Cambridge Dictionary of Philosophy* (New York, NY: Cambridge University Press, 1995).

Autry, Arden C., 'Dimensions of Hermeneutics in Pentecostal Focus', *Journal of Pentecostal Theology* 3 (October 1993), pp. 29–50.

Barrett, David B., 'Statistics Global' in Stanley M. Burgess and Gary B. McGee (eds.), *Dictionary of Pentecostal and Charismatic Movements* (Grand Rapids, MI: Zondervan, 1988), pp. 810-30.

Bartleman, Frank, *Azusa Street: The Roots of Modern-Day Pentecost* (South Plainfield, NJ: Bridge Publishing, 1980).

Barton, J., *Reading the Old Testament* (Philadelphia, PA: Westminster, 1984).

Bassett, Paul M., 'The Theological Identity of North American Holiness Movement: Its Understanding of the Nature and Role of the Bible' in D.W. Dayton and R.K. Johnston (eds.), *The Variety of American Evangelicalism* (Downers Grove, IL: InterVarsity Press, 1991), pp. 72–108.

Bauckham, Richard, *The Bible in Politics: How to Read the Bible Politically* (Louisville, KY: Westminster/John Knox Press, 1989).

—(ed.), *The Gospel For All Christians: Rethinking the Gospel Audiences* (Grand Rapids, MI: Eerdmans, 1998).

— 'Scripture and Authority', *Transformation* 15.2 (1998), pp. 5–11.

—*Scripture and Authority Today* (Cambridge, UK: Grove Books Limited, 1999).

—'Tradition in Relation to Scripture and Reason' in Richard Bauckham and Benjamin Drewery (eds.), *Scripture, Tradition and Reason* (Edinburgh, Scotland: T. & T. Clark, 1988), pp. 117–24.

Bauckham, Richard and Trevor Hart, *Hope Against Hope* (London: Darton, Longman and Todd, 1999).

Bebbington, D.W., *Evangelicalism in Modern Britain: A History from the 1730s to the 1980s* (Grand Rapids, MI: Baker Book House, 1989).

Bell, E.N. (ed.), *The Weekly Evangel* (1917–1919).

Belli, Humberto and Ronald Nash, *Beyond Liberation Theology* (Grand Rapids, MI: Baker Book House, 1992).

Bloesch, Donald G., *Essentials of Evangelical Theology* (2 vols.; San Francisco: HarperCollins Publishers, 1978).

Blumhofer, Edith, *The Assemblies of God: A Chapter in the Story of American Pentecostalism* (Springfield, MO: Gospel Publishing House, 1989).

—*Pentecost in My Soul: Exploration in the Meaning of Pentecostal Experience in the Assemblies of God* (Springfield, MO: Gospel Publishing House, 1989).

—'Purity and Perfection: A Study in the Pentecostal Perfectionist Heritage' in Richard Hughes (ed.), *The American Quest for the Primitive Church* (Urbana, IL: University of Illinois, 1988), pp. 256-82.

—'Restoration as Revival: Early American Pentecostalism' in Edith L. Blumhofer and Randall Balmer (eds.), *Modern Christian Revivals* (Urbana and Chicago, IL: The University of Illinois Press, 1993), pp. 145–60.

—*Restoring the Faith: The Assemblies of God, Pentecostalism, and American Culture* (Urbana and Chicago, IL: The University of Illinois Press, 1993).

Blumhofer, Edith L., Russell P. Spittler, and Grant A. Wacker (eds.), *Pentecostal Currents in American Protestantism* (Urbana and Chicago, IL: University of Illinois Press, 1999).

Boff, Leonardo and Clodovis Boff, *Introducing Liberation Theology* (London: Burns and Oates, 1987, reprint 1992).

Boone, R. Jerome, 'Community and Worship: The Key Components of Pentecostal Christian Formation', *Journal of Pentecostal Theology* 8 (April 1996), pp. 129–42.

Boone, Kathleen C., *The Bible Tells Them So: The Discourse of Protestant Fundamentalism* (New York, NY: State University of New York Press, 1989).

Bowman, Richard G., 'Narrative Criticism of Judges' in Gale A. Yee (ed.), *Judges and Method: New Approaches in Biblical Studies* (Minneapolis, MN: Fortress Press, 1995), pp. 17–44.

Bray, Gerald, *Biblical Interpretation: Past and Present* (Downers Grove, IL: InterVarsity Press, 1996).

Brooks, John P., *The Divine Church* (Columbia, MO: Herald Publishing House, 1891).

Brueggemann, Walter, *Texts Under Negotiation: The Bible and Postmodern Imagination* (Minneapolis, MN: Fortress Press, 1993).

Brumback, Carl, *Suddenly ... From Heaven: A History of the Assemblies of God* (Springfield, MO: Gospel Publishing House, 1961).

Bruner, Dale, *A Theology of the Holy Spirit: The Pentecostal Experience and the New Testament Witness* (Grand Rapids, MI: Eerdmans, 1970).

Bultmann, Rudolf, 'Is Exegesis Without Presuppositions Possible?' in Schubert M. Ogden (ed. and trans.), *New Testament and Mythology and Other Basic Writings* (Philadelphia, PA: Fortress Press, 1984), pp. 145-153.

Burgess, Stanley M. and Gary B. McGee (eds.), *Dictionary of Pentecostal and Charismatic Movements* (Grand Rapids, MI: Zondervan, 1988).

Bush, L. Russ, *A Handbook for Christian Philosophy* (Grand Rapids, MI: Zondervan, 1991).

Byrd, Joseph, 'Formulation of a Classical Pentecostal Homiletic in Doalogue With Contemporary Protestant Homiletics' (Unpublished Ph.D. dissertation, Southern Baptist Theological Seminary, 1990).

—'Paul Ricoeur's Hermeneutical Theory and Pentecostal Proclamation', *PNEUMA* 15.2 (Fall 1993), pp. 203–214.

Callinicos, Alex, *Theories and Narratives: Reflections on the Philosophy of History* (Durham, NC: Duke University Press, 1995).

Cargal, Timothy, 'Beyond the Fundamentalist-Modernist Controversy: Pentecostals and Hermeneutics in a Postmodern Age', *Pneuma* 15.2 (1993), pp. 163–87.

Carpenter, Joel A. (ed.), *Fundamentalist Versus Modernist: The Debates Between John Roach Straton and Charles Francis Potter* (New York: Garland Publishing, 1988).

Cerillo, Jr., Augustus, 'The Origins of American Pentecostalism', *Pneuma* 15.1 (Spring, 1993), pp. 77–88.

Chatman, Seymour, *Story and Discourse: Narrative Structure in Fiction and Film* (Ithaca, NY: Cornell University Press, 1978).

Chidester, David, *Patterns of Power: Religion and Politics in American Culture* (Englewood Cliffs, NJ: Prentice-Hall, 1988).

Christenson, Larry, 'Pentecostalism's Forgotten Forerunner' in Vinson Synan (ed.) *Aspects of Pentecostal-Charismatic Origins* (Plainfield, NJ: Logos International, 1975), pp. 15–37.

Clarke, William Newton, *The Use of Scriptures in Theology* (Edinburgh, Scotland: T. & T. Clark, 1907).

Clause, Robert G. (ed.), *The Meaning of the Millenium: Four Views* (Downers Grove, IL: InterVarsity Press, 1977).

Conn, Charles W., *Like a Mighty Army Moves the Church of God* (Cleveland, TN: Church of God Publishing House, 1955).

Cotterell, Peter and Max Turner (eds.), *Linguistics and Biblical Interpretation* (Downers Grove, IL: InterVarsity Press, 1989).

Cox, Harvey, *Fire from Heaven: The Rise of Pentecostal Spirituality and the Reshaping of Religion in the Twenty-first Century* (Reading, MA: Addison-Wesley Publishing Company, 1995).

Croatto, J. Severino, *Biblical Hermeneutics: Toward a Theory of Reading as the Production of Meaning* (Maryknoll, NY: Orbis Books, 1987).

Dake, Finis Jennings, *The Rapture and the Second Coming of Christ* (Atlanta, GA: Dake Bible Sales, 1977).

Dayton, Donald, 'Asa Mahan and The Development of American Holiness Theology', *The Wesleyan Theological Journal* 9 (Spring 1974), pp. 60–69.

—*Theological Roots of Pentecostalism* (Peabody, MA: Hendrickson Publishers, 1987).

—(ed.), 'Three Early Pentecostal Tracts' (vol. 14) in *idem* (ed.), *The Higher Christian Life* (New York: Garland Publishing, 1985).

—'The Use of Scripture in the Wesleyan Tradition' in Robert Johnston (ed.), *The Use of the Bible in Theology: Evangelical Options* (Atlanta, GA: John Knox Press, 1985), pp. 121–36.

—'Yet Another Layer of the Onion or Opening the Ecumenical Door to Let the Riffraff In', *The Ecumenical Review* 40.1 (January, 1988), pp. 87–110.

Dieter, Melvin, 'The Wesleyan/Holiness and Pentecostal Movements: Commonalities, Confrontation and Dialogue' (paper presented to the Society for Pentecostal Studies on November 11, 1988).

Dieter, Melvin E. *et al.*, *Five Views on Sanctification* (Grand Rapids, MI: Zondervan, 1987).

Dempster, M.W., 'The Search for Pentecostal Identity', *Pneuma* 15.1 (Spring 1993), pp. 1–8.

d'Epinay, Christian Lalive, *Haven of the Masses: A Study of the Pentecostal Movement in Chile* (London: Lutterworth, 1969).

Dunn, James D.G., *Baptism in the Holy Spirit: A Re-Examination of the New Testament Teaching on the Gift of the Spirit in Relation to Pentecostalism Today* (Philadelphia, PA: Westminster, 1970).

—'Baptism in the Spirit: A Response to Pentecostal Scholarship on Luke-Acts', *Journal of Pentecostal Theology* 3 (1993), pp. 3–27.

Eagleton, Terry, *Literary Theory: An Introduction* (Minneapolis, MN: University of MN Press, 2nd edn, 1998).

Eco, Umberto, *The Limits of Interpretation* (Bloomington and Indianapolis, IN: Indiana University Press, 1990).

—*The Role of the Reader: Explorations in the Semiotics of Texts* (London: Hutchinson, 1981).

Eco, Umberto *et al.*, *Interpretation and Overinterpretation* (ed. Stefan Collini; New York: Cambridge University Press, 1992).

Elbert, Paul (ed.), *Essays on Apostolic Themes* (Peabody, MA: Hendrickson Publishers, 1985).

Erickson, Millard J., *The Evangelical Heart and Mind: Perspectives on Theological Issues* (Grand Rapids, MI: Baker Books, 1993).

—*Evangelical Interpretation: Perspectives on Hermeneutical Issues* (Grand Rapids, MI: Baker Books, 1993).

Ervin, H., 'Hermeneutics: A Pentecostal Option' in Paul Elbert (ed.), *Essays on Apostolic Themes* (Peabody, MA: Hendrickson Publishers, 1985), pp. 23–35.

Evans, W., *Outline Study of the Bible* (Chicago, IL: Bible Institute Colportage Association, 1913).

Ewart, Frank J., *The Phenomenon of Pentecost* (Hazelwood, MO: Word Aflame Press, rev. edn, 1975).

—*The Revelation of Jesus Christ* (St. Louis, MO: Pentecostal Publishing House, nd).

Fackre, Gabriel, *The Christian Story: A Narrative of Basic Christian Doctrine* (Grand Rapids, MI: Eerdmans, 3rd edn, 1996).

Faupel, D. William, *The Everlasting Gospel: The Significance of Eschatology in the Development of Pentecostal Thought* (JPTSup, 10; Sheffield: Sheffield Academic Press, 1996).

—'Wither Pentecostalism? 22nd Presidential Address to the Society for Pentecostal Studies', *Pneuma* 15.1 (Spring 1993), pp. 9–27.

Fay, Brian, *Critical Social Science: Liberation and Its Limits* (New York: Cornell University Press, 1987).

Fee, Gordon, *God's Empowering Presence: The Holy Spirit in the Letters of Paul* (Peabody, MA: Hendrickson Publishers, 1994).

—*Gospel and Spirit: Issues in New Testament Hermeneutics* (Peabody, MA: Hendrickson Publishers, 1991).

—'Hermeneutics and the Historical Precedent: A Major Problem in Pentecostal Hermeneutics' in R.P. Spittler (ed.), *Perspectives on the New Pentecostalism* (Grand Rapids, MI: Baker Book House, 1976), pp. 118–132.

—*New Testament Exegesis: A Handbook for Students and Pastors* (Louisville, KY: Westminster/John Knox Press, rev. edn, 1993).

Ferguson, D.S., *Biblical Hermeneutics: An Introduction* (London: SCM,1987)

Fish, Stanley, *Is There a Text in This Class? The Authority of Interpretive Communities* (Cambridge, MA: Harvard University Press, 1980).

Fowl, Stephen E., *Engaging Scripture: A Model for Theological Interpretation* (Malden, MA: Blackwell Publishers, 1998).

Fowl, Stephen E. and L. Gregory Jones, *Reading in Communion: Scripture and Ethics in The Christian Life* (Grand Rapids, MI: Eerdmans, 1991).

Fowler, Robert, 'Reader Response Criticism' in *Mark and Method: New Approaches in Biblical Studies* (Minneapolis, MN: Fortress Press, 1992), pp. 59-94.

—'Reader-Response Criticism: Figuring Mark's Reader' in Janice Capel Anderson and Stephen D. Moore (eds.), *Mark and Method: New Approaches in Biblical Studies* (Minneapolis, MN: Fortress Press, 1992), pp. 50–83.

Frei, Hans, *The Eclipse of Biblical Narrative: A Study in Eighteenth and Nineteenth Century Hermeneutics* (New Haven, CT: Yale University Press, 1974).

—'The "Literal Reading" of Biblical Narrative in the Christian Tradition: Does It Stretch or Will It Break?' in

Frank McConnell (ed.), *The Bible and the Narrative Tradition* (New York, NY: Oxford University Press, 1986), pp. 36-77.

Funk, R.W., 'The Watershed of the American Biblical Tradition: The Chicago School, First Phase, 1892–1920', *Journal of Biblical Literature* 95 (1976), pp. 4–22.

Gadamer, Hans-Georg, *Truth and Method* (New York, NY: Crossroads Publishing company, 1985).

Gerlach, Luther P., 'Pentecostalism: Revolution or Counter-Revolution?' in I.I. Zarestsky and M.P. Leone (eds.), *Religious Movements in Contemporary America* (Princeton, NJ: Princeton University Press, 1974), pp. 669-99.

Gerlach, Luther P. and Virginia Hine, 'Five Factors Crucial to the growth and Spread of a Modern Religious Movement', *The Journal For the Scientific Study of Religion* 7.1 (Spring 1968), pp. 23–40.

—*People, Power, Change: Movements of Social Transformation* (Indianapolis, IN: Bobbs-Merril Educational Publishing, 1970).

Godbey, W.B., *Tongue Movement, Satanic* (Zarephath, NJ: Pillar of Fire Publishers, 1918).

Goen, C.C., *Revivalism and Separatism in New England, 1740–1800: Strict Congregationalists and Separate Baptists in the Great Awakening* (Middletown, CT: Wesleyan University Press, 1987).

Goff, Jr., James R., *Fields White unto Harvest: Charles F. Parham and the Missionary Origins of Pentecostalism* (Fayetteville, AR: The University of Arkansas Press, 1988).

Goldberg, Michael, *Theology and Narrative: A Critical Introduction* (Philadelphia, PA: Trinity Press International, 1991).

Goldingay, John, *Models for Interpretation of Scripture* (Grand Rapids, MI: Eerdmans, 1995).

—*Models for Scripture* (Grand Rapids, MI: Eerdmans, 1994).

Green, Garrett (ed.), *Scriptural Authority and Narrative Interpretation* (Philadelphia, PA: Fortress Press, 1987).

Green, Joel (ed.), *Hearing the New Testament: Strategies for Interpretation* (Grand Rapids, MI: Eerdmans, 1995).

Green, Joel, 'Hermeneutical Approaches to the Tradition' in J.D.G. Dunn and J.W. Rogerson (eds.), *Eerdmans Commentary on the Bible* (Grand Rapids, MI: Eerdmans, 2003), pp. 972-88.

Green, Joel and Max Turner (eds.), *Between Two Horizons: Spanning New Testament Studies and Systematic Theology* (Grand Rapids, MI: Eerdmans, 2000).

Grenz, Stanley J., *A Primer on Postmodernism* (Grand Rapids, MI: Eerdmans, 1996).

Grosvenor, Melville Bell (ed.), *American Mountain People* (Washington, DC: The National Geographic Society, 1973).

Gutierrez, Gustavo, *A Theology of Liberation* (Maryknoll, NY: Orbis Books, 1973).

Hague, Canon Dyson, 'The History of the Higher Criticism' in R.A. Torrey *et al.* (eds.), *The Fundamentals: A Testimony to the Truth* (Los Angeles, CA: The Bible Institute of Los Angeles, 1917, reprint by Baker Book House, 1998), pp. 9-42.

Hall, J. L., 'A Oneness Pentecostal Looks at Initial Evidence' in Gary B. McGee (ed.), *Initial Evidence: Historical and Biblical Perspectives on the Pentecostal Doctrine of Spirit Baptism* (Peabody, MA: Hendrickson Publishers, 1991), pp. 168-88.

Harris, R.W., *Spoken by the Spirit* (Springfield, MO: Gospel Publishing House, 1973).

Harrisville, Roy A. and Walter Sundberg, *The Bible in Modern Culture: Theology and Historical-Critical Method from Spinoza to Käsemann* (Grand Rapids, MI: Eerdmans, 1995).

Hart, Trevor, *Faith Thinking: The Dynamics of Christian Theology* (London: SPCK, 1995).

Hatch, Nathan O. and Mark A. Noll (eds.), *The Bible in America: Essays in Cultural History* (New York: Oxford University Press, 1982).

Hauerwas, Stanley, *The Peaceable Kingdom: A Primer in Christian Ethics* (Notre Dame: The University of Notre Dame, 1983).

Hauerwas, Stanley and L. Gregory Jones (eds.), *Why Narrative? Readings in Narrative Theology* (Grand Rapids, MI: Eerdmans, 1989).

Hawk, L. Daniel, *Every Promise Fulfilled: Contesting Plots in Joshua* (Louisville, KY: Westminster/John Knox press, 1991).

Hawkes, Terence, *Structuralism and Semiotics* (Berkeley and Los Angeles, CA: University of California Press, 1977).

Hays, Richard B., *Echoes of Scripture in the Letters of Paul* (New Haven, CT: Yale University Press, 1989).

Haywood, G.T., *Divine Names and Titles of Jehovah* (Indianapolis, IN: Christ Temple Book Store, nd).

—*The Birth of the Spirit in the Days of the Apostles* (Indianapolis, IN: Christ Temple Book Store, nd); republished in *The Life and Writings of Elder G.T. Haywood* (Oregon: Apostolic Book Publishers, 1984).

—*The Finest of Wheat* (Indianapolis, IN: Christ Temple Book Store, nd).

—*The Victim of the Flaming Sword* (Indianapolis, IN: Christ Temple Book Store, nd).

Hine, Virginia H., 'The Deprivation and Disorganization Theories of Social Movements' in I.I. Zarestsky and M.P. Leone (eds.), *Religious Movements in Contemporary America* (Princeton, NJ: Princeton University Press, 1974), pp. 646–61.

Hirsch, E.D., *Validity and Interpretation* (New Haven, CT: Yale University Press, 1967).

Hodge, Charles and B.B. Warfield, 'Inspiration' in *Presbyterian Review* (April 1881), reprinted by Philadelphia: PA: Presbyterian Board of Publication and Sabbath-School Work, no. 208, nd, pp. 5-71.

Hollenweger, Walter J., 'After Twenty Years' Research on Pentecostalism', *International Review of Mission* 75.297 (January 1986), pp. 3–12.

—'The Critical Tradition of Pentecostalism', *Journal of Pentecostal Theology* 1 (October 1992), pp. 7-17.

—'The Pentecostal Elites and the Pentecostal Poor: A Missed Dialogue?' in Karla Poewe (ed.), *Charismatic Christianity as a Global Culture* (Columbia, SC: University of South Carolina, 1994), pp. 200–214.

—*The Pentecostals* (Peabody, MA: Hendrickson Publishers, 1972).

Hunter, H.D., *Spirit-Baptism: A Pentecostal Alternative* (Lanham, MD: University Press of America, 1983).

—'Tomlinson, Ambrose Jessup' in Stanley M. Burgess and Gary B. McGee (eds.), *Dictionary of Pentecostal and Charismatic Movements* (Grand Rapids, MI: Zondervan, 1988), pp. 846-48.

Hunter, James D., *American Evangelicalism: Conservative Religion and the Quandary of Modernity* (New Brunswick, NJ: Rutgers University Press, 1983).

Iser, Wolfgang, *The Act of Reading: A Theory of Aesthetic-Response* (London: Routledge, 1978).

—*The Implied Reader: Patterns of Communication in Prose Fiction From Bunyan to Beckett* (Baltimore, MD: John Hopkins Press, 1974).

Jacobsen, Douglas, 'Pentecostal Hermeneutics in Comparative Perspective' (Collected Paper presented at the Annual Meeting of the Society for Pentecostal Studies, Oakland, CA, March 13–15, 1997).

Jeanrond, Werner G., *Theological Hermeneutics: Development and Significance* (New York: The Crossroad Publishing Company, 1991).

Jenkins, Keith, *Re-Thinking History* (New York: Routledge Press, 1991).

Johns, Cheryl Bridges, 'Partners in Scandal: Wesleyan and Pentecostal Scholarship', *Wesleyan Theological Journal* 34.1 (1999), pp. 7-23.

—'The Adolescence of Pentecostalism: In Search of a Legitimate Sectarian Identity', *Pneuma* 17.1 (Spring 1995), pp. 3–17.

—*Pentecostal Formation: A Pedagogy among the Oppressed* (JPTSup, 2; Sheffield: Sheffield Academic Press, 1993).

Johnson, Luke T., 'Imagining the World Scripture Imagines', *Modern Theology* 14.2 (April 1998), pp. 165-80.

—*Religious Experience in the Earliest Christianity: A Missing Dimension in New Testament Studies* (Minneapolis, MN: Augsburg Fortress Press, 1998).

—*Scripture and Discernment: Decision Making in the Church* (Nashville, TN: Abingdon Press, 1983).

Johnston, R., 'Pentecostalism and Theological Hermeneutics: Evangelical Options', *Pneuma* (Spring 1984), pp. 51–66.

—(ed.), *The Use of the Bible in Theology: Evangelical Options* (Atlanta, GA: John Knox Press, 1985.

Jones, L. Gregory, 'Alasdair MacIntyre on Narrative, Community, and the Moral Life', *Modern Theology* 4.1 (1987), pp. 53–69.

Joy, A.H., 'Rain' in J. Orr (ed.) *The International Standard Bible Encyclopedia* (Chicago, IL: Howard Severance Company, 1915), IV, pp. 2525-26.

Kallenberg, Brad J., 'The Master Argument of MacIntyre's *After Virtue*' in Murphy, Kallenberg and Nation (eds.), *Virtues and Practices in the Christian Tradition: Christian Ethics After MacIntyre* (Harrisburg, PA: Trinity Press International, 1997), pp. 7–29.

Keesey, Donald, *Contexts for Criticism* (Mountain View, CA: Mayfield Publishing Company, 1987).

Kenneson, Philip D., *Beyond Sectarianism: Re-Imagining Church and World* (Harrisburg, PA: Trinity Press International, 1999).

Kenyon, H.N., 'An Analysis of Ethical Issues in the History of the Assemblies of God' (Unpublished PhD dissertation, Baylor University, 1988).

—'An Analysis of Racial Separation within the Early Pentecostal Movement' (Unpublished MA thesis, Baylor University, Texas, 1979).

King, Joseph, *From Passover to Pentecost* (Franklin Springs, GA: Advocate, 1976, originally published 1911).

Kingsbury, Jack Dean, *Gospel Interpretation: Narrative-Critical and Social-Scientific Approaches* (Harrisburg, PA: Trinity Press International, 1997).

Klein, William, 'Evangelical Hermeneutics' in Simon Maimela and Adrio König (eds.), *Initiation into Theology: The Rich Variety of Theology and Hermeneutics* (Pretoria: J.L. van Schaik, 1988), pp. 319-36.

Klein, W., C. Blomberg and R. Hubbard, Jr., *Introduction to Biblical Interpretation* (Dallas: Word Publishing, 1993).

Knight III, Henry H., *A Future for Truth: Evangelical Theology in a Postmodern World* (Nashville, TN: Abingdon Press, 1997).

—'From Aldersgate to Azusa: Wesley and the Renewal of Pentecostal Spirituality', *Journal of Pentecostal Theology* 8 (April 1996), pp. 82–98.

Kraft, Charles, *Anthropology for Christian Witness* (Maryknoll, NY: Orbis Books, 1996).

Kuhn, Thomas, *The Structure of Scientific Revolutions* (Chicago: University of Chicago Press, 1970).

Land, Steven J., *Pentecostal Spirituality: A Passion for the Kingdom* (JPTSup, 1; Sheffield: Sheffield Academic Press, 1993).

Larkin, Clarence, *Dispensational Truth or God's Plan and Purpose in the Ages* (Philadelphia, PA: Clarence Larkin Est., 1920).

Lategan, Barnard C., 'Hermeneutics' in *The Anchor Bible Dictionary* (Doubleday: 1992), III, pp. 149-154.

Lawrence, B.F., *The Apostolic Faith Restored* (St. Louis, MO: Gospel Publishing House, 1961).

Lederle, H., 'Pre-Charismatic Interpretations of Spirit-Baptism' in *A Reader on the Holy Spirit: Anointing, Equipping and Empowering for Service* (Los Angeles, CA: International Church of the Foursquare Gospel, 1993), pp. 13-50.

Lennox, Stephan J. 'Biblical Interpretation in the American Holiness Movement, 1875–1920' (Unpublished PhD dissertation, Drew University, 1992).

Lincoln, Eric and Lawrence H. Mamiya, *The Black Church in the African American Experience* (Durham, NC: Duke University Press, 1990).

Lindsell, Harold, *The Battle for the Bible* (Grand Rapids, MI: Zondervan, 1976).

Linnemann, Eta, *Historical Criticism of the Bible: Methodology or Ideology* (Grand Rapids, MI: Baker Book House, 1990).

Longman III, Tremper, *Literary Approaches to Biblical Interpretation* (Grand Rapids, MI: Zondervan, 1987).

Loughlin, Gerald, *Telling God's Story: Bible, Church and Narrative Theology* (Cambridge, UK: Cambridge University Press, 1996).

Lovett, Leonard, 'Black Holiness-Pentecostalism: Implications for Ethics and Social Transformation' (PhD Dissertation, Emory University, 1979).

—'Black Holiness-Pentecostalism' in Stanley M. Burgess and Gary B. McGee (eds.), *Dictionary of Pentecostal and Charismatic Movements* (Grand Rapids, MI: Zondervan, 1988), pp. 76-84.

—'Black Origins of the Pentecostal Movement' in V. Synan (ed.), *Aspects of Pentecostal-Charismatic Origins* (Plainfield, NJ: Logos International, 1975), pp. 123–41.

Lundin, Roger, *Disciplining Hermeneutics: Interpretation in Christian Perspective* (Grand Rapids, MI: Eerdmans, 1997).

Lundin, Roger, Anthony C. Thiselton and Clarence Walhout (eds.), *The Responsibility of Hermeneutics* (Grand Rapids, MI: Eerdmans, 1985).

MacDonald, William, 'Pentecostal Theology: A Classical Viewpoint' in R.P. Spittler (ed.), *Perspectives on the New Pentecostalism* (Grand Rapids, MI: Baker Book House, 1976), pp. 58-75.

MacIntyre, Alasdair, *After Virtue: A Study in Moral Theory* (Notre Dame, IN: University of Notre Dame Press, 2nd edn, 1984).

—'Epistemological Crises, Dramatic Narrative, and the Philosophy of Science' in Stanley Hauerwas and L. Gregory Jones (eds.), *Why Narrative? Readings in Narrative Theology* (Grand Rapids, MI: Eerdmans, 1989), pp. 138-57.

—*Whose Justice? Which Rationality?* (Notre Dame, IN: University of Notre Dame Press, 1988).

MacRoberts, Ian, *The Black Roots and White Racism of Early Pentecostalism in the U.S.A.* (New York: St. Martin's Press, 1988).

Maimela, Simon and Adrio König (eds.), *Initiation into Theology: The Rich Variety of Theology and Hermeneutics* (Pretoria: J.L. van Schaik, 1988).

Marsden, George M., 'Everyone One's Own Interpreter?: The Bible, Science, and Authority in Mid-Nineteenth-Century America' in N. Hatch and M. Noll (eds.), *The Bible in America: Essays in Cultural History* (New York: Oxford University Press, 1982), pp. 79–100.

—*Fundamentalism and American Culture: The Shaping of Twentieth-Century Evangelicalism, 1870–1925* (New York: Oxford University Press, 1980).

—*Understanding Fundamentalism and Evangelicalism* (Grand Rapids, MI: Eerdmans, 1991).

Marshall, I. Howard, *New Testament Interpretation: Essays on Principles and Methods* (Carlisle: The Paternoster Press, rev. edn, 1985).

Martin, Lee Roy, *The Unheard Voice of God: A Pentecostal Hearing of the Book of Judges* (JPTSup, 32; Blandford Forum, UK: Deo Publishing, 2008).

Martin, James P., 'Toward a Post-Critical Paradigm', *New Testament Studies* 33 (1987), pp. 370–85.

Mauro, Philip, 'Modern Philosophy' in *The Fundamentals: A Testimony to the Truth* (Los Angeles, CA: The Bible Institute of Los Angeles, 1917, reprint by Baker Book House, 1998), pp. 9-29.

McCauley, Deborah, *Appalachian Mountain Religion: A History* (Urbana and Chicago: University of Illinois Press, 1995).

McClung, Jr., L. Grant (ed.), *Azusa Street and Beyond: Pentecostal Missions and Church Growth in the Twentieth Century* (South Plainfield, NJ: Bridge Publishing, 1986).

McGee, Gary B. (ed.), *Initial Evidence: Historical and Biblical Perspectives on the Doctrine of Spirit Baptism* (Peabody, MA: Hendrickson Publishers, 1991).

McGrath, Alister E., *A Passion for the Truth: The Intellectual Coherence of Evangelicalism* (Downers Grove, IL: InterVarsity Press, 1996).

—*Evangelicalism and the Future of Christianity* (Downers Grove, IL: InterVarsity Press, 1995).

—*The Genesis of Doctrine: A Study in the Foundation of Doctrinal Criticism* (Grand Rapids, MI: Eerdmans, 1997, copyright 1990).

McKay, John, 'When the Veil is Taken Away', *Journal of Pentecostal Theology* 5 (1994), pp. 17–40.

McKnight, Edgar V., *Post-Modern Use of the Bible: The Emergence of Reader-Oriented Criticism* (Nashville, TN: Abingdon Press, 1988).

McKnight, Edgar V. and Elizabeth Struthers Malbon (eds.), *The New Literary Criticism and the New Testament* (Valley Forge, PA: Trinity Press International, 1994).

McLean, Mark, 'Toward a Pentecostal Hermeneutic', *Pneuma* 6.2 (1984), pp. 35–56.

McLoughlin, William G., *Modern Revivalism* (New York: Ronald Press, 1959).

—*Revivals, Awakenings, and Reform* (Chicago: The University of Chicago Press, 1978).

McPherson, Aimee Semple, 'Death in the Pot' in *This is That: Personal Experiences, Sermons and Writings* (Los Angeles, CA: Echo Park Evangelistic Association, 1923), pp. 779-94.

McQueen, Larry R., *Joel and the Spirit: The Cry of a Prophetic Hermeneutic* (JPTSup, 8; Sheffield: Sheffield Academic Press, 1995).

McQuillian, Jeff, *The Literary Crisis: False Claims, Real Solutions* (Portsmouth, NH: Heinemann, 1998).

Menzies, Robert P., 'Coming to Terms with an Evangelical Heritage', *Paraclete* 28.3 (Summer 1994), pp. 18–28.

—*The Development of Early Christian Pneumatology with Special Reference to Luke-Acts* (JSNTSup, 54 ; Sheffield: Sheffield Academic Press).

—*Empowered for Witness: The Spirit in Luke-Acts* (JPTSup, 6; Sheffield: Sheffield Academic Press, 1994).

—'The Essence of Pentecostalism', *Paraclete* 26.3 (Summer 1992), pp. 1–9.

—'Jumping off the Postmodern Bandwagon', *Pneuma* 16.1 (1994), pp. 115–20.

—'Luke and the Spirit: A Reply to James Dunn', *Journal of Pentecostal Theology* 4 (1994), pp. 115–38.

—'Spirit and Power in Luke-Acts: A Response to Max Turner', *Journal for the Study of the New Testament* 49 (1993), pp. 11–20.

Menzies, William M., *Anointed to Serve: The Story of the Assemblies of God* (Springfield, MO: Gospel Publishing House, 1971).

—'The Methodology of Pentecostal Theology: An Essay on Hermeneutics' in Paul Elbert (ed.), *Essays on Apostolic Themes* (Peabody, MA: Hendrickson Publishers, 1985), pp. 1–14.

—'Non-Wesleyan Influences in the Pentecostal Revival From 1901 to 1910' in V. Synan (ed.), *Aspects of Pentecostal-Charismatic Origins* (Plainfield, NJ: Logos International, 1975), pp. 84-98.

—'The Non-Wesleyan Origins of the Pentecostal Movement' in V. Synan (ed.), *Aspects of Pentecostal-Charismatic Origins* (Plainfield, NJ: Logos International, 1975), pp. 81–98.

Middleton, J. Richard and Brian Walsh, *The Transforming Vision: Shaping a Christian World View* (Downers Grove, IL: InterVarsity Press, 1984).

—*Truth is Stranger Than It Used To Be: Biblical Faith in a Postmodern Age* (Downers Grove, IL: InterVarsity Press, 1995).

Miller, Albert G., 'Pentecostalism as a Social Movement: Beyond the Theory of Deprivation', *Journal of Pentecostal Theology* 9 (1996), pp. 81-98.

Moore, Rick D., 'A Pentecostal Approach to Scripture', *Seminary Viewpoint* 8.1 (1987), pp. 4-5.

—'Approaching God's Word Biblically: A Pentecostal Perspective' (Collected paper presented to the Society for Pentecostal Studies, Fresno, CA, 1989).

—'Canon and Charisma in the Book of Deuteronomy', *Journal of Pentecostal Theology* 1 (October 1992), pp. 75-92.

Moore, Stephen D., *Literary Criticism and the Gospels: The Theoretical Challenge* (New Haven, CT: Yale University Press, 1989).

—*Poststructuralism and the New Testament: Derrida and Foucault at the Foot of the Cross* (Minneapolis, MN: Fortress Press, 1994).

Morgan, Robert with John Barton, *Biblical Interpretation* (New York: Oxford University Press, 1988).

Munhall, L.W., 'Inspiration' in R.A. Torrey *et al.* (eds.), *The Fundamentals: Testimony to the Truth* (Los Angeles, CA: The Bible Institute of Los Angeles, 1917, reprint by Baker Book House, 1998), pp. 44-60.

Murphy Nancey, *Beyond Liberalism and Fundamentalism: How Modern and Postmodern Philosophy Set the Theological Agenda* (Valley Forge, PA: Trinity Press International, 1996).

Murphy, Nancey, Brad Kallenberg, Mark Nation (eds.), *Virtues and Practices in the Christian Tradition: Christian Ethics after MacIntyre* (Harrisburg, PA: Trinity Press International, 1997).

Myland, D. Wesley, *The Latter Rain Covenant and Pentecostal Power* (Chicago, IL: Evangel Publishing House, 1910).

Nash, Ronald H., *World-Views in Conflict: Choosing Christianity in a World of Ideas* (Grand Rapids, MI: Zondervan, 1992).

Nelson, Douglas J., 'For Such a Time as This: The Story of Bishop William J. Seymour and the Azusa Street Revival: A Search for Pentecostal Roots' (Unpublished PhD thesis, University of Birmingham, England, 1981).

Nida, Eugene A., *Signs, Sense, Translation* (Cape Town, SA: Bible Society of South Africa, 1984).

Nida, Eugene A. *et al.* (eds.), *Style and Discourse* (Cape Town, SA: Bible Society of South Africa, 1983).

Nienkrichen, Charles W., *A.B. Simpson and the Pentecostal Movement: A Study in Continuity, Crisis, and Change* (Peabody, MA: Hendrickson Publishers, 1992).

Noll, Mark A., 'Christianity and Culture in America' in Howard C. Kee (ed.) *Christianity: A Social and Cultural History* (New York: Macmillan, 1991), pp. 601–754.

—*A History of Christianity in the United States and Canada* (Grand Rapids, MI: Eerdmans, 1992).

—*Between Faith and Criticism: Evangelicals, Scholarship, and the Bible in America* (Grand Rapids, MI: Baker Book House, 1991).

—*The Princeton Theology, 1882–1921* (Grand Rapids, MI: Baker Book House, 1983).

—*The Scandal of the Evangelical Mind* (Leicester, England: InterVarsity Press, 1994).

Norwood, Frederick A., *The Story of American Methodism: A History of the United Methodists and Their Relations* (Nashville, TN: Abingdon Press, 1974).

Oden, Thomas C., *After Modernity...What? Agenda for Theology* (Grand Rapids, MI: Zondervan, 1990).

Ollenburger, Ben C., 'What Krister Stendahl "Meant"–A Normative Critique of "Descriptive Biblical Theology"', *Horizons in Biblical Theology* 8.1 (1986), pp. 61–98.

Orr, James, 'The Early Narratives of Genesis' in R.A. Torrey *et al.* (eds.), *The Fundamentals: A Testimony to the Truth* (Los Angeles, CA: The Bible Institute of Los Angeles, 1917, reprint by Baker Books, 1998), I, 9-42.

—'The Holy Scriptures and Modern Negations' in R.A. Torrey *et al.* (eds.), *The Fundamentals: A Testimony to the Truth* (Los Angeles, CA: The Bible Institute of Los Angeles, 1917, reprint by Baker Books, 1998), I, pp. 94-110.

Osborne, Grant R., *The Hermeneutical Spiral: A Comprehensive Introduction to Biblical Interpretation* (Downers Grove, IL: InterVarsity Press, 1991).

Packer, J.I., *Fundamentalism and the Word of God: Some Evangelical Principles* (Grand Rapids, MI: Eerdmans, 1992, first edition 1958).

Parham, Charles, *The Everlasting Gospel* (Baxter Springs, KS: Apostolic Faith Bible College, 1911 reprint).

Parham, Sarah F., 'Earnestly Contend for the Faith Once Delivered to the Saints' in Robert L. Parham (com.), *Selected Sermons of the Late Charles F. Parham, Sarah E. Parham: Co-Founders of the Original Apostolic Faith Movement* (Baxter Springs, KS: Apostolic Faith Bible College, 1941), pp. 9-22.

—*The Life of Charles F. Parham: Founder of the Apostolic Faith Movement* (Joplin, MO: Hunter Publishing Company, 1930, reprint 1969).

Patte, Daniel, *What is Structural Exegesis?* (Philadelphia, PA: Fortress Press, 1976).

Pelikan, Jarsolav, *From Luther to Kierkegaard* (St. Louis, MO: Concordia, 1950).

Perkins, Jonathan E., *Pentecostalism on the Washboard* (Fort Worth, TX: Jonathan Elsworth Perkins, nd).

Petersen, Douglas, 'The Kingdom of God and The Hermeneutical Circle: Pentecostal Praxis in the Third World' in Murray A. Dempster, Byron D. Klaus and Douglas Petersen (eds.), *Called & Empowered: Global Mission in Pentecostal Perspective* (Peabody, MA: Hendrickson Publishers, 1991), pp. 44–58.

Petersen, Norman R., *Rediscovering Paul: Philemon and the Sociology of Paul's Narrative World* (Philadelphia, PA: Fortress Press, 1985).

Pierson, Arthur, T., 'The Coming of the Lord: The Doctrinal Center of the Bible' in *Addresses on the Second Coming of the Lord: Delivered at the Prophetic Conference, Allegheny, PA, December 3–6, 1895* (Pittsburgh, PA, 1895).

—'The Testimony to the Organic Unity of the Bible to its Inspiration' in R.A. Torrey *et al.* (eds.), *The Fundamentals: Testimony to the Truth* (Los Angeles, CA: The Bible Institute of Los Angeles, 1917, reprint by Baker Books, 1998), pp. 97-111.

Pinnock, Clark, 'Biblical Texts: Past and Future Meanings', *Wesleyan Theological Journal* 34.2 (Fall 1999), pp. 136-51.

—'The Work of the Holy Spirit in Hermeneutics', *Journal of Pentecostal Theology* 2 (1993), pp. 3–23.

Poewe, Karla (ed.), *Charismatic Christianity as a Global Culture* (Columbia, SC: University of South Carolina Press, 1994)

Poloma, Margaret M., 'By their Fruits …: A Sociological Assessment of the To-
ronto Blessing' (paper presented to the Annual Meeting of the Society for Pentecostal Studies, University of Toronto, Ontario, Canada, March 7–9, 1996).
—*The Assemblies of God at the Crossroads* (Knoxville, TN: University of Tennessee
Press, 1989).
Powell, Mark Allan, 'Narrative Criticism' in Joel Green (ed.), *Hearing the New Testa-
ment: Strategies for Interpretation* (Grand Rapids, MI: Eerdmans, 1995), pp. 239–55.
—'Toward a Narrative-Critical Understanding of Matthew' in Jack Dean Kingsbury
(ed.), *Gospel Interpretation: Narrative-Critical and Social-Scientific Approaches* (Harris-
burg, PA: Trinity Press International, 1997), pp. 9–15.
—*What is Narrative Criticism?* (Minneapolis, MN: Fortress Press, 1990).
Ramm, B., *Protestant Biblical Interpretation: A Textbook of Hermeneutics* (Grand Rapids,
MI: Baker Book House, 1970).
Reed, David A., 'Origins and Development of the Theology of Oneness Pentecos-
talism in the United States' (PhD Dissertation, Boston University, 1978).
—'Oneness Pentecostalism' in Stanley M. Burgess and Gary B. McGee (eds.), *Dic-
tionary of Pentecostal and Charismatic Movements* (Grand Rapids, MI: Zondervan,
1988), pp. 644-51.
—'Oneness Pentecostalism: Problems and Possibilities for Pentecostalism', *Journal
of Pentecostal Theology* 11 (1997), pp. 73–93.
Rhoads, David, Joanna Dewey and Donald Michie (eds.), *Mark as Story: An Introduc-
tion to the Narrative of a Gospel* (Minneapolis, MN: Fortress Press, 1999).
Ricoeur, Paul, *Freud and Philosophy: An Essay on Interpretations* (New Haven, CT: Yale
University Press, 1970).
—'Biblical Hermeneutics', *Semeia* 4 (1975), pp. 29–48.
—*The Symbolism of Evil* (New York: Harper and Row, 1967)
Rimmon-Kenan, Shlomith, *Narrative Fiction: Contemporary Poetics* (New York: Rout-
ledge Press, 1997).
Riss, R. A., 'Finished Work Controversy' in Stanley M. Burgess and Gary B. McGee
(eds.), *Dictionary of Pentecostal and Charismatic Movements* (Grand Rapids, MI: Zon-
dervan, 1988), pp. 306-309.
Robbins, Vernon K., *Exploring the texture of Texts: A Guide to Socio-Rhetorical Interpreta-
tion* (Valley Forge, PA: Trinity Press International, 1996).
—*The Tapestry of Early Christian Discourse: Rhetoric, Society and Ideology* (New York:
Routledge Press, 1996).
Robeck, Jr., Cecil M., 'Taking Stock of Pentecostalism: The Personal Reflections of
a Retiring Editor', *Pneuma* 15.1 (Spring, 1993), pp. 35–60.
Robinson, E.B., 'Myland, David Wesley' in Stanley M. Burgess and Gary B. McGee
(eds.), *Dictionary of Pentecostal and Charismatic Movements* (Grand Rapids, MI: Zon-
dervan, 1988), pp. 632-33.
'The Role of Women in Ministry as Described in Holy Scripture' (Position paper of
the General Council of the Assemblies of God adopted by the General Presbytery, Springfield, MO: Gospel Publishing House, 1990).
Russell, Bertrand, *A History of Western Philosophy* (New York: Simon and Schuster,
1972).
Ruthven, Jon, *On the Cessation of the Charismata: The Protestant Polemic on Postbiblical
Miracles* (JPTSup, 3; Sheffield: Sheffield Academic Press, 1993).

Ryrie, Charles C., *Dispensationalism Today* (Chicago: Moody Press, 1965).

Sandeen, Ernest R., *The Roots of Fundamentalism: British and American Millenarianism, 1880–1930* (Chicago: The University of Chicago Press, 1970).

Sanders, Cheryl J., *Saints in Exile: The Holiness-Pentecostal Experience in African American Religion and Culture* (New York: Oxford University Press, 1996).

Scalise, Charles J., *Hermeneutics as Theological Prolegomena: A Canonical Approach* (Macon, GA: Mercer University Press, 1994).

Schneiders, Sandra M. 'Feminist Hermeneutics' in Joel Green (ed.), *Hearing the New Testament: Strategies for Interpretation* (Grand Rapids, MI: Eerdmans, 1995), pp. 349–69.

Schweizer, E. 'Πνεῦμα' in *TDNT*, VI, pp. 389–455;

Scofield, C.I., *Rightly Dividing the Word of Truth* (Neptune, New Jersey: Loizeaux Brothers (undated), first edition 1896).

—(ed.), *The Scofield Bible Correspondence Course: Volume One, Old Testament* (Chicago, IL: The Moody Bible Institute of Chicago, 1907).

—*The Scofield Reference Bible* (New York: Oxford University Press, 1917, first published 1909).

Seung, T.K., *Semiotics and Thematics in Hermeneutics* (New York, NY: Columbia University Press, 1982).

Seymour, William (ed.), *The Apostolic Faith* (Los Angeles: The Pacific Apostolic Faith Movement, 1906–1908).

Sheppard, Gerald T., 'Biblical Interpretation after Gadamer', *Pneuma* 28.2 (Spring 1994), pp. 121–41.

—'Pentecostals and the Hermeneutics of Dispensationalism', *Pneuma* 16.2 (1984), pp. 5–33.

—'Word and Spirit Scripture in the Pentecostal Tradition, Part II', in *Agora* (Summer 1978), pp. 4-5, 21.

Smelser, Neil J., 'Culture: Coherent or Incoherent' in Vernon K. Robbins, *The Tapestry of Early Christian Discourse: Rhetoric, Society and Ideology* (New York: Routledge, 1996), pp. 3-28.

Smith, James K.A., *The Fall of Interpretation: Philosophical Foundations for a Creational Hermeneutic* (Downers Grove, IL: InterVarsity Press, 2000)

Smith, Timothy L., *Called Unto Holiness: The Story of the Nazarenes: The Formative Years* (Kansas City, MO: Nazarene Publishing House, 1962).

Spittler, Russell P., 'Are Pentecostals and Charismatics Fundamentalists? A Review of American Uses of These Categories' in Karla Poewe (ed.), *Charismatic Christianity as a Global Culture* (Columbia, SC: The University of South Carolina, 1994), pp. 103–116.

—(ed.), *Perspectives on the New Pentecostalism* (Grand Rapids, MI: Baker Book House, 1976).

—'Scripture and the Theological Enterprise: View from a Big Canoe' in Robert K. Johnston (ed.), *The Use of the Bible in Theology: Evangelical Options* (Atlanta, GA: John Knox Press, 1985), pp. 56–77.

Stanton, G., 'Presuppositions in New Testament Criticism' in I. Howard Marshall (ed.), *New Testament Interpretation* (Carlisle: The Paternoster Press, rev. edn, 1985), pp. 60–71.

Stendahl, Krister, 'Biblical Theology, Contemporary' in *Interpreter's Bible Dictionary* (Nashville, TN: Abingdon Press, 1962), I, pp. 67–106.

Stiener, George, 'Critic/Reader', *New Literary History* 10 (1979), pp. 423–52.

Steinmetz, David C., 'The Superiority of the Pre-Critical Exegesis' in *Ex Auditu* 1 (1985), pp. 74–82.

Stout, Harry S. 'Theological Commitment and American Religious History', *Theological Education* 25 (Spring 1989), pp. 44–59.

Strachan, Gordon, *The Pentecostal Theology of Edward Irving* (Peabody, MA: Hendrickson Publishers, 1988).

Stronstad, Roger, *The Charismatic Theology of St. Luke* (Peabody, MA: Hendrickson Press, 1984).

—'Pentecostal Hermeneutics: A Review of Gordon D. Fee', *Pneuma* 15.2 (Fall 1993), pp. 215–22.

—'Pentecostal Experience and Hermeneutics', *Paraclete* 26.1 (Winter 1992), pp. 14–30.

Stuhlmacher, Peter, *Historical Criticism and Theological Interpretation of Scripture: Towards a Hermeneutic of Consent* (Philadelphia, PA: Fortress Press, 1977).

Suurmound, Jean-Jacques, *Word and Spirit at Play: Towards a Charismatic Theology* (London: SCM Press, 1994).

Swartley, Willard, *Slavery, Sabbath, War and Women* (Scottsdale, PA: Herald Press, 1983).

Synan, Vinson (ed.), *Aspects of Pentecostal-Charismatic Origins* (Plainfield, NJ: Logos International, 1975).

—'Classical Pentecostalism' in Stanley M. Burgess and Gary B. McGee (eds.), *Dictionary of Pentecostal and Charismatic Movements* (Grand Rapids, MI: Zondervan, 1988), pp. 219-22.

—*The Holiness-Pentecostal Movement in the United States* (Grand Rapids, MI: Eerdmans, 1971).

Tate, W. Randolph, *Biblical Interpretation: An Integrated Approach* (Peabody, MA: Hendrickson Publishers, rev. edn, 1997).

Taylor, G.F., *The Spirit and the Bride* (no publisher or publishing date given, but ca. 1907).

Thiselton, Anthony, *Interpreting God and the Postmodern Self: On Meaning, Manipulation and Promise* (Grand Rapids, MI: Eerdmans, 1995).

—'The New Hermeneutic' in I. Howard Marshall (ed.), *New Testament Interpretation* (Grand Rapids, MI: Eerdmans, 1977), pp. 308–333.

—*New Horizons in Hermeneutics* (Grand Rapids: Zondervan, 1992).

—*The Two Horizons* (Grand Rapids, MI: Eerdmans, 1980).

Thomas, John Christopher, 'Max Turner's *The Holy Spirit and Spiritual Gifts: Then and Now* (Carlisle: Paternoster Press, 1996): An Appreciation and Critique', *Journal of Pentecostal Theology* 12 (April 1998), pp. 3–121.

—'Reading the Bible From Within Our Traditions: A Pentecostal Hermeneutic as Test Case' in Joel Green and Max Turner (eds.), *Between Two Horizons: Spanning New Testament Studies and Systematic Theology* (Grand Rapids, MI and Cambridge, England: Eerdmans, 2000), pp. 108–122.

—'Women, Pentecostals and the Bible', *Journal of Pentecostal Theology* 5 (1994), pp. 41–56.

Tinny, James S.,'Competing Strains of Hidden and Manifest Theologies in Black Pentecostalism' (a paper presented to the Society for Pentecostal Studies held November 14, 1980 at Oral Roberts University, Tulsa, OK).

—'Exclusivist Tendencies in Pentecostal Self-Definition: A Critique from Black Theology', *The Journal of Religious Thought* 36.1 (Spring-Summer, 1979), pp. 32–49.

Torrey, R.A., *The Baptism with the Holy Spirit* (Chicago, IL: The Bible Institute Colportage Association, Copyright 1895, by Fleming H. Revel Company).

—*First Course – Bible Doctrine* (New York: Garland Publishing 1988, facsimile of 1901 publication).

—*The Person and Work of the Holy Spirit* (Grand Rapids, MI: Zondervan, rev. edn, 1974).

Torrey, R.A. *et al.* (eds.), *The Fundamentals: Testimony to the Truth* (Los Angeles, CA: The Bible Institute of Los Angeles, 1917, reprint by Baker Book House, 1998).

Traina, R., 'Inductive Bible Study Reexamined in the Light of Contemporary Hermeneutics' in McCown and Massey (eds.), *Wesleyan Theological Perspectives* (vol. 2): *Interpreting God's Word for Today* (Anderson, IN: Warner Press, 1982), pp. 53–83.

—*Methodical Bible Study: A New Approach to Hermeneutics* (New York: Ganis and Harris, 1952).

Turner, Bryan S. (ed.), *Theories of Modernity and Postmodernity* (London: Sage Publications, 1990).

Turner, Max, *The Holy Spirit and Spiritual Gifts: In the New Testament Church and Today* (Peabody, MA: Hendrickson Publishers, 1998).

Turner, Max, 'Readings and Paradigms: A Response to John Christopher Thomas', *Journal of Pentecostal Theology* 12 (April 1998), pp. 23–38.

Turner, Jr., William Clair, 'The United Holy Church of America: A Study in Black Holiness-Pentecostalism' (Unpublished PhD dissertation, Duke University,1984).

Vander Stelt, John C., *Philosophy and Scripture: A Study in Old Princeton and Westminster Theology* (Martlon: NJ: Mack, 1978).

Vanhoozer, Kevin J., 'The Reader in the New Testament Interpretation' in Joel Green (ed.), *Hearing the New Testament: Strategies for Interpretation* (Grand Rapids, MI: Eerdmans, 1995), pp. 301–328.

Virkler, Henry A., *Hermeneutics: Principles and Processes of Biblical Interpretation* (Grand Rapids, MI: Baker Book House, 1981).

Wacker, Grant, 'Character and Modernization of North American Pentecostalism' (Paper presented to the Annual Meeting for the Society of Pentecostal Studies, 1991).

—'The Demise of Biblical Civilization' in N. Hatch and M. Noll (eds.), *The Bible in America: Essays in Cultural History* (New York: Oxford University Press, 1982), pp. 121–38.

—'The Functions of Faith in Primitive Pentecostalism', *Harvard Theological Review* 77 (1984), pp. 353–75.

—'The Holy Spirit and the Spirit of the Age in American Protestantism, 1880–1910',*The Journal of American History* 72.1 (June 1985), pp. 45–62.

—'Marching to Zion: Religion in a Modern Utopian Community', *Church History* 54.4 (December 1985), pp. 496–511.

—'Playing for Keeps: The Primitivist Impulse in Early Pentecostalism' in Richard T. Hughes (ed.), *The American Quest for the Primitive Church* (Urbana, IL: University of Illinois, 1988), pp. 196–219.

Waddell, Robby. *The Spirit of the Book of Revelation* (JPTSup, 30; Blandford Forum, UK: Deo Publishing, 2006)

Wagner, C. Peter, 'Church Growth' in Stanley M. Burgess and Gary B. McGee (eds.), *Dictionary of Pentecostal and Charismatic Movements* (Grand Rapids, MI: Zondervan, 1988), pp. 180-95.

Waldvogel, E.D., 'The Overcoming Life: A Study in the Reformed Evangelical Origins of Pentecostalism' (PhD dissertation, Harvard University, 1977).

Wallace, Mark I., *The Second Naïveté: Barth, Ricoeur, and the New Yale Theology* (Macon, GA: Mercer University Press, 1990).

Ware, Steven L., 'Restoring the New Testament Church: Varieties of Restorationism in the Radical Holiness Movement of the Late Nineteenth and Early Twentieth Centuries', *Pneuma* 21.2 (Fall 1999), pp. 233–50.

Warfield, B.B., 'Review of R.A. Torrey, *What the Bible Teaches*', *Presbyterian and Reformed Review* 39 (July 1899), pp. 562-64.

Warfield, E.D., W.P. Armstrong and C.W. Hodge (eds.), *The Works of Benjamin B. Warfield* (New York: Oxford University Press, 1931, reprint 1981 by Baker Book House).

Warner, W. (ed.) *Touched by the Fire* (Plainfield, NJ: Logos International, 1978).

Watson, George D., *A Holiness Manual* (Jamestown, NC: Newby Book Room, 1882).

Watson, Francis, *Text, Church and World* (Edinburgh, Scotland: T. & T. Clark, 1994).

Weber, Timothy P. *Living in the Shadow of the Second Coming: American Premillennialism, 1875–1982* (Chicago, IL: University of Chicago Press, 1987).

—'The Two-Edged Sword: The Fundamentalist Use of the Bible' in N. Hatch and M. Noll (eds.), *The Bible in America: Essays in Cultural History* (New York: Oxford University Press, 1982), pp. 101–120.

Welch, Claude, *Protestant Thought in the Nineteenth Century* (New Haven, CT: Yale University Press, 1985).

Wenham, Gordon J., *Genesis 1–15* (WBC 1; Waco, Texas, 1987).

White, Alma, *Demons and Tongues* (Zarephath, NJ: Pillar of Fire Publishers, 1936).

Whittaker, Colin C. *Seven Pentecostal Pioneers* (Springfield, MO: Gospel Publishing House, 1985).

Williams, J.R., 'Baptism in the Holy Spirit' in Stanley M. Burgess and Gary B. McGee (eds.), *Dictionary of Pentecostal and Charismatic Movements* (Grand Rapids, MI: Zondervan, 1988), pp. 40-48.

Williams, Peter W., *America's Religions: Traditions and Cultures* (New York: Macmillan, 1990).

Willis, Lewis J. (compiler), *Assembly Addresses of the General Overseers: Sermons that Guided the Church* (Cleveland, TN: Pathway Press, 1986).

Wilson, D.J., 'Pacifism' in Stanley M. Burgess and Gary B. McGee (eds.) *Dictionary of Pentecostal and Charismatic Movements* (Grand Rapids, MI: Zondervan, 1988), pp. 658-60.

Witherington III, Ben, *Paul's Narrative Thought World: The Tapestry of Tragedy and Triumph* (Louisville, KY: Westminster/John Knox Press, 1994).

Wright, N.T., *The New Testament and the People of God* (Minneapolis, MN: Fortress Press, 1992).

Wyckoff, John W., 'The Relationship of the Holy Spirit to Biblical Hermeneutics' (Unpublished PhD dissertation, Baylor University, 1990).

Yee, Gale A. (ed.), *Judges & Method: New Approaches in Biblical Studies* (Minneapolis, MN: Fortress Press, 1995).

Yoder, John H., *The Politics of Jesus: Vicit Agnus Noster* (Grand Rapids, MI: Eerdmans, 1971).

Yong, Amos, *Discerning the Spirit(s): A Pentecostal-Charismatic Contribution to Christian Theology of Religions* (JPTSup, 20; Sheffield: Sheffield Academic Press, 2000).

INDEX OF AUTHORS

INDEX OF BIBLICAL REFERENCES